TOP WALKS
in TASMANIA

Melanie Ball

CONTENTS

Introduction		v
What to take		viii
Bushwalkers' code		xi
How to use this book		xii
Map		xiv

WALKS

no.	walk	kms	time	grade	page

HOBART REGION

no.	walk	kms	time	grade	page
1	kunanyi/Mount Wellington Summit	13.8	5–7 hrs	Hard	2
2	Lost World	5	3–4 hrs	Moderate–hard	9
3	Truganini	5.1	2 hrs	Easy–moderate	14
4	Alum Cliffs & Brickfields	4.7	2–3 hrs	Easy	18
5	Chauncy Vale Caves	7	2–3 hrs	Easy	23
6	Historic Richmond Town	4	2 hrs	Easy	28
7	Lady Barron Falls	7.5	2.5 hrs	Easy	34
8	Tarn Shelf	15	5–6 hrs	Moderate	38
9	Growling Swallet & Junee Cave	3.6	2 hrs	Easy	44
10	Marriotts Falls	6	2 hrs	Easy	49
11	Tolkien Track – The Styx	3	1.5 hrs	Easy–moderate	54
12	Mount Misery	8.6	3–4 hrs	Easy	58
13	Cape Queen Elizabeth (Bruny Island)	13	4 hrs	Easy–moderate	62
14	Fluted Cape (Bruny Island)	7.5	2–3 hrs	Easy–moderate	67
15	Slide Track (Bruny Island)	13	5–6 hrs	Moderate	72

TASMAN PENINSULA

no.	walk	kms	time	grade	page
16	Cape Hauy	10.3	3–4 hrs	Moderate	80
17	Cape Raoul	15	5–6 hrs	Moderate	85
18	Crescent Bay & Mount Brown	11.5	4–5 hrs	Easy–moderate	90
19	Coal Mines Historic Site	4.7	2 hrs	Easy	95
20	Fortescue Bay to Devils Kitchen	21	6–9 hrs	Moderate	101
21	Three Capes Track	48	4 days	Easy–moderate	107

CONTENTS iii

no.	walk	kms	time	grade	page
EAST COAST					
22	Maria Island	18	5–6 hrs (or 2 days)	Moderate–hard	124
23	Mount Amos	6	3–5 hrs	Moderate–hard	132
24	Wineglass Bay & Hazards Beach	12	4 hrs	Moderate	137
25	Freycinet Peninsula	42	4 days	Moderate	142
26	Bay of Fires	8.5–22	3 hrs – all day	Easy	152
27	Apsley Gorge	6	2.5 hrs	Easy–moderate	156
28	Moon Valley Rim	4.5	2–3 hrs	Easy	160
29	wukalina/Mount William	13.5	4–5 hrs	Easy	165
FLINDERS ISLAND					
30	Strzelecki Peak	7.2	4–5 hrs	Moderate–hard	172
31	Cameron Inlet	9.4	2–3 hrs	Easy	178
32	The Docks to Killiecrankie	8.2	4 hrs	Easy–moderate	182
LAUNCESTON REGION					
33	Bridport Walking Track	12.5	3–4 hrs	Easy	190
34	Cataract Gorge	9	3–4 hrs	Easy–moderate	196
35	Tamar Island	4.6	1.5 hrs	Easy	202
36	Liffey Falls	8.5	3–4 hrs	Easy	206
37	Higgs Track to Lady Lake	7.2	3–5 hrs	Moderate	210
38	Meander Falls	10	4.5–6 hrs	Moderate–hard	215
39	Quamby Bluff	7.5	3–5 hrs	Moderate	220
40	Ben Lomond Snow Pole	11.5	3–5 hrs	Moderate	225
41	Narawntapu National Park	12	3–4 hrs	Easy	231
NORTH-WEST					
42	Mount Roland	17	5–6 hrs	Moderate	238
43	Leven Canyon	6.5–10	2–3 hrs	Moderate	243
44	Rocky Cape	19	5–6 hrs	Moderate	248
45	The Nut	5.5	2 hrs	Easy	254

WALKS CONT.

no.	walk	kms	time	grade	page
CENTRAL HIGHLANDS					
46	Dove Lake	6.5	2-3 hrs	Easy	262
47	Dove Lake High	11	4-5 hrs	Moderate	267
48	Dove Gorge	6.5	3 hrs	Easy-moderate	273
49	Lakes Loop	7.3	3 hrs	Easy	277
50	Cradle Mountain Summit	15.4	7-9 hrs	Hard	282
51	Shadow Lake	14	4-5 hrs	Easy-moderate	289
52	The Labyrinth	30	3 days	Moderate	294
53	Overland Track	65	6 days+	Moderate	303
54	Walls of Jerusalem	28.6	3 days	Moderate	318
WEST & WILDERNESS					
55	Philosopher Falls	3.6	1.5 hrs	Easy-moderate	328
56	West Point to Black Rocks	10	3 hrs	Easy	333
57	Mount Donaldson to Corinna via Savage River	14.5	4.5-6 hrs	Moderate	337
58	Montezuma Falls	11	3 hrs	Easy	342
59	Mount Farrell & Lake Herbert	10.5	4-6 hrs	Moderate	346
60	Pillinger Point	10-15	3-4 hrs (or 5-6 hrs without car shuffle)	Easy	352
61	Frenchmans Cap	50	3-5 days	Hard	357
62	Donaghys Hill	2.4	1 hr	Easy	368
63	The Needles	3	2-3 hrs	Moderate	371
64	Mount Eliza Plateau	10	5-6 hrs	Hard	375
65	Hartz Peak	8.7	3-4 hrs	Moderate	380
66	Mystery Creek Cave	4.7	2 hrs	Easy	386
67	South Cape Bay	15	5 hrs	Easy-moderate	390

Index	396

TOP WALKS IN TASMANIA

Tassie, as Australia's island state is colloquially and affectionately known, has impressive environmental credentials. Almost half of it is protected within national parks, reserves and World Heritage sites, some secured by hard-fought, high-profile and contentious campaigns and protests that gave rise to the Australian Greens political party. And swathes of that protected land is genuine wilderness, accessible only by experienced and determined adventurers.

Mere mortals, however, can choose from hundreds of less demanding walks. You can poke your toes over the edge of Australia's highest sea cliffs and dip them in alpine tarns ringed by ice-carved mountains; feel the spray off a hundred metres of single-drop waterfall and trail footprints along remote beaches; knock off Australia's most popular multi-day hike and escape the crowds in treasure-trove rainforest hidden behind a locked gate; walk through convict-era underground isolation cells and watch white-bellied sea eagles free fly over a mountain plateau.

But, I hear you ask, 'What about the weather?' Tasmania's climate is officially cool temperate and even in the depths of winter you can usually step out on the more sheltered east coast. Some parts of the state, however, receive annual rainfalls measured in metres and snow can blanket mountain ridges and elevated plains at any time of year. So, yes, Tassie's reputation for unpredictable weather is deserved – particularly in the west and the central highlands, where conditions can deteriorate dramatically at short notice. But preparing for the worst sets you up for some of the best bushwalking of your life.

Part of continental Australia until about 10,000 years ago, when rising seas last submerged the connecting land bridge and created the infamous Bass Strait, Tasmania is Australia's smallest state. It sits in the path of strong westerlies known as the Roaring Forties that have partnered with Antarctic southerlies, ice and water over time to shape mountains, alpine plateaus, low-lying plains and the wild and welcoming coast that encircles them.

Geographic and genetic isolation has produced unique flora and fauna and diverse rock types, including the world's largest area of exposed dolerite (hexagonal, columnar magma intrusions). Together, these create awesome settings that intrigue and captivate.

Child-migrant Peter Dombrovskis (1945–1996) was a photographer with a visceral love of Tasmania. His images revealed the stunning beauty of once-remote and inaccessible parts of the island and together with photographs by his mentor, Olegas Truchanas, raised awareness about the importance

Stepping out on the Overland Track

of Tasmania's south-west. Some commentators credit Dombrovskis' most famous photograph, *Morning Mist, Rock Island Bend, Franklin River*, as a critical element in the successful campaign to save the Franklin River from being dammed for hydro-electric power.

Australia's most mountainous state, Tassie is also home to the country's largest expanse of temperate rainforest: a staggering 3800 square kilometres. Only on foot can you begin to appreciate the grand scale of this physical drama and its exquisitely wrought detailing.

Describing all the top walks in Tasmania would result in a multi-volume guide, so the main challenge in compiling this book was shortening the initial working list. Asked for their suggestions, several hiking aficionados unhelpfully added walks rather than deleting, some saying 'You must include...!'

A few of these walks might test an uber-fit hiker's fortitude and fondness for hills but there are no epic bush-bashes or off-track expeditions here and most are suitable for groups of mixed ages and abilities. And while some of the walks require a high fitness level, all are routes to fitness that leave gym workouts for dead. How could anyone prefer air-conditioning to an alpine breeze? Or pumping techno music to the rattle of pandani curls as you brush past, or the squawk of yellow-tailed black cockatoos, or water tumbling over a cascade? Studies have also shown that exercising outdoors raises levels of serotonin, melatonin and endorphins, which in turn reduces stress. So if you need an excuse to go walking in Tasmania, you can always say you are improving your physical and mental health.

Whether you want to escape civilisation for days with survival rations on your back or take a half-day break from happening Hobart; whether you want to venture beyond your comfort zone or induct your children into the wonders of going bush on a stroll through mining history; whether you want to feast your eyes on mountain scapes so rugged they leave you slack-jawed or narrow your focus to a tiny fungi jewelled with pearls of rain, Tasmania has a walk for you.

Slow down, walk with respect, and have fun.

With thanks

This book is dedicated to all the people who have walked across Tasmania: the First Tasmanians who have done so for millennia and the men and women who followed them, their hearts stolen by its unique natural beauty.

Thanks to the friends who have hiked with me, and posed for more photographs than is reasonable, in particular my husband Simon who recovered from hip-replacement surgery in time to join me on the last few tracks; thanks as well to the Tasmanian Parks and Wildlife Service.

But my loudest thank you is for my dad, Richard Ball, who died while I was scaling the heights of Walls of Jerusalem National Park. Without you I wouldn't have discovered the joys of walking, travelling and writing, and this book would not have eventuated.

Melanie Ball

PARK FEES

Fees apply to enter all Tasmanian national parks. Parks passes can be purchased at Parks and Wildlife Service offices, Tasmanian travel centres, on the Spirit of Tasmania ferry, online (www.parks.tas.gov.au) and at some parks. The Holiday Pass is the best value for interstate and international visitors hiking in more than one park over a two-month period while an annual or two-year pass is recommended for Tasmanians and frequent bushwalkers.

WHAT TO TAKE

To enjoy bushwalking you need to be comfortable – which doesn't mean you should never push yourself. It's just that blistered feet, bruised shoulders and clothes that chafe can turn a great walk into a trial – and getting wet and cold or sunburnt and dehydrated can endanger your life.

There have been remarkable innovations in outdoor clothing and equipment since Livingstone went tropo in the African jungle and Robert Falcon Scott forced hands into frozen fur gloves in Antarctica. But while it's fun to flex your credit card on a load of latest gear in adventure stores, you essentially only need walking clothes appropriate for the environment and weather. Never wear cotton, which is cold when wet, in alpine environments, whatever the forecast.

Poles

There are traditionalists who hate walking poles and converts who promote them. But poles can aid balance when crossing creeks and ease pressure on knees during descents. Using poles also lessens or prevents the fat fingers that some walkers suffer as a consequence of pack-strapped shoulders; and countless websites claim that walking with poles burns almost half as many calories again as walking without. Poles or not? One or two? It's up to you. As is how you carry water.

Water

Water is essential on walks longer than an hour in hilly country or in hot weather – but on a short wildflower ramble? Leave your water in the car and discover the joys of going bush empty-handed. In other situations, consider the weather and climate and your drinking habits; some walkers need considerably more than others. If you don't drink much and have to be reminded/encouraged, a water bladder with tube might be the best option because it enables you to drink small amounts on the move rather than have to stop to pull out a bottle. Consider whether there is water to fill up your bottle en route, or whether you need to take enough for the duration of your walk.

Footwear

The last thing you want on a walk is sore feet so footwear should be appropriate for the conditions and comfortable for long periods of time. Closed shoes or boots provide some protection from sticks and stones and a twisted ankle, but walking sandals may be more comfortable in open country or with creek crossings because the water drains out. Some people still reminisce about hiking in Dunlop Volleys while others pull on 'barefoot shoes' with individual toes. Whatever you choose it should fit properly, not move around on your feet – thongs/flip flops/jandals are asking for trouble - and be worn in. The road to bushwalking hell is littered with people wearing brand new boots on long hikes.

Gear list

The ideal on any walk is to carry as little as is safe.

Moderate walk of a few hours

Daypack with at least 1L of water
Whistle (for attracting attention)
High-energy snack such as muesli bar, nuts or chocolate
Rain- and wind-proof jacket/and or second layer
Sunglasses, sunhat and sunscreen for warm weather
Gloves and beanie for cold weather
Camera
A map (unless the trail is clearly marked – local tourist maps may be enough)

Half-day, tougher walk

Daypack with at least 1.5L of water
Whistle (for attracting attention)
Lunch and high-energy snack such as muesli bar, nuts or chocolate
Rain- and wind-proof jacket/and or second layer
Sunglasses, sunhat and sunscreen for warm weather
Gloves and beanie for cold weather
Basic first-aid kit – bandages, blister treatments, perhaps some antihistamine
Map, compass and GPS
Camera and phone (turned off for safety)

x   WHAT TO TAKE

Full-day, more remote walk

Daypack with at least 2L of water
Whistle (for attracting attention)
Lunch and high-energy snacks
Rain- and wind-proof jacket, and second layer; thermals, beanie and gloves if in alpine environment (even if fine weather is forecast)
Torch and waterproof matches
Full first-aid kit including a foil heat blanket
Compass, map and GPS
Camera
Leave plans of your walk with someone to alert authorities if you don't return
Phone for safety (turned off to save batteries)

Very remote long walk

All the above, plus a personal locator beacon (PLB). You can hire one from Service Tasmania shops in Hobart, Launceston, Burnie and Devonport (www.parks.tas.gov.au – search 'EBIRBs' or phone 1300 135 513).

TOP LEFT: *A Tasmanian waratah burns bright on hike into The Labyrinth;* **TOP RIGHT:** *Tree ferns within cooee of lower Liffey Falls parking area have gained many metres in height;* **BOTTOM LEFT:** *Mosses festoon forested areas of Walls of Jerusalem National Park;* **BOTTOM RIGHT:** *Tea-tree flowers put on a show on the Cape Hauy Track, Tasman National Park*

BUSHWALKERS' CODE

The 'take only photos, leave only footprints' philosophy is an oldie but a goodie. It is confounding - and infuriating - how many hikers despoil the landscapes that their pursuit would otherwise suggest they love. It may be as minor as a dropped muesli bar wrapper or as extreme as pooing beside a creek and leaving an 'I was here' toilet-paper marker. The bushwalkers' code is a common-sense approach to limiting impact on the country. When you're on the track, this includes keeping groups small and not making or using short cuts, which cause erosion and increase the risk of others losing their way.

Mud is a celebrated enemy of bushwalkers in Tasmania and every experienced hiker has a yarn to tell about getting bogged. Detouring around bogs in fragile environments to avoid getting your boots dirty only exacerbates the environmental damage. Of course, sometimes you will need to take an alternate path, but otherwise channel your inner child and embrace the mud!

For minimal impact, camp only on existing tent sites (unless bushcamping is permitted); light campfires (where permitted) only in existing fireplaces and don't cut wood to burn; carry out what you take in; and wash and toilet away from water. Minimal impact bushwalking is described in detail at www.parks.tas.gov.au (search for 'Leave No Trace').

Looking after yourself and your walking companions is as important as respecting the environment. Enhance your enjoyment and safety by appointing a friend or family member as your safety contact. They need to know where you are going, when you expect to be back and who to contact should you not return by a designated time. Choose walks that suit a group's experience and fitness. Prepare for weather changes even on 'perfect' walking days and be prepared to cancel a walk, even at the last minute, if conditions deteriorate. Know what to do if someone gets injured and be even more cautious about timing, walk choice, weather and injuries if you're walking solo. Walking alone is considered dangerous on longer and more remote overnight walks.

References
For bushwalking hints, suggested walks, walking clubs and more go to:
Bushwalking Australia: www.bushwalkingaustralia.org.au
Bushwalk Australia forum: bushwalk.com
Hobart Walking Club (Tasmania's oldest and largest walking club): www.hobartwalkingclub.org.au
TasTrails: http://tastrails.com

HOW TO USE THIS BOOK

Designed to motivate you to explore Tasmania on foot and help you do so, this book includes descriptions of routes, wildlife and plants, and simple maps. On overnight and more remote walks you'll need a contour map, compass and a GPS, and know how to use them, and additional maps are suggested. In most cases, however, you should be able to safely do the walks with the maps provided.

DISTANCE AND WALK TYPE

Some walk lengths given in this book vary from those found on websites, and park signs and notes (which often don't tally in any case). All were measured using a Garmin GPSmap 62s and distances in the walk introductions and descriptions refer to these readings.

Some of the walks are loop walks (returning to the start point a different way), others are return walks (out-and-back on the same track) and others are one-way (A to B) walks which require a shuttle from the end to the start.

LEVEL OF DIFFICULTY

Most of the walks in this book demand some effort. Some follow formed tracks, with a crushed rock or sandy surface, however many hiking tracks are unsurfaced; the narrowest of these, often just a trail worn by feet, are commonly called footpads, a term used in this book.

TIME REQUIRED

A major challenge in writing a bushwalking guide is estimating how long a route will take, because everyone walks at different speeds in flat terrain and even more so in hills; some hikers power from A to B, others stop frequently for photographs. Food breaks, track finding, weather conditions, group size (large groups move slower than small groups) and stopping for a refreshing swim all alter completion times.

Times in this book are estimated for fit, enthusiastic, middle-aged walkers who enjoy taking photographs but who do not linger over lunch and snack breaks. Some people will take longer than the estimated time, some will finish earlier. Hopefully fit walkers will find these estimates reasonably accurate.

WHEN TO WALK

Many top Tasmanian walks are in environments where extreme weather can occur even at the height of summer, turning an otherwise moderate walk into a tough gig even for experienced hikers. Peak times for views, wildflowers and events are noted, as are more challenging or even dangerous walking times. Walks that require protective gear whatever the forecast are also noted.

GRADE
The detail in each walk description will help you decide whether it is right for you, as will the grading. Walks in this book are graded as follows:

Easy: these walks are reasonably flat and on well-formed tracks, although longer distances might elevate some otherwise-easy walks to a higher grade.

Moderate: these walks may include stairs, hills, rough tracks and some scrambling.

Hard: difficult terrain, steep or long hills, remoteness and distance are all features of 'hard' walks.

FLORA AND FAUNA REFERENCES
The University of Tasmania produces three invaluable waterproof, folding 'flip guides' for identifying the state's remarkable flora: *FungiFlip*, *TreeFlip* and *EucaFlip*. These are available online and at many shops and tourist centres.
A Guide to Flowers & Plants of Tasmania, by the Launceston Field Naturalists Club, is a handy travel size.
The Slater Field Guide to Australian Birds is small enough to pop in a daypack.

Author Melanie Ball takes a break in lush forest on the Three Capes Track, Tasman Peninsula

Map symbols

—— 850 ——	Contour with height
▬ ▬ ▬ ▬ ◆	Walking route with direction, steep track
- - - - - - -	Walking track
══════	Freeway/highway
══════	Major road
══════	Other road
●	Point of interest
∧	Cave
▲	Hill/mountain
●	Landform
●	Vegetation
○	Water feature
═	Waterfall
—	Weir
⊗	Trail junction
⚒	Mine/diggings
⏚	Lighthouse
ER	Emergency radio
H	Helipad
⚓	Ferry terminal
🚇	Bus stop
🚆	Train station

LOCALITY

WORLD HERITAGE AREA

NATIONAL PARK

	Accommodation
	Attraction
	Barbecue
	Beach
	Bench
	Cafe/restaurant
	Campsite
	Indigenous culture
	Information
	Lookout
	Parking
	Picnic area
	Playground
	Stairs
	Toilet
	View
	Wildlife
	Walk start
	Walk finish

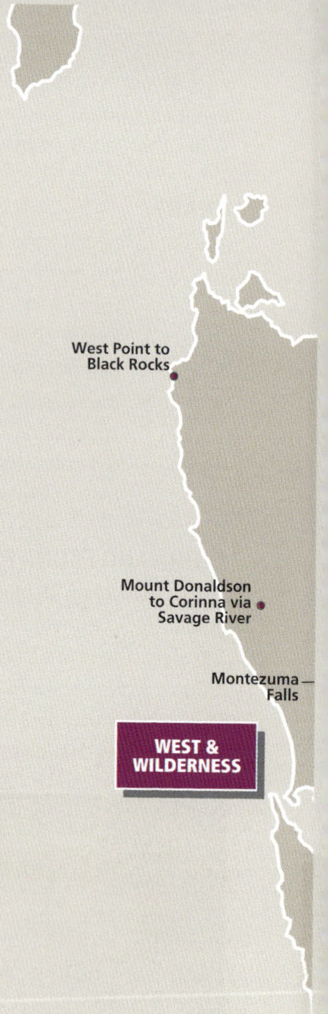

West Point to Black Rocks

Mount Donaldson to Corinna via Savage River

Montezuma Falls

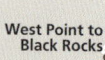

Moorina Bay and South Bruny Island from Cape Queen Elizabeth

HOBART REGION

Wonderful walking awaits within an hour of Tasmania's waterfront capital city. Wander among the world's tallest heath plants and in the company of sea birds on a deserted beach; marvel at in-your-face geology and exquisite fungi. Just do it!

1	kunanyi/Mount Wellington Summit	2
2	Lost World	9
3	Truganini	14
4	Alum Cliffs & Brickfields	18
5	Chauncy Vale Caves	23
6	Historic Richmond Town	28
7	Lady Barron Falls	34
8	Tarn Shelf	38
9	Growling Swallet & Junee Cave	44
10	Marriotts Falls	49
11	Tolkien Track – The Styx	54
12	Mount Misery	58
13	Cape Queen Elizabeth (Bruny Island)	62
14	Fluted Cape (Bruny Island)	67
15	Slide Track (Bruny Island)	72

HOBART REGION

1 KUNANYI/MOUNT WELLINGTON SUMMIT

Walk:	13.8km loop
Time required:	5–7 hours
Best time:	Clear day
Grade:	Hard
Environment:	Tree-fern gullies, eucalypt forest, exposed alpine plateau
Best map:	TASMAP's *Wellington Park Recreation Map & Notes* 1:20,000
Toilets:	Flushing toilets at The Springs picnic area and on the summit
Food:	Pub lunches and dinners, takeaway pizzas and homemade cakes are all on offer at Fern Tree Tavern.
Tips:	There is no drinking water on this walk, so take enough for the whole day.

Loop through fern-filled gullies and eucalypt forest and traverse exposed slopes as you summit Hobart's landmark mountain for a hard-to-better view of southern Tasmania.

Tasmania's capital spreads over the Derwent River estuary like a colony of colourful molluscs, and from nowhere is this description more apt than the top of kunanyi/Mt Wellington, the natural sentinel that protects Hobart from the worst of westerly storms. Often covered in snow, which can fall here even in summer, the mountain is both the city's spectacular backdrop and the barometer by which residents check the weather.

Spectacular views abound on the walk to Hobart's high point

KUNANYI/MOUNT WELLINGTON SUMMIT   3

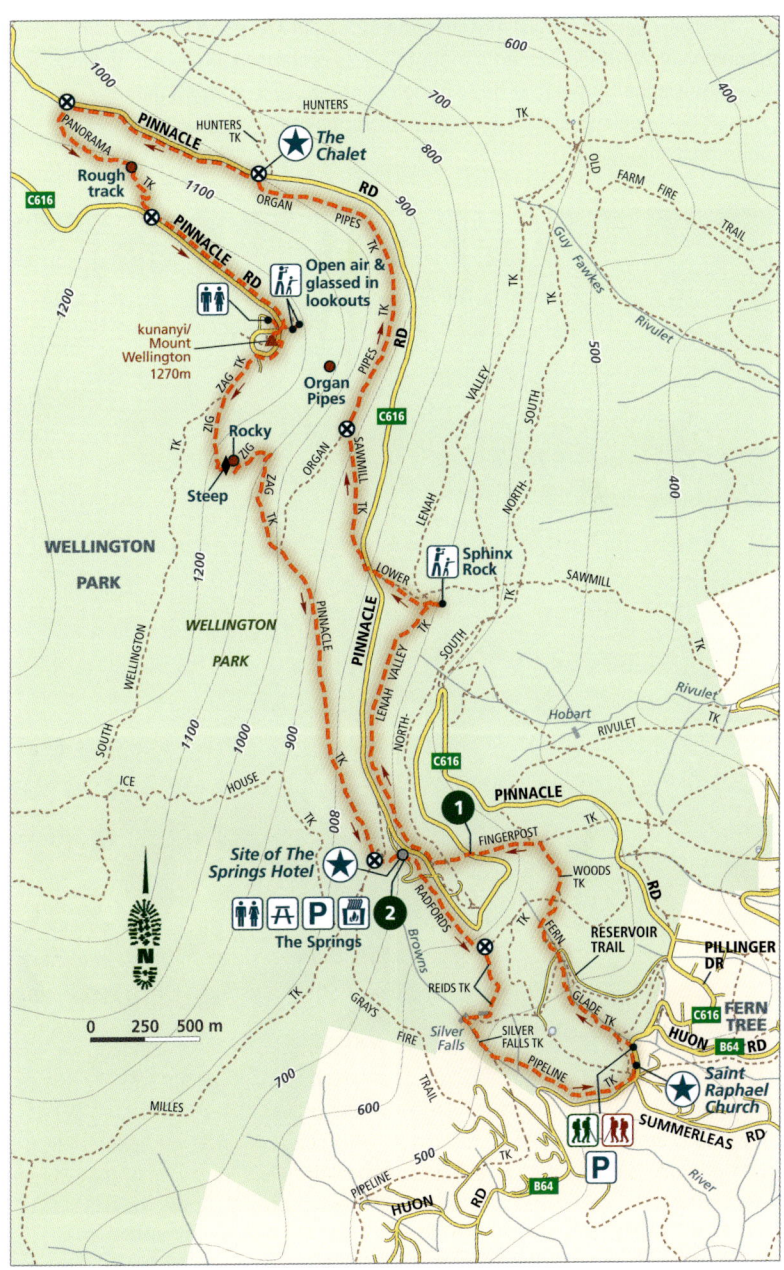

Officially named Mt Wellington in the 1820s, in honour of the duke who beat Napoleon at Waterloo, Hobart's mountain was renamed kunanyi/Mt Wellington to acknowledge that places had Aboriginal names first. kunanyi means 'mountain' in palawa kani, a constructed composite of original Tasmanian Aboriginal languages.

TOP: *Rocky track leads to Sphinx Rock;* **BOTTOM LEFT:** *Wildflowers decorate the mountain scrub;* **BOTTOM RIGHT:** *Tasmanian snow berries abound summer to autumn*

Walking tracks in Wellington Park reveal the 'noble forest', 'most extensive views', 'elegant parasols' of tree ferns, and the 'huge angular masses of naked greenstone [dolerite]' that Charles Darwin described in his book, *The Voyage of The Beagle*, after climbing kunanyi/Mt Wellington in 1836. This walk links several tracks into a grand day tour.

The walk starts in a small parking and picnic area on the mountain side of Summerleas Rd, just short of Fern Tree village, 13km from Hobart's CBD. The parking area can accommodate half a dozen sensibly parked cars. There is roadside space for a couple more, but the road is narrow and winding, so it's safer to park in Fern Tree and walk back.

The track disappears into thick forest from the picnic area, up stone steps beside a small seasonal waterfall. Follow the creek feeding the fall up a ferny gully, ignoring other tracks and footbridges left and right. Cross a restricted-use vehicular track and scale the stone steps opposite, up which you'll see a fabulous old gum tree.

Climbing from tree ferns into smooth-barked eucalypts, you'll intersect multi-use Radfords Track (mountain bikes permitted). Here stands a memorial to George H. Radford, who died coming down Mt Wellington on 19 Sept 1903 during the first recorded footrace from Hobart to the pinnacle. The modern-day equivalent is the annual Point to Pinnacle, promoted as the world's toughest half-marathon.

Cross Radfords Track, and continue north on an easy, vehicle-wide track through tall eucalypt forest for about 300m, then turn left up Fingerpost Track, a steeper, narrower, rocky track. Cross sealed Pinnacle Rd, which snakes to the summit, and ascend the stone steps opposite (*see* point 1 on map), shortly after which you reach another track junction with the road immediately ahead. Watching for mountain bikes, cross North–South Track (there are toilets in The Springs parking area, down to your left) and turn right onto Lenah Valley Track, parallel with the road.

Lined with prickly mountain-berry bushes – the females produce plump pink-to-red fruit – this flattish track ambles through eucalypts and traverses a boulder slope. Gaps between tree trunks provide a preview of the view to come.

About 1.3km from The Springs, on a sharp left bend, a side trail tunnels through tea tree to Sphinx Rock (a childproof gate prevents overeager youngsters from rushing out onto this unfenced lookout).

While you obviously need to view this sandstone outcrop from afar to see any similarity to the famous Egyptian monolithic creature, the impressive view from Sphinx Rock takes in Hobart, the Derwent estuary and the Tasman Peninsula. Up to your left is the spectacular dolerite Organ Pipes formation.

Immediately beyond the Sphinx Rock side trail, turn left onto Lower Sawmill Track, and climb through a swathe of spiky heath plants from which soar alpine gums. The track becomes rougher here, and crosses another boulder slope, the rocks underfoot decorated with rosettes of white lichen.

Lower Sawmill Track ends at Pinnacle Rd. Continue on Sawmill Track, which starts about 20m north up the road and climbs through sedgy grass, tea tree, elegantly striped eucalypts and alpine mintbush to the Organ Pipes.

A mountain-side wall of dolerite columns visible from afar, the Organ Pipes is one of Tasmania's most popular rock-climbing venues. As you walk north, with stone columns reaching skyward above and Hobart and surrounds spread below, you may hear voices and the tinkle of rock-climbing gear.

After descending to The Chalet, a stone shelter beside Pinnacle Rd, walk about a kilometre up the road to Panorama Track (on the left). A bit of a stretch up stone steps puts you on a rocky track that scrambles up through alpine gums and scratchy alpine heath, and rounds boulders.

Steep steps put you on Pinnacle Rd, with kunanyi/Mt Wellington's signal tower ahead. Follow the road to the top, where you'll find toilets, boardwalk-linked viewing platforms and a stone-and-glass lookout that shelters you from the bitter winds that often blow here.

When you're done ooh-ing and aah-ing at Hobart and southern Tasmania spread at your feet, and have ticked off the summit proper (a trig point on a rock pile), keep on along the road (a one-way loop) to the television and radio signal broadcasting tower.

Turn left immediately beyond the tower onto ZigZag Track, and traverse kunanyi/Mt Wellington's wind-scoured rocky plateau, treading a slightly uneven but beautifully stone-paved pathway through metre-high heath towards another fabulous dolerite wall.

South Hobart and Bruny Island (see p. 62) come into view beyond this tubular wall, and the view reaches to the east to take in Hobart as you descend further.

Now it's down the ZigZag Track, steep and rocky, with chains running between posts in places where nothing would prevent a rapid descent if you went over the edge. Go steadily and enjoy the 180° panorama of estuary and islands bookended by fabulous vertical geology.

The view vanishes as you drop into trees, there coming to another junction, with Organ Pipes Track running uphill. Turn right down Pinnacle Track and cross the path of a landslide, looking up at the swathe of damage and down at the boulder that caused it, resting just off the trail.

TOP: *More spectacular views from the mountain;* **BOTTOM:** *New myrtle beech leaves gild the forest*

Wider and less rocky now, so you can step out at last, the track crosses a grassy fire trail running along power lines and proceeds down into tea tree forest, towards The Springs. Stone track and stone steps descend through leafy forest to a one-way bitumen road. Turn right towards the 'No Entry' sign and pick up the walking track again opposite the grassy site of The Springs Hotel (1907), following this downhill. Cross the one-way loop road again (The Springs picnic area is to the left), then step down onto an unmarked walking track (*see* point 2 on map).

Signs a short way along announce this is a multi-use track, so watch for mountain bikes as you navigate chicanes fashioned from fallen trees and rocks, designed to slow cyclists.

Turn right down Reids Track (no bikes permitted), a steep track lined with mossy rocks and tall gum trees. Turn right again at the bottom, towards the swish of running water, and amble to Silver Falls, where Brown's River cascades prettily from a low ledge into a walled pool that empties into a stone-lined creek. (The stonework is part of the Waterworks scheme (1861), which took water from Mt Wellington to South Hobart.)

Cross the footbridge and follow the wide, formed Pipeline Track down the burbling river beneath a canopy of fern fronds. The track then recrosses the creek and diverges from the water. Benches along here might tempt you to stop and listen to the forest, but soon the loudest sound will be cars.

You come out on Pinnacle Rd opposite Fern Tree Tavern. Stay on this side of the road and walk left to the car park, passing the pretty, Swiss-style Anglican Church of St Raphael, one of the few Fern Tree buildings to survive the devastating 1967 bushfires.

Taking in the Hobart view from the exposed track to Sphinx Rock

HOBART REGION

2 LOST WORLD

Walk:	5km loop
Time required:	3-4 hours
Best time:	Clear, dry day. Can be snowbound in winter.
Grade:	Moderate–hard (predominantly clambering and rock-hopping)
Environment:	Mountain road, dolerite cliffs, boulder field, snow-gum forest
Best map:	This one
Toilets:	None
Food:	None
Tips:	How long this walk takes, depends on your prowess on rocks. If you prefer clambering downhill, walk clockwise as described here or if uphill suits you better, walk anticlockwise. Track signs are positioned for walking anticlockwise. Dolerite can be slippery when wet so reconsider if it rains; good-gripping, secure footwear is essential in all conditions.

Come all ye rock hoppers: fun times await in a natural adventure playground high on kunanyi/Mt Wellington.

Children shouldn't have all the fun and the Lost World, on kunanyi/Mt Wellington, above Hobart, is packed with physical fun for the young at heart. This walk's not about kilometres covered; it's about rocks trodden, sat on, skirted, slid down and ducked under.

Ferns add colour and texture to rock crevices

HOBART REGION

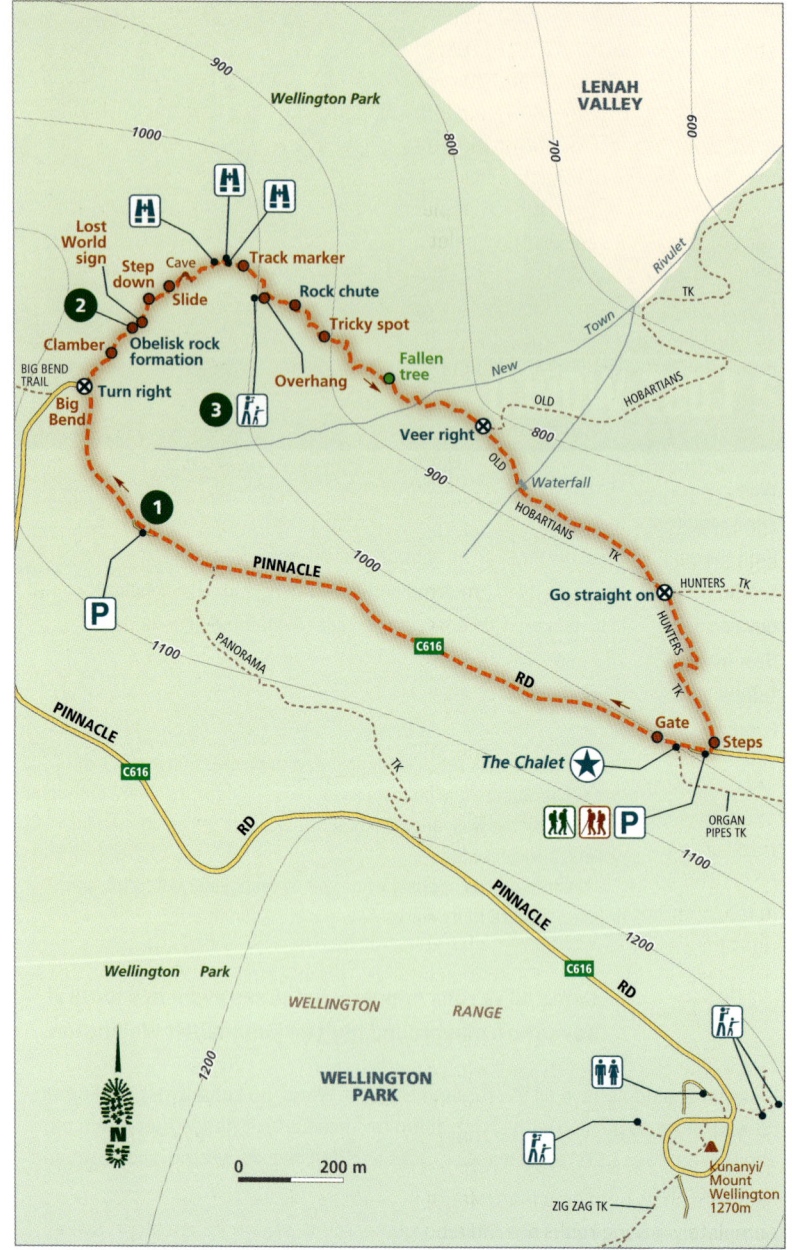

The get go is a small road-side parking area below The Chalet (picnic shelter) on Pinnacle Rd (C616): 1.5km below Big Bend and 4km from the top of kunanyi/Mt Wellington, and 20 minutes' drive from Hobart's waterfront, via Davey St (A6), Huon Rd (B64) and Pinnacle Road. The Hunters Track, which drops down the mountainside directly opposite the parking area is either the first (anticlockwise) or last (clockwise) leg of the Lost World loop.

Clockwise hikers – you are happier clambering down rocks than up? Great, walk up the road, passing The Chalet on your left. Perched 1000m above sea level, this stone shelter is the perfect place for a pre-walk picnic breakfast. It's also the trailhead for a great short walk to the Organ Pipes, visited on the kunanyi/Mt Wellington Loop (see page 2). Watching and listening for cars, continue up the road, past a couple of snow gates closed when conditions beyond make driving unsafe.

Alpine shrubs and yellow gums, shedding grey bark to reveal skin-smooth yellow, crowd the rocky slopes – those nearest the road cling with finger-like roots to a bank undermined by rock falls and water. But none of this distracts you for long from the view of Hobart (right), and the Lost World's dolerite column-cliff ahead.

Just short of Big Bend, where Pinnacle Rd makes its final turn before gaining the summit, you cross a narrow boulder field running down the mountain (see point 1 on map). The Lost World track goes right about 200m further up, opposite a three-car parking space and before a gated vehicular track on the bend.

The going is immediately rocky but can be boggy too; stick to the track and get dirty rather than skirt trouble spots. To the right is a Derwent Valley vista and further right, kunanyi/Mt Wellington towers over the spectacle. The rough track crests small boulders as it climbs through alpine heath, twisted snow gums and copperleaf snow-berry bushes, identifiable by their plump white fruit in late summer to autumn, towards a dolerite crown. Note the obelisk, to the right (see point 2 on map), which has split from the main formation; an elegant dead tree stands over it. Footpads clamber through and around these volcanic rocks but treading the most obvious track brings you to a Lost World track sign: welcome reassurance that you're going the right way!

Take in the Derwent view through the trees before continuing on a less distinct route with only occasional markers. You'll come to a natural rock sculpture that's split from the main formation but not yet toppled. Soon after, you've got a big step-down (easier than it looks) immediately below an exquisite snow gum on a lean. Marginally more obvious track then disappears completely among rocks around a gorgeous multi-stemmed eucalypt. Swing

A fallen dolerite column presents an on-the-edge Derwent Valley view

left around the tree onto a short rock slide roughly 2km into the walk. Once safely down – some walkers find it easier on their backsides although this can rip your shorts asunder – look back up at the tree, which grows out of savagely undercut rock.

Descend steeply now through dolerite, sometimes stepping down, sometimes slowing to find a boot-and-hand route. Snow gums are everywhere, striped trunks slicing through Hobart views. Then you're among fagus (deciduous beech); their crinkle-cut leaves decorate a track that works east to an expanse of fallen and broken dolerite extending out from the base of the columnar cliff you saw from the road. kunanyi/Mt Wellington is ahead and Hobart and the Derwent River laid out like a tableau below. As if the footing isn't enough to slow you down, now there are photographs everywhere, just waiting to be taken!

Footpads and then occasional orange arrows (the odd lolly wrapper too) lead across and down through boulders with micro caves between. Fern gardens and mountain-berry bushes grow in hollows underfoot. A massive dolerite column that's fallen away from the cliff towards the view makes an excellent half-way picnic platform (*see* point 3 on map).

Fuel up here for more steep descents, with too many big step-downs to mark on the map. Watch for orange arrows and occasional red reflectors sited

LOST WORLD   13

for walkers coming up the hill. Drop down and cross under balancing rocks, below which there's a small cave; navigate a chute between lumps of mossy rock. Mere mortals unrelated to mountain goats can find it slow-going but that only increases the fun. Take your time, helping companions where needed, and enjoy this geological escapade.

Suddenly you've got leaves and bark underfoot rather than rock and you're descending through massed snow berries, spiky grass with red flower heads, fagus and eucalypts. The track is indistinct in places, despite the addition of marker tape and yellow-and-red bullseyes painted on rocks so pay close attention: employ the leap-frog method for safety, letting party members take turns going ahead to find the next marker before others follow.

Having stepped over a fallen log, ducked under another felled tree and forded a rocky creek, you're finally on something approximating a good walking track; it crosses a slope thick with shrubs and shadow-casting eucalypts to a junction, 750m from the end, where the Old Hobartians Track goes left.

Turn right for The Chalet (40 minutes), treading firm, metre-wide track uphill into rough-barked eucalypts and banksias, and passing a little waterfall. Keep right and uphill on the Hunters Track at the next junction. Rock and wood steps put you on the road opposite your car.

Derwent Valley views await you all along this geological escapade

HOBART REGION

3 TRUGANINI

Walk:	5.1km out-and-back
Time required:	2 hours
Best time:	Clear day for the best views from the Signal Station
Grade:	Easy–moderate
Environment:	Wet riparian forest, eucalypt scrub, hill top, communication history, 19th century historic site
Best map:	This one
Toilets:	Flushing toilets in Signal Station car park
Food:	Pull up a seat in the Signal Station Brasserie, in the signalman's cottage, for breakfast or lunch and all-day sweet and savoury treats, including lemonade scones.
Tips:	You can drive to Signal Station, so if anyone in your party doesn't fancy walking, and/or you only want to walk the track one way, rendezvous up top, perhaps with a picnic or barbecue in the boot.

A memorial to Tasmanian Aboriginal culture and communication history, with sweeping views thrown in, this mostly-forest walk climbs from riverbank to 19th century signal station.

This walk is named in honour of Truganini, the most famous historical Tasmanian Aborigine, whose work with (and against) European settlers to save her people

Enjoy late afternoon light from the Signal Station Brasserie

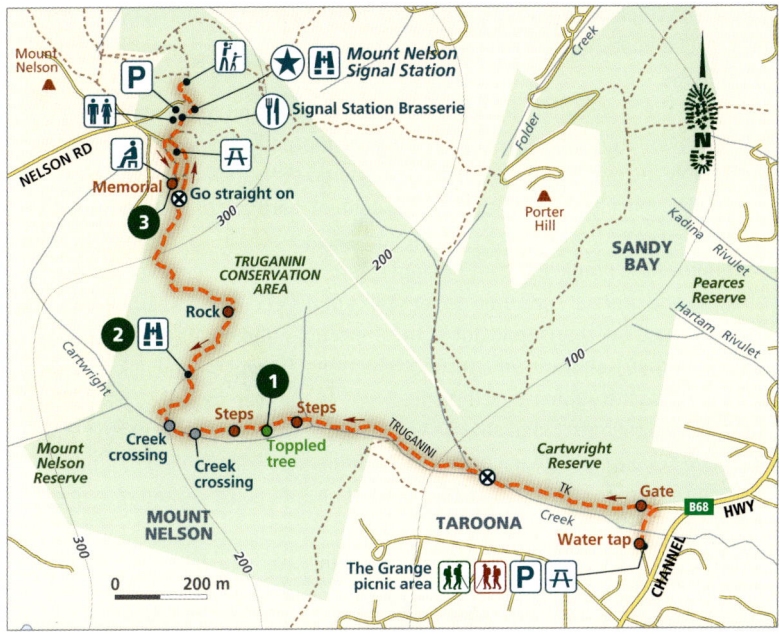

from annihilation saw her described as ambassador, guerrilla fighter and survivor. Truganini Track climbs Cartwright Creek to historic Mt Nelson Signal Station in south Hobart.

It starts from shady Truganini Reserve (where you'll find parking and picnic tables) on the western side of Sandy Bay Rd, a couple of hundred metres from the Derwent River, in the southern suburb of Cartwright Creek. About 20m into the bush from the yellow-and-white sign at the rear of the reserve, the track is gated against vehicles.

Initially wide enough for two people, the bark-covered track threads through untidy eucalypt forest, in the main creek gully, with houses just visible beyond the trees. Having crossed a smaller tributary, ignore a lower track with rocks across it and instead keep right, but staying beside the creek. Veer left at the next junction, ignoring a fire trail to private property, and down into the creek gully. Narrower and rockier track continues upstream, through bracken and moss and occasional tall eucalypts far outnumbered by ganglier immature ones.

You'll come to a junction where a track with an old wooden sign goes left, over the creek. Ignore this and remain on this side of the creek, climbing more steeply up man-made steps, rocks and roots, with Cartwright Creek still below. The track slices through a long-toppled tree that's covered in moss, ferns and miniature mushrooms (see point 1 on map). Look out for colourful jelly fungus.

Cross the creek where it's piled with mossy rocks and thick with tree ferns and continue on the opposite bank. The footpad coming up on this side is probably the continuation of the track ignored at the last crossing point. Beyond the majestic eucalypts standing sentinel here you enter drier forest with fewer ferns. The air cracks with whipbirds too.

Recross the creek and continue upstream; note the diversity of moss textures and greens. Look out too for stalks of pink common heath bell flowers. The track then steps out of the creek gully and heads uphill (see point 2 on map), showing you, through the trees, fingers of land poking south beyond Hobart. Truganini's birthplace, Bruny Island (see page 62), pokes its head around the next ridge east as you climb. Several step-ups stretch your legs as you walk through eucalypts with coarse grey bark peeling to smooth buttermilk trunks. The track skirts a lump of granite polka-dotted with grey-and-white lichens.

LEFT: Fungi sprout in gullies and on fallen trees; **RIGHT:** The track climbs from Cartwright Creek to the old Signal Station

Almost at the top, there's a T-junction with a narrow track going left onto a granite slab. Keep right and walk on through another four-way junction, leaving the memorial track (left) for your return. Ignoring another track going right almost immediately after, walk the final 50m or so to the top, across picnic lawns with electric barbecues and past Signal Station Brasserie (delights with a view) in the signalman's cottage (1897).

Beyond, squats boxy Mt Nelson Signal Station. Founded in 1811 to convey information about shipping traffic in and out of the Port of Hobart to marine authorities, and later modified to also accommodate messages to and from Port Arthur, Mt Nelson Signal Station is an integral part of Tasmania's communication history. (See also Coal Mines Historic Site page 95). Flag, lamp, semaphore, telegraph, telephone and radio signalling techniques were used here before it was decommissioned in 1969.

Within the tiny building you'll find memorabilia, photographs, books, the International Code of Signals and a chart showing how the semaphore system operated across south-east Tasmania. The last semaphore message ('Forgotten') was sent from here to Battery Point in 1890.

Three signalmen operated the station, so life wasn't as isolated as at a lighthouse. And while they had to work in all weathers, few workplaces have views to compare: over Hobart and its waterways, including the Tasman Bridge spanning the Derwent River and ships and boats navigating the river; and Mt Wellington standing above the city, with its signal tower poking the sky. The view takes in the Tasman Peninsula to the south-east, and narrow Eaglehawk Neck. On clear days you can see Cape Raoul (see page 85). Bruny Island is visible just beyond the trees to the right.

Past and below the signal station is another lookout. A walking track leads from here down to the suburb of Sandy Bay. With a car shuffle or public transport, you could do this as a through walk.

Otherwise, retrace your steps to the memorial junction and take the right-hand track, towards a house. A few metres along there is a seat facing a granite boulder on which is a sculpted metal plaque dedicated to the Tasmanian Aboriginal people and their descendants (see point 3 on map).

Continue past the memorial and swing left to the track you walked up. Retrace your steps down Cartwright Creek to finish.

HOBART REGION

4 ALUM CLIFFS & BRICKFIELDS

Walk:	4.7km A to B
Time required:	2-3 hours
Best time:	Year-round
Grade:	Easy
Environment:	Eucalypt forest, heathland, coastal cliffs, beach, historic shot tower
Best map:	This one
Toilets:	Flushing toilets in the Shot Tower grounds and at Kingston Beach
Food:	Cafes and restaurants in Kingston Beach
Tips:	Check out bus times at www.metrotas.com.au – search: Kingston Beach.

Tread a path along coastal cliffs from Australia's oldest shot tower to a dog-friendly, beach-front suburb that dishes up delicious food and great coffee.

More than 140 years after it rose from the cliffs 9km south of Hobart town, the sandstone Shot Tower at Taroona still ranks as one of the tallest structures in Tasmania's capital. Australia's first-built, and one of only three surviving, Scotsman Joseph Moir's shot tower operated for 30 years from 1870, manufacturing lead shot for muzzle-loading sports guns. This industrial landmark is the starting point for a Hobart-fringe coastal ramble on a track long-used by locals.

Insect feeding tracks decorate a dead eucalypt

ALUM CLIFFS & BRICKFIELDS 19

While you could car shuffle, public transport works well for walkers with one vehicle. Park at Kingston Beach's foreshore (Osborne Esplanade), 13km south of Hobart via the A6, and round the corner into Beach Road. The bus stop is a hundred metres or so up on the left. Weekdays and Saturdays catch a route 407 bus to Kingston, changing there to route 427; on Sundays the route 427 bus travels to Hobart via Kingston Beach and Taroona so you don't need to change.

A scenic bus ride on a winding coastal road brings you to stop #32, directly opposite the shot tower; ask the bus driver to alert you. You're on a bend with double lines so cross the road with care.

For $8 you can climb from the tower's 10m diameter base to its 4m top. Multiple timber steps spiral upwards from a small information room – a video shows how shot was made – to a broad view over Taroona and neighbouring peninsulas. Looking south you can see Bruny Island (see page 62).

The rusty cauldron at the top of the stairs is a relic of operational days. Molten lead mixed with arsenic (to decrease the surface tension) and antimony (to harden the shot) was poured through colanders, the resulting droplets becoming spherical as they fell the height of the tower into water. The cooled shot was dried, polished in a revolving drum and graded by size. Moir's factory produced 100 tons of shot a year at its peak.

From the shot tower, follow the bitumen down through the historic site, around Moir's castle-like house and clockwise below the toilet. The Alum Cliffs walking track comes in on the left, from Taroona (an alternative starting point), but keep right towards an obvious red-and-green Alum Cliffs track sign.

Having descended between a paddock with water views and a house hiding behind a high metal fence, the vehicle-wide walking track swings left and into a gully (the track is loose and shaly and you could easily slip without the wood-plank steps leading steeply down and up the other side). Climbing out, note the shallow soil layer laid over base rock. Turn around up top for a shot tower view.

Past a home with an enviable view you come to a cliff-edge picnic table and a close-up view of the layered and textured cliffs. The rocks to the right have fallen away, leaving a powdery slope dropping to rock shelving – don't climb over the fence for a better view!

Continuing south, eucalypts and she-oaks make up for less exciting views of some backyard fences – as do an old water race (see point 1 on map) and the nearness of the cliff. The track descends from house level into a gully and swings left through grassy forest with a delicious aroma and a noisy bird chorus. Back up out of the gully you come to the Brickfield's track junction. There's not a great deal to see but detour right a couple of hundred metres up to the remains of convict-era brickworks. Wooden steps and decking lead to an information board.

Back on the main track, you'll start glimpsing water and shore through the trees. For now, though, the trees remain the focus of the walk. Few are bigger than about 90cm diameter but their colours and textures are attractive; some have thick and almost spongy brown bark that comes loose in pieces and litters

TOP LEFT: *Treading the Alum Cliffs track;* **TOP RIGHT:** *A bee feeds on a daisy field near Moir's Shot Tower;* **BOTTOM:** *Kingston Beach is a popular dog walking stretch*

the track with leaves, giving the forest the scruffy appeal of gold country. On warm days the forest hums with insects.

About 400m from the Brickfields junction there's a lookout on the lip of a drop to blue-green water from which, on a breezy day, you often see yachts. Keep looking left to see water-level rock shelving as you push on.

Beyond a gnarly, old-timer gum on the left (see point 2 on map), the track goes inland along a gully, passing the hollowed and blackened stump of what would have been a majestic gum; moss and insects have colonised its charcoal lining. The track U-turns over a little creek where walkers have worn a footpad to what is probably a pretty cascade after good rains. Note the drop in humidity and rise in temperature as you leave behind the gully's moss and fallen logs and regain drier eucalypt scrub.

Steps give a good view north of the layered cliffs you followed here, and east-ish across the water. Rougher steps lead to another fenced lookout soon after. On the right of the track, directly opposite the lookout, is a splendid old gum several metres around its base and almost immediately after there's another, on the left, with three mature trunks growing from one base. The vibrant green trees with cypress-like foliage and small orange berries are native cherry, an indigenous root parasite. Watch for green rosellas – they can be difficult to see among the trees – and listen for the distinctive swallowing sound of yellow-cheeked wattle birds, found only in Tasmania.

Up another gully the track U-turns over a deep channel, with exposed roots and rocks; water must rush through underfoot after rain. Out again, you cross a grassy hill, with water views and rock paving at the base of the cliffs. Skirting more backyards, you come to a junction: the right-hand track (see point 3 on map) follows the Alum Cliffs track to the car park (no steps) but the route described here goes left to Tyndall Beach (uneven track with multiple steps), because what's a coastal walk without sand?

Descend steeply, through gum trees to the wash of waves and dog barks. Tyndall is a leash-free dog beach and you often pass people and sandy, tongue-lolling canines coming up as you step down.

A walking track goes right just before you hit the sand. Ignore this and step down onto the beach. Head left and fossick around the rocky outcrop on the beach just before sand runs into cliff. Then turn back and walk the length of the beach, about 400m to Browns River. Depending on the tide and your footwear, you can often wade through the water and follow the foreshore to your car. Otherwise, you'll need to head slightly inland, past the Kingston Sea Scouts Group club building and over a footbridge.

HOBART REGION

5 CHAUNCY VALE CAVES

Walk:	7km loop
Time required:	2-3 hours
Best time:	Mild, clear day in spring or autumn (the lagoon and creek dry up in summer and Caves Track can be slippery in winter after rain)
Grade:	Easy (with short climb)
Environment:	Dry sclerophyll forest, sandstone caves
Best map:	This one
Toilets:	Toilet at start of walk
Food:	None
Tips:	Day Dawn, the house built in 1916-18 and given to original owners of the land (Nan and Anton Chauncy) as a wedding present, is open to the public on the 1st Sunday of each month from 2pm til 4pm.

Leave underground caving to the wetsuit-clad and discover the joys of dry caving on an easy walk in the heart of Tasmania.

Chauncy Vale Wildlife Sanctuary (www.chauncyvale.com.au) is one of Tasmania's oldest private conservation areas. Gazetted in 1946 after an application by Nan and Anton Chauncy, it was bequeathed to the local council on Anton's death in 1988 and is now managed by a council sub-committee. Chauncy Vale, adjoining

Looking out over the sanctuary from Brown's Caves

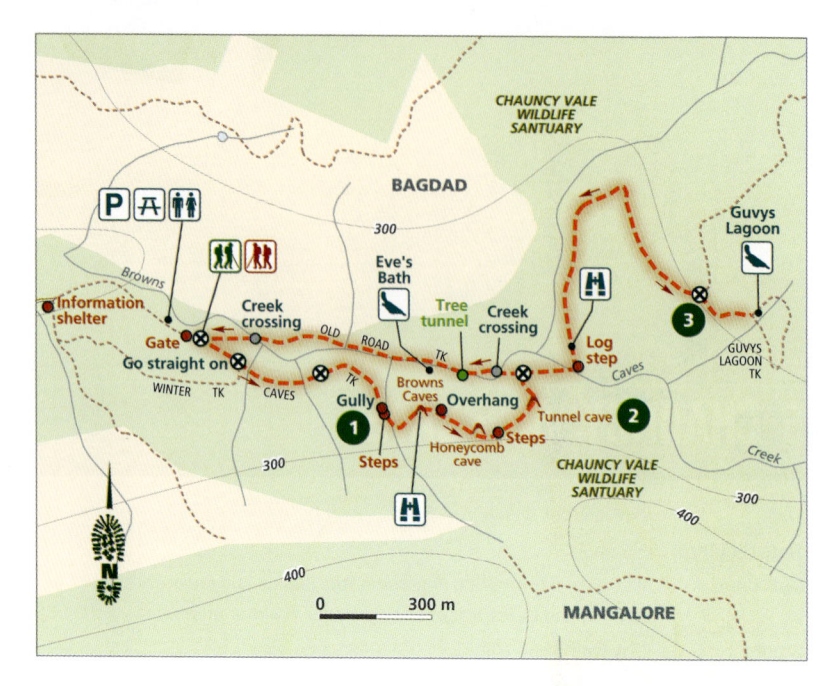

Flat Rock Reserve, purchased by the Tasmanian Land Conservancy in 2006, and Alpha Pinnacle Conservation Area together protect over 1000 hectares of the Southern Midlands.

Chauncy Vale is a sanctuary for resident nomadic and migratory birds, including ten of Tasmania's 12 endemic species. You may see wombats, Bennett's wallabies, pademelons, bandicoots, perhaps even an endangered Tasmanian devil or uncommon eastern quoll. Snakes number among the reptiles that thrive here, so watch your step. The long list of native and endemic plants recorded on the property includes more than two dozen orchids.

Walking tracks extend through the sanctuary to Flat Rock Reserve but the walk described here shows off the sanctuary's geology and flora; the more observant you are, the more wildlife you will see.

Chauncy Vale is 4km east of Bagdad, a small town 40km north of Hobart on the Midland Hwy (Route 1). In Bagdad turn east into Chauncy Vale Rd and follow it 4km to the gated sanctuary boundary (entry is a $2 donation). Having closed the gate after you, drive about 700m to the end of the road, beyond the information shelter and picnic area. The walking track starts past the gate across the road here.

A handsome eucalypt reaches skyward from the rock on the approach to Brown's Caves

Much of Chauncy Vale is dry sclerophyll forest of white peppermints (eucalypts) and the walk begins among these tall trees with smooth, cream-streaked grey trunks. At a junction about 50m beyond the gate keep right on vehicle-wide Caves Track and then ignore the right-hand Winter Track, which loops back to the information shelter. At the next junction, step from the vehicle track onto the narrower Caves Track, which heads right and uphill towards a rocky ridge, through cutting grass, wattles, almost fluffy green native cherry trees and tall gums. The track crosses and then steps up beside a narrow gully (see point 1 on map), the climb bringing you face to face with squared-off rock faces above the valley floor. Keep a look out for camouflaged grey-and-white mountain dragons (small thorny lizards) among the leaf litter and rocks.

Following the track left past a beautiful leaning gum tree, you come to undercut sandstone sculpted into sedimentary tiers and drilled with holes; this is the first of Brown's Caves and from here you can see down Brown's Caves Creek valley and out to the plains beyond. Past a slab of sandstone jutting from the cliff you'll come to steps leading up into a sandstone 'vestibule' opening into a roomier cave, both with sculpted walls. Sandstone wears to powder that can make the rock slippery so take care as you step up into the first cave and duck through into the bigger one; they could have been purpose-built for sitting and looking out over the treed sanctuary. Beyond those open caves you pass a hole naturally drilled up into the hill and 50m or so further along you can clamber up into another cave with honeycomb internal walls. As you zigzag down the hill, you'll pass a tunnel cave drilled into the sandstone (see point 2 on map), its mouth right beside the track.

Sanctuary co-founder Nan Chauncy was a celebrated children's author who died in 1970 a year after the publication of her twelfth novel. These caves possibly and probably inspired her first, published in 1947, a best-seller called *They Found a Cave*. Early in his illustrious career, Launceston composer Peter Sculthorpe wrote the score for the successful film version of the book, which was released in 1962.

Down on the valley floor in a sea of bracken there's a junction marked with a wooden post. You could turn left here for a shorter loop back to the parking area but even in summer it's worth turning right for Guvys Lagoon, a great bird-watching spot when there's water.

Cross Brown's Caves Creek, often bone dry in summer, and continue upstream along the opposite bank. You are now treading the Old Road Track, which shortly turns left away from the creek and doglegs up and around a low ridge through scruffy eucalypt forest. This track gives a good view back to the cave and the cliffs above. Protecting the peregrine falcons that nest in these cliffs was a major impetus for Nan and Anton making their home a wildlife reserve. The cliffs are out-of-bounds for visitors.

Invaded by shrubs in a couple of spots but easy to follow, the Old Road Track brings you to another junction. Ignore the Flat Rock Lookout option to the left (see point 3 on map) and keep right for Guvys Lagoon, about 200m further on and gently downhill through eucalypts trailing bark streamers.

Dry sclerophyll forest becomes very dry sclerophyll forest in summer and Guvys Lagoon shrinks to a puddle; animal droppings on the mossy lagoon floor indicate the importance of every water source to sanctuary wildlife in hot weather. Multiple shades of green, yellow and brown also make it unexpectedly photogenic. At wetter times the lagoon is a wonderful bird-watching spot and you can identify what you see from photos at the information shelter on the road out.

Backtrack from the lagoon to the Caves Track junction and follow the valley-floor track over the rock-floored creek and downstream. The Chauncy family used to wash in the creek at Eves Bath (signed); in summer it dries to another puddle fed by a trickle, down a water-cut incision in the creek bed. You may see eels here, and wallabies and echidnas on the final 800m walk to the car.

The track shelters in a patch of dense, leafier trees before pushing on through open eucalypt forest to finish.

Take a short, shaded break in Brown's Caves overlooking the sanctuary

HOBART REGION

6 HISTORIC RICHMOND TOWN

Walk:	4km loop
Time required:	2 hours
Best time:	Sunny day
Grade:	Easy
Environment:	Village streets, convict-era gaol, colonial buildings, riverbank
Best map:	This one
Toilets:	Flushing toilets in the Forth St parking area near Richmond Gaol
Food:	Everything from oven-fresh scones to pub fare is available along Richmond's main street
Tips:	Richmond is on the Convict Trail (www.tasmanian-convict-trail.com), a fascinating 205km self-drive tour from Hobart to Port Arthur and back, highlighting the region's history and scenery

Follow in the footsteps of convicts, military officers, innkeepers and a Dickens character as you explore the streets of one of Tasmania's most historic towns.

Settled in the early 19th century after the discovery of coal, the fertile Coal River region north-east of Hobart became known, with neighbouring Pitt Water, as 'the granary of Australia' – and is now a renowned wine region. This walk dips into the fascinating history of Richmond, the town established at the point where a

Richmond Bridge is said to be haunted by several ghosts

HISTORIC RICHMOND TOWN 29

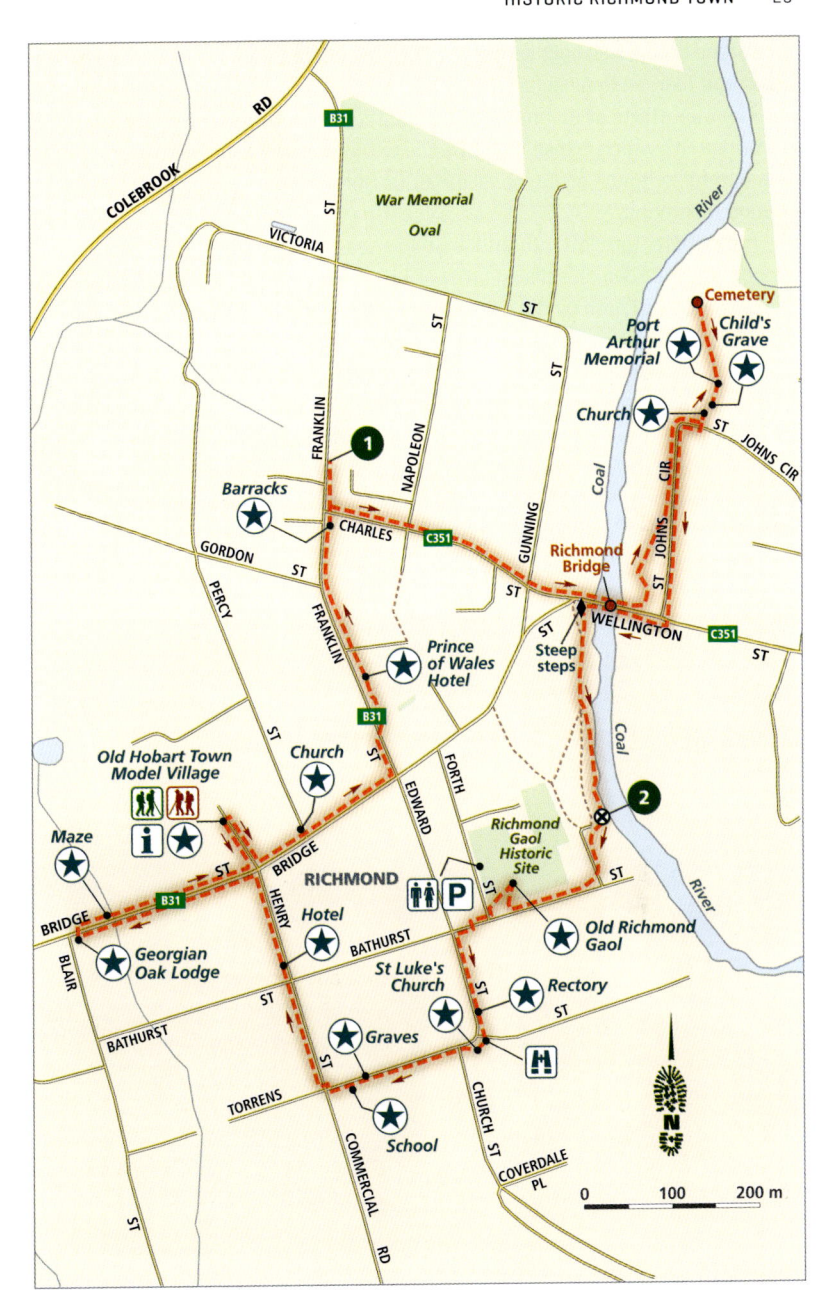

sandstone bridge was built across the Coal River to facilitate travel to the east coast and Tasman Peninsula.

The walk starts at Richmond's visitor information centre (up a laneway off Bridge St), which is also the entrance to Old Hobart Town. Wander around this faithful, outdoor, scale model of 1820s Hobart before heading off around Richmond.

From there, turn left into Bridge St and pass Fry Cottage (1835), now the Woodcraft Shop, which sells an array of Tasmanian timber products. Note the stone front step, worn by the passage of feet over nearly 200 years. Imagine what stories it could tell!

The congregational church on the next corner was built in 1873, making it a youngster, but the supermarket, just before the next corner, dates from 1836.

Turn left at the supermarket car park and walk along the east side of Franklin Street. Now a private residence, the two-storey red-brick building was once the Prince of Wales Hotel, one of numerous hotels that accommodated early travellers quenching their thirsts.

Start the walk with a stroll around Old Hobart Town, a scale model of 1820s Hobart

Have a stickybeak over the picket fence at the old hotel's elegant Georgian lines before strolling on to the cluster of white-painted cottages on the corner of Charles Street. Now holiday accommodation, these buildings were the Richmond Barracks, built of convict-made bricks in 1830, when Richmond became one of Governor Arthur's police districts.

You are going to turn right here, but first walk a bit further along Franklin St and look across the road at the early workers' cottages (see point 1 on map). On this side you'll see some new houses, built in sympathy with the original, simple historic design.

Retrace your steps, then turn down Charles St and walk east and downhill to a junction with more lovely old brick cottages on your right. Directly ahead is Richmond Bridge, the oldest bridge in Australia still in use.

The construction of a bridge over the Coal River enabled settlers to push further east, to the coast and Tasman Peninsula in search of good land. Commenced in 1823 and built by convicts from sandstone (quarried by convicts) and hauled in hand carts to the river (yes, by convicts), Richmond Bridge is said to be haunted by several ghosts, including George Grover. Himself a convict, transported for stealing, Grover was by all accounts a nasty piece of work who whipped prisoners like horses during the rebuilding of the bridge piers in 1829. Three years later, the 27-year old 'wicked Flagellator' was thrown over the bridge to his death while drunk, probably by some of the men he brutalised; he is buried in the grounds of St Luke's Church, which you'll pass later on the walk.

Turn left immediately across the bridge and walk down the grassy bank to view its beautiful arches. Then head up St John's Cirque to the oldest Catholic Church in Australia still in use, which sits prettily on a rise behind some beautiful gum trees. The church interior is fairly plain but, inside and out, you can see convict tool marks in every stone.

A historic burial ground overlooks the Coal River from a rise behind the church. Some of the oldest and most interesting headstones, at the back, have developed severe lists.

Return to the bridge and cross back over the river, turning hard left at the end of the stonework and heading down the steep, worn original steps – if you can cope with the pitch (otherwise just amble down the wheel-friendly path beyond). The three-storey Georgian building sitting proudly on the opposite bank was convict-built as a steam mill in 1853. It later became a butter factory.

Walk downstream through linear parkland, keeping to the lower walking track, which passes lovely old wooden boats for hire and awful plastic swans you can paddle on the river.

Many original cottages line Richmond's streets

Continue along the river to a track (*see* point 2 on map) up to a car park, and from there walk up Bathurst St, between almond trees, with the clocktower/spire of St Luke's Church to your left. Just before the crossroad, turn right to Richmond Gaol (1825), the oldest gaol in Australia.

Allow at least an hour to wander around this remarkable piece of history and read about the people who lived and worked here. One notorious prisoner was Ikey Solomon, London fence and pawnbroker and repeat escapee, who was transported to Van Diemen's Land in 1831 (having sailed to Australia voluntarily after his wife was transported from Britain). Solomon is widely believed to have been the inspiration for Fagin in Charles Dickens' novel *Oliver Twist*.

On exiting the gaol, head back across the lawns and towards the church seen earlier. Wander up Edward St (the little sandstone cottage on the corner was Richmond Dispensary, c. 1830) to St Luke's Church, passing the stone-block rectory on the left.

As you approach the church gate you are treated to a watercolour view of river and farmland to the left.

St Luke's Anglican Church is the oldest church in Richmond, its foundation stone having been laid in 1834 by Governor Phillip himself. Convict James Thompson was granted his freedom as a reward for the interior timberwork.

Now walk up Torrens St, passing the burial ground (1845) on the site of the original congregational church. Directly opposite is the oldest still-operating primary school in Australia (1834). Turn right into Commercial Rd and walk to Bridge St, passing the old Richmond Hotel – note the faded 'wine and spirits' paintwork.

Turn left into Bridge St and walk to Georgian Oak Lodge (1830), perhaps via the homewares shops along the way, all in stone cottages. Built as a gentleman's town residence and subsequently used as a rectory, school, doctor's surgery and family home, Oak Lodge is run by volunteers as a local museum and is open most days 11.30am–3.30pm (or by appointment).

Cross the street and head back up to the visitor information centre, perhaps getting lost in Richmond Maze on the way.

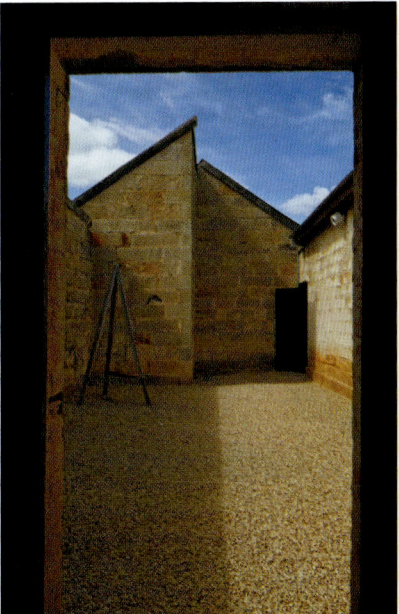

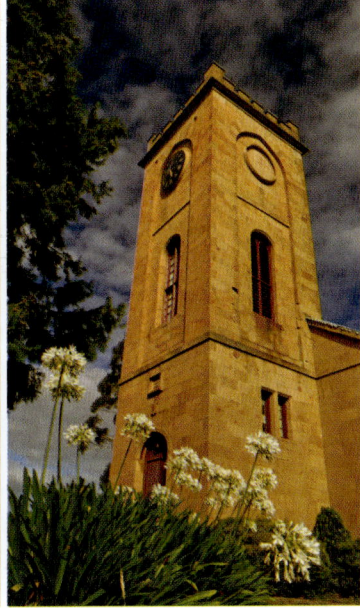

LEFT: *Looking into the whipping yard in Richmond Gaol;* **RIGHT:** *St Luke's Anglican Church (1834) is the oldest church in Richmond*

HOBART REGION

7 LADY BARRON FALLS

Walk:	7.5km loop
Time required:	2.5 hours
Best time:	Any time of year; richest hues and shadow-free photographs on overcast days. Most spectacular cascades after rain.
Grade:	Easy
Environment:	Tall eucalypt forest, rainforest, waterfalls
Best map:	This one
Toilets:	Flushing toilets at Mt Field National Park Visitor Centre
Food:	Good range of food at the café within the visitor centre
Tips:	Take a picnic or buy takeaway at the café and lunch on the lawns at the entry to the park.

Bag three beautiful waterfalls on this easy loop through towering timbers in the lower reaches of Mt Field National Park

Who can resist a waterfall? Seeing waterfalls (broad and voluminous, delicate and elongated), hearing them (crashing, trickling, dripping) and the kiss of their spray all energise and relax. They can entertain for hours. Tasmania boasts many cascades (http://waterfallsoftasmania.com.au/waterfalls) and this easy loop visits Mt Field National Park's triumvirate.

Russell Falls cascades in veils over three tiers of layered rock

LADY BARRON FALLS   35

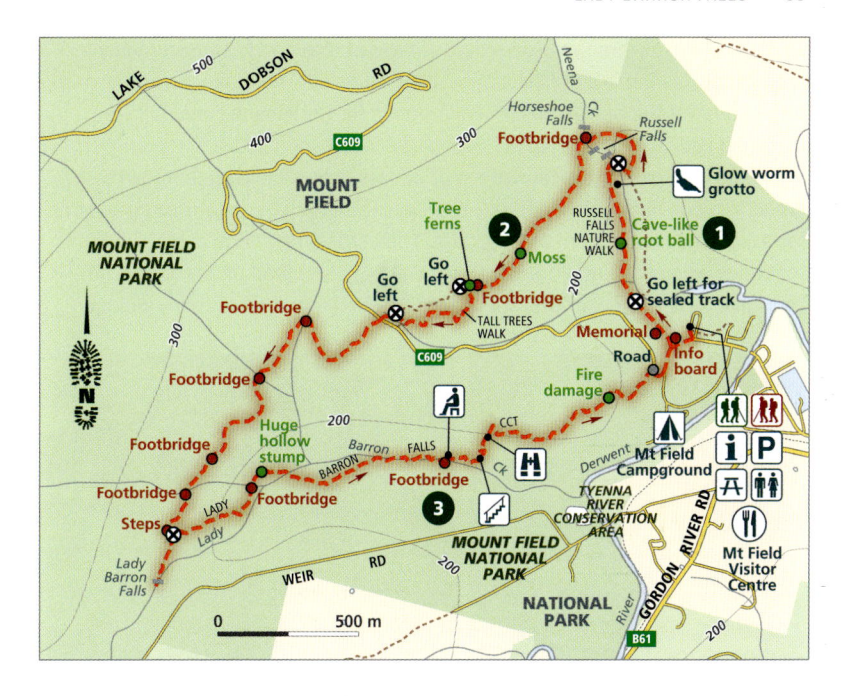

The walk begins at Mt Field National Park Visitor Centre, on Gordon River Rd, about 80km north-west of Hobart via New Norfolk and the rolling Derwent River valley. Wander through the informative park visitor centre and out the back door. From the Russell Falls sign, to your left, follow sealed track into a forest of swamp gums (*Eucalyptus regnans*, called mountain ash in Victoria), the world's tallest flowering plant. You will pass a memorial to people who played important roles in the development of Mt Field National Park, which was founded in 1916 and is Tasmania's joint oldest national park with Freycinet (see page 142).

A track junction offers a choice: stay on the sealed track or turn right, over Russell Falls Creek, and tread an alternate, slightly rougher track; they meet further on. You can tread both, one before and the other after visiting Russell and Horseshoe falls, on a shorter loop walk. Both options follow the creek, through swamp gums, sassafras, blackwoods and myrtle. The sealed track passes a tree that came down eons back and whose cave-like root ball has become a popular selfie spot (see point 1 on map). Mossy fallen branches litter the creek gully and tree ferns add a lattice texture.

Soon after passing a glow-worm grotto (come back at night), you reach another junction. Go left onto a deck giving the best view of Russell Falls, which cascades 45m in three veils over tiers of layered rock and is considered by many to be Tasmania's prettiest cascade – a big call! Then take the stone steps and wooden stairs beside Russell Falls signed for Horseshoe Falls, Tall Tree Walk and Lady Barron Falls.

About 100m after the fenced top of Russell Falls a footbridge fords the creek. You can hear and see Horseshoe Falls from here but continue straight on for a closer look at the smaller cascade. Then cross the bridge and follow signs for Lady Barron Falls and the Tall Trees Walk. A short climb puts you on a flat track in a flotilla of eucalypts, some broad around their bases, many younger

Foliage creates beautiful patterns around and above you on this walk

and thinner. Note the variety of mosses that have colonised the root ball of a fallen giant you pass (see point 2 on map).

Another footbridge puts you amid abundant tree ferns on the official Tall Trees Walk (a 30-minute loop). Take the track going left. A sign describes how to calculate the age of a tree by counting growth rings but explains that swamp gums sometimes produce false rings.

The swamp gum, a big tree when mature with a dark, fibrous bark stocking low on its trunk and contrasting smooth, white-ish upper bark, is the main timber in this forest but assorted species weave the canopy. Looking at the leaf litter is a great way to identify the species.

At the next junction, turn left again to Lady Barron Falls. The track crosses the unsealed road running the length of the park to Lake Dobson, a departure point for Mt Field alpine walks (see page 38). Cross and walk through handsome trees. Easy, compacted gravel descends into moister forest to a footbridge, after which you're back in fern forest, with dead eucalypts reaching high and live ones appearing to have climbed up the ferns towards the light. There's a distinct change in temperature as you drop into sheltered creek gullies – one especially thick with ferns and moss – and climb into drier forest.

Step down to a junction, with the visitor centre to your left and Lady Barron Falls five minutes to your right. As you stroll up the falls track, the water becomes louder and you glimpse foaming white ahead. Boardwalk and more steps deliver you to a cascade that pours over two broad steps before foaming through a chute into a plunge pool full of logs washed down in the rain.

This beauty is the last of the waterfalls, so drink your fill before returning to the junction and walking on towards the visitor centre: downhill along pretty Lady Barron Creek, across it and along the opposite bank among handsome old trees and bright green ferns. Here too are fagus (deciduous beech) so this section is prettiest in autumn when the leaves turn yellow and red before falling.

Cross another footbridge – fantastic plate fungi project from the tree where you step off (see point 3 on map) – and keep along the opposite bank, past stumps of logged trees. From the top of the steep stairs exiting the creek gully you get a good look at the surrounding ranges and pine plantations. A broad gravel track flattens out in drier forest of coarse-barked eucalypts quite different from the swamp gums.

Buildings appear to your right and then left and you emerge from trees beside a house on the main park road. Head right and follow the road downhill about 100m to the visitor centre.

HOBART REGION

8 TARN SHELF

Walk:	15km loop
Time required:	5-6 hours
Best time:	Clear, mild day spring-to-autumn; often snowbound in winter but wintry conditions can occur any time of year
Grade:	Moderate
Environment:	Tarns, ancient pencil pines, alpine heathland, dolerite, mountains
Best map:	This one or TASMAP's *Mt Field National Park Map & Notes 1:50,000*
Toilets:	Flush toilets at the Mt Field National Park Visitor Centre, composting at Lake Dobson
Food:	Hot and cold food and drinks available from visitor centre café
Tips:	Defer your walk if bad conditions are forecast and take a wind- and waterproof jacket whatever the weather. When it's warm take a towel so you can have a swim or dip your feet.

Climb from the weird and wonderful world of giant heath to a raw, glaciated, alpine plateau studded with tarns on a day-trip from Tasmania's capital.

Mt Field National Park is Tasmania's most diverse national park, and joint oldest with Freycinet (*see* page 137 and 142), both declared in 1916. The park is a scenic 80km drive north-west of Hobart via the Derwent Valley. The capital's

Alpine gums find enough nutrients among the rocks to thrive in often-harsh conditions

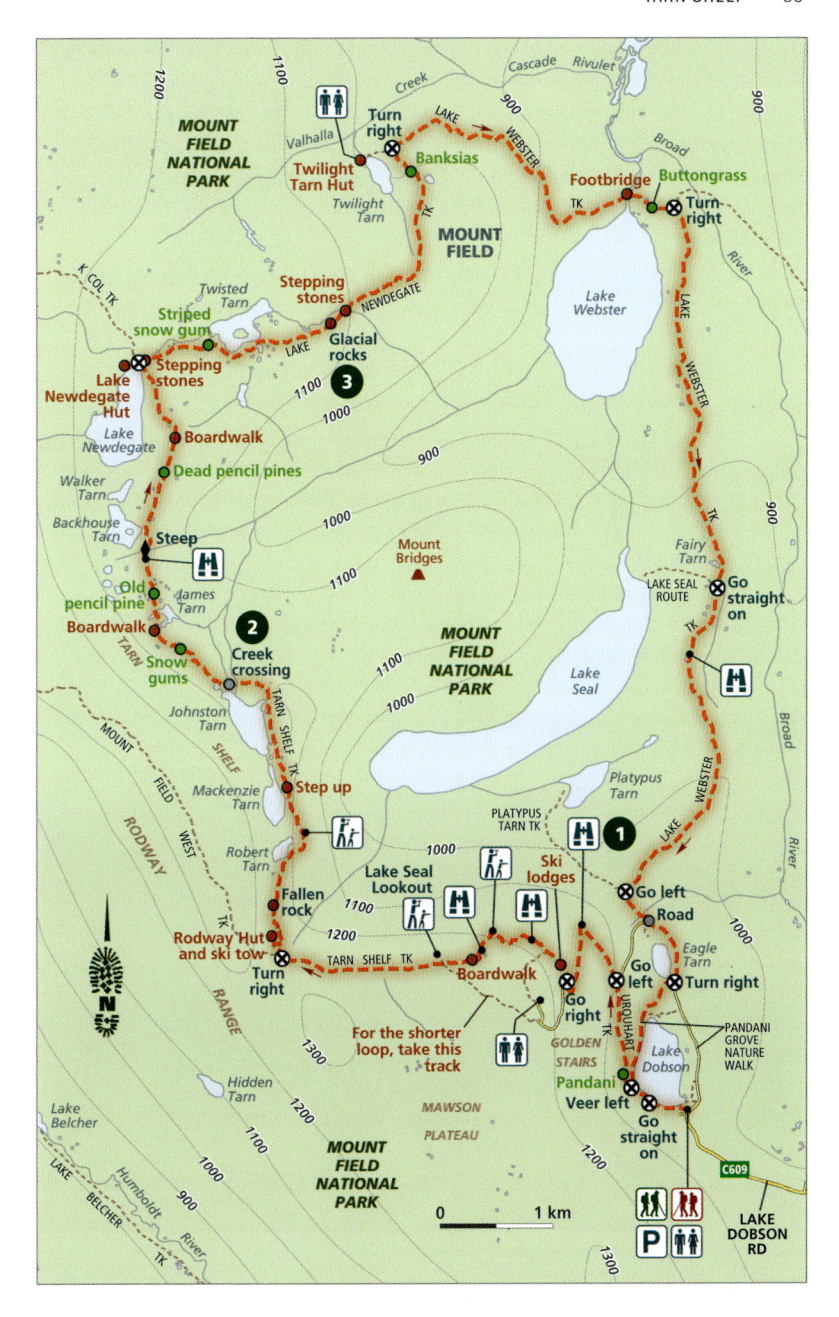

TARN SHELF 39

'backyard' playground, it is equipped with downhill ski runs for lovers of white stuff and kilometres of walking trails.

The popular but never crowded Tarn Shelf walk, in the park's west, kicks off from Lake Dobson car park, 15km beyond the visitor centre, on a gravel road that begins beneath towering gums. The car park marks the end of public road access; in summer ski-club members with a gate key can drive further on a jeep track.

The walking track drops obliquely from car park to water's edge. Tread the boardwalk clockwise around Lake Dobson, watching for platypus in the toffee-coloured water.

Ignore the path to Wellington Ski Club and veer left at the next junction onto Urquhart Track, which pulls away and uphill from the lake. (For an easy short walk, stay on the lower track and circle the lake.) The shaggy, Dr Seuss-ish plants on the hillside are pandani, the world's tallest heath, and Mt Field is the most accessible place in Tasmania to see these Gondwana-era relics. A short climb puts you in forest given height by alpine gums and deciduous beech and texture by pandani and scoparia.

You emerge from the trees at a U-bend on the jeep track. Head up the 'road', turning off it at the third U-bend where Snowgum Track is marked right. The walking track goes bush beyond two ski lodges, undulates through snow

Two of the jewel-like tarns that give the shelf its name

LEFT: *Tasmanian snow berries grow plump in this alpine environment;* **RIGHT:** *A pandani tendril curls around an elongated leaf*

gums with impressive girths and turns sharply left at a jumble of granite rocks with an 'OMG' view of Lake Seal and the park's exposed interior (see point 1 on map). There are so many lookouts up here that this one isn't named, let alone signed, but there is no better place on this walk to stop and ponder the nature of things.

With your back to the panorama, follow occasional arrows up rocks to a boardwalk junction with ski runs left and Lake Seal Lookout signed right. This lookout is an area rather than a specific spot and a web of footpads leads to the cliff edge for a vista of Lake Seal (in its tell-tale U-shaped valley), the Tarn Shelf, and the dolerite plateau. Glaciation is writ large on this landscape!

For a shorter loop (5.2km), head south-east, across the ski tow and down past tow huts and winter-season emergency shelters to the jeep track. Follow it past Snowgum Track (left), the Lake Dobson footpad (right) and Platypus Tarn Track (left) to Eagle Tarn.

For the full Tarn Shelf experience (don't embark on this option on the spur of the moment because it is a much longer walk into more remote country) head right towards the Tarn Shelf and Rodway Range. This takes you through scoparia and alpine daisies, tea tree and creek-watered herb fields at the foot of a dolerite battlement. Missing and broken timbers attest to the difficulty of maintaining walking tracks in extreme environments.

From Eagle Tarn and as you approach a hut and ski tow, you'll start to see the tarns that give the shelf its name. Lake Seal comes into view on your right, too, with a backdrop of blue mountain ridges. There isn't a tree in sight until you duck down slopes offering a little shelter.

Ignore the wooden-signed track to the Rodway Range and K Kol. (This harder alternative loop-walk, which includes considerable clambering, treads the K Kol track along the ridge top from here and return via the Tarn Shelf.) Instead, keep right towards lakes Webster and Newdegate. Metal posts wrapped in faded yellow reflectors mark the descent to the buildings seen earlier, through scoparia that puts on a colourful spectacle in summer. In sunshine, Lake Seal glitters and the tarns ahead look like jewels.

Duck under ski tow wires and pass fallen, fractured rock at the base of a cliff studded with boulders that appear at risk of losing their grip. Rocky track leads to the first tarn, which deepens from gin-clear shallows to greenstone. On a still day there's hardly a sound except occasional insect buzz.

The track is now sparingly marked but fairly easy to follow – in clear conditions! Cairns lead up rocks to a view of Lake Seal and, to its right, Platypus Tarn. After squeezing between a jagged boulder and a rounded one, step up an outcrop for another eyeful of Lake Seal. Beyond pencil pines and rock embellished with orange, white and black lichens, you pass two tiddler tarns beside a larger one, stepping stones leading to its shore.

Take care as you navigate another boulder pile, about 1km from the ski tow (*see* point 2 on map), because the distracting view can lead you astray and

An ancient pencil pine grows over a shallow tarn

towards the valley rim. Essentially keep left over natural pavement, towards the Rodway Range, crossing a creek trickling out of Johnston Tarn.

Ice has cracked the rock here and conditions have pruned the pencil pines to 2m tall; there's a six-trunk old-timer on the right. Ascending from Backhouse Tarn, which has an island, you pass a smaller pool with an ancient, silver pencil pine growing over the water.

Pandani rattle like bones as you brush past on the descent to Lake Newdegate, through platinum-coloured, dead pencil pines, victims of bushfire. Boardwalk leads to the lake's shore and stepping stones ford a creek flowing between Newdegate and Twisted Tarn. Lake Newdegate Hut, left at the next junction, is a rustic emergency shelter and a better lunch spot is the wooden platform beside the junction.

Refuelled, head downstream on a part-boarded, part-boggy, part-rooty track to a striped snow gum standing sentinel on the flats beside Twisted Tarn. Skirt the water and continue through pandani, heath and pencil pines and red-striped gums contrasting the dead trees. More tree skeletons and the odd route-marker post await over a slight rise. Now in the direct path of the glacier that fashioned this landscape, you pass a river of rocks deposited by moving ice (see point 3 on map).

After a relatively easy run along the lakes, you've got about 2km of steep descent to button-grass marshland studded with the tallest trees so far; welcome to the Broad River Valley. For a break, head left at Twilight Tarn to a day shelter and emergency hut. Otherwise stay right, towards lakes Webster, Fenton and Dobson on flatter track enabling greater speed. Lake Webster shows itself just beyond the walk's first red marker arrow.

Beyond the junction to Lake Fenton (left), amid banksias, you've got about 3km of climbing in a forest of eucalypts whose peeling grey bark reveals smooth peachy yellow and which is raucous with birds. Ignore the side track to Lake Seal (you get a view right up the lake valley to the ski tow visited earlier just beyond) and the detour (about 1km return) to Platypus Tarn, unless you've boundless energy. Walk on and turn left onto the jeep track descending from the ski fields. Turn right onto the Pandani Grove track immediately after Eagle Tarn, into fantastical ancient pencil pines.

Pencil pines are one of Tasmania's nine endemic conifers. All are slow-growing and long-lived, with the Huon pine, famed for its buttery timber, living more than 2000 years in favourable conditions. Conical pencil pines, predominantly found fringing sub-alpine lakes, can live 1200 years and some of these may be of that vintage.

Continue through slightly more open forest around the lake to the car park.

HOBART REGION

9 GROWLING SWALLET & JUNEE CAVE

Walk:	3.6km (two out-and-back walks with a short drive in between)
Time required:	2 hours (plus 15-minute drive)
Best time:	Misty day for the best atmosphere
Grade:	Easy (but can be muddy)
Environment:	Rainforest, river, karst cave system
Best map:	This one
Toilets:	None
Food:	Waterfalls Cafe, within Mt Field National Park Visitor Centre, sells a range of drinks, takeaway food and table meals
Tips:	The forestry road into Growling Swallet is gated and locked. You must pre-book the key with the national park rangers (03 6288 1149) and pay a $300 security deposit when you collect it at the visitor centre at the Mt Field National Park entrance. The forestry road can be rough in winter, so check the road condition with the park rangers.

Pairing one of Tasmania's best rainforest walks with a leafy riverside ramble, this easy two-part walk initiates you in the mystery and magic of limestone caves and underground rivers.

Water has piled rocks and logs in the mouth of Growling Swallet

Nature performs a now-you-see-it-now-you-don't conjuring trick with the Junee River, whose peat-stained mountain tributaries disappear into an extensive karst (limestone) cave system only to reappear on the far side of the range as a gin-clear river. These two short walks visit one of the most spectacular entrances into the system and the cave through which the Junee River resurfaces.

The delightfully named Growling Swallet (sinkhole) is tucked inside Mt Field National Park's southern boundary, but access is through plantation forest. From the turn-off to the national park proper, and the visitor centre, 67km north-west of Hobart, via North Norfolk, drive about 15km further along Gordon River Rd (B61) and through Maydena until you see large tourist signs for the Styx Valley and Big Tree pointing up Florentine Road. Follow this wide, well-maintained forestry road about 16km north to gated F8 East, on the right. Beyond the gate (see point 1 on map where the lock is tucked under a small metal canopy on the left upright), drive 2km east on a rougher, narrower, occasionally sandy road best travelled in a 4WD or AWD vehicle (some conventional vehicles get through).

If you can't be bothered arranging to pick up the key from the visitor centre and are up for 4km extra leg work you could walk in from the gate; however, there are commercial beehives along here and the mosquitoes can be fierce, so reconsider this option if you are allergic to either.

F8 East ends at a wall of forest, where there's space for a handful of cars, and the walking track disappears into the foliage at around one o'clock (with the road directly behind you). A sign about 5m in warns that there are numerous deep hidden shafts in this area and that flash flooding can occur in the creek and cave system; there's a Mt Field National Park sign shortly after.

This track doesn't appear on park maps and isn't permanently marked, but you'll often spot pink and orange ribbons guiding the way. The route is easy to follow, with the only possible confusion at the end.

Beyond the national park sign, the trail rambles through thick myrtle and sassafras forest, whose leafy canopy looks like green confetti tossed into the air, passing centuries-old eucalypts and the stumps of others felled for timber. About 300m in there's a magnificent tree, its coarse, red-barked trunk about 20m around, and lumpy with burls. A hundred metres further on there's another old-timer whose trunk is limbless for about 30m before bursting into a Rastafarian top knot of leafy branches.

Immediately beyond this second notable forest character, a tree branch has grown down towards the track and then looped skyward again, creating a throat-high booby trap for the distracted.

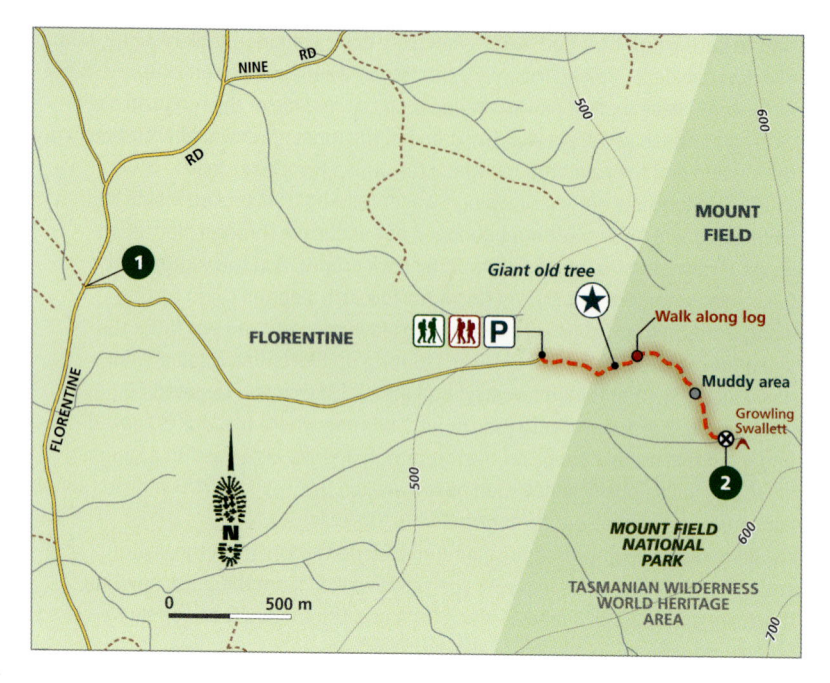

Rooty in parts and boggy after rain – boots and gaiters are recommended and walking poles handy – the track snakes between, over and around fallen trees colonised by lichens and velvety mosses. It also runs 20m along a toppled trunk.

About 1.3km into the walk, with the sound of rushing water now quite loud, you'll see a tree festooned with coloured ribbons (see point 2 on map). Turn right and walk down into the creek gully. (If you come to a small cavers' camping clearing with old fireplaces, you have gone a few metres too far.)

Descending right and then scrambling steeply left lands you beside a stream that washes around and over mossy rocks before disappearing into a cave mouth at the base of a limestone formation, like an ancient temple being reclaimed by the jungle. Tree ferns umbrella overhead and every branch and trunk is shaggy with old man's beard.

Work your way across to the boulders in the creek for a better look down into Growling Swallet, so named because it growls after heavy rain when water pours into the cave. Getting your feet damp is usually the only risk here, though extra care is needed to navigate a fallen tree and rocks to get closer to the mouth.

GROWLING SWALLET & JUNEE CAVE

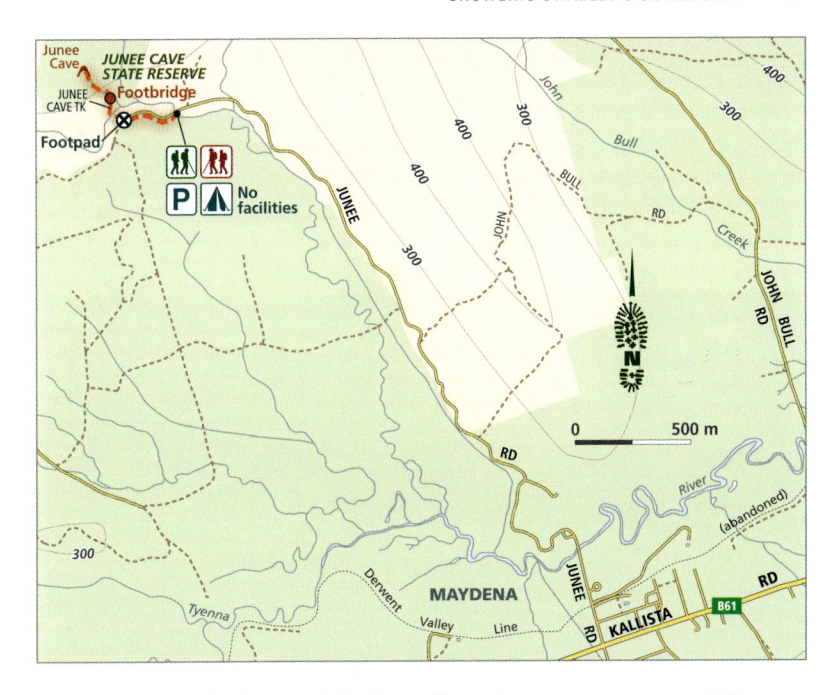

Growling Swallet is part of the Junee Florentine cave system, consisting of 30km of passages and more than 295 cave entrances. Decorated with limestone formations and home to creatures such as Tasmania's cave spider (the females have a leg span up to 180mm), this cave system is hard, wet, technical and includes the deepest cave in Australia. Only experienced, fully-equipped cavers should venture beyond the logs stacked at Growling Swallet's mouth.

From the growling – or perhaps just grumbling, or even gurgling – sinkhole, retrace your steps to the car and drive south back to the bitumen and then left, back towards the visitor centre. Turn left again onto Junee Rd (signed for Junee Cave) just as you come into Maydena, and follow this narrowing, dirt road to its end, at a turning area beside pretty Junee River.

Continue in the same direction on foot (there's an orange arrow and sign), treading a forestry road between the river and plantation timber, with Mt Field National Park mountains on your left. The Junee Cave walking track heads right off the road about 300m up.

Starting downhill, this easy track curves through thick forest noisy with birds and fords a footbridge over the fast-flowing clear river. Walk upstream and through a tree-fern tunnel to a boarded platform in the shadow-filled mouth of Junee Cave, through which the river re-emerges into the light.

The tannin-browned river that disappeared underground through Growling Swallet is filtered by the limestone before it surfaces again and runs clear past this platform. Imagine the twists and turns along that journey, the cracks and caverns through which the river works, as you watch the river and listen to it burble. Then return to your car when you're done.

Water runs between ferns and over rocks towards Growling Swallet, the mouth of the Junee Florentine cave system

HOBART REGION

10 MARRIOTTS FALLS

Walk:	6km out-and-back
Time required:	2 hours
Best time:	Overcast day after rain (best forest colours and most spectacular cascade) but can be walked any time of year.
Grade:	Easy
Environment:	Wet eucalypt forest, rainforest, river, waterfall
Best map:	This one
Toilets:	Mt Field National Park Visitor Centre, 7km east
Food:	The café at Mt Field National Park serves hot and cold meals, snacks and drinks. The National Park Hotel, on Gordon River Rd just outside the park entrance, plates good tucker.
Tips:	Don't be put off if it's raining. Water only makes the forest more beautiful and adds to the flow over the cascade.

Up for a test of willpower? Tread this less-beaten track along a rocky river in verdant forest to one of Tasmania's top waterfalls and then resist the temptation to tell everyone about it!

Visitors to Tasmania are at severe risk of contracting NAW (Not Another Waterfall) Syndrome but Marriotts Falls, 75km north-west of Hobart, is not 'just another waterfall'. It is one of the island state's prettiest, rivalling more-visited

Mosses and lichens thrive in the damp forest conditions

50　HOBART REGION

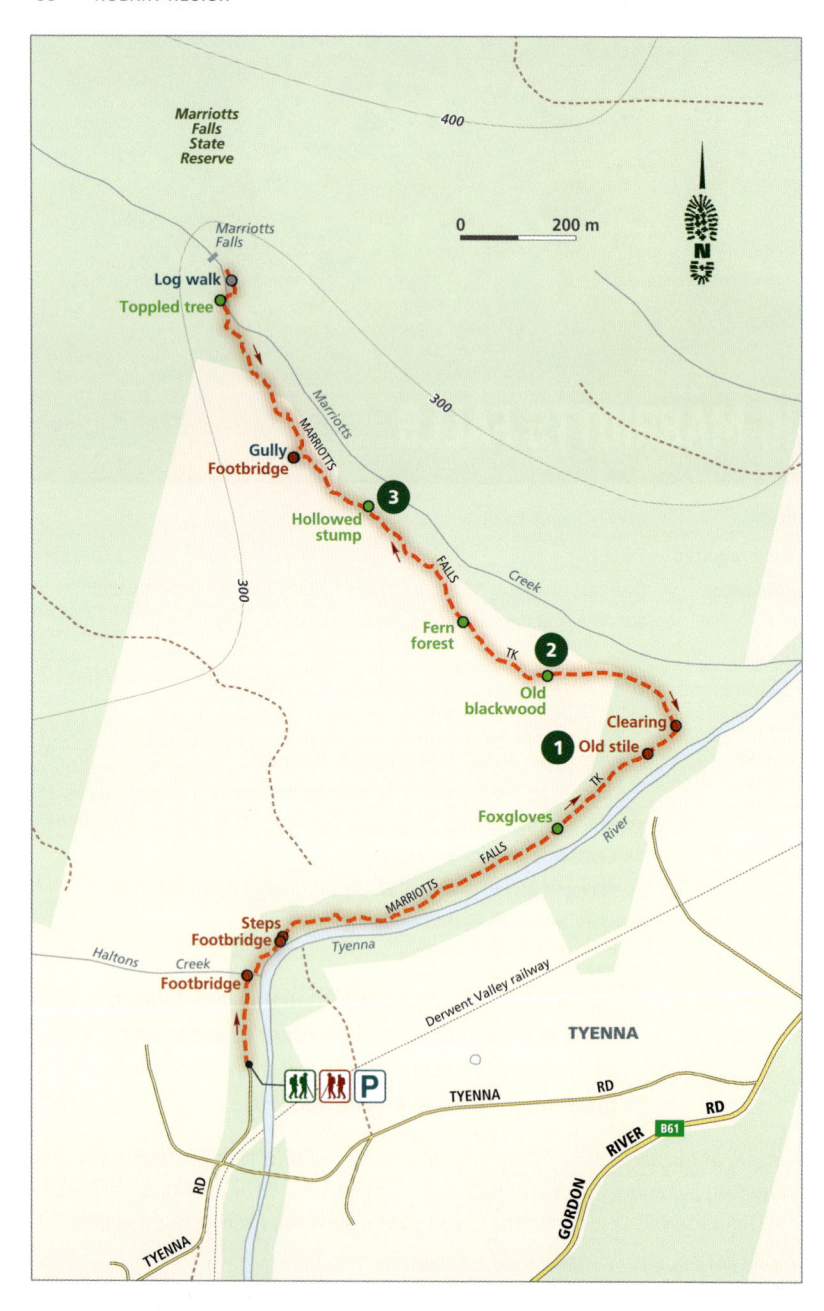

Russell Falls, in neighbouring Mt Field National Park, and the walk to it is easy – a combination promising family-friendly fun.

The Marriotts Falls walk is signed off Gordon River Rd (B61), 7km beyond the national park entry and 70 minutes by road from Hobart. Drive about 700m down unsealed and sometimes potholed Tyenna Rd, crossing the Tyenna River and the closed Derwent Valley rail line. Immediately turn right (the walk is signed) into a gravel parking area (no facilities) beside a logging coup.

Marriotts Creek spills and sometimes thunders down a curved wall of tiered stone

Clear-felled ground may greet you on exiting your car but so does the sound of running water; the blue-signed walking track follows the Tyenna River downstream towards tall eucalypts. Cross a footbridge fording a stone-floored creek feeding into the river and turn hard right onto wide walking track.

Continuing downstream, you pass rocks, on your left, undercut to the point of being cave-like, topped with silver-and-grey barked trees and covered in disparate mosses. Beyond another gully that can rush with water, steps climb past fallen trees angled down the steep bank before returning you to the water's edge where the Tyenna cascades over shelved rock. Boards keep you relatively mud-free in boggy areas.

Continue through more open forest of bracken, cutting grass and tree ferns and robust eucalypts with spongy, fibrous bark. The stalky, pink, bell-shaped flowers decorating an open area are foxgloves, a poisonous introduced plant – don't touch them! – and are classed as a weed. Bumblebees, another foreigner, love these garden escapees, their fluffy bodies fitting perfectly up the flower tubes.

In spring, native bush peas decorate an area on the left as you approach an old stile (see point 1 on map) beside the Tyenna, about 1km from the car park. Weathered timbers and rusty wires, and a sign ('Gross load limit 2t') indicate there was a river crossing here.

Shortly past the stile the track turns left into a clearing and works away from the river, star pickets topped with orange arrows marking the uphill route through rafts of bracken. A magnificent old blackwood (acacia) (see point 2 on map) with wide-reaching branches and many years' growth of the Spanish moss 'old man's beard' stands on the right about 300m from the river. The impressive mountains at your back and to your left disappear again when you plunge back into wet forest at the top of the clearing.

Climbing just enough to make you aware of height gain, a track – shot with roots – winds through aged ferns whose fronds form lacy umbrellas, towering swamp gums trailing bark streamers and past the hollowed stump of what must have been a mammoth eucalypt (see point 3 on map). Planks and a footbridge ford boggy sections and a fern-filled gully; look right for a lattice of mossy roots.

To the thump of falling water, veer right and down a hill thick with ferns on a narrowing track, ducking under a toppled tree. A footbridge over a gully brings you almost to the cascade. Walk along another fallen giant or take a footpad just prior to it; both routes bring you to steps cut into the wood that can be slippery with spray. Find your own way over the last 30m or so of the foot of the falls, beyond another tree fallen more recently across them.

On its run from the Mt Field Range to the Tyenna River, Marriotts Creek spills and sometimes thunders more than 10m down a curved wall of tiered stone, creating an exquisite large-scale hanging garden. Poke and wade around as near the cascade as water volume allows, noting the diversity of mosses, lichens and ferns – and staying alert for leeches in search of their annual meal.

When you're done, retrace your steps to the car, there checking exposed skin for blood-sucking worms.

Metallic beetles festoon a tree, like Christmas baubles

HOBART REGION
11 TOLKIEN TRACK – THE STYX

Walk:	3km out-and-back
Time required:	1.5 hours
Best time:	Cloudy day for most intense forest hues
Grade:	Easy-moderate (a short, steep and uneven pitch to the waterfall)
Environment:	Tall wet eucalypt forest and waterfall
Best map:	This one plus the Styx Valley of the Giants pdf (*See* Tips below).
Toilets:	Toilet at Big Tree Reserve
Food:	Drinks, fried fast food and some groceries are available from the Corner Store in Maydena
Tips:	There are no road signs to this walk and it is not shown on the information boards at the popular Big Tree Reserve. Download the Wilderness Society's *Styx Valley of the Giants Visitor Learning Guide* pdf for a map and comprehensive information about the forest, its importance and the fight to protect it.

Arboreal giants saved from logging by passionate protestors await you in Middle Earth forest a day-trip from Hobart

Arguably the most successful of the protest actions that saved the Styx Valley from being logged and saw its rivers and ancient forests added to the Tasmanian Wilderness World Heritage Area in 2013, was the launch, ten years earlier, of the

This way to the waterfall!

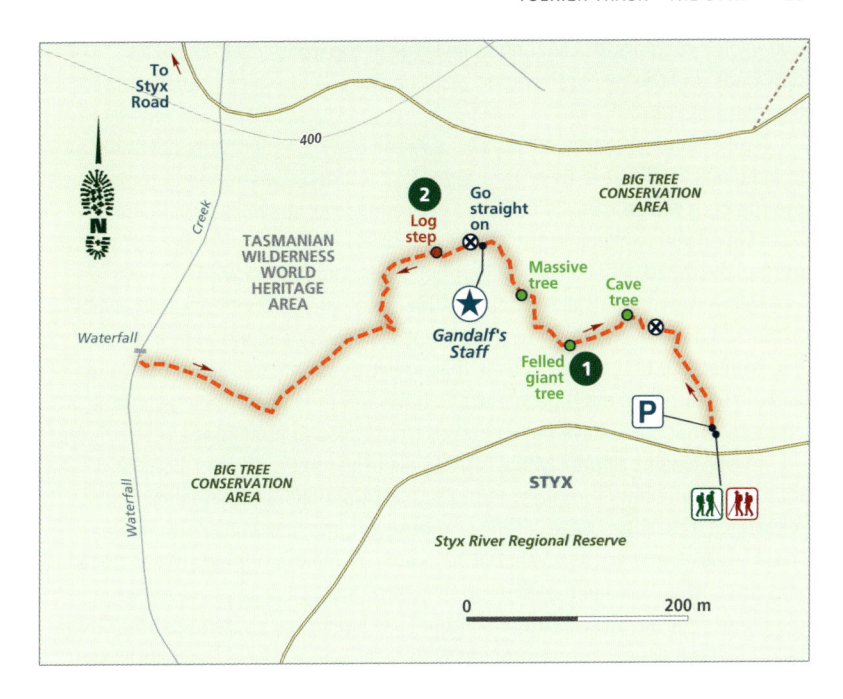

Global Rescue Station. A collaboration between Greenpeace and the Wilderness Society, the Station was a series of platforms perched in a magnificent swamp gum where activists from around Australia and the planet lived aloft, sending interviews, photographs and video footage to the world. The tree was known as Gandalfs Staff, and it is the star of this walk through the Valley of the Giants, a wonderland of tall timbers suggestive of Tolkein's Middle Earth.

A 75-minute drive (85km) from Hobart, via New Norfolk and the Derwent Valley, brings you to the Styx Rd junction on the left of Gordon River Road (B61). Drive about 12km along Styx Rd's winding gravel (there is some signage but ignore smaller side forestry tracks) brings you to the Big Tree Reserve (where there is also a toilet). Continue another 2km and turn right onto unsigned Waterfall Creek Road. Look for a small, green wooden roadside Tolkien Track sign and cairn about 1km from the junction. Park and step into the forest on a leaf-littered and infrequently trodden track (a boardwalk does a shorter loop through magnificent trees at Big Tree Reserve).

Push through the ferns reaching across the track and follow a trail of pink ribbons into a leafy forest of tree ferns and huge old eucalypts. Commonly called swamp gums in Tasmania and mountain ash in Victoria, these are

Eucalyptus regnans, the second tallest tree in the world after America's redwoods and the tallest flowering plant on the planet, which produces white blossoms in autumn.

A pink ribbon in a tree fern marks a vague track junction. Just beyond a bit of old plank you'll see a 'Cave Tree' sign. Turn left and then right into a massive swamp gum whose trunk is hollowed at ground level. Inside is a rustic bench from which you can look at the blackened walls and up at the 'cave' roof a few metres overhead. Mosquitoes will probably cut short your stay.

Follow the ribbon trail further into the forest, past a huge tree, long-since felled and now covered in moss (*see* point 1 on map), and a tree fern whose two trunks split and merge. Beside it is an extraordinary merger of two gums and a tree fern, twisted together at the base and then doing their own thing: a character that could have been plucked from Tolkien's imaginings.

As well as pink ribbons you will find yellow-on-green wooden signs at important junctions. Turn right at the sign for Gandalfs Staff and descend to a massive tree whose base is tens of metres around and whose grey-striped trunk trails streamers as it reaches skywards. Fungi often grow around the tree and you can see a huge burl high up the trunk. Swing left past this unnamed giant and walk down a hill littered with myrtle beech leaves through other huge trees. A steep descent criss-crossed with roots brings you to Gandalfs Staff.

A Valley of the Giants information board depicts a logger showing the size of some of the trees before logging came to an end

Giant swamp gums dwarf fungi and ferns

Eighty-four metres high and estimated to be 350 to 400 years old, this is a tree to which Tolkien's wizard would have been proud to lend his name. Looking up you can see wires in situ from the aerial protest platforms. Yellow-tailed black cockatoos hang out in these treetops too, giving themselves away with croaky whistling calls. Research has found that mature *Eucalypt regnans*-dominated forests store more carbon than any other forest type so trees such as this are important; but they are also fabulous to see, hug and sit beneath.

Visible beyond the tree are pink ribbon trails leading straight on and uphill. Leaving the climb (perhaps for later) follow the lower trail, which skirts an unnamed tree only 15m around and a baby compared with Gandalfs staff! Step over logs and climb steeply up and around fallen eucalypts (*see* point 2 on map), layers of forest debris making the track spongy underfoot. Now descend steeply into fabulously lush rainforest and further into a fern-filled gully to the sound of falling water. Two small, broken footbridges cross a creek that drops over a rocky lip. Ribbons lead right and down a bank to where water pours down rock dripping with moss and ferns into a gully full of tree ferns. A steeper few metres, with root footholds and handholds, take you to a rickety footbridge greened with moss at the base of the falls. Two fallen trees roof this little gully.

Having retraced your steps to Gandalfs Staff, you can turn right and up the ribboned hill from the giant gum and loop left back to the main track or keep walking, returning to your car the way you came earlier.

HOBART REGION
12 MOUNT MISERY

Walk:	8.6km loop
Time required:	3–4 hours
Best time:	Sunny day
Grade:	Easy
Environment:	Rainforest, tall eucalypt forest, sub-alpine heathland, waterfalls
Best map:	This one
Toilets:	Flush toilets in the car park/reserve
Food:	None
Tips:	Access to walking tracks is included in Huon Bush Retreats' accommodation rates (www.huonbushretreats.com); day visitors are asked to make a donation (at the walk registration booth) to contribute to track maintenance.

Aboriginal cultural connections and colourful geology, lush rainforest and exposed hilltops make this walk, on private property, a delight rather than the misery its name suggests.

About 42% of Tasmania is protected and managed as national parks and reserves, but that's not enough for some people, who establish private conservation areas and invite the public to share their vision. Huon Bush Retreats

Take in a wide-angle view from Flat Rock on Mt Misery's sub-alpine plateau

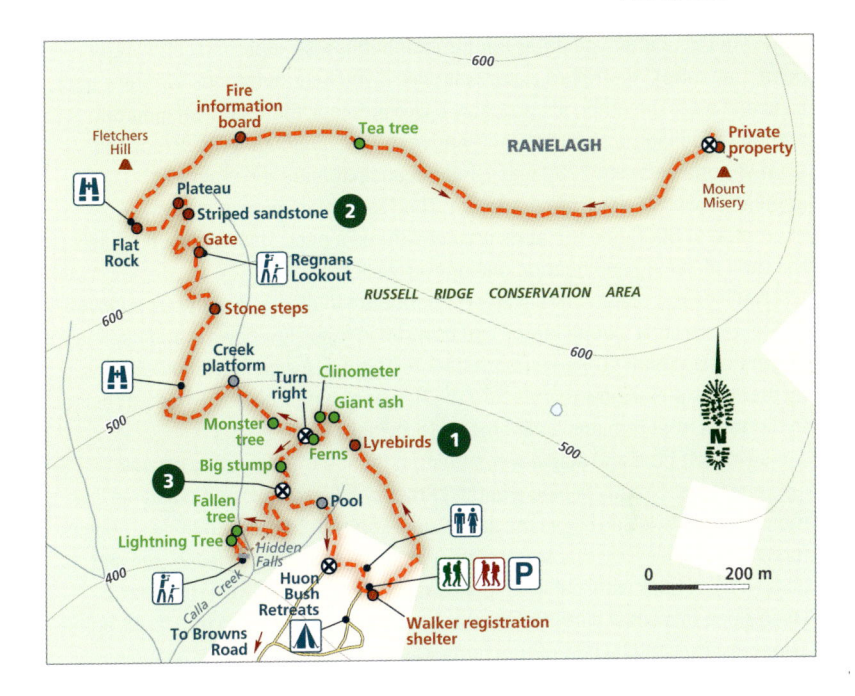

is such an enterprise. This nature-based carbon-positive tourism village in the Huon Valley was founded by two environmentalists who also established the Huon Nature Trust. They work with other like-minded landowners to conserve Mt Misery and surrounds and walking here reveals why they bother.

The four walks at Huon Bush Retreats range from a 20-minute village loop to the longer loop described here. Each has an Aboriginal theme and the longest walk is the Dreaming; you are invited to drift back in time and appreciate the Palawa (Tasmanian Aboriginal) people's concepts of time and place. Interpretive signs on the walks provide alternative and even conflicting Aboriginal perspectives, early European viewpoints, and modern concepts.

Huon Bush Retreats is 50 minutes' drive south-west of Hobart. Exit the city on the A6 Southern Outlet and head for Huonville. The property is signed 2.5km south of Grove, at the C619 (North Huon Rd) turnoff to Judbury. Follow the C619 and 'Retreat' signs and turn right onto Browns Rd about 3km beyond Ranelagh. From here there's 3km of narrow, winding gravel to the property gate and another kilometre to reception; the last 500m is steep so don't stop. Take care and watch for wildlife. Drive through the property until you see the walker registration shelter on the right. There are roadside parking spots.

From the shelter you enter rainforest inhabited by superb lyrebirds (see point 1 on map), Australia's expert mimics. If you hear numerous different bird calls one after the other, it's probably a lyrebird; look for a harp-shaped tail among the foliage. Lyrebirds aren't native to Tasmania; 22 were introduced from Victoria between 1934 and 1949 because of fears the mainland population was at risk from predation. The Tasmanian population is now estimated at 8000 and the birds are considered a pest. This doesn't diminish the thrill of seeing and hearing one on this walk.

You'll pass a giant ash (eucalypt) about 20m in diameter that has survived losing its crown; it's quite lumpy and covered in moss low down – and peeling to grey-and-cream striped smooth bark further up. A sign in a small clearing further on explains how to measure the height of a nearby tree (marked) using Pythagoras' theorem and a clinometer (provided).

Swing left here and step down, turning right at a track junction beyond luscious ferns. Directly behind a patch of mossy fallen trunks and branches is a monster tree, twice as big as the earlier one. Look out for fungi in this damper forest and the leeches that counter their beauty! Duck under a fallen tree and climb a track thick with leaf litter. Boardwalk (slippery when wet) traverses a treed slope to a small platform spanning a creek crammed with tree ferns, some 10m tall. (The starchy part of tree ferns was an important food for Aborigines.)

Stone steps continue uphill into beech forest. Then, suddenly, the fern forest is behind and below – and young, strappy trees outnumber big ones. Zigzag upwards into tea tree and giant ash (*Eucalyptus regnans*) to gated Regnans Lookout, for a miniature view of the Huon Valley through the treetops. The track zigs and zags some more, and runs along curved, layered stone, to a sandstone lip striped and swirled red, orange, yellow and white (see point 2 on map).

A short climb and you're on Mt Misery's sub-alpine plateau. Neighbouring hills reach across the horizon as you walk through banksias, stunted tea tree and other hardy heath shrubs to Flat Rock, about 2.5km into the walk. This naturally crazed rock, imprinted with historic European engravings, presents a wide-angle view of D'Entrecasteaux Channel and Bruny Island (see page 62), Tasman Peninsula (see page 78), and the peaks of Southwest National Park.

Poles mark the route beyond Flat Rock and on warm, sunny days, insect hum adds a metallic soundscape to a pleasant roof-top walk. The track swings right and down into tall eucalypts and bracken burned in a 2007 bushfire, then continues predominantly slightly uphill to another information board. The boulder pile beyond is the end of the track, and a short scramble puts you on top. Despite the 700m altitude there is no fantastic view here, just the tops of some peaks, but the geology is interesting and it's a lovely lunch spot.

A footpad on the right as you approach (left going back) leads about 75m to a better Huon Valley view but it is on a neighbouring property, whose owner forbids entry and has erected a 'private property' sign a short way in.

Backtrack about 3km to the last junction and turn right towards the village. Continue to another junction, over one fallen tree, down another and past a tree stump (see point 3 on map) – why did axemen fell this one and not others? The village is a few minutes to the left but turn right for the Lightning Tree and Hidden Falls.

Longer than the suggested 10 minutes but worth it, this detour descends steeply through fern forest, on boardwalk and rock steps and leaf-littered track, all slippery when damp. About 350m from the junction, you walk through a giant tree blackened and hollowed; imagine the sound when the lightning struck!

Several more minutes down are the falls. Panels describe how this once reliable cascade has almost ceased flowing, due to global warming, but it's a pretty gully. Ferns crown the opposite cliff, down which water trickles, and Christmas-bauble ferns crowd the limbs of a tree growing out of the rock.

Back at the main track, turn right. You'll shortly arrive at a gravel road; the walker registration shelter is a hundred metres up to your left, village reception to your right.

Scribbly gum moth graffiti adorns a tree beside the recommended lunch spot

HOBART REGION

13 CAPE QUEEN ELIZABETH (BRUNY ISLAND)

Walk:	13km return
Time required:	4 hours (longer if you loll on the beach)
Best time:	Sunny day
Grade:	Easy–moderate
Environment:	White beaches, rocky cape, rock stacks, coastal heathland
Best map:	This one
Toilets:	None
Food:	Bruny Island Cheese (http://brunyislandcheese.com.au), which sells artisan cheeses, coffee and cake and seasonal homemade ice-cream, and the Oyster Bar at Get Shucked (www.getshucked.com.au) are just up Bruny Island Main Rd from the walk car park
Tips:	Time your walk so you can include the low-tide route around Mars Bluff. Check times at www.surf-forecast.com/breaks/Neck-Bay/tides/latest.

White sand, turquoise water, geological artistry, massed wildflowers and only moderate hills make this one of Australia's great short coastal walks.

Treading any Bruny Island walking track gives you an appreciation of why Hobart's long-time secret backyard playground is now attracting visitors from further afield. Do you love birds? Jaw-dropping geology? Verdant forests? Lighthouses? Beachcombing? Colonial history? Take your pick of walks, none prettier than the

Miles Beach, looking towards Cape Queen Elizabeth

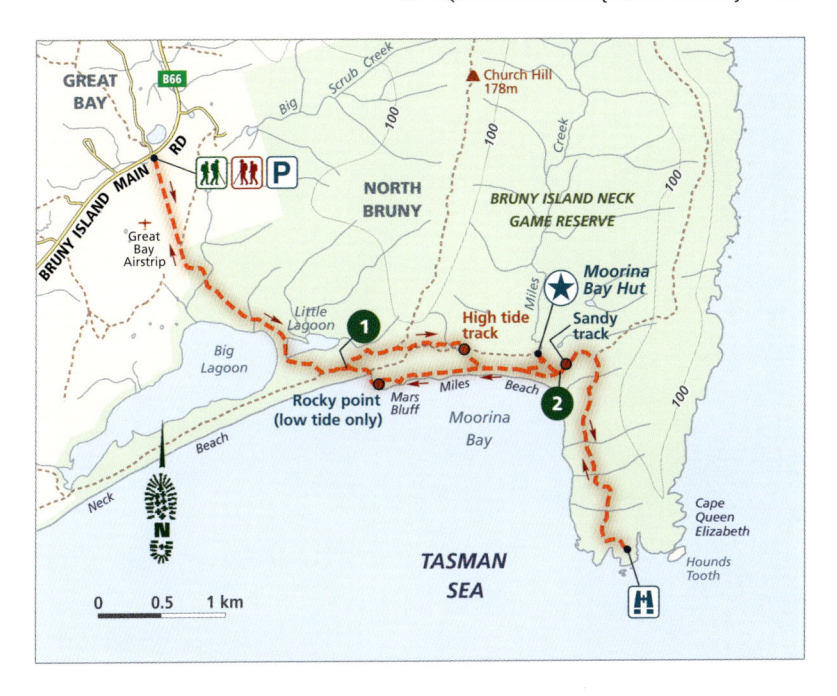

amble to Cape Queen Elizabeth, North Bruny Island's south-east point – and all within easy reach of the state capital.

To get there drive 33km south-west from Hobart on the A6 and B68 to Kettering, there catching the vehicular ferry across D'Entrecasteaux Channel.

The Cape Queen Elizabeth walk starts in a small parking area beside Bruny Island Main Rd, about 18km south of the ferry landing and 4km before the ribbon-like isthmus – The Neck – linking North Bruny Island and hillier, more forested South Bruny. Head east from here on a flat, gated and unused 4WD track, through a corridor of eucalypts and banksias separating farmland and Bruny's airstrip, where scenic flights take to the air (www.islandscenicflights.com). The trees are often a-chatter with birds, and on warm days hum with bees (and flies).

About 700m along, the track sweeps left through bracken, she-oaks and tea tree, and from the next bend you can look across Big Lagoon to the distinctive dolerite columns that give South Bruny's Fluted Cape (*see* page 67) its name. Tasmania's 12 endemic bird species can all be seen on Bruny Island – including the rare forty-spotted pardalote, if you are very lucky – and more than

The walk ends on a rocky cape where cliffs plunge into the sea

a hundred other species live on or visit the island. Look for waterbirds on Big Lagoon and majestic white-bellied sea eagles overhead.

Cape Queen Elizabeth comes into full view as you pass smaller, ephemeral Little Lagoon on the left.

Narrower and sandier but still easy going, the track wanders through twisted rough-barked eucalypts and into dunes greened with sand-hugging heath. You'll hear waves and taste salty breeze before the ocean shows itself.

About 300m beyond the lagoons the track divides (see point 1 on map). The tide determines which way you go: right, on the low-tide route to Moorina Bay via the beach (fantastic and fun geology) or, if the tide is high, left, up and over Mars Bluff (with sweeping views of lagoons and The Neck). Don't attempt the low-tide beach route more than an hour or so either side of low water – and even then you'll probably get wet feet! If conditions give you the choice, take the 'high road' first and come back from the cape on the lower route, as described here, which gifts you the rugged geology at the foot of the Bluff as a grand finale.

Assuming conditions allow this, turn left at the junction and work your way up and over Mars Bluff on a footpad, remembering to look back at the broadening view over the lagoons and isthmus and South Bruny's dolerite sea cliffs. From the top you descend gently to wooden steps that deposit you in soft sand behind a dune. (The lone post with sun-bleached marker arrow atop this dune helps people walking in the reverse direction find this track after visiting the cape.) Stroll along Miles Beach, with Moorina Bay to your right.

Moorina Bay is named after a sister of Truganini, the famous Indigenous woman born on Bruny Island around 1812. A spokesperson and leader of Tasmanian Aboriginal people, and briefly a guerrilla fighter with Victoria's first Australians, Truganini was for many years described, erroneously, as the last Tasmanian Aboriginal person.

About 600m along the beach, detour left, up Miles Creek, to Moorina Bay Hut in the dunes. Two walkers built this rustic shelter in the 1950s, from planks of sawn timber they found in the wreck of the *Swift*, a ketch abandoned after grounding and washing ashore in a heavy storm in 1935.

Back on the beach, continue along the bay. Just before the sand ends in a pile of rocks (see point 2 on map) turn off the beach onto a narrow, sandy track that climbs into the dunes. Above the beach, turn right onto a track running along the cape's southern flank. This undulates through eucalypts with thick, coarse trunks and others peeling in streamers of bark; through stands of tea tree; through bristling banksias and drooping she-oaks; with views to the south.

As you near the cape's point, trees give way to shrubs and then stunted coastal heath, and you pass through an area drilled with shearwater (muttonbird) burrows. The smell of these birds infuses the rest of the walk.

Cape Queen Elizabeth's crown is a web of tracks, but finding your way is only an issue coming down, and even then, the plants are low enough to keep your bearings: look for rock cairns and occasional ribbons.

The wonderful view from the top sweeps from The Neck, Adventure Bay and Fluted Cape (another great walk) to the south, around to the Tasman Peninsula and north into the nooks and crannies of Hobart's waterways. And immediately below, over the precipitous edge, is a fist of dolerite columns.

Now retrace your steps to Miles Beach and amble to its southern end (tide permitting) for the walk's geological climax.

In the lee of the cliff just short of a rock stack is an extraordinary arch fashioned from layered, crazed dolerite. Walk around and through this architectural natural sculpture, before rounding the rock stack that blocks passage into the tiny next bay at high tide. Continue through a taller, narrower archway and a rock corridor to elongated Neck Beach, passing undercut and eroded stone.

It's a short walk from here to the high-tide junction and the track back to the car.

Allow time to look at the shells strewn along Miles Beach

HOBART REGION

14 FLUTED CAPE (BRUNY ISLAND)

Walk:	7.5km loop
Time required:	2–3 hours
Best time:	Dry weather year-round; take care near the edge on windy days
Grade:	Easy–moderate (long, steep descent to end/ascent to begin)
Environment:	Bay, beach, eucalypt forest, dolerite sea cliffs
Best map:	This one or TASMAP's *Bruny Island Walks 1:75,000*
Toilets:	Flushing toilets on the foreshore in Adventure Bay
Food:	Bruny boasts some of Tasmania's best food, with oysters, cheese, chocolate, berries, lamb, wallaby, wine, cider and whisky on the menu. The nearest option for this walk is fast food from the Adventure Bay store.
Tips:	This walk treads unfenced sea cliffs; it is unsuited to young children and people afraid of heights. Don't leave Bruny without experiencing Fluted Cape and the continuation of South Bruny's spectacular sea cliffs from water level with Bruny Island Cruises (www.brunycruises.com.au).

Walk from a safe harbour where historically celebrated navigators dropped anchor to the knee-trembling edge of vertiginous volcanic cliffs.

Sunset gilds Adventure Bay and its enfolding ranges

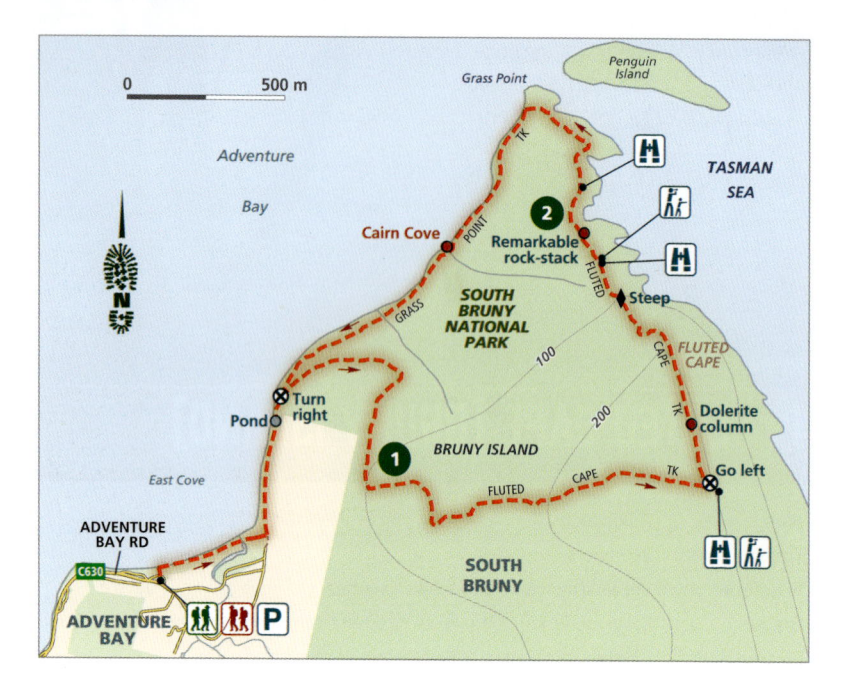

The long-time 'backyard' playground of Hobartians, Bruny Island is a half-hour drive – and a world away – from Tasmania's capital. About 80km long and thirty across at its widest, it is essentially two islands linked by an isthmus called The Neck. South Bruny is bigger, more rugged, more treed and more popular with tourists.

Bruny's headline attractions – after its food and wildlife – are the dolerite cliffs, blowholes, caves and smaller islands along South Bruny's south-east coast. And the most accessible part of this extraordinary land edge is Fluted Cape, a dolerite parapet rearing 272m out of the Southern Ocean.

One of a handful of good Bruny Island walks, the Fluted Cape track begins in Adventure Bay, the most important bay in Australia's European history. The who's-who of mariners who found safe harbour here includes Dutch navigator Abel Janszoon Tasman, in 1642, and 150 years later French Rear Admiral Bruni D'Entrecasteaux, after whom the island and the channel separating it from mainland Tasmania are named. Captains Tobias Furneaux, James Cook, Matthew Flinders and William Bligh (en route to mutiny in the Pacific) all anchored ships here in the late 1700s.

Nuenonne Aboriginal people, who called the island Lunnawannalonna, hunted its hills and fished its waters for millennia before tall ships sailed into

FLUTED CAPE (BRUNY ISLAND) 69

Adventure Bay. Truganini (*see* page 14), the most famous historical Tasmanian Aborigine, was born on Bruny Island.

Driving 33km south-west from Hobart to Kettering on routes A6 and B68, riding the Bruny island vehicular ferry across D'Entrecasteaux Channel, and driving another 29km south lands you in Adventure Bay. The lasso-shaped

Cracked and crazed, this remarkable column looks like it was stacked by human hands

walk to the edge of Bruny's awesome geology starts at the eastern end, in Cookville. Here, the botanists sailing with Bligh planted apple seeds and founded Tasmania's ongoing apple industry. From the car park at the end of the bitumen, step onto the beach and head right. The mountain directly across the bay, to your north, is Hobart's kunanyi/Mt Wellington, another top walking destination (see kunanyi/Mt Wellington Summit Loop page 2).

The signed track proper leaves the beach just before the end of the sand. Turn left and follow a vehicular track between fenced private land and beach lined with blue gums. One tree lives on despite being hollowed and teetering on an A-frame trunk. If you see a white wallaby grazing here you're not hallucinating; Bruny Island's white Bennett's wallabies are world-famous. While some are albino, most are a dark-eyed, light-furred variant of the more familiar brown macropods.

The track passes a pond before entering South Bruny National Park. And a magnificent eucalypt guards the junction where Fluted Cape is signed uphill to the right. This walk features a long, steep slope so turn right (as described here) if your knees prefer descending, and continue to Grass Point and walk clockwise if you are happier climbing.

LEFT: *Every eucalypt has a different character;* **RIGHT:** *Look closely at the wonder of banksias*

Turning right, tread a well-trodden track with occasional roots up through eucalypt forest carpeted with spheres of sedgy grass. Here too are yellow banksias, she-oaks, hakeas and scribbly gums (see point 1 on map). Scribbly gum moths lay their eggs under the trees' smooth bark and feeding larvae leave the distinctive graffiti-like scrawls. Also note an entwined pair of different eucalypts: one smooth-barked, one rough.

After climbing steadily, the track stops abruptly on the edge of Fluted Cape, where rock nosedives to inky ocean. The walk continues left but winning views await from a small promontory to your right. You can see kunanyi/Mt Wellington and South Arm Peninsula to the north; Tasman Peninsula to the east; and along the columnar cliff underfoot (where a single dolerite pillar has split away from the rock face). If you're blessed, a white-bellied sea eagle, Australia's second largest raptor after the wedge-tailed eagle, will cruise past.

The return track follows the cliff line and coast back to Adventure Bay, so closely you can (stomach permitting) peer down sheer drops to rocks and rolling ocean. As you descend you'll see another dolerite column leaning out from the main body of stone and other pillars and chunks that have lost their grip and fallen. Banksias and the odd gum thrive on the cliff edge and eucalypts grow taller back from the brink. Fallen needles soften your footfalls through a stand of she-oaks but can also make the track slippery. As the track swings around the cape, you'll see elongated Penguin Island, off the point, and then Adventure Bay.

The descent steepens now so watch your step, and stop often to look at the dramatic cliff you're navigating; nature's stonemasonry glows red in the late sun as if blushing. You'll pass a remarkable rock-stack standing out from the cliff; cracked and crazed, it looks as though it was stacked by human hands (see point 2 on map). Below it, bull kelp, the largest form of brown algae, which can grow to 30m long, washes against rock shelves. The track bottoms out at Grass Point where you might find wallabies grazing and see seals frolicking in the shallows.

Back in the 1830s, up to 90 men at a time worked at four whaling stations along this short stretch of coast (there were eight whaling stations across Bruny Island), hauling in mostly southern right whales for their oil. The station at Grass Point is the best preserved, where you can explore the remains of 12 stone structures, the only physical relics of the bloody, smelly, boom-and-bust trade that collapsed in 1840.

Imagine the shouts and bubbling pots, the smoke and stench, as you follow the track through she-oaks with the tranquil bay lapping the shore past the junction and back to the beach for a sandy stroll to your car.

HOBART REGION

15 SLIDE TRACK (BRUNY ISLAND)

Walk:	13km A to B
Time required:	5–6 hours
Best time:	Any time; overcast day after recent rain for the most intense forest hues (but worst leeches).
Grade:	Moderate (poorly marked, unmaintained track)
Environment:	Damp coastal forest, old logging tramway, dolerite cliffs
Best map:	This one
Toilets:	Flushing toilets in Adventure Bay at end of walk
Food:	Bruny Island tantalises with oysters, wine, whisky, cheese and more. The Adventure Bay General Store sells groceries and takeaway fare.
Tips:	The Slide Track is not included on TASMAP's *Bruny Island Walks* map but is listed on some websites. The suggested 3.5 hours is out of date because of the track conditions. Some Bruny outlets can supply an information sheet on the walk but many markers are missing or impossible to find. Leeches abound so wear gaiters and check yourself and your companions often. Bruny Island has no taxis so you need to car shuffle.

Tread a long-abandoned timber tramway through verdant forest to one of Australia's most historic bays.

A second view of rocky shore emphasises that this timber tramway was an engineering feat

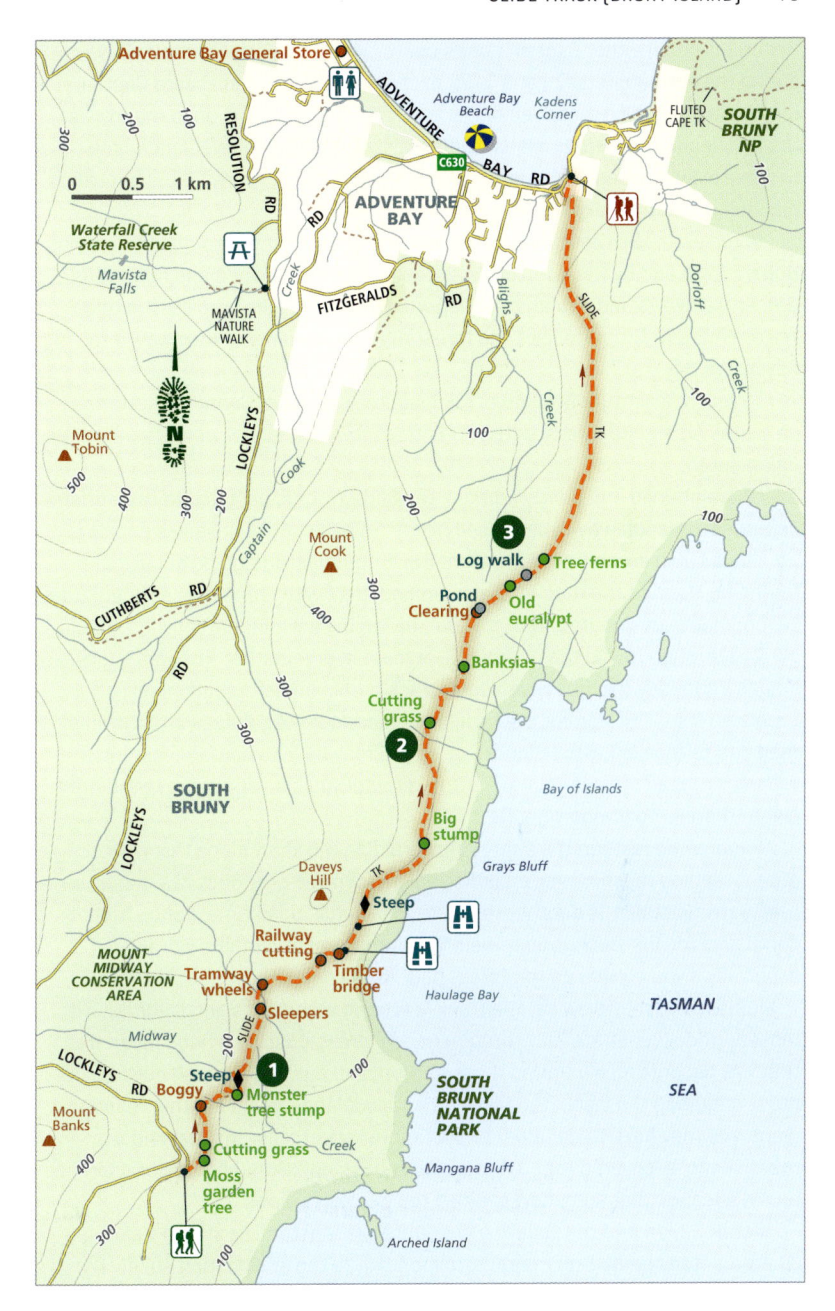

SLIDE TRACK (BRUNY ISLAND) 73

Historians credit either Captain Cook's crews, who sailed into Adventure Bay during the navigator's 1773 and 1777 expeditions, or the men aboard Captain Bligh's *Bounty*, which made repairs here in 1788 before sailing on to mutiny, as the first 'loggers' on Bruny Island, south-west of Hobart. Whoever landed the first axe blow founded an industry that continued until the early 2010s but which hopefully – there is no guarantee – won't resume.

In the early 19th century Bruny became the main timber source for growing Hobart Town and by the late 1800s sawmills were established and numerous timber tramways and haulages transported logs from hills to mills. The Slide Track, on South Bruny, follows the forest route of the longest tramway, into Adventure Bay.

To reach Adventure Bay, drive 33km south-west from Hobart to Kettering on routes A6 and B68, ferry across D'Entrecasteaux Channel, and drive another 29km south.

Unmaintained and poorly marked, the Slide Track is unsuited to first-timers unless accompanied by experienced hikers. To begin, drive unsealed Lockleys Rd about 10km south from Adventure Bay through post-logging eucalypt regrowth. Much of the road is 'stone pitched' (laid with stones) so although the second half is designated 4WD, careful driving in conventional vehicles should get you through (avoid the potholes!), at least in dry weather. The walking track begins 200m down a mossy vehicular track branching left (south-east) off Lockleys Road. The sign for the turn-off is hidden among foliage and the side road can be blocked with fallen trees, so you may have to hoof the last bit. If you get dropped off, ask your driver to wait until you confirm you're in the right place (there is no phone signal).

Fungi often festoon the approach, heralding the show along this walk; photographing mushrooms, including yellow-centred grey ones like miniature fried eggs on stalks, is another threat to finishing in good time. Fungi-friendly damp also means leeches so remain vigilant for these vampiric worms, especially if you crouch on the forest floor for pics.

Initially two metres wide, the track is littered with leaves and trimmed with mosses. It descends steadily through beech forest, passing a huge fallen tree that has become an elongated moss garden, and pushing through cutting grass engulfing the track. You traverse a hillside and around another fallen giant; you may have to go under or over more recent falls. Just beyond a massive moss-covered root ball the track goes right, through lacy coral fern, at an old eucalypt that somehow avoided the axemen's blows.

About 1.5km into the walk you encounter a monster tree stump wearing a '2' marker (*see* point 1 on map) corresponding to the information sheet. The

SLIDE TRACK (BRUNY ISLAND) 75

TOP: *Fabulous fungi festoon this walk;* **BOTTOM:** *Tramway wheels rust into the forest floor*

broad track continues several more metres towards a small barricade of logs but the Slide Track drops downhill to the right. Pink ribbons mark the narrow descent to burbling Midway Creek and leeches!

Once out of the creek gully the steepest walking is behind you and you start one of the prettiest legs of the walk, often strung with spiders' webs. Clamber over a huge fallen log cut with footholds that are slippery when wet, duck under another log, and walk the length of a third between two more. The mossy wooden plank part-way along the log walk is a platform on which timber fellers

TOP: *Clumps of fungi herald the fungi show to come;* **BOTTOM LEFT:** *Coral ferns provide lacy decoration;* **BOTTOM RIGHT:** *A red beauty stands out among the green*

once stood, swinging their axes and hauling on saws. Having walked-the-plank along another log that keeps your boots clear of pooled water, you'll pass a tree many metres around its gnarly base.

Water now audible, you step over your first timber tramway sleepers about 3km into the walk. The old tramway leads to a leafy creek where you have to clamber down the damp bank and through old bridge timbers. The mossy stumps beyond hint at the forest's majesty prior to logging.

From a lush gully where two tramway wheels rust into the forest floor, push on through ferns crossing the track. It's not hard going but you can't get up any speed. More-open canopy reveals the remains of another timber bridge.

Thumping waves herald a sudden glimpse, about 5km into the walk, of ocean, foam and cliff down to your right. A second view of rocky shore, from another light-filled opening, emphasises that this tramway was an engineering feat. The track immediately beyond is poor and hugs the steep slope but is negotiable with care.

Now for the most interesting section of the old line, where multiple surviving sleepers and side beams hide under a layer of moss: the line is broken in places with some step-ups and -downs, but that only increases the fun. Flatter terrain awaits when the track veers inland but you still have to push through swathes of tangling cutting grass (see point 2 on map) (lift your feet rather than shuffle): watch for snakes in summer.

Having passed a pond in a small clearing and stepped back into trees at an orange ribbon, you come to a tumbledown length of track beams and sleepers, marked with information tag '10'. The track can be extremely overgrown here so follow the tramway to find it again, passing an old eucalypt that appears to have wrapped around and grown up another tree.

Easy going leads to another log walk (see point 3 on map); step up and walk left (there's a pink ribbon on a tree), and walk through ferns and gums.

Only about 2km from the end of the walk the track can again be hard to follow. Look for ribbons and follow the tramway relics. The timber fellers' slots on one big, old stump have been fashioned into marker arrows.

More pink ribbons than are necessary mark the final easy and obvious descent to Adventure Bay, near backyard fences. At unsealed Sawdust Rd turn right and walk down to the water, swinging left onto the main town road and your car.

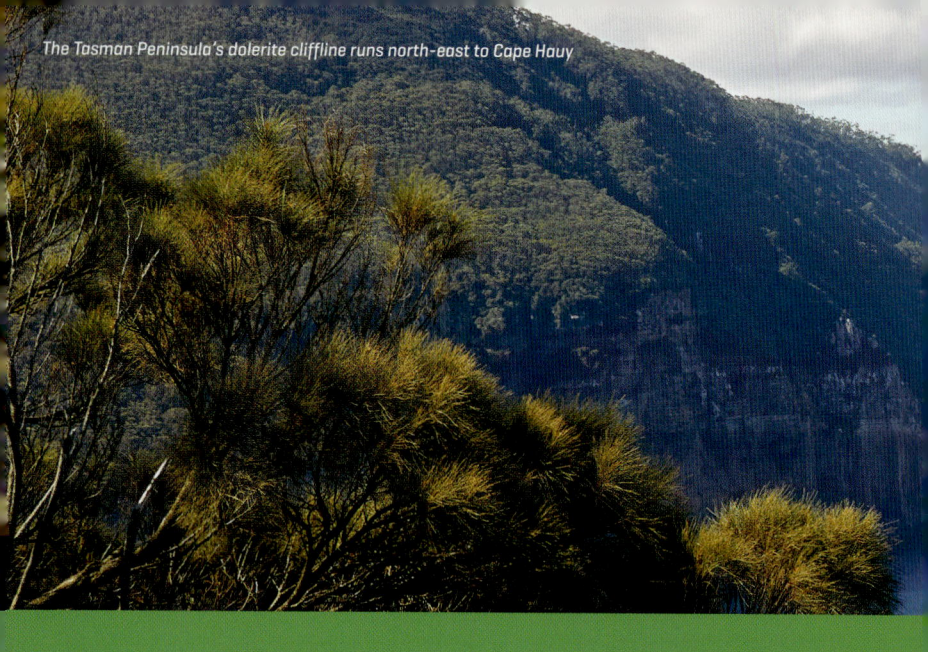

The Tasman Peninsula's dolerite cliffline runs north-east to Cape Hauy

TASMAN PENINSULA

Follow in the footsteps of convicts around a Colonial-era coal mine and poke your toes over Australia's highest sea cliffs; inhale sea spray from blowholes and the pungent aroma of fur seals; tread boardwalks through a sea of wildflowers and feel the drip of drizzle from rainforest ferns. The Tasman Peninsula is a gobsmacking place to walk.

16	Cape Hauy	80
17	Cape Raoul	85
18	Crescent Bay & Mount Brown	90
19	Coal Mines Historic Site	95
20	Fortescue Bay to Devils Kitchen	101
21	Three Capes Track	107

TASMAN PENINSULA

16 CAPE HAUY

Walk:	10.3km return
Time required:	3–4 hours
Best time:	Sunny day (much of the walk is exposed, and it can be unsafe in bad weather)
Grade:	Moderate (with quite a few steps and some steep sections)
Environment:	Tranquil bay, coastal forest, exposed saddles, sheer sea cliffs and precipitous drops
Best map:	TASMAP's *Tasman Peninsula Walks Maps & Details 1:75,000*
Toilets:	Pump-out pit toilets at Fortescue Bay
Food:	Scallop pies, a Tasmanian tasting plate and lavender panna cotta are among the treats on the menu (and in the display fridge) at Port Arthur Lavender (http://portarthurlavender.com.au), on Arthur Hwy just south of the Fortescue Bay turnoff.
Tips:	While most children of all ages will love the thrill of this walk, there are dangerous unfenced drop-offs, so don't let youngsters walk ahead unsupervised. Book a Tasman Island Cruises tour (www.tasmancruises.com.au) for a gobsmacking sea-level perspective of Cape Hauy.

The opportunity to poke your nose over a cliff plunging more than a hundred metres into inky ocean makes this much more than just a spectacular coastal walk.

Dolerite cliffs rear out of the inky ocean off Cape Hauy

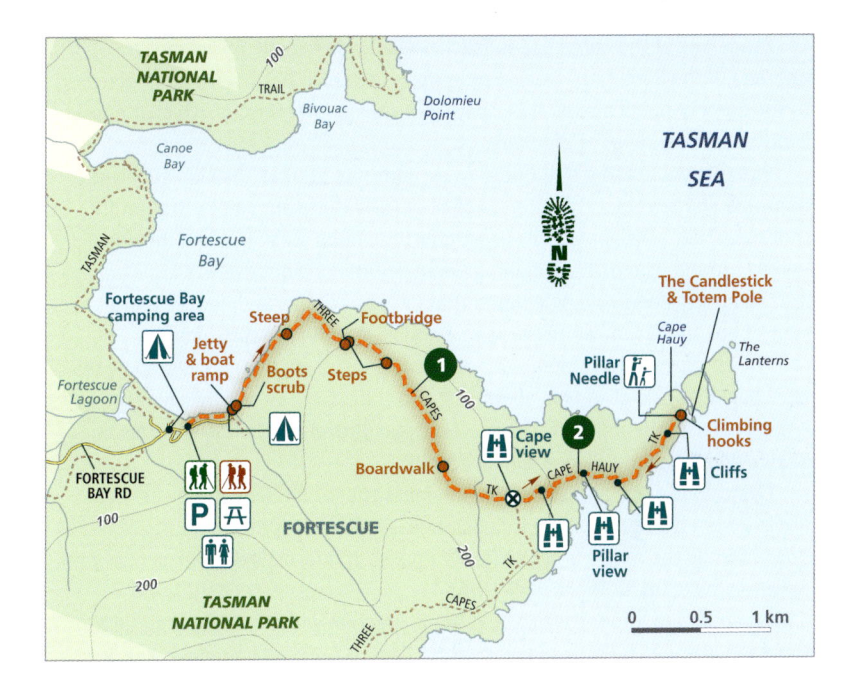

Tasmania boasts thousands of kilometres of shoreline, from wild and rugged to ridiculously pretty. Trying to nominate any one section as the most spectacular would be asking for trouble. But it would take award-winning debating skills to argue against the title going to the Tasman Peninsula, where the ocean slams into the highest sea cliffs in the southern hemisphere.

Lodge accommodation with cooking facilities and ranger assistance/interpretation are part of the package on the 4-day Three Capes Track (see page 107)(www.threecapestrack.com.au) between Port Arthur and Fortescue Bay, but you can also enjoy the drama of Capes Pillar, Raoul and Hauy on day walks and overnight camping hikes.

Half-day walks don't have more wow-factor than the return tramp to Cape Hauy, which points seaward from Fortescue Bay like an ancient, gnarled finger. The walk starts in Fortescue Bay's day-use car park, 12 unsealed kilometres off the Arthur Hwy, an often rough drive that takes you through regrowth eucalypt forest logged in 1971. The signed walking track starts at the eastern end of the day use area. Fortescue Bay laps the rocks to your left as you follow the track east through a camping area and into the bush beyond a jetty and boat ramp.

Stage one of the Three Capes Track project was a multi-million dollar upgrade of the Cape Hauy track. Some walkers think it has been over engineered to the point of being almost a footpath, but the country through which it passes is no less astounding for this work.

First up, you tread a flat, metre-wide compacted track through eucalypts, banksias and tea tree. Then the steps start, and there are plenty. Stonework that would set a stonemason's heart aflutter climbs steadily along the coast before turning inland, there gaining about 150m in height over a kilometre, among stringybarks and blue gums that dwarf banksias and native cherry trees. Look for pink or white Parson's Bands (orchids) growing beneath.

The steps end on a plateau of sorts (see point 1 on map) populated by tea tree, banksias and grand old eucalypts, and the trail rises and falls gently as it continues south and east. The pretty white-dotted purple flowers growing beside a long boardwalk are fairies' aprons.

Oyster Bay pines and she-oaks dominate the forest here. If the she-oaks are in bloom it's worth taking a closer look – the females erupt in tufts of red flowers while the males produce flower spikes. The forest's diverse colours and textures make up for the lack of a view.

About 3.5km into the walk you reach a junction with signs pointing right to Cape Pillar via Mt Fortescue and left to Cape Hauy (two hours' return). Turn left for your first glimpse of the sea and a faceful of wind (the remainder of the walk is very exposed to the elements). Descending steeply on stone steps and packed earth you can clearly see the walking track snaking out along the cape below, a yellow line through wind-cropped green heath bookended by dolerite columns and cliffs.

The track skirts the edge of a steep, rocky cove before climbing again (see point 2 on the map). As you start uphill you'll see Cape Pillar around to your right. Both the Three Capes Track and a 3-day camping hike put you atop Australia's tallest sea cliffs, at Cape Pillar, with 300m drops into the ocean. A stand-alone dolerite column sticks out from the sentinel-like cliff just south of the cove, and Fortescue Bay is now visible behind. From further along the narrowing cape you can see the battlement-like cliffs that run north from Fortescue Bay (see page 101) to Tasman Arch, one of the peninsula's most visited tourist spots. The walking track continues through a waist-deep sea of coastal heath often awash with stalks of candy-floss pink common heath bells.

Gaps in the natural rock wall along the cape's southern edge give vertiginous views of the Tasman Sea and a 20m long rock shard that has split from the cliff but not yet let go.

TOP LEFT: *Multiple steps lead out to Cape Hauy;* **TOP RIGHT:** *A 20m long rock shard has split away from the cliff;* **BOTTOM LEFT:** *The Cape's cliffs plunge from just beyond your feet;* **BOTTOM RIGHT:** *Rocks litter Fortescue Bay's eastern shore*

After dipping down to the left and doing an S-bend, the track ends suddenly on a small, unsigned rock shelf with a view sweeping clockwise from the sea cliffs north of Fortescue Bay to Cape Pillar and the neighbouring, upthrust Tasman Island, beyond which the next landfall is Antarctica.

It appears as if the cape extends further, but the dolerite formations beyond this rocky aerie are separated from it by a sheer drop. If you dare, crawl to the edge and poke your nose over the cliff: you'll see inky water thumping into rock more than a hundred metres below. Visible to your left is the top of the Totem Pole, a dolerite needle that looks like it was pushed through from below by a subterranean stitcher.

The subject of many photographs promoting Tasmania, this remarkable geological exclamation mark is popular with freestyle sports climbers, and voices and the tinkle of climbing equipment sometimes carry across the gap. The two metal D-rings bolted to the cliff beneath your nose are rock climbing anchor points!

When you've had your fill of this jaw-dropping view, raise yourself from horizontal and retrace your steps to Fortescue Bay.

The Cape Hauy walking track snakes along the cliff edge

TASMAN PENINSULA
17 CAPE RAOUL

Walk:	15km out-and-back
Time required:	5-6 hours
Best time:	Clear, mild day (but also under a moody sky for added drama). The last section of the walk offers no protection from high winds that make the cliff edges even more dangerous; turn back in extreme conditions.
Grade:	Moderate
Environment:	Eucalypt forest, heathland, dolerite cape, coastal cliffs, gulches
Best map:	This one
Toilets:	Toilet (gold-coin donation) at Raoul Bay Retreat, adjoining the parking area
Food:	Raoul Bay Retreat sells home-made jam, honey and rhupagne (rhubarb champagne) to jazz up your picnic lunch.
Tips:	Don't leave Tasman Peninsula without experiencing its extraordinary dolerite cliffs from sea level on an adventure cruise with Tasman Island Cruises (www.tasmancruises.com.au).

Precipitous dolerite sea cliffs and the smelly seals that haul out at their base, towering eucalypts and stunted heath all compete for headline status on this day walk to the edge of the world.

You may also spot rock climbers on the spectacular dolerite spike at the end of Cape Raoul

86 TASMAN PENINSULA

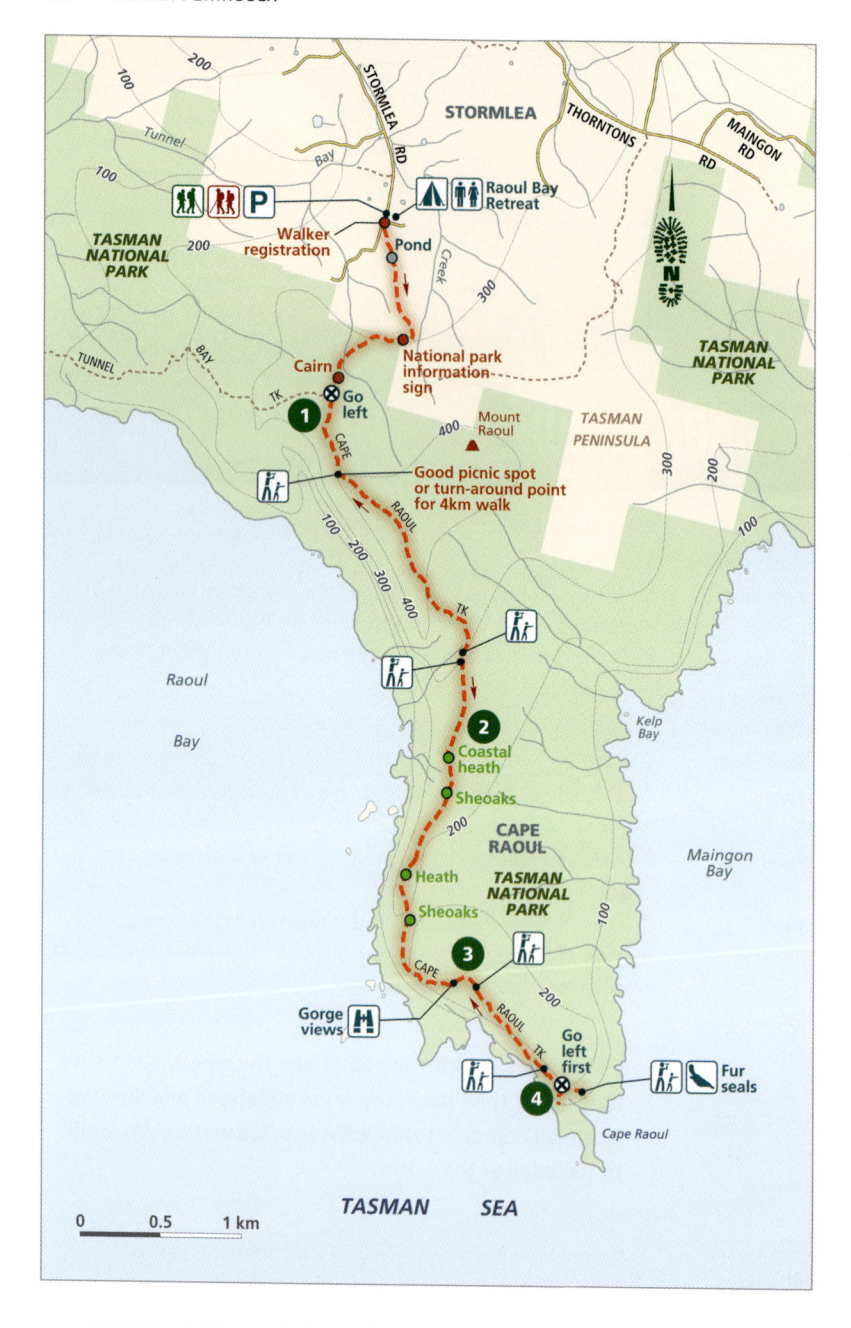

Cape Raoul, the Tasman Peninsula's southernmost point, thrusts into the ocean like a massive club wielded in warning. The walk to its wind- and water-chipped head visits one of Tasmania's most spectacular lookouts.

The walk starts at the end of Stormlea Rd, near Port Arthur penal settlement, 80 minutes from Hobart. Drive 8km west from Port Arthur on Nubeena Rd to Parsons Bay Creek, there turning south and driving another 10km on good gravel Stormlea Rd; the turnoff is signed 'Highcroft 3 Stormlea 9'. (If you reach Nubeena you have gone 3km too far on the bitumen.)

Park at the end of Stormlea Rd, beside Raoul Bay Retreat, an ongoing project with mudbrick retreat, self-contained cottage accommodation and camping. For a coin donation you can use a cute toilet with a weighted door, in the field. You'll have to ask whether the same deal applies for the sauna!

The well-marked walking track starts at the end of the parking area and follows a fence before going bush. Boards and compacted gravel climb from scrubby tea tree and mountain-berry bushes into blue gums and stringybarks – or looming out of the sea mists that often linger here, their trucks and limbs painting black-and-grey stripes on the grainy backdrop. Look for stand-out pink trigger plants, curly beaked hakea flowers and pademelons (rufous wallabies).

The trees become shorter and less streamlined as you ascend and find yourself among banksias and common heath on reaching the junction with the Shipstern Bluff track (another great walk) going right (*see* point 1 on map). Head left and uphill, stepping from scrub onto a natural rock platform on the edge of a dolerite cliff with a jaw-dropping view over Cape Raoul and west to Bruny Island (*see* page 62). This is an unforgettable spot for a snack break or picnic or to hangout before turning back if you opt for only a 4km return walk.

The longer walk, to the cape, heads south-east from the lookout, hugging the cliff edge and gifting amazing views through striped gums twisted and bent by salty sea winds. Having pulled clear of the cliff into she-oaks, banksias, beaked hakea and taller eucalypts with shaggy grey trunks, you've got a long descent in damper forest, where moss cloaks fallen trees, and rocks and bracken carpet the ground. The next leg, back on the cliff edge, is one continuous lookout, with more and more inlets coming into view to the west, then Bruny Island and south-west Tasmania behind. Nearer is Shipstern Bluff, rock shelving extending into the sea from its foot. (Huge breaks at the Bluff attract big-wave surfers.)

Every time you look there's more cliff and coast telling an action-packed story of deposition, compaction, continental shift, lava flow, faulting and erosion. The slope you've just come down (and have to climb back up) is impressive from here! Watch for stumpy tailed lizards and skinks among the rocks and be alert for snakes, particularly in warm weather.

She-oaks, banksias and mountain-berry bushes flourish along the cliff, tea tree and contorted eucalypts with scaly bark collars back from the edge. Then you step from she-oaks into classic coastal heath (see point 2 on map), the track thrust through a sea of bristling flowering plants a-metre-and-a-half deep. Firetails (finches), with red beaks and tails, and black-and-white barred chests, are common here. Weather permitting, you'll see Cape Pillar and Tasman Island (see the Three Capes Track page 107) and other Tasman Peninsula landmarks to the left.

The track crosses the cape's exposed plateau – some of Australia's strongest winds have been recorded here – to a massive gorge (see point 3 on map) that draws your gaze down cliffs fashioned from dolerite columns that look like boxed pencils, to deep blue water and white foam. See the fracture lines running from cliff top to bottom, and to the right where some have broken away and fallen. (The Royal Navy apparently used the cliffs for target practice in the late 19th century!)

This spot – actually, anywhere on Cape Raoul – is a grandstand for watching migrating humpback and southern right whales in spring and

One of Tasmania's most spectacular lookouts comes up early in the walk

TOP LEFT: *Lichen adorns many trees;* **RIGHT:** *Eucalypts loom out of the sea mist;*
BOTTOM LEFT: *A metallic skink gleams in the sun*

autumn, and Sydney-to-Hobart racing yachts round the Tasman Peninsula for their run into Hobart at year's end.

Continue on a flat track through heath to the edge of the Cape, turning left when the track branches. About 150m on you'll step onto cliff-edge rock overlooking a spectacular spine of dolerite columns snapped off at different heights. Depending on your mood and imagination you'll see all sorts of characters in the stonework, including Ned Kelly; you may also spot the ant-like figures of rock climbers. Australian fur seals frolic in the dark depths off the cape and haul themselves out at its seaward foot, lolling on a ledge white-washed with faeces. You'll probably hear them grunting and also catch their unforgettable aroma on the ocean breeze. Keep an eye out too for big pods of dolphins slipping through the water. An uninterrupted view of Tasman Island and Australia's tallest sea cliffs (300m high) on Cape Pillar make this a gobsmacking lunch spot.

Back at the previous track junction, keep left to the crenellated top of Cape Raoul's dolerite spine (*see* point 4 on map). Vantage points among the stone columns reveal the sheerness of Cape Raoul and the cliffs atop which you just lunched.

Refuelled, backtrack to your car.

TASMAN PENINSULA

18 CRESCENT BAY & MOUNT BROWN

Walk:	11.5km out-and-back
Time required:	4–5 hours
Best time:	Spring for the wildflowers; any time for rugged coastal scenery
Grade:	Easy–moderate
Environment:	Coastal cliffs, beach, rocky promontories, blowholes, dunes
Best map:	This one
Toilets:	Flushing toilet in Remarkable Cave car park
Food:	The tiny village of Port Arthur has a supermarket and general store; the Tudor Fox & Hounds Inn serves tasty evening meals.
Tips:	Allow time before or after the walk for the 15-minute stroll down to remarkable Remarkable Cave, a two-pronged tunnel drilled through the coastal cliff by the sea. Mosquitoes mass in patches of heath protected from sea breezes so wear protective clothing and don't stand still for long.

An easy Tasman Peninsular walk combines blowholes, beach, yellow-tailed black cockatoos and masterful geology.

Yellow-tailed black cockatoos take flight

CRESCENT BAY & MOUNT BROWN   91

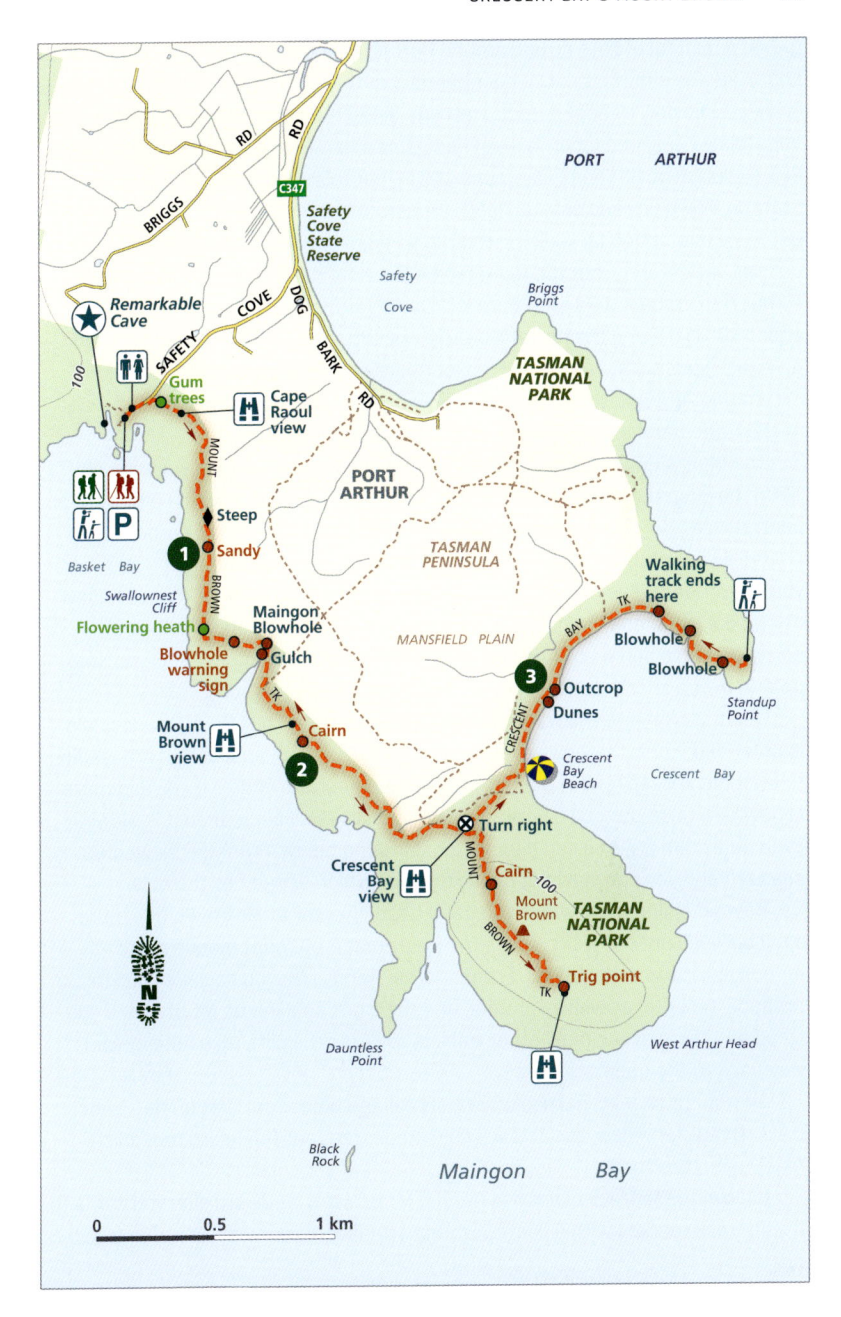

One of a handful of bays strung around Port Arthur, the body of water on whose shore sits the infamous convict penitentiary of the same name, Crescent Bay is accessible only by boat or foot. The cliffs along the pedestrian route lack the body-blow visual impact of Tasman Peninsula's famous capes – Hauy (see page 80), Raoul (page 85) and Pillar (page 109) – but this walk is less energetic. Starring blowholes and coastal heath that erupts in spring and summer colours, this is a great option for walkers wanting a Peninsula warm-up or cool-down.

The walk starts from the Remarkable Cave car park. To get there, turn off Arthur Hwy/Nubeena Rd onto Safety Cove Rd (signed for Remarkable Cave) about 600m beyond the Port Arthur Historic Site and follow the road to its end, on a rocky point. The land's-end lookout here provides a great view of layered cliff to the right and the weaknesses on which the sea works to fashion caves. At the right-hand extreme you can just make out Cape Raoul.

The blue-signed Maingon Blowhole, Crescent Bay and Mt Brown track starts 150m back up the access road, on the right. Skirting a gulch with a phallic rock centrepiece, you climb dunes topped with a cluster of gums and carpeted in a coarse weave of pink-, yellow- and white-flowering heath. Spring and summer you will probably see pale-yellow scented paperbark, bush peas, mauve honey myrtle balls and many more. The pale green or yellow cylindrical bells are common apple berry. Look for animal tracks – some like zippers – as you step up and over a short, steep, sandy section (see point 1 on map).

About 1.5km into the walk you pass a sign warning that Maingon Blowhole is unfenced. Enjoy the views along the cliff line to Cape Raoul before proceeding to the hole, a deep rent in the rocks. Take care near the edge – if you slip there is nowhere to go but down into the sea – and stay well back when it is blowing. Even on a calm day you can hear water slumping below. From the blowhole's seaward end you can view the ravine through which ocean fills the hole.

Beyond Maingon Blowhole you get a head-on view of Mt Brown (it's more a hill but let's not nit-pick) and cairns (see point 2 on map) mark a route across natural granite paving. From another sandy rise you can see black rock, probably dolerite, as well as granite, and the track snaking up Mt Brown. If you tread any footpads worn by other walkers towards the cliff, take note of your way back to the main track.

Watch for snakes, particularly where foliage hides your feet on narrower track. Beautiful yellow-tailed black cockatoos frequent the heath too, noisily feasting on the seeds.

Following the track clockwise around Mt Brown's landward side you come to a side track marked with a cairn. Turn right and work your way up rough track.

CRESCENT BAY & MOUNT BROWN   93

You soon get a fabulous view left of Crescent Bay and its yellow beach. Across Port Arthur's mouth is Budget Head, Arthurs Peak rising above it.

The view from a large cairn swings 180° from Cape Pillar and Tasman Island to Cape Raoul but this isn't the top. A gentler final climb marked with cairns leads to the trig point, from where you can see the beautiful sand dunes backing Crescent Bay beach and the blowholes drilled into the rocky point at the bay's eastern end. You can also see way up Port Arthur and all the way back along the walking track to the car park. Just visible are one of Remarkable Cave's two exits and you can sometimes glimpse the northern tip of Bruny Island (see page 62) beyond Cape Raoul.

Note the eroded cliff line to Cape Pillar as you work your way back down to the main track. (There is such a network of footpads you will probably tread

The unmarked walk to Standup Point takes you to the lip of a blowhole

paths you didn't tread coming up.) As well as its dolerite structure you can see the crenellations where columns have broken away.

A sandy track with occasional roots and then rocks, works around Mt Brown and steeply down onto Crescent Bay's squeaky yellow sand, which you may share with pied oystercatchers and plovers. With the dunes rising to your left, walk the length of the bay; at high tide you may have to walk over the rock outcrop, crazed into terrazzo patterns (see point 3 on map), that breaks the beach about half way along.

There is no track but you can continue 500m beyond the beach on rocks to Standup Point. It's dangerous to proceed in rain or when the sea is rough but on a clear, calm day the point gifts an elongated view up Port Arthur, a wide angle across Crescent Bay to Mt Brown, which looks like a whale's head from here, and along the impressive cliffs running from Port Arthur to Cape Pillar.

Heading out to the point you cross sloping granite decorated with yellow, orange and white lichen; pass vertically fractured rock; divert inland through tea tree around one blowhole and tread the edge of another. Look for helpful blue ribbons towards the end.

Adventuring done, turn around and head back to your car.

TOP LEFT: *Honey myrtle shrubs produce explosions of pink flowers;* **RIGHT:** *The rocky outcrop on Crescent Bay beach is naturally terrazzo tiled;* **BOTTOM LEFT:** *Fracturing rock forms brick-like patterns*

TASMAN PENINSULA
19 COAL MINES HISTORIC SITE

Walk:	4.7km loop
Time required:	2 hours
Best time:	Any time
Grade:	Easy
Environment:	Coastal eucalypt scrub, convict-era ruins
Best map:	This one
Toilets:	Pit toilet in car park
Food:	No food on site; bakery, cafe and pub fare in Nubeena, 11km south of Premaydena
Tips:	Don't be put off by grey skies; they only add to the atmosphere of this historic site.

Walk in the footsteps of convict labourers and their minders on this disarmingly pretty stretch of Tasmanian coast.

Convicts who reoffended after transportation to Van Diemen's Land, as Tasmania was known in the early 19th century, found themselves at Port Arthur, the infamous penal settlement on the Tasman Peninsula. Port Arthur targeted reform through hard physical labour and severe punishment, and conditions were harsh. An even more dreaded destination, however, were the coal mines on the peninsula's north-west coast.

Chain creates an evocative timeline for the site

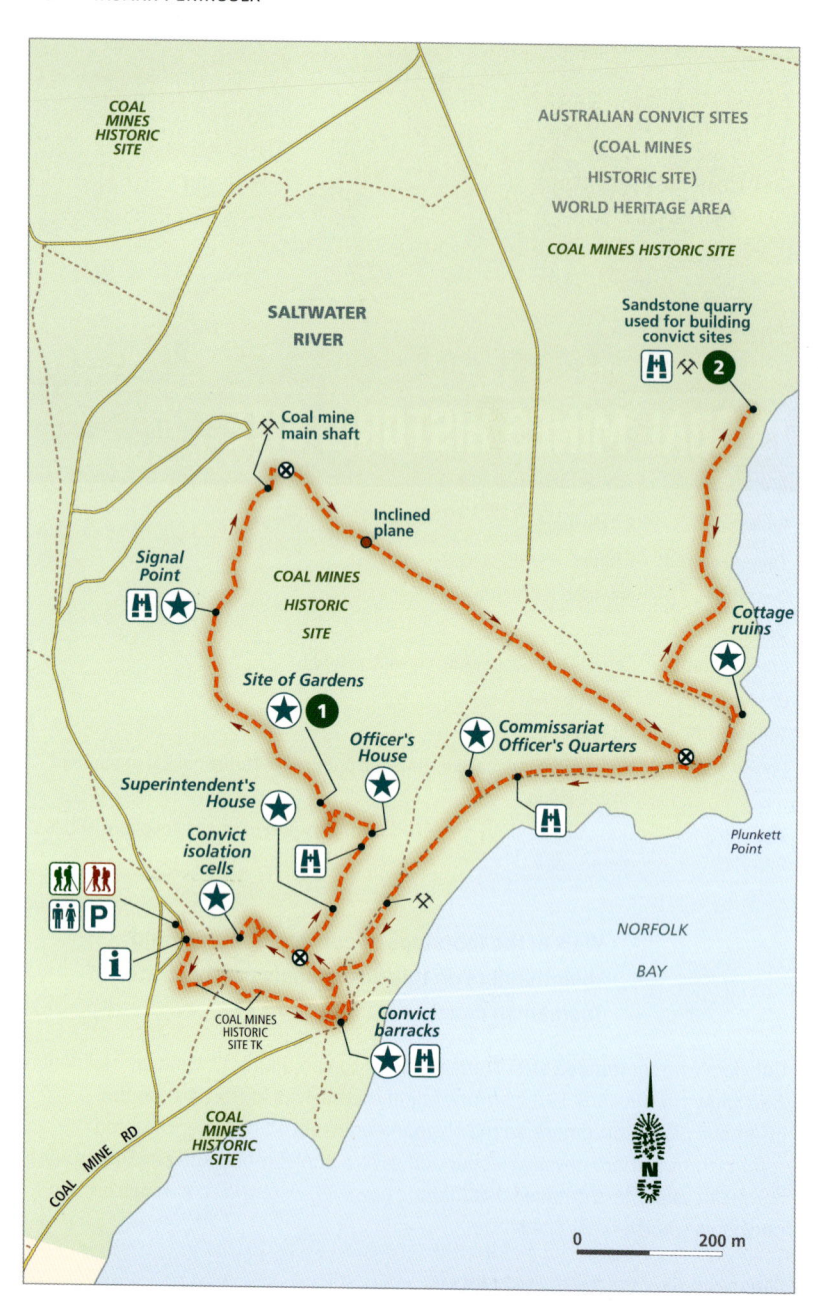

TASMAN PENINSULA

AUSTRALIAN CONVICT SITES (COAL MINES HISTORIC SITE) WORLD HERITAGE AREA

COAL MINES HISTORIC SITE

- COAL MINES HISTORIC SITE
- SALTWATER RIVER
- Sandstone quarry used for building convict sites — **2**
- Coal mine main shaft
- Inclined plane
- Signal Point
- COAL MINES HISTORIC SITE
- Cottage ruins
- Site of Gardens — **1**
- Officer's House
- Commissariat Officer's Quarters
- Superintendent's House
- Convict isolation cells
- Plunkett Point
- NORFOLK BAY
- COAL MINES HISTORIC SITE TK
- Convict barracks
- COAL MINE RD
- COAL MINES HISTORIC SITE

0 — 200 m

Colourful ruins of the Commissariat Officer's Quarters

But this reputation may have been unjust. While the 'worst class' of convicts laboured underground in unstable mine shafts, often harnessed to others and always under threat of solitary confinement in subterranean punishment cells, most men at the coal mines worked above ground, quarrying rock, building prisoner barracks and civilian quarters, splitting timber and tending vegetables.

The Coal Mines Historic Site is one of 11 sites in Tasmania (*see* Maria Island Loop, page 124), Norfolk Island, Western Australia and New South Wales that form the Australian Convict Sites World Heritage property. This walk revisits a dramatic chapter in Australia's short but action-packed European history.

To get there you turn west off the Arthur Hwy at Taranna, south of Eaglehawk Neck, the infamous isthmus that links the Tasman and Forestier peninsulas, which in Port Arthur's day was guarded by a chain gang of vicious dogs. Drive along the B37 to Premaydena then turn north up the C341, following this road 13km (mostly unsealed) north.

Your journey back in time begins when you step through an obvious break in the tea tree fringing the parking area, and continues on a flat walking track that snakes through woodland to a chicane of timber and rammed earth.

Information plaques on the wall above a rusty chain outline the site's timeline. Watch for superb fairy-wrens flitting about the leaf litter as you continue through woodland into the site.

The track emerges from the trees beside the main settlement or 'square', founded in 1838, and swings around in front of the ruined convict barracks, their every sandstone block pitted with tool marks. Climb the rise and wander around the settlement. A second-floor fenced area within the first building gives a view down into the solitary confinement cells (and out over the blue water of Norfolk Bay).

Now head towards the rear of the square and take the right-hand track to the Military Precinct. Ascending gradually through banksias and tall eucalypts, with a broadening view of water and peninsula, you pass the remains of the Superintendent's House (built in 1837), home to tyrannical Superintendent Cook and more moderate managers.

The track turns left at the remains of the brick six-room Senior Military Officer's House, which from 1837 to 1842 housed the garrison commander, who also acted as magistrate. Under the sadistic Lieutenant Barclay, the miners became known as Barclay's Tigers because of the flogging scars on their backs.

After a short detour left to the beautiful remains of the sandstone officers' outbuilding, you reach the garden site (*see* point 1 on map), a grassy clearing where convicts once grew hectares of potatoes, carrots, turnips, cabbages and leeks.

From here the track, now lined with delineating logs, climbs through cypress pines, thick, velvety moss growing in their shade, and tops out at Signal Point. The convict-manned signal station operated here was a branch line of the semaphore system that enabled Port Arthur to communicate with Hobart in just 15 minutes (*see* Truganini Track page 14). There must have been far fewer trees back then, to facilitate signal-flag sightings, but now eucalypts frame scraps of farmland and water views.

Descend slightly from here to the deepest coal mining shaft, down which convicts were lowered by windlass to work a coal face, or run out the coal-laden boxes, or pull and push them to the shaft. This shaft reached 92m into the hill but is now a fairly shallow fenced hole. The rusty boiler behind powered the steam engine, which superseded convict labour to pump water from the constantly flooding mine.

Turn right at the track junction immediately beyond the shaft and descend the inclined plane. A gravity-powered cable transfer system operated on this

COAL MINES HISTORIC SITE   99

TOP: One of the convict-built ruins of the Coal Mines Site settlement; **BOTTOM LEFT:** Stone windows frame the convict ruins; **BOTTOM RIGHT:** Eucalypts frame scraps of view from the signal station site

slope, with empty wagons being hauled back up to the mine by the weight of those laden with coal running down to the jetty.

There are unfenced shafts either side of the inclined plane, so don't leave the wagon route. Just continue downhill (ignoring a crossroad) to Plunkett Point, where aqua water laps white sand.

You could turn right here and make your way back to the settlement area, but we're making the 1.4km return detour to the quarry first. So turn left and follow a sandy track with occasional exposed roots north along the bay's rocky shore to the quarry via photogenic stone cottage ruins. The track tunnels through tea tree, which blocks the breeze, but you still get refreshing views of Norfolk Bay.

Unfinished stone blocks (see point 2 on the map) that were abandoned on the track the day the mine closed signal you've reached the quarry. Ignore the rougher track going left and continue ahead and down. Walk into the quarry area and compare the clean stone faces cut by convicts with the voluptuous curves nature has fashioned in the rock face.

Back at Plunkett Point, walk south-west along the shore on a sandy track often lined with stalks of pink and white common heath. Ignore the intersecting wide track on the left but do step up to the right to the ruins of the Commissariat Officers' Quarters (1842). There are some particularly colourful stone blocks here.

On your return to the Coal Mines settlement square, which soon comes into view through the trees, walk up through the buildings again, passing the track to the Officers' Quarters you took earlier and continuing to the punishment cells at the rear of the site. Tread the mesh walkway through the building and past the restored and original isolation cells, in which convicts were locked for days at a time, deprived of light, sound and human company. Then escape along the track heading west to the car park.

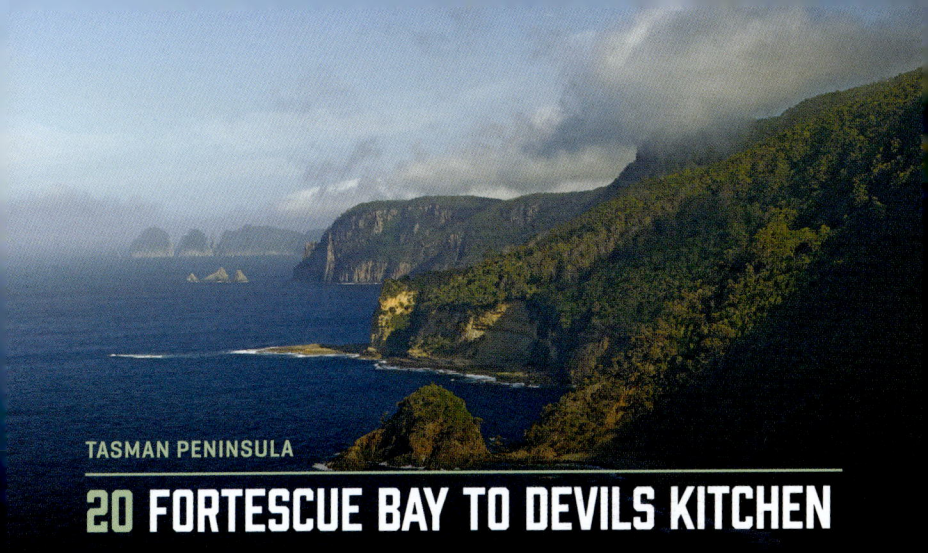

TASMAN PENINSULA
20 FORTESCUE BAY TO DEVILS KITCHEN

Walk:	21km A to B
Time required:	6–9 hours
Best time:	Mild, clear weather; after rain for forest and waterfalls at their best
Grade:	Moderate; long with multiple ups and downs
Environment:	Beach, bay, dolerite coastal cliffs, rainforest, fern gullies, waterfalls
Best map:	This one or TASMAP's *Peninsula Walks (Tasman Peninsula) Walk Map and Details 1:50,000*
Toilets:	Composting toilets at Fortescue Bay and Bivouac Bay
Food:	Port Arthur town, 4km south, has a pub, supermarket, café, and takeaways. There's also a great café at the Port Arthur historic site.
Tips:	This walk follows unfenced cliffs; take extreme care.
	You'll need to car shuffle or arrange a drop-off/pick-up to do the walk as described.
	Allow time to explore Port Arthur and the Tasman Peninsula by land and view the spectacular coast from the water with Tasman Island Cruises (www.tasmancruises.com.au).

Plunging sea cliffs, sweeping coastal vistas, towering trees, lush rainforest and dripping ferns make this a contender for Tasmania's 'best' all-day hike.

What a view: south to Cape Hauy

102　TASMAN PENINSULA

FORTESCUE BAY TO DEVILS KITCHEN

Cut by Hobart Walking Club volunteers in the 1970s, the Tasman Coastal Trail, between Fortescue Bay and Waterfalls Bay, on the rugged east coast of Tasman Peninsula, is a stunner, thanks to the diverse environments it traverses and the remarkable dolerite battlement it follows north. Add the stroll from Waterfall Bay to the Devils Kitchen and you've got a hell of a hike.

One of several dozen walks on Tasman Peninsula, an hour's drive south-east of Hobart, this all-dayer starts/ends in beautiful Fortescue Bay in Tasman National Park, as does the Cape Hauy walk (see page 80). To reach this popular camping and day-use destination, turn off the Arthur Hwy (A9) 4km north of Port Arthur and drive 12km east on forestry road.

While not a designated 4WD road, this access road in is often rough and potholed. So you may still be shaken and stirred from the drive as you start your walk north along the bay beach, with Fortescue's fine white sand squeaking underfoot. From September to February, walk closer to the water, to avoid birds' nests, eggs and chicks above the high-tide line. You may need to wade if water is flowing out of the lagoon behind the beach.

The walking track begins near the end of the sand (the marker comes in and out of view). It follows the shoreline to a rocky cove exited via a rise thick with banksias, tea tree, stringybarks, blue gums, common heath and mountain-berry bushes. The rise offers a view back along Fortescue Bay's white crescent beach and your first good look (there are plenty to come) at the coast's columnar dolerite construction. (Dolerite is volcanic rock, injected in molten form up into older sedimentary rock and then exposed by time.) Higher still the view takes in Cape Hauy's cliffs, east of Fortescue Bay.

She-oak needles soften footsteps down to Canoe Bay. The rusty metal protruding from the water is an old dredge sunk in 1970 to create a breakwater that's now a popular bird perch (see point 1 on map). Cross the swing bridge over Walkers Creek and pass from tree ferns into tea tree and gums. Note the multiple moss varieties, including shaggy rosettes, as you scale the next headland; the view back to Cape Hauy improves with each step.

Impressive natural stonework appears through the trees as you approach Bivouac Bay, a south-facing sheltered anchorage with grassy camping, pit toilet and permanent creek water. Sea lettuce scattered on the rocky beach appears luminous on cloudy days. Ford the creek running into the bay on stepping stones and climb Dolomieu Point, stopping within centimetres of oblivion on unfenced cliff that rears 100m from inky depths and extends kilometres north.

Sea mist commonly shrouds this natural fortification but when the coast is clear you come face-to-face with grand-scale geology. In several places you

104 TASMAN PENINSULA

The last leg of the walk leads to lookouts over ocean-cut caves and arches

can look straight down cracked rock to swell thumping into the base of the cliff. Depending on wind conditions and your proximity to the edge, the percussion can be loud or like brush strokes.

There are countless ups and downs over the next 6km but effectively you climb. Minimal changes in altitude produce dramatic changes in forest: native conifers and scribbly gums scrawled with moth-larva feeding trails give way to taller eucalypts that draw black stripes in mist; stepped steep descents navigate gullies criss-crossed with fallen trees and boulders covered with moss and ferns.

About 4km north the track kisses the lip of the cliff before veering inland, into cutting grass so tall you might feel like Alice in Wonderland after drinking shrinking potion. Climb; descend; climb amid stringybarks, blackwoods, grass trees, and mountain berries, keeping watch for leeches.

Now it's steeply up Tatnells Hill, on narrow track through snow-berry shrubs (plump white fruit) and candleheath bushes (see point 2 on map) that are fantastically spiky and spiraly, and which produce sculptural white flowers in spring. Old man's beard and lichens hang from practically every plant.

The climb lands you on an open false summit with fragments of view through leaves, a lovely spot for a break on a sunny day. The weathered Balts Spur and Lichen Hill sign here is confusing because Balts Spur climbs Tatnells Hill from the south-west and Lichen Hill is to the north-west. But immediately to the right of the sign there's a footpad and a marker ribbon. This is the unsigned side track to the top of Tatnells Hill.

LEFT: *Spiky candle heath starts to bloom;* **MIDDLE:** *Eucalypts soar into grainy sea mist;* **RIGHT:** *Raindrops jewel a spider's web*

Faded yellow and pink ribbons keep you on track (lumpy with rocks and roots in places but okay) through beech tunnels towards a dead tree and up to the summit.

At 571m, Tatnells Hill is the highest point on the peninsula and the panoramic view from the top reaches north to Maria Island, north-west to kunanyi/Mt Wellington, south-west to Bruny Island and south to Cape Pillar. On wet days, however, or when cloud enfolds the 'hill', and even the false summit feels more alpine than coastal, it's not worth doing the detour.

A small cairn marks where the Tasman Trail continues north off the false summit, down into textural fern forest. Ignore a footpad to Clemes Peak and descend through myrtle beech, eucalypts trailing bark streamers, and more Alice-in-Wonderland cutting grass, passing greened, fallen trees and stumps. Cross Waterfall Creek on stepping stones and follow it down a gully crisscrossed with trees into shadow-filled rainforest.

The descent ends at a T-junction where the creek drops over a ledge at Camp Falls (just a trickle in drier months). Waterfall Bay is left but walk about 600m to the right for ocean vistas from Waterfall Bluff. Back at the junction, cross a footbridge over the creek and listen for yellow-tailed black cockatoos as you amble north close to the lip of Waterfall Bay.

The Tasman Trail officially ends at a vehicle turnaround. Walk to its fenced southern border for the best of Waterfall Bay (*see* point 3 on map), a rock horseshoe thrust 100m out of deep, dark water. When the creeks flow, they pour over the edge and plunge white and frothy into the sea.

You could park a car, or arrange for a pick-up here rather than at the Devils Kitchen, but you'd miss the grand finale stroll.

A wide, flat gravel track, starting opposite where you emerged from the forest, follows a fenced cliff strung with lookouts over rock stacks, shelving and ocean-carved arches. It continues through heathland to the Devils Kitchen car park, from where it's another short walk (or drive) to Tasman Arch.

Two of the Tasman Peninsula's biggest tourist attractions, these neighbouring geological fascinators testify to the sea's power to work on weaknesses, opening and enlarging great archways through apparently solid rock.

TASMAN PENINSULA

21 THREE CAPES TRACK

Walk:	48km A to B
Time required:	4 days (you can't stay more than one night at each cabin)
Best time:	Year-round but spring wildflowers put on an unforgettable show
Grade:	Easy-moderate
Environment:	Beaches, coastal heath, eucalypts, rainforest, dolerite cliffs, capes
Best map:	This one and TASMAP's *Peninsula Walks Tasman Peninsula, 1:50,000*
Toilets:	Flushing toilets at Port Arthur Historic Site (start), composting toilets at each cabin and Fortescue Bay (finish).
Food:	No food on the track. Bring your own.
Tips:	The Three Capes Track must be booked via www.threecapestrack.com.au. In 2018, the fee was $495 per adult and $396 concession including boat cruise to the start and bus back to Port Arthur; accommodation with bunk beds and share kitchens; luggage storage and parking at Port Arthur; a Port Arthur pass; and a guidebook of walking notes, maps, profiles, and information for 40 'story-seats' that you'll find along the track. Several companies operate coach services between Hobart and Port Arthur. Book a post-track passage with Tasman Island Cruises (www.tasmancruises.com.au) to see the where you've walked from the water.

Walk to Australia's highest coastal cliffs and overnight on bespoke mattresses in hard-top accommodations: welcome to the Three Capes Track experience!

The geological wonder of Cape Hauy is on show all the way along the Three Capes Track

108 TASMAN PENINSULA

THREE CAPES TRACK 109

Let's get one thing straight first off: the Three Capes Track visits only two Tasman Peninsula capes. Bagging the triumvirate involves doing an additional day walk to Cape Raoul (see page 85). But whether you opt for the add-on or not, you will find yourself on what is arguably Australia's most extraordinary coast, where land ends in toe-curling dolerite cliffs plunging into inky waters.

The Three Capes Track has proved more popular than even its most enthusiastic proponents expected since opening in December 2015 and the 48-bed 'cabins' are often full over peak holiday periods. The walk is unguided, however, so you set your start time – some hikers love early light, others prefer to sleep in – and pace themselves. You don't have to walk in a group and there are countless places to enjoy the majesty of the scenery in solitude.

Another option, for the price of a Parks Pass, is a two-to-three-day, anticlockwise, full-pack camping loop from Fortescue Bay to Cape Pillar and back via Cape Hauy, a route that excludes the first two days of the Three Capes Track. Some people behind the track initially proposed closing all camping on the entire peninsula but saw the light – or, perhaps, felt the glare of the spotlight – when local bushwalkers declared they would walk and camp anyway.

At the other end of the scale you've got the Three Capes Lodge Walk (www.taswalkingco.com.au/three-capes-lodge-walk), opened in September 2018, a guided, fully-catered day-pack walking experience, with accommodation in private lodges starts at $2790 per person.

Three Capes Track

DAY 1: Cruise (1 hour) plus 4km walk (2 hours)

The Three Capes Track launches with an adventure boat cruise – you're asked to don voluminous, unflattering red rubber cover-alls to keep dry – departing Port Arthur Historic Site, 75 minutes' drive south-east of Hobart. Weather permitting, the purpose-built boat runs down Port Arthur to Crescent Bay (see page 90) and around West Arthur Head to visit Australian fur seals before dropping you in Tasman National Park at Denmans Cove, opposite the convict station.

Pied oystercatchers, plovers and other birds nest in the soft sand of Denmans Cove beach during breeding season (August to April); posts along the creek that flows into the ocean show you where not to tread.

Bollards engraved with banksias mark the beginning of the Three Capes Track proper at the top of the beach. Nearby is a boot wash station; clean your boots to keep this section of the park free of rootrot fungus (*Phytophthora cinnamomi*).

From here you've got an easy, undulating warm-up walk that initially hugs Port Arthur's shoreline, so you can see the convict-era buildings across the water and, as you go, Cape Raoul's crenellated profile to the south-west.

Among eucalypt woodland you come to a timber bench with leg irons attached. This is 'Dear Eliza' the first of the 40 story seats, their stories told in *Encounters on the Edge*. This one relates to correspondence from a convict, Henry, to his dear Eliza that begins, 'Torn from you as I am, perhaps forever, has blasted my hopes in life...' Reading the guidebook at these spots lends the walk a human and historic dimension.

Continue on track, boardwalk and footbridges over gullies and through white-flowering common tea tree, yellow bush pea, pink-and-white bushman's bootlace, needle-leafed hakea, and mauve blushes of Tasman hairy boronia. About 2.5km into the walk you'll pass a eucalypt blackened and hollowed by the ferocious 2003 bushfire; and shortly after come to the cobblestoned Surveyors Cove (*see* point 1 on map) beach where you could unclip your pack and poke around for ages.

Stone steps zigzag steeply uphill from the bay and a long boardwalk climbs gently through coral fern and button grass to Surveyors Cabin, which – at the whim of the weather gods – welcomes walkers with a spectacular view south-west to Cape Raoul.

The word 'cabin' belittles the true Three Capes Track accommodation experience. Central to each architect-designed complex are shared kitchens

Weather permitting, Surveyors Cabin welcomes walkers with a view south-west to Cape Raoul

with gas burners, pots and utensils, tables and chairs, reference books, playing cards and board games. Off these branch decked wings of four- and eight-bed rooms with purpose-designed, locally made and very comfy memory-foam mattresses. There's also a changeroom and wash room and Munro Cabin (Night 2) has a canvas bag-shower you can fill with gas-warmed water. There are, however, no garbage bins so you need to carry all rubbish out with you.

A ranger meets and greets walkers and gives a nightly talk about the weather forecast and following day's route, and tells stories about the track and peninsula.

DAY 2: 11km, 3.5–5 hours (+ 2km detour to campsite)

Day 2 starts with you cutting the corner off Surveyors Cabin's button-grass moor and re-entering eucalypt scrub. The track now climbs slightly, offering a view over Port Arthur waters, layered cliffs and Cape Raoul. There are too many short footbridges to mark them all on the map.

Soon after the 'Punishment to playground' seat, about 400m into the day, the track veers from shoreline into heathland which transforms into a rough embroidery stitched in pink, yellow, orange and white. Look out for grazing wallabies, particularly early-morning, as you cross and climb a small hill that traverses button-grass plains.

Having navigated a creek gully thick with eucalypts and cutting grass, you pass another survivor of the 2003 fire. The guidebook notes for 'Fire is food', immediately beyond, explains that many Australian plants need fire and that Australia's first peoples used it as a tool. The mosaic of moorland, heathlands, scrub and forest through which the track passes, reflects not just geology, aspect and soil, but years of deliberate burning. A couple of hundred metres on you can find out why messy forests are healthy forests.

Boardwalk crosses a heathy plain scattered plentifully with cuboid wombat droppings, and stone steps and gravel ascend a treed headland offering fragmented views of Port Arthur waters through foliage. Soon after a sign warning of cliffs ahead (*see* point 2 on map), you reach the first of the day's many viewpoints. Three hundred more metres of climbing puts you atop Arthurs Peak (312m), with dolerite cliffs at your feet and Tasman Island (look for the lighthouse) poking around the next headland south-east. To your right are Crescent Bay and Mt Brown and beyond them, Cape Raoul. Watch for dolphins and migrating whales (winter and spring) in the sea and wedge-tailed eagles and white-bellied sea eagles overhead. This would also be an enviable position from which to watch Sydney to Hobart competitors sail past en route to the finish line.

TOP LEFT: *Tasmanian waratah;* **RIGHT:** *Dolerite columns stand tall on the walk to Cape Pillar;*
MIDDLE LEFT: *Male she-oak flowers are worth a closer look;* **BOTTOM LEFT:** *Curlicue hakea adds texture to the bush*

The walking track is clearly visible ahead now, snaking over a saddle and up a rise. From the saddle you can see the cliff on which you were just standing and the rise gives an extended view back over your route and out to Cape Raoul.

Once at Jurassic Crack lookout (see point 3 on map), stand on the boulder and take in the view of the commanding dolerite cliffs. First described in 1807 by French mineralogist Rene Just Hauy (hence Cape Hauy's name), dolerite is an igneous rock that covers two-thirds of Tasmania. It is created by magma (molten rock) being forced into and widening, fractures in older sedimentary rock, then cracking into polygonal columns as it cools. Erosion of the older rock here at Jurassic Crack reveals these distinctive structures, other fine examples being kunanyi/Mt Wellington (Hobart), Mt Ossa (Tasmania's highest mountain) and Cradle Mountain on The Overland Track (see page 303).

From Jurassic Crack tread compacted gravel down through damper, greener, mossier, more aromatic cloud forest that's home to many more birds than sing in the open. This patch of remarkably different forest is created by the cliff shape, which sucks cold air up from the sea and condenses it.

You step from cloud forest into windswept Ellarwey Valley. Common heath is one of the many flowering plants that weave the valley's coarse-piled carpet; even the eucalypts and she-oaks here are only a metre tall. The heath was sliced open to build the walking track but plants are starting to heal the wound.

Tall stringybarks and vivid-green cutting grass await on the next rise, as does 'Love in the woods' (see point 4 on map), a double seat positioned for laying back and resting while you think about all the different places in which forest dwellers reproduce – hollows, nests, tussocks – the list is never-ending.

Turn right for Munro Cabin (tonight's destination) and Cape Pillar at the four-way junction 300m on. Retakunna (Night 3 cabin), Cape Hauy and Fortescue Bay are straight ahead – and immediately left at this junction is Old Cape Pillar track, the lower-grade trail that non-Three Capes Trackers tread from Fortescue Bay. Meander through scrub to a seat sited for identifying some of the many plants growing in the forest and listening to chattering birds.

The steep, rooted side track at the next junction drops down to Wughalee, the lone camping area for Cape Pillar at the time of writing. If you want to see some of the biggest gum trees on the peninsula, drop your pack here and take this 45-minute return detour.

A narrower, leaf-littered track, with roots and steps, descends about 1km to eight wooden camping platforms watered by a creek and shaded by towering trees (see point 5 on map). The steepness of this track and the risk of tree falls in high wind have prompted discussions about re-opening an old camp on the main track. A signed but poorly maintained track pushing north-east from

THREE CAPES TRACK   115

TOP LEFT: *Cape Hauy rears out of inky sea;* **TOP RIGHT:** *Surveying the stepped track out to Cape Hauy;* **MIDDLE RIGHT:** *An insectivorous sundew glistens in afternoon light;* **BOTTOM LEFT:** *The dolerite walls of a deep slice into Cape Pillar herald the remarkable geology to come;* **BOTTOM RIGHT:** *Fluffy honey myrtle blooms contrast stone steps*

The top of the Blade gives you a fabulous view of Tasman Island

Wughalee links up with the Cape Hauy track. Don't go this way on the spur of the moment; it is a long loop back to your pack.

Back up on the main track, you'll come to a gorgeous patch of forest thick with ferns and dripping moss. There are 11 red hand prints along this stretch, sprayed with a traditional Aboriginal mix of ochre, animal blood and saliva, but they are hard to see; one of the rangers, who knows where to look, has still only managed to identify a handful.

You often meet people walking the other way over today's final three kilometres. Most will be Three Capers who've spent the morning on Cape Pillar, lunched at Munro Cabin and are headed for Retakunna Cabin for the night.

Munro Cabin sits among trees on a cliff edge and a metal lookout platform projects north-east to Cape Hauy. Hippolyte Rock, off Cape Hauy's tip, is the southernmost extent of the land bridge that once joined Tasmania to mainland Australia. Other remnants include Wilsons Promontory (Vic.) and Flinders Island (Tas., *see* page 170). Standing binoculars – no coin needed – give a voyeur's view of shearwaters (also known as mutton birds) stuffing themselves with fish in preparation for nesting (in spring), dolphins and cooperative whales. But the best view is from the helicopter pad, beyond the toilet block, back up the entry track and right.

DAY 3: 19km 6 hours

One of the most scenically dramatic walking days in Australia, Day 3 starts at dawn if you want to witness first sun kissing Cape Hauy. Leave your pack in the shed 50m beyond Munro Cabin and continue with a daypack (stuffed with superlatives and exclamations to toss at the views), initially through eucalypt forest inhabited by old and twisted trees. Look out for spring-flowering Tasmanian waratahs, their blooms smaller and looser than their showy NSW counterparts.

Cape Pillar is shaped like a foot and today's route, much of it boardwalk, takes you south and east from the ankle bone (Munro Cabin) to the ball and then out beneath the toes. You travel via Lunchtime Creek, Corruption Gully, Perdition Plateau and Desolation Gully, mostly named by Tim Christie and Reg Williams, who made several attempts to bush-bash through 'menacing scrub' from Fortescue Bay to Cape Pillar in 1965–67 to scale Cathedral Rock, off the Cape's big toe. It's a great yarn, colourfully described in folders in the cabins' reference libraries.

Three Capes Track story seats get you thinking as you walk through heathland and along sheer cliffs boasting sweeping views: about endangered purple-flowering eyebrights, animal reproduction, and snakes! (Tasmanian snakes give birth to live young rather than lay eggs that would chill if buried in cold ground.) The ocean offshore from 'Converging on the shelf' is a biodiversity hotspot. It is, unfortunately, also a hotspot of another kind; the ocean here is warming at more than four times the global average.

About 2.5km into the walk out to Cape Pillar you get your first good look at Cape Pillar (see point 6 on map), and a clear view of the boarded walk traversing the next hill like a mock Great Wall of China.

A warning sign announces your approach to a a deep slice into the Cape whose dolerite walls are a foretaste of the extraordinary geology to come and about 150m further on the track turns east along the cliff line, footpads leading off the main track towards oblivion! An obvious, open rocky area is a top perch for a porridge breakfast if you bring your gas stove.

Vertiginous lookouts, including 'The Lightkeeper's Daughter', are strung along the next 2km of track, which works through rocky scrub and along the cliff culminating in The Blade a remarkable geological formation. As you step down to the brink you won't know which way to look, with Tasman Island right, Australia's highest sea cliffs ahead, and Cape Hauy and mainland Tasmania left. The view disappears as you tunnel through tea tree but The Blade awaits you on emerging.

Turn left for Seal Spa at a track junction and walk for three minutes to a view of The Blade, Tasman Island and seals, which can usually be found frolicking in the plunge pool at the island's northern base. This side track extends another 700m to Chasm Lookout, which hiker and Cape Pillar adventurer Tim Christie described as 'a mighty chasm, the vertical walls of which fell a thousand feet from their summit to the sea'.

Time now for The Blade (see point 7 on map). There are steps and good dry-weather footing to the top however the climb tests your head for heights: the ridge narrows to about 10m along its 200m length. What sort of photographs you capture will depend on your faith in nature's stonemasonry; one step beyond sensible and the only way is straight down.

Safely off The Blade, return to Munro Cabin for lunch, enjoying the reverse perspective of Cape Pillar. From Munro you've got about an hour back to the four-way junction and right to Retakunna Cabin at the foot of Mt Fortescue.

DAY 4: 14km 7–9 hours

To call Fortescue a mountain is flattery, because the hill rises only 250m from the cliff-top plain but the climb starts 750m into the day so hearts and lungs get an early workout.

Boardwalk snakes north-east from Retakunna Cabin through open eucalypt forest bristling with banksias. Only two banksia species grow in Tasmania: these silver banksia (*Banksia marginata*), found across the state, and sawtooth banksia (*Banksia serrata*), known only in Rocky Cape National Park (see page 248). *Banksia serrata* is one of the four original banksia species collected by botanist Joseph Banks in 1770.

Two tall-backed wooden chairs mark the transition from plains environment to the damper, darker, cooler forest on Mt Fortescue's southern slopes. Smooth, white-trunked peppermints make way for stringybark

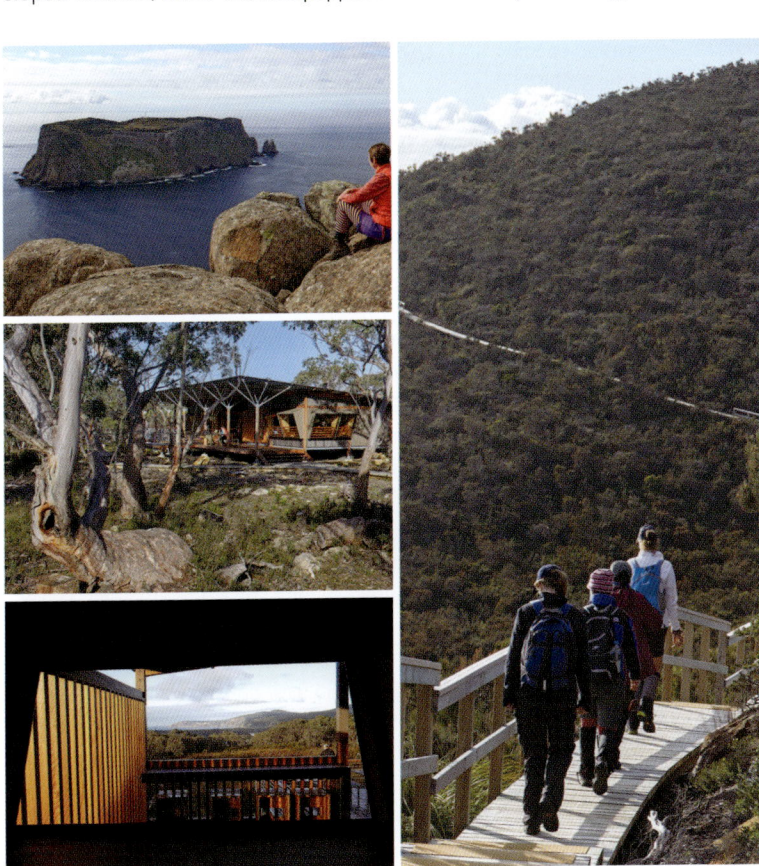

TOP LEFT: Sit and enjoy a view of Tasman Island from the Cape Pillar track; **RIGHT:** Boardwalk traverses a hill on the way out to Cape Pillar; **MIDDLE LEFT:** Retakunna Cabin sits among open eucalypt forest; **BOTTOM LEFT:** Surveyors Cabin window from Cape Raoul

eucalypts with furrowed, brown bark. Sassafras, a rainforest species, grows here and beech myrtle drop hole-punch sized leaves.

After all the boardwalk, you might enjoy the more traditional bushwalking track that scales Fortescue, rounding mossy boulders and trees. Near the top (482m) – there is no designated summit – you pass a helicopter pad (see point 8 on map) in dryer, more open forest but you're back among moss and ferns on reaching a gobsmacking natural vantage point with a view along Cape Pillar's magnificent north-east wall to Tasman Island; you can just see the boardwalk followed yesterday.

This lookout is named 'Far Flung' in reference to the marathon round-trips that migrating species, such as humpback whales, make each year from Antarctic feeding grounds to warmer Australian waters.

Despite the odd gully and occasional rises, you essentially descend for the next five kilometres: from rainforest dating back 100 million years to when dinosaurs, rather than bushwalkers, roamed Earth, into tea tree and cutting grass, eucalypts and heath. About 1.5km along you pass a tree with multiple trunks (see point 9 on map). And the lookouts keep coming, revealing sea caves in the cliffs. Take particular care on unnamed lookouts as many contain hidden dangers.

Pushing on through button grass you'll see, to the left, the battlement-like cliffs that run north from Fortescue Bay to Tasman Arch, one of the peninsula's major natural tourist attractions. There is a fabulous day walk along those cliffs (see Fortescue Bay to Devils Kitchen page 101).

Finally Cape Hauy appears on the right and gravel track brings you to a track junction (see point 10 on map). The 3.5km, two-hour return detour to Cape Hauy, which has the profile of a roller-coaster, is worth every one of its multiple steps, so leave your pack at the seated rest area right of the junction and descend to a saddle sandwiched between cliffs and a dolerite gulch. A huge dolerite hole over the next hill squeezes the track to a few metres of rock between it and another gulch.

Safety demands that you focus on the track now but you won't be able to resist peering through gaps in the narrowing dolerite spine at snapshots of sea and stone columns clinging to the cliff. The track ends suddenly on a small, fenced column-top with 360° views.

Don't be deceived. The rocky upthrusts beyond this aerie are not connected to the Cape. They are separated from it by a stomach-turning drop to deep waters centimetres from the fence. The single, 65m-tall needle of dolerite below left is the Totem Pole, a much-photographed landmark and rock-climbing pitch that 20–30 climbers attempt each year.

The Totem Pole was dubbed 'the most difficult place to be rescued from' in 1988 when leading British climber Paul Pritchard nearly lost his life here: look up the story of his ordeal and inspirational return from the injury he sustained here. Your return to the main track will be considerably easier than his!

Back at the pack-drop, load up and head anticlockwise around the cape to Fortescue Bay. Gravel and then impressive stone-paving and stone steps work through open eucalypt forest and the most southerly extreme of Oyster Bay pines on Earth (see point 11 on map). The skeletal 'stags' (dead pines) were killed in the 2003 bushfire. One of ten native Tasmanian conifers (nine found nowhere else), Oyster Bay pines produce male and female cones on the same plant.

Eventually you glimpse bay water and about 2.5km from the Cape Hauy junction come to a sculpture called 'Photo Finish'. These marble mother-of-pearl shell basins sit against a backdrop of turquoise bay and white beach.

The track returns to sea level, for the first time since Denmans Cove, at Fortescue Bay's rocky southern end. Pass a jetty and boat launch, with a camping area to your left, and follow the walkway near the water's edge to the day-use shelter, which is expected to be the walk's finishing point from 2019.

If you've time before your transfer (bus times are allocated), cool your feet in the bay's refreshing waters or brave a whole-body immersion to celebrate walking around one of the most remarkable coasts on the planet.

One of the many jaw-dropping views from the track out to Cape Pillar

Stormy sky only adds to the drama of The Hazards and Wineglass Bay from Mt Graham, on the Freycinet Peninsula loop walk

EAST COAST

A refuge when wintry weather batters the west, and gorgeous year-round, Tasmania's east coast tempts with a mixed assortment of walking options on islands, in gorges, up mountains and out to lookouts perched above arguably the most beautiful beach in Australia. Lace up your shoes and prepare to indulge in this lolly bag of walks.

22	Maria Island	124
23	Mount Amos	132
24	Wineglass Bay & Hazards Beach	137
25	Freycinet Peninsula	142
26	Bay of Fires	152
27	Apsley Gorge	156
28	Moon Valley Rim	160
29	wukalina/Mount William	165

EAST COAST
22 MARIA ISLAND

Walk:	18km loop
Time required:	2 days (or 5-6 hours if not spending the night)
Best time:	Clear, dry day
Grade:	Moderate-hard (easy without the mountain climb)
Environment:	Sea cliffs, primordial forest, mountains, beach, convict settlement
Best map:	This one or TASMAP's *Maria Island National Park Map & Notes*
Toilets:	Flushing toilets beside Commissariat Store and in Darlington
Food:	None on the island; Triabunna (where the ferry departs) has a pub, tea house, fish-and-chip caravan, and a supermarket for supplies
Tips:	There are multiple departures daily to Maria Island September to April, and five times a week in winter (http://encountermaria.com.au); return fares include national park entry. For a less rushed Maria Island experience divide this walk into two day walks either side of a night spent in a penitentiary cell; book at http://encountermaria.com.au/accommodation.

Mountains, tangled forest and windswept cliffs provide a stunning backdrop for this walk through another fascinating chapter in Tasmania's history.

Allow time to appreciate the extraordinary Painted Cliffs

'... to find a gaol in one of the loveliest spots formed by the hand of Nature in one of her loveliest solitudes creates a revulsion of feeling I cannot describe ...' So wrote Irish political prisoner William Smith O'Brien, transported to Van Diemen's Land in 1849, of first seeing Maria Island.

Settled in 1825 as a convict station, and subsequently home to Italian business entrepreneur Diego Bernacchi (silk, wine and concrete) in the late 19th century, and a concrete factory in the 1920s, Maria Island remains one of the loveliest spots formed by nature's hand – and now people visit voluntarily.

This walk, coincidentally shaped on the map like convict leg irons and chain, showcases north Maria's geological and human history. Boot-camp pace would have you completing this walk between the first incoming ferry from Triabunna and the last departing one, but it's more rewarding to take it slower and stay overnight. You can camp or unroll a sleeping bag in the penitentiary (booking required; see 'Tips'), in a six-bed dorm with wood-burning stove that once slept 66 convicts. More indulgent again would be to splurge on a private guided four-day walking holiday with Maria Island Walk (www.mariaislandwalk.com.au).

This walk begins and ends at the Commissariat Store, Maria's oldest building, which overlooks the ferry jetty. Built in 1825, the two-storey dolerite-and-limestone store, designed to house months of supplies, is now the national park visitor centre, where you collect maps and find out which 'cell'

Stepping out towards mist-capped Bishop of Clerk

EAST COAST

DARLINGTON
- Apartment Site 1842
- Bakehouse & clothing store 1843
- Coffee Palace 1888
- Cook house & bread store 1842
- Mess hall
- Penitentiary 1830
- Visiting Managers' Office 1846

MARIA ISLAND NATIONAL PARK

Cape Boullanger

Landing Ground

Mainland view

Whale bones

Fossil Cliffs

FOSSIL CLIFFS

Cemetery

Boatshed (ruins) 1828

Convict Barn (ruins)

Triabunna–Maria Island passenger ferry

Concrete silos 1922
Clink 1922

MERCURY PASSAGE

Commissariat Store & ranger office

Darlington Bay

AUSTRALIAN CONVICT SITES (DARLINGTON PROBATION STATION) WORLD HERITAGE AREA

Darlington camping area

A Super 1849

DARLINGTON (see list of places)

CIRCUIT

Schoolmaster's House 1922 & ranger station

Mrs Hunt's Cottage

FOSSIL CLIFFS

Cliffs

Engine house

B Terraces 1886

Cottage sites 1888

RESERVOIR

Bernacchi House 1890

Bernacchi's Creek

Wombats 2

OAST HOUSE TK

Darlington view

Hopground Beach

PAINTED CLIFFS TK

Bridge

Oast House (ruins)

OAST

Footbridge

AUSTRALIAN CONVICT SITES (DARLINGTON PROBATION STATION BUFFER ZONE) WORLD HERITAGE AREA

100

'Painted' sandstone cliffs (access low tide)

MARIA ISLAND

100

MARIA ISLAND NATIONAL PARK

MARIA ISLAND 127

you've been assigned. Trolleys are provided to wheel your gear 400m up to the cluster of buildings of Darlington settlement.

From the store, walk back towards the jetty and past the National Portland Cement Company concrete silos (1920s). The bleached whale bones on the shore are evidence of a bloody earlier industry.

You'll already have seen Cape Barren geese – and probably stepped in their poo – because the small population of these elegant grey birds, introduced in 1968 as part of a program to save several endangered species, has thrived. A similar philosophy saw the controversial release of captive-bred Tasmanian Devils on Maria in November 2012 in the hope of saving the carnivorous marsupial from the contagious tumour disease threatening its survival, so look out for white-spotted black devils bowling along the harbour.

Gravel road becomes grassy track as you loop right and up to a red-brick Convict Barn (1844) on Cape Boullanger that houses rusty machines and wooden wagons. Hugging the cape's contour, the easy trail then passes the picket-fenced cemetery (half a dozen marked graves with unimpeded views of Tasmania's east coast) and the airstrip.

Step down into the Fossil Cliffs quarry site to fossick, or just look along Maria's sea cliffs to Bishop and Clerk, your mountain destination (weather

LEFT: *Red brick frames the view out of an engine house;* **RIGHT:** *Cape Barren geese graze the lawns in Darlington*

permitting). Named for its perceived likeness to a clergyman following a bishop wearing a mitre (can you see it?) Bishop and Clerk (620m) is the second highest point on the island after Mt Maria (711m).

About 500m beyond the cliffs is a junction: climb Bishop and Clerk (8km return from here) or loop right back to Darlington? Leaving out the mountain climb shortens the walk to an easy 10km day trip. The way to the top is almost unremittingly uphill and increasingly rocky, the stone is slippery when wet, and there is no view in rain and mist. But on a sunny day, you're rewarded with a gobsmacking panorama, and you can straddle a deep crevice for a photo that will curl the toes of your less-adventurous friends and family, making the ascent very worthwhile.

If climbing, keep along the cliff-line and uphill, past a eucalypt that looks like it was hand-wrapped in its twisted bark. She-oak needles soften your footfalls as you continue through flatter woodland.

Now for the push to the top, on a narrowing, rocky track through thicker, damper forest dripping with bark streamers and old man's beard and patched with lichen and moss. It feels so like the land that time forgot, you might almost expect a dinosaur to poke its head through the canopy.

A tree tunnel pops you out at the bottom of a scree slope (see point 1 on map). Follow orange arrow markers up the switchback track, catching your breath at old eucalypts with roots buried beneath the stones. From the top of the scree slope, the trail winds through forest and around boulders.

An expanding view encourages you up a short but steep boulder face (with a couple of okay footholds) to the jaw-dropping summit sweep of island, sea and mainland.

Back down at the Darlington junction, turn left and follow the signs to the settlement, turning left again onto a gravel road at the red-brick engine house (1888). Ignoring tracks coming in from the sides (the ends of Reservoir Circuit), walk through scruffy eucalypt forest and step into the heart of the village between the mess hall (on your right) and the penitentiary (long building on your left).

The penitentiary verandah is a great late lunch spot, with seats and posts to lean against as you watch Cape Barren geese grazing. Common wombats also trundle around the settlement in the late afternoon and evening. This is the place to end Day 1 of the walk if you are staying overnight.

Darlington comprises a dozen or so red-brick and whitewashed stone buildings dating from the convict era and Diego Bernacchi's reign. Read about transported young Irelander William Smith O'Brien in the single-storey terrace

A simple 1920s cottage overlooks the town and harbour

cottage where he lived. Listen to taped anecdotes of more comfortable island life in the elegant, weatherboard Coffee Palace (1888). Then continue south-west to the red-brick and weatherboard Bernacchi houses.

From here, walk down to the colonnade of Cypress pines and turn left onto Maria's only road, following it uphill past the camping area (right) and a simple 1920s cottage overlooking the town and harbour. Heading downhill now you'll see a ribbon of white beach ending in shallow cliffs, whose stripes are just visible, even from this distance.

A sign immediately before a bridge directs you right onto Counsel Beach for a sandy stroll to the cliffs. You can also stay on the road, passing wetlands (see point 2 on map) where you are almost guaranteed to see a wombat (ignore the Oast House track going left and continue to the Painted Cliffs sign).

Counsel Beach ends in a delicious toffee-like swirl of smooth and pitted sandstone striped yellow, white and red. Low tide gives you the best access to these Painted Cliffs, which continue well around the point.

Head back to Darlington by walking north along the road and turning right onto the Oast House Track, which forks a few hundred metres into a sea of bracken. Follow the Oast House track left (Mt Maria, the highest point on Maria Island, is straight ahead), through eucalypts peeling rough bark to yellow trunks. Beyond a wetland thrumming with insects and frogs, you come to the Oast House (1884) ruins. Hops were dried here for making beer during the Bernacchi era, and one of the two circular kilns still stands, several metres tall, but minus its conical roof and cowl.

From the clearing's eastern corner the track curls through woodland littered with bark streamers to the road. Follow it back to Darlington – and down to the jetty for the ferry, when you can bring yourself to leave.

TOP: *Common wombats trundle around the Darlington settlement late afternoon and evening;*
BOTTOM: *The view from atop Bishop of Clerk will leave you open-mouthed*

EAST COAST

23 MOUNT AMOS

Walk:	6km return
Time required:	3–5 hours
Best time:	Dry, mild day
Grade:	Moderate–hard (considerable clambering)
Environment:	Exposed granite slopes, mountain-top lookouts
Best map:	This one
Toilets:	Flushing toilets in Wineglass Bay car park
Food:	There are small supermarkets, cafés, restaurants and a pub in Coles Bay. Freycinet Marine Farm (www.freycinetmarinefarm.com) sells freshly shucked Coles Bay oysters and other local seafood.
Tips:	Granite is slippery when wet so don't set off on this walk in rain or if rain is forecast. Whatever the weather, wear good-gripping footwear with some ankle support. Gloves protect hands and rings from rock scratches
	There is little protection from the sun so take drinking water.

Escape the crowds on this adventurous climb to a Wineglass Bay lookout that leaves the more popular paved one for dead.

Stop and look at Coles Bay and mainland Tasmania on your way up Mt Amos

MOUNT AMOS 133

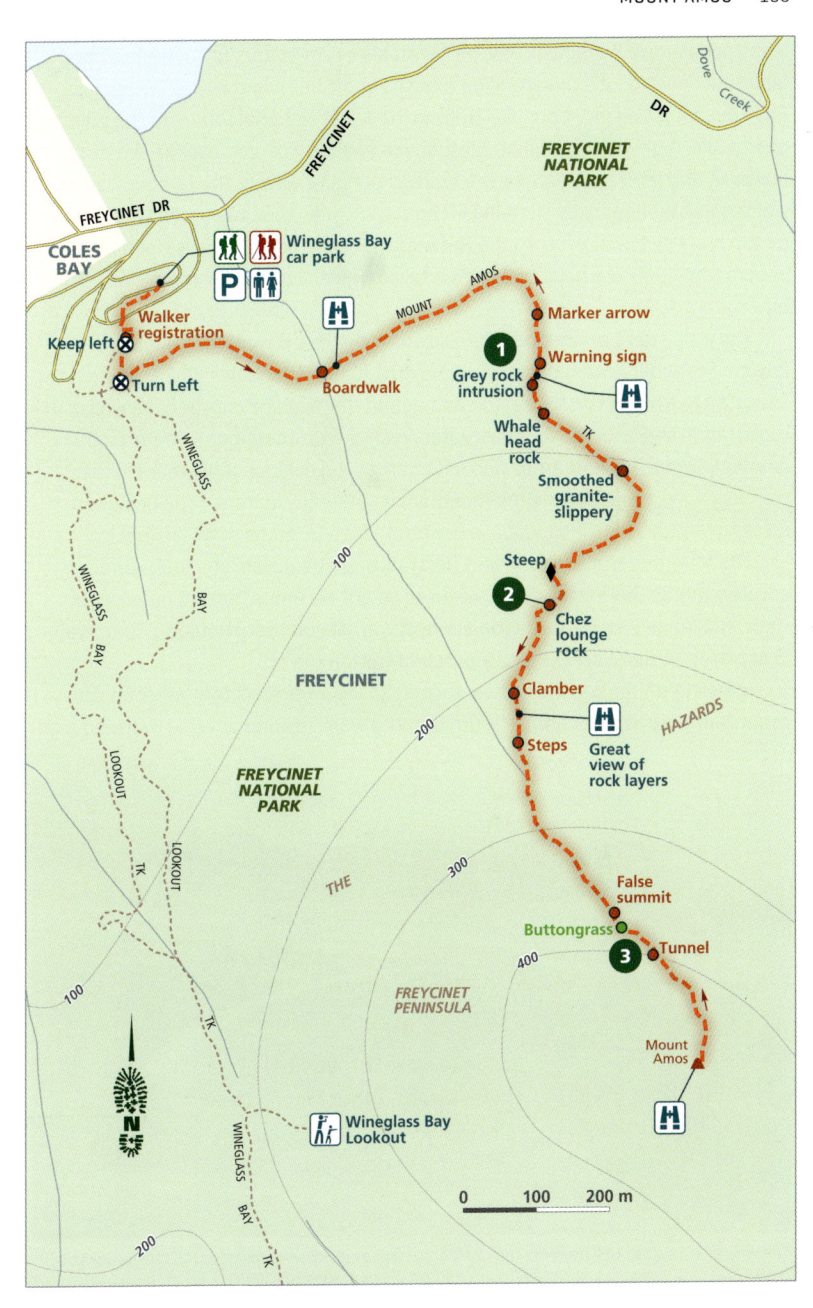

Many people rate Wineglass Bay, on Tasmania's east coast, as Australia's most beautiful beach so it's unsurprising that the short but steep walk to Wineglass Bay Lookout is the most popular track in Freycinet National Park – to the point of city-like, rush-hour crowding on sunny weekends. You can escape the throng, however, and later boast about the more impressive view of the famous bay and white crescent beach, by climbing Mt Amos, second (west to east) of the four pink granite peaks making up the Hazards mountain range. This is not a walk for people who don't like heights but it's a rewarding adventure for the sound-of-hip-and-knee.

The walk starts on the mountainside of Wineglass Bay car park, about 3km beyond Freycinet National Park visitor centre, just east of Coles Bay, and about two hours' drive from both Launceston and Hobart. Immediately beyond the walker registration shelter – for your own safety record your intentions – there's a track junction. Turn left for Mt Amos and left again at the next junction, marked with warning signs about scaling the mountain now directly in front. (The unsigned straight-on track at the junction is the return loop from the main lookout.)

The Mt Amos track heads east (left) through banksias, she-oaks and scruffy, coarse-barked eucalypts, so you've got Mt Amos rearing up on your right and Coles Bay, glittering on sunny days, off your left shoulder. Boardwalk crosses ephemeral creeks and a patch of button grass.

Ignoring unmarked side trails, follow the yellow arrows that start up the mountain's north flank about 900m into the walk, beyond another warning sign.

The view of Wineglass Bay from the top of Mt Amos leaves the more popular paved one for dead

The Mt Amos walk takes you up exposed granite slopes

Take your time, take care and enjoy yourself, stopping often to look over Coles Bay and the waterfront town of the same name. The view widens as you go, taking in Honeymoon Bay and the many coves indenting the shoreline.

About 200m up you find yourself on a micro plateau facing tiers of sloping pink granite artistically striped by water. A remarkable intrusion of grey rock slices through the pink mountaintop overhead (see point 1 on map). And behind you is an ascent-stowing vista of water, bay, peninsula and mainland Tasmania.

Further uphill, past a balancing rock that looks like a whale's head, (migrating whales sometimes mosey into Coles Bay) there's a section of granite smoothed by running water. A slightly rougher route up the middle provides the securest footing in the dry but this is one of many sections where you could well slip in the wet. More striped tiers are stacked to the left.

You shortly reach a particularly steep section where you have to clamber up those tiers; dry weather provides good footholds through she-oaks, massed tea tree and smooth-barked small eucalypts. A chaise-lounge rock (see point 2 on map) about 1.7km into the walk is a fun photo prop.

After another steep climb, on earthier track with roots underfoot, you weave between trees and boulders for a great view of that intruded layer of grey stone seen earlier. Here, too, is an outstanding example of a scribbly gum.

Now for a couple of hundred metres of full-on clambering, following a fold or fault line in the granite that runs with water in the wet, which supports miniature gardens. When dry, the footing is surer than appearance suggests and you can usually work up it without drama, but this section defeats some walkers. Unless you feel really uneasy, push on – there are no exposed cliffs and you are nearly at the top.

Finally, the track flattens out on a false summit and ahead sits Amos's boulder crown. The hard work is behind you, for now. Follow arrows across a button-grass plain ringed by rock, through massed tea tree hugging a natural rock wall (*see* point 3 on map), over a rocky rise with a gully to your right; and hard right to the top for a spectacular view.

Some people embark on this walk in darkness so they are on the summit to watch dawn's light play over Wineglass Bay, Hazards Beach and the isthmus separating them – and south down the peninsula's mountainous spine. On clear days, Cape Tourville lighthouse, on the peninsula's east coast, is visible to the left.

Another arrow, right of the summit, leads 20-odd metres down to a flattish area even nearer Amos's south face. You can potter here, locating photo angles seen in postcards and books, but take care near the edge.

When you're done, retrace your steps down the mountain, watching for skinks enjoying the warm rocks on sunny days.

LEFT: *A crow waits for hikers' crumbs atop Mt Amos;* **TOP RIGHT:** *The climb ascends tiers of pink granite artistically striped by water;* **BOTTOM RIGHT:** *Look out for wallabies along the track and in the car park*

EAST COAST
24 WINEGLASS BAY & HAZARDS BEACH

Walk:	12km loop
Time required:	4 hours
Best time:	Sunny day for the bay at its beautiful best
Grade:	Moderate
Environment:	Granite peaks, beach, forested isthmus, rocky shore
Best map:	TASMAP's *Freycinet National Park 1:50,000 Map & Notes*
Toilets:	Flushing toilets in Wineglass Bay car park
Food:	There are two options at Freycinet Lodge, within the national park: snacks and tasty, casual lunches in Richardson's Bistro; and dinners of scrumptious, seasonal Tasmanian produce in The Bay Restaurant (bookings essential). Pub, takeaway and other food is available in Coles Bay, outside the park; and fresh local seafood at Freycinet Marine Farm, on Coles Bay Road.
Tips:	Don't be put off by a crowd on the track; on a sunny day the elevated view of Wineglass Bay makes it worth it. Start early to minimise crowds.

One of the most beautiful beaches in Australia? Undoubtedly. THE most beautiful? You decide on this loop walk up Wineglass Bay and back via beach and rugged shore.

Freycinet Peninsula and Wineglass Bay from the main bay lookout

BIG4 Iluka on Freycinet Holiday Park
Picnic Island
C302
COLES BAY
Camping area
Visitor centre
Richardsons Beach (powered sites) camping area
Richardsons Beach
FREYCINET DR
Coles Bay
Richardsons Beach (the Sand Dunes) camping area
0
0.5
1 km
N
Freycinet Lodge
Honeymoon Bay camping area
Honeymoon Bay
GREAT OYSTER BAY
Wineglass Bay carpark
FREYCINET
FREYCINET DR
Parsons Cove
Old granite quarry
Footbridge
Grass trees
Walker registration post
Striped Eucalypt
Bay view
Footbridge
Steps
1
Balancing rock
Flat rock (no tables)
BEACH
TK
100
200
300
400
Mount Dove 485m
Boulder
Coles Bay Lookout
Hollowed rock
HAZARDS
Mount Amos 454m
THE HAZARDS
Boulder
Main bay lookout
WINEGLASS BAY
Mount Mayson 415m
Steps
Standing stone
Striped Eucalypts
Granite slab
Hawksnest Cove
Fleurieu Point
HAZARDS Cove
BEACH
ISTHMUS
2
Boardwalk
Wetland
Wineglass Bay
Wineglass PENINSULA Bay Beach
Refuge Island
Promise Rock
Promise Bay
Hazards PENINSULA Beach
FREYCINET NATIONAL PARK
Wineglass Bay camping area

Most visitors to Freycinet National Park, halfway up Tasmania's east coast, come for one thing: to walk to Wineglass Bay lookout and add to the already countless pixels that have captured this picture-postcard view. Fewer continue down to the beach itself; fewer still walk on from there across the isthmus to Hazards Beach to complete a scenic loop. But that doesn't mean you'll have this walk to yourself: it is very much about sharing!

Starting in Wineglass Bay car park, about 4km from Coles Bay and the national park boundary, just go with the flow, treading a fairly easy gravel track up through white-flowering tea tree, grey-and-yellow striped peppermint eucalypts, and the pretty pink granite featured in all Freycinet promotions, usually blushing at dawn or sunset. (A combination of pink feldspar and orange lichen produces this distinctive hue.) Look for a particularly beautiful twisted and striped eucalypt soon after the track ducks under a balancing rock and squeezes between lumps of rock.

Wineglass Bay lookout sits in the saddle between mounts Mayson and Amos, two of the landmark five-in-a-row granite knuckles collectively called The Hazards. These rocky rises, as well as Coles Bay, come into view as you climb.

Part-way up there's a junction, where a one-way descent track disappears downhill on the left – yes, it gets that busy! The climb continues up stone steps (*see* point 1 on map).

A voluminous bowl of water contained by a crescent of sand and forested mountains, Wineglass Bay is impressive even on a cloudy day. But when sunshine blues the sea and greens the hills, and the white sand gleams, you'd be hard-pressed to argue that this isn't Australia's prettiest beach.

When you tire of the view or the crowd (whichever comes first) keep on the south-east, heading down Wineglass Bay Track. A sign warns that this is steep and can be slippery, and it is certainly very different from the formed track you came up. With stone steps, exposed roots and granite underfoot, descend through tea tree, smooth and rough eucalypts, drooping she-oaks and banksias to Wineglass Bay beach.

This is a beautiful spot to picnic on a granite boulder, have a cooling swim or leave footprints in the sand; it's 1.7km to the end of the beach, where you'll find a camping area used mostly by hikers treading the multi-day Freycinet loop down the main peninsula. But remember that it's another 8km and about three hours to the car park.

When you're ready to push on, leave the beach where you stepped onto it and head south-west on a flat track that crosses the isthmus tethering The

TOP: *The Hazards from Coles Bay;* **BOTTOM LEFT:** *Fungi sprout from trees and rocks in the moister forest;* **BOTTOM RIGHT:** *A black-faced cormorant watches walkers from the rocks*

Hazards to the main peninsula. Visible through the trunks of eucalypt woodland trees is broad Hazards Lagoon, often noisy with frogs.

Six frog species have been recorded in the park, including the nationally threatened green and gold frog, which lives in Hazards Lagoon. Some two-thirds of Tasmania's endemic bird species frequent the Freycinet Peninsula region too, and you'll probably hear many different calls on this leg of the walk.

Having forded an area of sedgy grass and coral fern on boardwalk (see point 2 on map), climb up and over white dunes and down onto yellow Hazards Beach, then walk right (north-west) along sand littered with oyster shells.

For millennia before European settlement, Aboriginal people harvested oysters and marine vegetables in these waters during autumn and winter. Native oysters still grow here, but Pacific oysters, mussels, scallops, abalone and sea urchins are farmed in Great Oyster Bay and Mercury Passage. You can savour the harvest at Freycinet Marine Farm, on the Coles Bay road.

At the end of Hazards Beach, the track heads inland and works its way around Mt Mayson's rocky base, snaking in and out of forest. Bennett's (red-necked) wallabies are often seen among the tea tree and she-oaks. Rock slabs, slippery in places, present fantastic views into pretty rocky coves whose lapping green water contrasts the pink-orange granite. As you dip down steps and emerge from gullies, look up at the fantastic boulders decorating the Hazards' jagged ridgeline. Slow down when the track emerges from trees and enjoy the extended views across Coles Bay and up the bald granite mountain slopes.

With only a kilometre to go you'll start to see grass trees. The track then doubles back on itself and heads down a leafier, greener creek gully, flattening and widening as it continues through an area of young and mature tea trees sandwiched between bay water and sky-reaching rock.

At the junction with the Wineglass Bay Lookout track, turn left and wind your way back to the car park.

EAST COAST

25 FREYCINET PENINSULA

Walk:	42km loop
Time required:	4 days
Best time:	Mild weather year-round (limited drinking water can make summer walking a challenge)
Grade:	Moderate
Environment:	Granite ranges, beaches, bays, eucalypt forest, mountain tops
Best map:	This one or TASMAP's *Freycinet National Park Map & Notes 1:50,000*
Toilets:	Flushing toilets at Wineglass Bay car park; composting toilets at Hazards Beach camp, Cooks Beach camp and Wineglass Bay
Food:	Coles Bay has a supermarket, cafés and restaurants. For eat-in or takeaway freshly shucked local oysters head to Freycinet Marine Farm (www.freycinetmarinefarm.com).
Tips:	Drinking water is a major issue on Freycinet Peninsula, particularly in summer. The only tanks are at Cooks Beach camp and these can be empty. Otherwise you are reliant on creeks that don't flow year-round. Because of poor toileting by campers, Parks staff discourage drinking from the creek at Wineglass Bay which, in any case, is often dry. Check the water situation by phone before setting out.

Get off the beaten track on a four-day pack walk and discover how much more there is to Freycinet Peninsula than Wineglass Bay.

You'll probably share Hazards Beach with daily walkers doing the Wineglass Bay loop

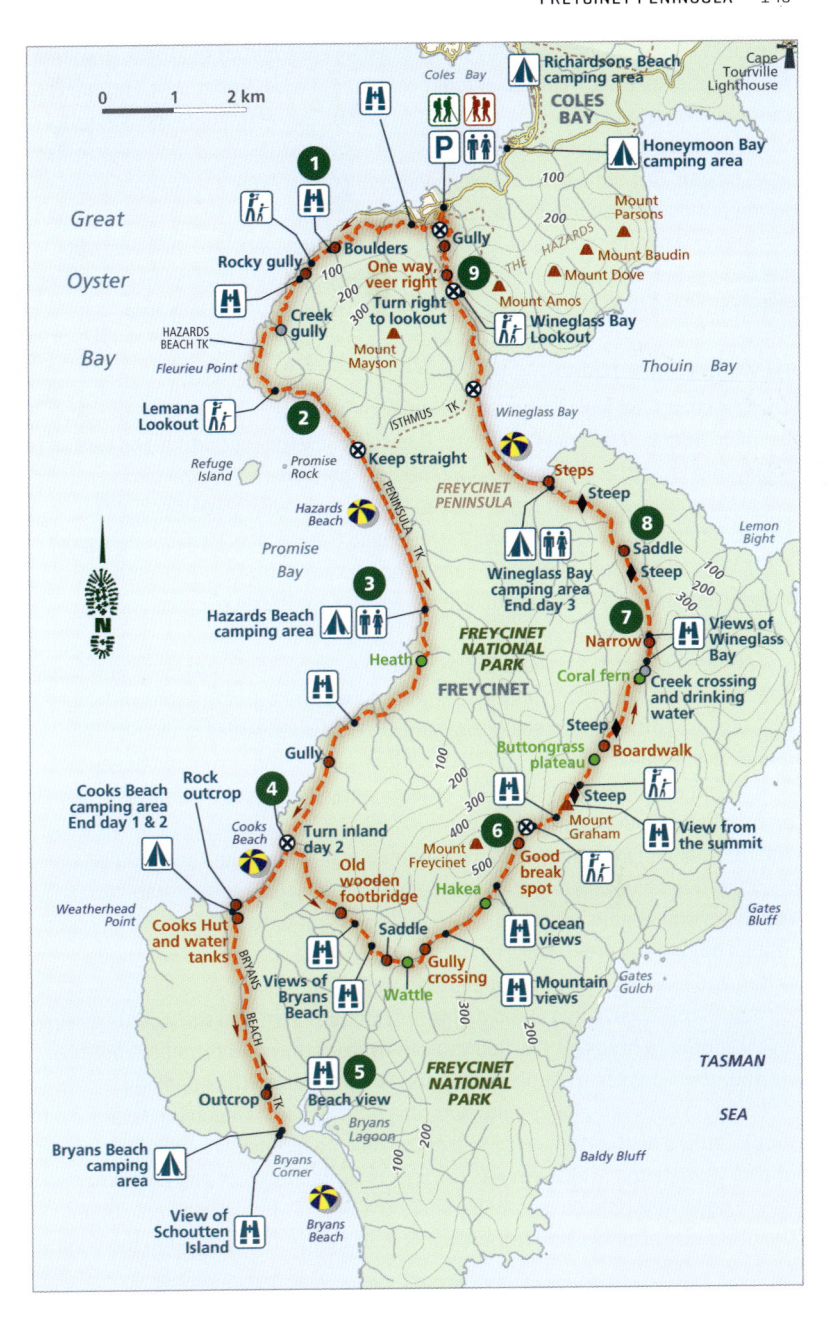

FREYCINET PENINSULA   143

Freycinet Peninsula, on Tasmania's east coast, is essentially two eroded granite blocks – the Hazards, made up of four peaks, and the Mt Graham–Mt Freycinet range, linked by an isthmus. Wineglass Bay, on the eastern side of the isthmus, is the peninsula's major drawcard, with most visitors walking up to the Wineglass Bay Lookout. But the Freycinet Peninsula Circuit reveals how much more there is to the peninsula than one beautiful white-sand beach.

Many hikers do the circuit in two nights/three days but the walk described here extends the trip by a night, giving you a lazy day walk from Cooks Beach to Bryans Beach before heading up and over the range to Wineglass Bay.

DAY 1: 15.1km (4–6 hours)

The Freycinet Peninsula Circuit starts and ends at Wineglass Bay car park, 3km beyond Freycinet National Park Visitor Centre. Follow the footpath to the walker registration booth and record your intentions. Then, briefly, join the throng (there are crowds on most sunny days) headed for the main Wineglass Bay lookout, keeping right at the first junction (the left-hand track scales Mt Amos, see page 132). With Mt Mayson, the fourth Hazard, on your right, tread compacted gravel through scrubby tea tree and eucalypt forest and around an elegant, striped silver peppermint tree.

At the next junction, about 500m in, keep right for Hazards Beach and fewer people. For the next 2km you wind through scruffy forest of tea tree and she-oak, dip into (often dry) creek gullies and walk between Mt Mayson and Great Oyster Bay. While it shelters you from wilder weather, the scrub can be stuffy in warm temperatures so it's lovely to emerge onto steep, rocky coast (see point 1 on map) and breathe salty air as you overlook the bay and mainland Tasmania. The rocks balancing up to your left give the Hazards a castle-keep profile.

Continue on undulating track: through tea tree scrub, coarse-barked eucalypts and needle-carpeted she-oak stands; out onto pink granite lookouts, into an ephemeral creek gully, past a miniature sandy cove filled with aqua water, and towards pyramid-shaped Fleurieu Point.

Another tiny cove in a stand of she-oaks, about 5km into the walk, is a lovely spot for a break. At low tide you can keep on the sand from here but the walking track passes a couple more coves and rounds a little headland before descending between pink granite outcrops onto Hazards Beach (see point 2 on map). Today's destination is the end of the next beach visible beyond this string of pale yellow sand, which sweeps towards mounts Freycinet and Graham.

In good weather you'll probably share the beach with day walkers coming the other way after walking from Wineglass Bay and cutting through the dunes

1km along. A great day walk (Wineglass Bay and Hazards Beach, see page 137) loops from the car park to the lookout, across the isthmus and back the way you've just come.

The scallop and oyster shells littering Hazards Beach speak of the bounty of these waters. Bird guano gives a snowy effect to the islet just offshore.

Check out the beach rock where the sand ends and the track continues inland, at the foot of Mt Freycinet: distinctly different black rock has 'wedged' into the pink granite, creating geological art (see point 3 on map). Spacious Hazards Beach camping area, under the she-oaks, is a shady lunch spot. Watch for green parrots as you dine.

The common disparity between park signs and maps is evident here: the map says the walk to Cooks Beach camp from the car park is 12km yet the signage says it's 8km to here and another 6km to Cooks Beach (14km); the GPS ups it to fifteen kilometres.

LEFT: *Looking back at the Hazards from Cooks Beach;* **TOP RIGHT:** *A pied oyster catcher patrols Cooks Beach;* **BOTTOM RIGHT:** *Hairy boronia splashes pink through the bush*

The walk continues just off the beach on an easy track that meanders through dry forest and woodland. The shrubs that produce winter and spring stalks of vaguely bell-shaped white flowers with ten petals are Tasmania's only thryptomene, an endangered species restricted to Freycinet and environs.

Mount Freycinet appears left as you walk through massed, yellow bush peas in open heath and a gentle climb provides a view to mainland Tasmania, over water that glitters with sunlight sequins on clear days. Arachnophobes should beware of spiders' webs across the track.

Perhaps an hour after lunch you'll reach a junction above Cooks Beach, with Wineglass Bay (via Mt Graham) signed an optimistic six hours left (*see* point 4 on map); you'll return to here but for now descend onto the white beach and follow it about 1.2km to camp. Remember to look back to the Hazards during this warm-down.

Camp is among she-oaks just past an outcrop of lichen-covered rocks that trap piles of shells. Nature has positioned these rocks perfectly for watching the sunset while cooling de-booted feet in the bay's shallows. Watch for sea eagles on the wing.

Cooks Beach is named after two brothers who grazed sheep on the flats behind the beach and a hundred metres into the bush is their stone hut, beside which are water tanks that collect rainwater off the roof. Rangers monitor levels every few weeks and you can check this at the information centre. Wallabies and wombats graze around the hut and some people camp here but the mosquitoes can be vicious; pitching a tent in a breezier spot near the beach reduces the risk of attack.

DAY 2: 6.8km return
(2–3 hours, plus beachcombing, lounging, swimming)

The Bryans Beach track heads south-east from behind Cooks Hut, through tall mixed eucalypts and open heathland of bush pea, thryptomene and many other flowering plants – again, beware spiders' webs. The trees with brighter-green fine foliage that's surprisingly 'crunchy' to touch are cherry ballarts (often called native cherries). Green parrots and exquisite eastern spine bills frequent this forest. Look out too for orchids in the rough beside the track; eighty-three species have been recorded in the park.

You cross occasional ephemeral creek gullies but the walking is mostly easy and flat, on a track that traverses a hill dropping left into a valley only to rise again into the main range you'll climb tomorrow. As you navigate scattered boulders, about 2.5km from camp (*see* point 5 on map), you'll glimpse beach

TOP: *Approaching the end of Hazards Beach;* **BOTTOM LEFT:** *Sunset illuminates a gem of a shell on Cooks Beach;* **BOTTOM RIGHT:** *A crab peeks from its shell house*

and bay through the trees, and the tempting visions increase as you swing left and descend gently, then steeply for about 50m, to Bryans Beach.

Another gorgeous crescent beach, of very fine, high-silica white sand, Bryans Beach sweeps clockwise about 2km from the rocks and shaded camping area where you land; the peninsula extends the same distance again, with dolerite Schouten Island sitting off the end. Sea mist sometimes drifts through Schouten Passage, engulfing the daily cruise boat on its loop around the peninsula.

Walk the length of the beach or snooze under a tree, read a book, and fossick through the oyster and scallop shells piled up against the rocks. Shells exposed in the treed, compacted sand at the top of the beach tell of millennia of winter gatherings of Toorernomairremener people, part of the Oyster Bay tribe of First Australians.

Then it's back to Cooks Beach for a second night.

DAY 3: 14.6km (6–9 hours)

Walk back along Cooks Beach to begin Day 3 and turn inland at the track junction passed two days ago. You're not hallucinating if you see black swans just off the beach; they're adventurers from the more protected waters of Moulting Lagoon, an internationally recognised breeding ground for birds and a stopover for migrating species.

The early walking's easy, on compacted track with an odd root and rock. Well signed with orange arrows, it meanders from open eucalypt forest into heathland that erupts with spring flowers. This gorgeous patch of tweedy white and yellow is the calm before the storm of climbing.

The ascent starts up a creek gully, which you cross via an old wooden footbridge sturdier than it looks, and continues up the other side. Bryans Beach and wetland appear over your shoulder as narrower track climbs through banksias, eucalypts and she-oaks into taller gums.

A saddle of sorts provides a chance to step out after the climbing, among tall gums, their peeling grey bark revealing peachy yellow bark beneath. You might also see orchids here, too, and *Austral clematis* (also called traveller's joy), a climber with star-shaped white flowers.

Between this saddle and another, the track dips into a gully awash with wattles, ferns and cutting grass, and climbs out through peeling gums and hakeas with 10cm-long, needle-like leaves and curly white flowers. Yellow and orange arrows lead around the back of Mt Freycinet, with Mt Graham ahead.

Then the forest opens out and – weather Gods be praised – you'll see the Southern Ocean to your right as you walk between mounts Freycinet and

The Hazards shrink behind as you near Cooks Beach camp

Graham. The track continues through grass trees and lemon-scented boronia dusting the bush the palest pink.

Having climbed a bouldered slope, you reach a flat patch among rocks that's perfect for a break (see point 6 on map). Mount Freycinet sits on your left shoulder as you step up rooted track to the saddle between Freycinet and Graham. A blue sign marks the start of the Mt Freycinet summit track (750m each way) on the left.

The views from Mt Graham are remarkable, so only make the Freycinet detour if it's a glorious day, you're full of energy or just determined. It takes 1–2 hours to the top and back – take a jacket and some water. But on a grey day you might want to conserve your energy for Mt Graham, which you have to summit. Even in moody weather it's spectacular here among the heath and buttongrass, an impressive view of Mt Amos and its fellow Hazards rewarding your progress.

From the saddle you climb rock. A natural lookout on the left grants another sweeping view of the Hazards, Hazards Beach, isthmus wetlands, and a splinter of Wineglass Bay. The famous beach looks close but cliffs prevent a direct route. Instead it's up and over Mt Graham – but the climb's nowhere near as bad as some suggest, in dry weather at least, and you might not even register the supposed 'vertigo' spot demanding three-point contact. Perhaps it's one of the short granite slopes where a helping hand can be welcome. Find your own pace, while keeping in sight of group members, and you should be fine.

As you climb, the expanding view takes in more of the peninsula and Schouten Island; the button grass and other plants hunker closer to the rock and even the she-oaks and banksias grow no taller than 1.2 metres.

A sweeping view down the peninsula's east coast to Schouten Island greets you on reaching a cluster of big, columnar rocks. Steep, rough tracks lead from there to a pile of stone, on the left, that looks like sliced bread. The vista from a button-grassed plateau below Mt Graham's summit draws your gaze from Mt Freycinet to the mainland, south to Schouten Island and around to the Southern Ocean. For the 360° summit panorama, you've got a couple more short-but-steep granite slopes and a rocky track worn through the heath groundcover.

Up top are two granite rises. A few steps right and you are looking south down the peninsula, while footpads up the taller granite crown, on the bay side of the summit, gifts a three-points-of-the-compass view that robs you of breath whether the sun is shining or the sky a stormy drama.

After the steep Mt Graham climb, the descent to Wineglass Bay might feel longer than the six kilometres it is. But there's more than views to distract you along the way.

Track markers beyond the summit are limited to occasional arrows and a few cairns but the route is obvious and sometimes visible well ahead – just don't get distracted by the views! Initially the track is eroded and a bit of a knee-trembler with some big steps, but it soon eases onto a saddle. You have rocks above and below now, and from the next rise you can see sculptural boulders to the right, one combination resembling a storm trooper's helmet from *Star Wars*.

Watch and listen for yellow-tailed black cockatoos as you traverse a wind-pruned button-grass plateau whose few eucalypts crown low to the ground. Sections of wooden planking indicate it can be boggy up here.

The track parallels a major gully with a prominent cliff (right) before descending towards that gully. A 5m-drop and you're among substantial, striped eucalypts, some peeling to a creamier underbark. The difference between the exposed plateau and this more protected country is dramatic. The track descends steeply through boulders and gums, many heavily decorated with moth larvae scribbles, into a gully before climbing out towards a rocky ridge; when the creek's running this is a good place to get water but it's often dry in late summer. Beyond the creek you're back in exposed heath with an eye-full of mounts Graham and Freycinet behind you.

After traversing button-grass plain and crossing a granite mound you enter a stand of fallen trees with the Hazards on show to your left. Another descent puts you in a gully carpeted with lacy coral fern. The roots of big, fibrous eucalypts reach across the walking track, which follows the gully downstream, the cliffs behind Wineglass Bay appearing ahead.

The narrow gully widens and, continuously descending, you round a hill. Good handholds help you along 4m of boot-wide track with a sheer drop-off (*see* point 7 on map) and, coming around this, you get a view of Wineglass Bay and the isthmus wetlands to the left. But look right too; the track skirts an eroded hill from which boulders have been carved, some leaning so far out they appear ready to fall on you!

About 3.5km from the top of Mt Graham you start down a ridge between the Southern Ocean (right) and Hazards Bay and mainland Tasmania (left), the track steepening, and roots and erosion requiring some big steps down. You can usually hear waves washing Wineglass Bay from here.

Still descending, you see the Hazards and Mt Amos' distinctive, flat summit and after an unwelcome climb (*see* point 8 on map) the view opens up, taking in mainland, mountains, beaches, bays and cliffs. After the pink rock of the Hazards you've got white rock underfoot here – in bigger and bigger pieces as you snake downhill. The volume of breaking waves increases until finally you reach sea level.

Wineglass Bay camping area has a composting toilet and numerous tent spots, most just metres from the much-photographed white beach. White-bellied sea eagles patrol the bay and you'll wake to an enthusiastic dawn chorus. But beware the possums, which can undo zips! Double-bag your food and keep your pack in your tent.

Wineglass Bay is usually calm enough for a swim or feet-cooling wade and sunset often projects a lightshow on the Hazards. Walk down the steps at the eastern end of the campsite to the sand rather than step over the eroding bank. The whalebone standing beside the steps is a relic of bloody days when a whaling station operated from Wineglass Bay's eastern end.

DAY 4: 5.3km (2 hours)

Rise early for pastel hues and playful shadows as you walk the length of Wineglass Bay beach, first sun turning wheeling gulls into strobe lights and, in calm weather, waves forming long breaks that curl over into an elongation of froth.

Wooden steps about 1.8km around the beach lead to a track junction among bracken and banksias. Day walkers doing the Wineglass Bay–Hazards Bay loop go left here after descending from the lookout. This walk takes you right, up a wide, compacted track with multiple steps (wood down low, stone higher up) built in 2017. A 1.5km climb in eucalypt forest between Mt Amos and Mt Mayson brings you to a track junction and rest area amid granite boulders (see point 9 on map); looking back at Wineglass Bay gives you time to catch your breath as you ascend.

The lookout is roughly 100m to the right, up wide stone steps, and if you started early from camp you will probably have this often crowded spot to yourself – a rare treat. It's a beautiful view but doesn't compare with the vista from Mt Amos (see page 132).

Coles Bay greets you on rounding the boulders at the rest area and the distinctive curved roof of exclusive Saffire Lodge is visible through the gap in the trees as you start down to the car park, initially on expert stonework beneath striped eucalypts. Veer right at Boulder Field Junction onto the one-way, return loop (it gets that busy on this lookout walk) and follow the track down through a gallery of boulder making and lesser chunks that have fallen off Mt Amos.

Across a gorgeous gully you zigzag downhill and past the Mt Amos track junction to the main Freycinet Peninsula walking track. Turn right and return to your car, remembering to record your return in the walkers' registration book.

EAST COAST
26 BAY OF FIRES

Walk:	8.5–22km return (walk as long as you like!)
Time required:	Between 3 hours and all day (plus swimming, paddling and picnicking time)
Best time:	Sunny day (or stormy, for a shorter, dramatic walk)
Grade:	Easy
Environment:	White sand ocean beach, lichen-covered granite outcrops, coastal heath and lagoons
Best map:	This one
Toilets:	Flushing toilets on Binalong Bay foreshore and pit toilets in Swimcart Lagoon day-use area
Food:	Slim pickings in Binalong Bay; cafes, coffee, restaurants, fast food and a supermarket in St Helen, 11km south-west
Tips:	Take your bathers and a picnic lunch and spend the day soaking up the natural beauty, or pack a tent and camp out overlooking the waves

White beaches, blue water and orange granite give this easy beach walk a visual punch, making it a walk unlike any other in Tasmania.

The Bay of Fires, on Tasmania's north-east coast, was named by English navigator Tobias Furneaux, who saw numerous fires, lit by coastal Aboriginal people, burning along this shore when he captained HMS *Adventure* up the coast

Signature granite boulders glow like hot coals in early and late sunlight

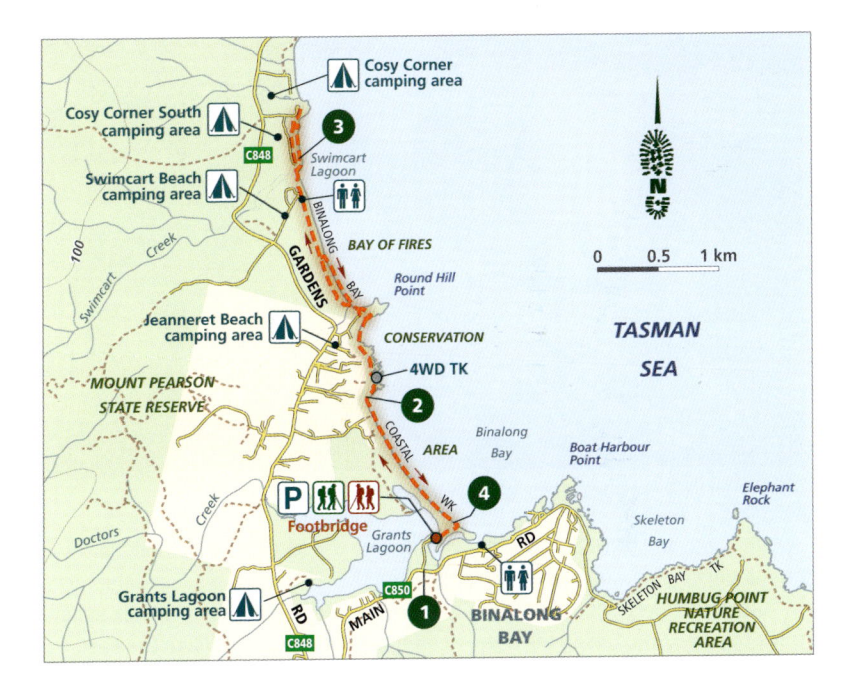

in March 1773. But this stunningly gorgeous region might just as well be named for its signature granite boulders, which are covered in orange lichen and glow like hot coals in early and late sunlight.

The beauty extends for many kilometres, protected within conservation areas, state reserves and Mt William National Park. One of the simplest walking pleasures in the island state is leaving footprints in the white sand and clambering about the low-slung granite outcrops that separate the beaches. Walk for an hour, all day, or even take a tent and camp overnight before heading back. Or spoil yourself with a luxurious four-day guided Bay of Fires Lodge Walk (www.bayoffires.com.au) further up the coast.

The area is of continuing cultural significance to Tasmania's Aboriginal community, and Aboriginal sites should be respected and left untouched (there are middens in the dunes).

The walk described here is on the most accessible stretch of coast, immediately north of the village of Binalong Bay, 11km north-east of St Helens. It starts in the Grants Lagoon day area, a sandy parking spot beside a footbridge in Humbug Point State Reserve. As you come into Binalong Bay look for an unsigned dirt road on the left (see point 1 on map), just after Main Rd

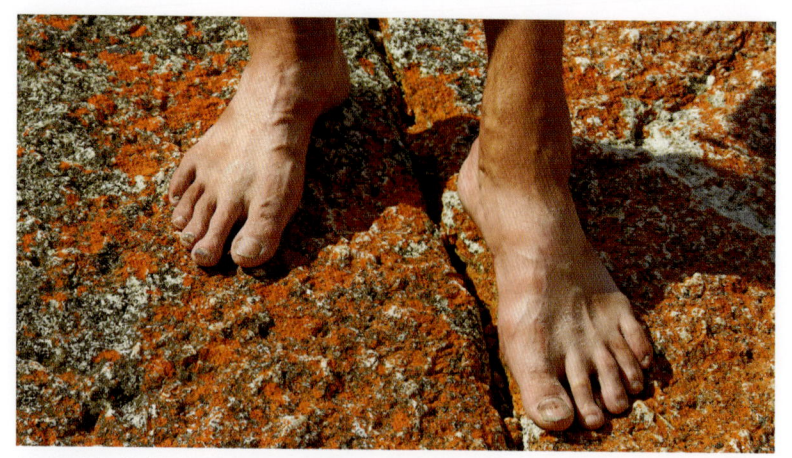

Get a feel for the lichen-covered granite with your bare feet

swings right, and drive down it about 300m into the reserve. If you reach a grassy picnic area with toilets and parking on the left you have missed the turn.

Cross the footbridge over the serpentine lagoon outlet and follow the sandy track to a junction, taking the right-hand track, with Humbug Hill to the east, its slopes colonised by Binalong Bay houses. Step down onto a beautiful white beach and head left (north) along the sand towards its rocky end, accompanied by a rhythmic wash of waves and passing holiday homes nestled in the dunes.

A footpad on the land side of the first rocky point (*see* point 2 on map) leads to a spectacular gulch among the granite. Follow the narrow track going bush from here, which gives rocky and rooty passage through tea tree and she-oaks and around the point to another couple of hundred metres of white beach.

The colour of the sand is a product of the granite's high quartz content. Lichen, a symbiosis between a fungus and an alga, gives the crazed, cracked granite points separating the beaches their distinctive and vibrant orange hue.

You'll probably see camps set up in the scrub to your left as you amble along this beach. Behind you is a great view of Binalong Bay township.

Tread the sandy track that clambers over Hill Point to gorgeous Swimcart Beach, a longer sweep of sand, with campsites strung along its edge and a day-use area with toilets tucked back in the scrub.

Along here you'll come to Swimcart Lagoon, on Swimcart Creek, its tannin-stained water contrasting the pale sand through which the creek sometimes breaks to meet the blue ocean. Salmon, flounder, eastern king prawns and black bream inhabit the lagoon, and if you're really lucky a magnificent white-bellied sea eagle, Australia's second largest bird of prey, with a wingspan reaching 2m, will pluck a meal from its waters in front of you.

Continue along the track and explore the next beach (see point 3 on map), over another rocky point, before turning back.

If prepared for a long day out, with water, food and sunscreen, you can tread another 7km or so along beach, headland and unsealed road to The Gardens, a place of stunning beauty, with a white-sand bay nestled against a mass of sculpted granite covered in orange lichen.

Also accessible by car, The Gardens was named by Lady Jane Franklin, wife of Sir John Franklin, Lieutenant Governor of Van Diemen's Land (now Tasmania) from 1837 to 1843. Lady Franklin rode her horse here from Georges Bay and found it abloom with wildflowers. If you're tempted to walk to The Gardens from Binalong Bay just remember that you'll have to walk back again or arrange a lift.

Packing a tent opens up even more options. Walking another 16km north from The Gardens up the coast puts you on Policeman's Point at the outlet of Ansons Bay. You can't cross the outlet and it's a long walk around this bay, so northward travel on foot stops here.

However far you go along this glorious shoreline, look for wooden steps up off the beach (see point 4 on map) as you return to Binalong Bay, near the walk's end. Leave the beach here and follow a sandy track along a fence line, which is part of a Landcare project, turning left at the next track back to your car.

LEFT: *Sea and lichen-covered rock creates a remarkable show of colours and textures;*
RIGHT: *Time and tide have shaped and smoothed granite beside Swimcart Lagoon*

EAST COAST

27 APSLEY GORGE

Walk:	6km out-and-back
Time required:	2.5 hours plus swimming!
Best time:	Spring to autumn (winter water can make it impossible to cross the Apsley River to start the walk)
Grade:	Easy-moderate
Environment:	River, dolerite gorge, swimming holes, eucalypt forest
Best map:	This one
Toilets:	There's a toilet in the camping area, off the walking track near Apsley Waterhole
Food:	None; there are cafes and a supermarket in Bicheno, 12km east on the coast.
Tips:	In summer months, when the water level is low, it is possible to turn this walk into a loop by returning to the main waterhole via the gorge. There is no designated track or markers and this adventurous and demanding alternative, which takes at least three hours, involves rock-hopping, clambering, multiple gorge crossings and, sometimes, backtracking. It should be planned and not done on the spur of the moment.

Score a trifecta on this east-coast hinterland bushwalk: waterholes, spectacular dolerite geology and virgin eucalypt forest.

Sit quietly in Apsley Gorge and marvel at the power of water and time

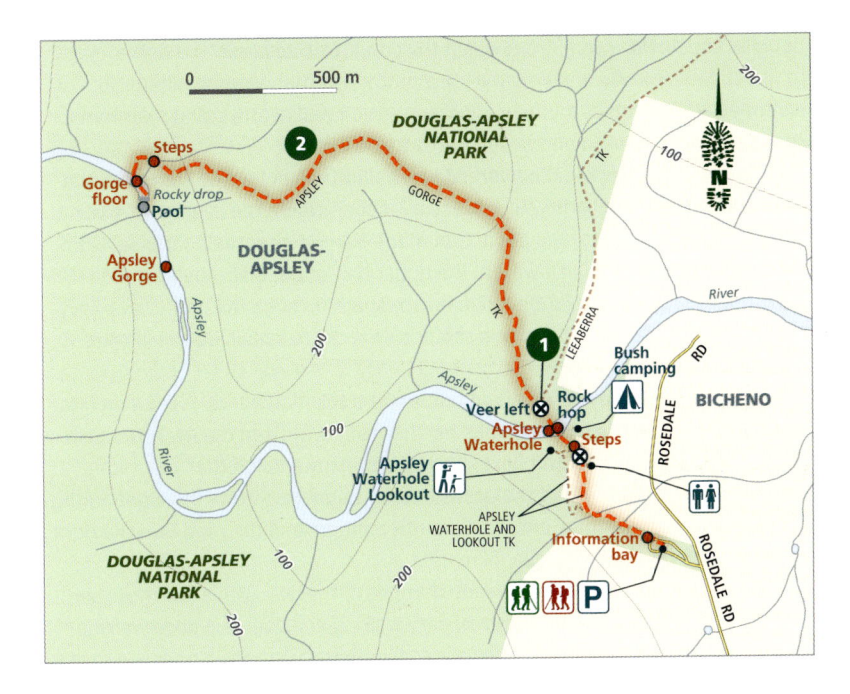

A short drive inland from Bicheno, about two-thirds of the way up Tasmania's east coast, Douglas-Apsley National Park protects an expanse of dolerite-capped plateau deeply dissected by the boulder-strewn river gorges of the Douglas and Apsley rivers. Many park visitors venture no further than Apsley Waterhole, 500m from the car park, a popular swimming spot at the mouth of Apsley Gorge, but a fairly easy forest walk to the body of the gorge reveals its geological splendour and water's role in its formation and continual shaping.

The walk starts from Apsley Gorge car park, 12km west of Bicheno. To get there turn left into Rosedale Rd off the Tasman Hwy (A3) 5km north of Bicheno and drive 7km to the national park. The final 6km is unsealed and subject to flooding but generally suitable for 2WD vehicles and mountain bikes.

Head west from the car park on broad, well-formed gravel track, passing an information bay where you can buy a pay-and-display parks pass if you don't already have one. The track climbs marginally through open eucalypt forest, with trackside signs identifying some of the trees, including bull oak, blackwood, dogwood, wattle and blue gum.

Ignoring the 10-minute loop track on the left, you come to Apsley Waterhole, a broad permanent pool in the Apsley River's rocky bed. The

Douglas and Apsley rivers, from which the park takes its name, are home to the endangered Australian grayling, a native fish that grows to about 30 centimetres. To protect the fish, apply sunscreen well before going swimming, so it has time to soak in and doesn't pollute the water.

Work your way across the riverbed just below the pool. A few steps into the trees on the opposite bank you come to a junction where the Leeaberra Track comes in from the right (see point 1 on map). Named after the Aboriginal word for the Douglas River, which waters the upper half of Douglas-Apsley National Park, the Leeaberra Track runs 28km north–south through the park, traversing eucalypt forest, rainforest and marshlands en route to scenic waterfalls and natural lookouts.

Keep left for Apsley Gorge on an unformed track marked with yellow arrows. Beginning flat, the track then climbs north-west, away from the river. You gain about 150m altitude over the next kilometre, steeply enough that you might need to catch your breath at the occasional through-tree views of neighbouring hills and blue-gum plantations. If you're not panting, and the wind is in the right direction, you may hear the sea, 8km east.

The track is less than a metre wide this side of the river with a few rocks and the odd exposed root but it's relatively easy walking and doable in good walking sandals (no need for boots). But beware snakes, particularly in warmer weather.

The Apsley River falls over a rocky drop and fills a pool at the foot of a building-block dolerite cliff

Note the different types of bark on the trees and the colours of stones on the gorge floor

Despite a history of farming, mining, timber felling and animal trapping, Douglas-Apsley National Park protects one of Tasmania's few tracts of uncleared dry sclerophyll forest and the largest on the state's east coast. Cutting grass, banksias, bull oaks, grass trees, wattles (acacias), tea tree and native cherry fruit, abound in this attractively scruffy forest. Also called cherry ballart, native cherry trees have distinctive, bright green, fir-like leaves and tiny orange fruit. In spring and summer you will probably see grass trigger plants (a close look at the pink flowers reveals a cocked 'trigger' that deposits pollen on unsuspecting insects) and stalks of purple-spotted pink hyacinth orchids. Less flamboyant orchids also grow here.

Eucalypts dominate, however; fourteen species have been recorded in Douglas-Apsley National Park, five of them endemic to Tasmania, and it is fun trying to identify the different ones as you continue west and then gently downhill. Among the rough-trunked stringybarks and peppermints stand occasional smoother-trunked beauties peeling to smooth, yellow inner bark.

After a short, flat stretch (*see* point 2 on map) the track descends gently for a kilometre, then steps steeply down a gully onto the gorge floor amid shallow pools. Note the different coloured pebbles and rocks underfoot as you work your way about 100m downstream (left) to where the riverbed drops several metres. The Apsley River falls over this rocky drop and fills a pool at the foot of a building-block dolerite cliff.

You can easily lose track of time picnicking and swimming here and exploring the surrounding rocks. Just leave enough time to retrace your steps to the car in daylight.

EAST COAST

28 MOON VALLEY RIM

Walk:	4.5km loop
Time required:	2-3 hours
Best time:	Clear day
Grade:	Easy
Environment:	Rocky hilltop, heath, old tin mine site, forest, unsealed road
Best map:	This one
Toilets:	Composting toilets in the Poimena Day Use Area
Food:	None
Tips:	Take a jacket to protect against the windy tops, even on warm days.

An unlikely pairing of tin mining history and sweeping views make for a lovely few hours in the state's north-east high country.

A sub-alpine granite plateau crowning just over 800m above sea level, the Blue Tier was named (presumably because it looked blue) in the 1830s by government surveyor Charles Gould, who also named its surrounds Gould's Country. Hardships awaited the English, Scottish and German settlers who came to farm the flat lands some thirty years later but the discovery of 'grey gold', as tin was called, in the 1870s changed their lot. Over the next 20 years, mines were dug across the range, dams constructed, water wheels erected, and the ring of picks and shovels became the soundtrack for life.

A wide-angle view awaits at the top of Mt Poimena

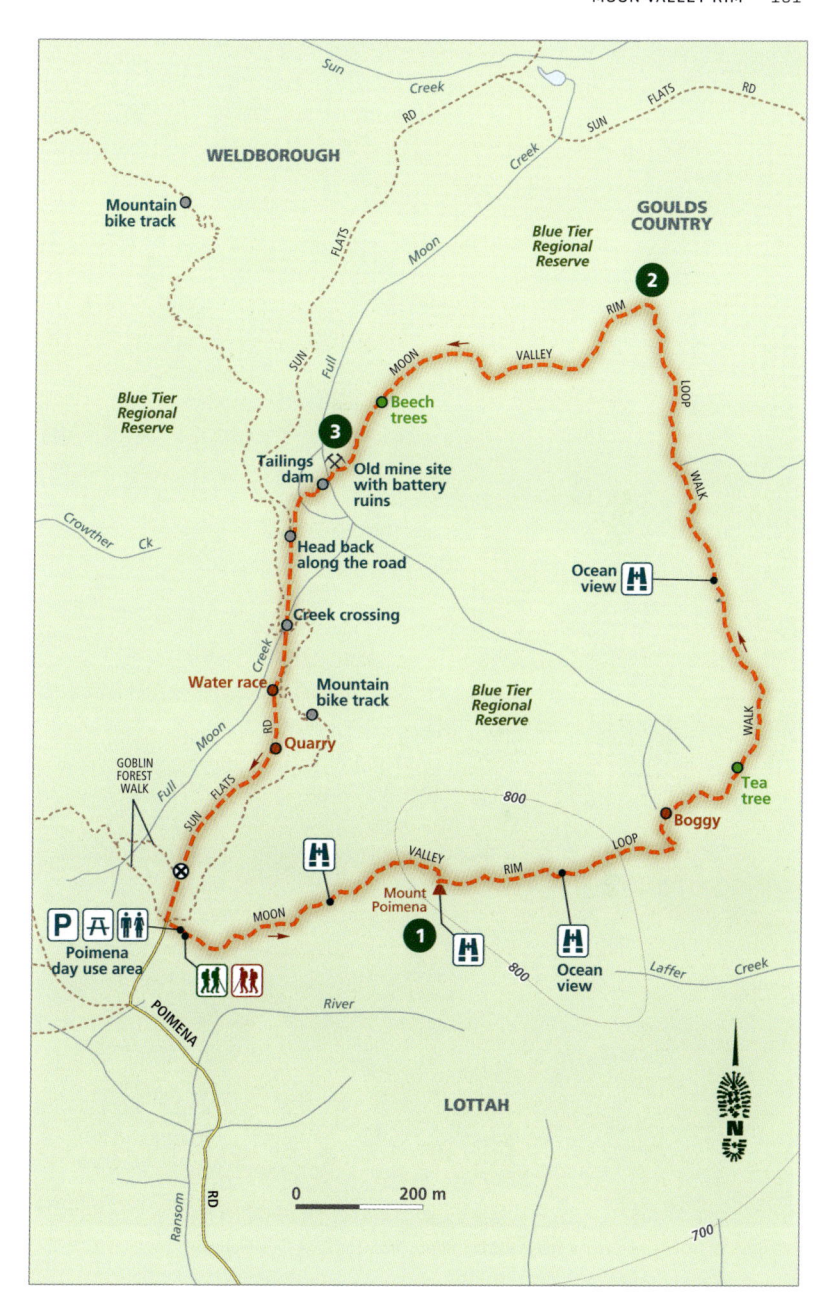

MOON VALLEY RIM 161

Weathered fallen trees, rocks and flowering shrubs litter The Blue Tiers Plateau

More than 11,000 tonnes of tin was won from the hills between 1875 and 1996 and north-east Tasmania gained the tag 'Tin Province'.

The Moon Valley Rim loop walk, one of several in Blue Tiers Forest Reserve, reveals aspects of the local mining industry and its stunning setting, which the miners may not have appreciated. It starts from Poimena Day Use Area (with composting toilets), on Sun Flat Rd, about 25kms north-west of St Helens. To get there, turn on to Lottah Rd off the Tasman Hwy (A3), 15km north-west of St Helens and north again onto gravel Poimena Rd just short of Lottah. You can also approach from Launceston and Scottsdale, turning north onto Lottah Rd about 7km south-east of Weldborough.

Marked with orange arrows on poles, the track heads east from Poimena car park up a grassy slope littered with marsupial scats and into tea tree forest often carpeted with frothy white coral lichen.

Your first destination is Mt Poimena (816m) and the track takes the easiest route uphill, swinging left as you approach the summit. At the top (see point 1 on map), drop your daypack and explore the granite boulders and their views of the Blue Tier range and Bass Strait coast.

When you're done, follow orange markers across the plateau: through tough and wiry sub-alpine scrub, softened with flowers and berries at different times of year, and around boulders and weathered fallen trees. A gorgeous ocean view greets you over a slight rise. Swinging north, continue over granite and down a slope patched with thick moss and embroidered with minuscule yellow fungi.

The track descends further into taller forest where delicate ferns enjoy protection not offered up top. You're at risk of muddy feet treading ground carpeted with green lichen and moss through shapely, shaggy tea tree and native pines. When you emerge, Mt Poimena's granite-boulder crown dominates the view to your left.

The track shadows Full Moon Creek (see point 2 on map) across more exposed slope, with compact plants and only occasional taller trees. Look out for native pepper-berry bushes with elongated leaves and black berries on red stalks. Pepper berry is a popular bush tucker. Tasmania's north coast and a sliver of beach appear briefly before you descend again, into a grove of myrtle beech.

Turn off the main track at the sign for Gough's Battery (see point 3 on map) and check out the rusty mining relics tucked into the forest. Mining commenced hereabouts in 1875 but operations were at a standstill by 1932 and the lease relinquished in the 1950s. Some relics have been stolen/souvenired over the years and campers have burned timbers but you'll find interesting and photogenic remains of a ten-head stamp battery, which was powered by a gas-converting Hornsby Rushton engine, a cylindrical boiler and a bucket head, all rusty and perished through. You can see a battery in good condition at the Anchor Mine site to the south-east.

Immediately on leaving the battery you pass a man-made tailings dam now prettily trimmed with lichen.

Walk on through old myrtle beech, a natural grotto having developed under trees on the right, and turn left onto gravel Sun Flat Rd, which runs through the reserve. This takes you back to the car park, via more gorgeous beech. Look for pretty purple-and-white fairies' aprons flowers and assorted fungi on the road's rubbly verge.

The track crosses Full Moon Creek and a shared mountain-bike-walker track and passes a quarry with a central unexcavated tree-topped rock island. Soon after you come to one end of the 400m Goblin Walk, which starts in the car park. Turn right here to see how the forest is regenerating after mining or just stay on the road back to your car.

LEFT: Check out the rusty mining relics at Goughs Battery; **TOP RIGHT:** The track is well marked with arrows; **BOTTOM RIGHT:** Look out for tiny fungi as you go

EAST COAST

29 WUKALINA/MOUNT WILLIAM

Walk:	13.5km out-and-back
Time required:	4-5 hours
Best time:	Clear, sunny day
Grade:	Easy
Environment:	Coastal plains, banksia scrub, rocky rise with views, wildlife
Best map:	This one
Toilets:	Pit toilets in coastal campsites and in the summit car park
Food:	None
Tips:	Bring drinking water because only bore water is available in the park. Allow time after climbing wukalina/Mt William to get pure-white granite sand between your toes on Stumpys Bay beach, at the northern end of Tasmania's Bay of Fires (see page 152) coastline. Good meals, cute rooms and a cosy guest lounge make the Gladstone Hotel a great budget base for exploring and enjoying the northern reaches of wukalina/Mt William National Park.

Coastal plains, wildlife and wonderful views from an easy 'mountain' top make for a wonderful day out in Tasmania's far north-east.

It's not much of a climb but the view from wukalina/Mt William is panoramic

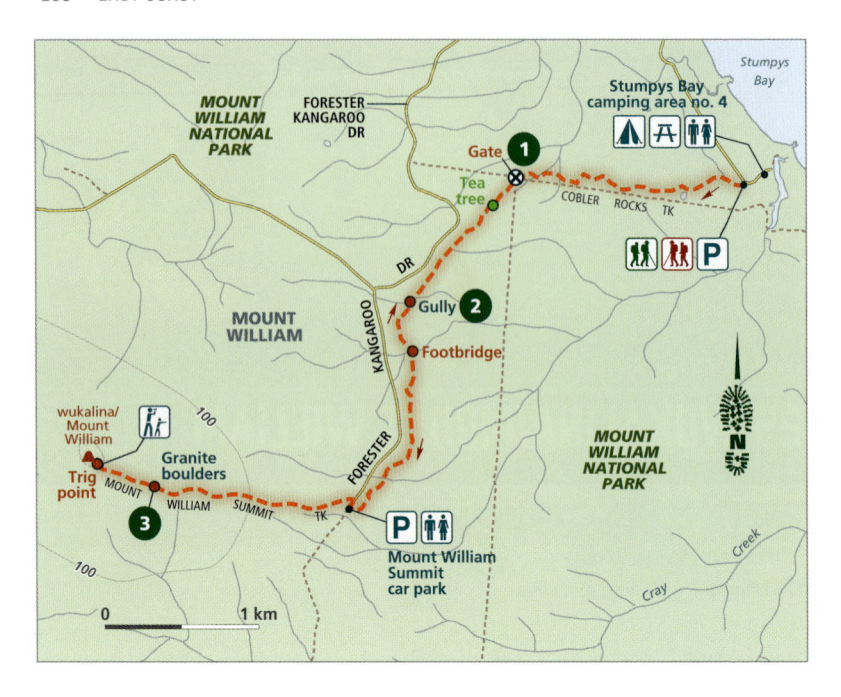

Rising a mere 216m from north-east Tasmanian coastal heathland, wukalina/Mt William is more blip than mountain. But that small elevation rewards big time and the mostly flat walk leading to the top is a gem. (There is a shorter walk from the summit car park but that robs you of the lazy plains traverse.)

The closest town to wukalina/Mt William National Park is the north-east town of Gladstone, from where you've got 17km of good gravel road into the park. A scenic, clockwise loop drive brings you to the wukalina/Mt William walking track trailhead, in a small parking area between coastal Stumpys Bay campsites numbers three and four.

A flat, compacted-sand track heads straight for the 'mountain' rising from the plain, giving you an easy walk though grass trees and coarse-barked eucalypts with narrow leaves, tea tree and stands of banksias, many blackened by fuel-reduction burns. Pink and white bell-shaped common heath flowers poke from the ground-hugging heath shrubs that grow everywhere here.

The black-white-and-yellow New Holland honeyeaters that love this heath are one of the nearly 100 bird species recorded in the park. Many of the others are better camouflaged so you'll hear more birds than you see but there's no

TOP: *A flat track provides an easy walk through banksias blackened by fire;* **BOTTOM LEFT:** *Grass trees festoon the plains;* **BOTTOM RIGHT:** *You'll likely meet a wallaby at the wukalina/Mt William car park*

missing yellow-tailed black cockatoos, Tasmania's largest parrot species, flying overhead.

wukalina/Mt William National Park was established in the 1970s, in part to provide a refuge for the Forester kangaroo, a Tasmanian subspecies of mainland Australia's eastern grey, then in grave danger of extinction, and you'll often see them grazing the plain. More sightings of Foresters, and of wombats, pademelons and wallabies, are almost guaranteed if you leave the park via Forester Kangaroo Drive.

Lucky walkers might also see a Tasmanian devil: several healthy devils were released here in 2017 to live with the existing population, 20 years after a contagious disease (devil facial tumour disease or DFTD) was discovered here. The disease has killed 80% of the island state's iconic carnivores. This was the third Wild Devil Recovery (WDR) trial, which followed encouraging results with immunotherapy trialled elsewhere; the first animals were released, in September 2015, in Narawntapu National Park (*see* page 231).

About 1.8km from the car park you reach a gate and fence (*see* point 1 on map), on the left. Vehicular tracks run west along the fence line and left, through the gate, where the walking track resumes (marked with yellow arrow). wukalina/Mt William peeps over the scrub as you walk on between tea tree and long-leafed wattles (acacia) strung with creamy yellow flower baubles from autumn to spring. Here too are banksias, eucalypts and grass trees; in places she-oak needles cushion your footfalls.

The track swings hard left and crosses an eroded creek fitted with a water pipe under the track (*see* point 2 on map). A vehicle-wide track leads to another eucalypt-lined eroded creek with recent pipework and a handrail, beyond which you enter the parking area where the shorter summit walk (45 minutes return) starts.

Here you'll likely meet a friendly wallaby practised at photographic modelling. It's probably familiar with being hand-fed by visitors but resist the temptation; as well as creating an expectation of food, which can lead to aggression, feeding wild animals can cause illness and death.

From this parking area the summit track steps into forest quite different from that on the plain: greener grasses, taller eucalypts, denser banksias, and a canopy that casts striped shadows on a sunny day. Compacted track, with the odd exposed root, passes granite boulders (*see* point 3 on map) on its approach to the summit, swinging right and giving you a short ascent through needle-sharp shrubs with fragmented coastal views between the trees. Look for an orange post on the left marking the final up.

WUKALINA/MOUNT WILLIAM 169

Step around the trig point and go another 20m east to a granite slab where water pools after rain. This is a top spot for lunch or to just overlook the park listening to the hum of bees collecting nectar from the flowering shrubs encircling you. It's also a great spot to lie back watching a wedge-tailed eagle riding the thermals.

Given how little you have climbed, the view is remarkable: a panorama swinging anticlockwise from the inland Blue Tiers (see page 160), to the sea, up the rocky coast, dotted with fragments of offshore islands, to the Furneaux Islands (see page 172) in Bass Strait.

From the top, retrace your steps down through the banksias and bracken forest to the car park.

TOP: *The Furneaux Islands are visible to the north from the park's north shore;* **MIDDLE LEFT:** *Look out, too, for colourful fungi;* **BOTTOM LEFT:** *Look closely at the beautiful tea tree flowers;* **BOTTOM RIGHT:** *Tea tree produces gorgeous nuts*

Strzelecki Peak's rocky crown frames crescent-shaped Fotheringate Beach

FLINDERS ISLAND

A combination of history, wildlife and geology fill up a Flinders Island itinerary that will take you to both beaches and mountains. You can leave footprints on white sand trimmed with lichen-festooned rocks or climb the island's tallest peak for a view extending to Tasmania and across Bass Strait to mainland Australia. Book your flight or ferry ride now!

30	Strzelecki Peak	172
31	Camerons Inlet	178
32	The Docks to Killiecrankie	182

FLINDERS ISLAND
30 STRZELECKI PEAK

Walk:	7.2km out-and-back
Time required:	4–5 hours
Best time:	Mild, sunny day; do not attempt in wet or misty weather
Grade:	Moderate–hard
Environment:	Forest, rocky slopes, unprotected cliff edges, exposed mountain top
Best map:	This one
Toilets:	None
Food:	Whitemark, 12km north, has a pub, cafe, provedore, butcher (Flinders Island wallaby is delicious) and supermarket.
Tips:	Whatever the forecast carry water, a snack and a rain jacket; wear good-gripping footwear.

Climb Flinders Island's highest peak for rainbow-hued land-and-sea views reaching to Tasmania and the Australian mainland

The largest of 52 islands in the Furneaux Group, ruggedly beautiful Flinders Island is a remnant of the land bridge that once linked Australia and Tasmania, one of a string of granite massifs created hundreds of millions of years ago by continental collision. The high point of Flinders' granite spine, and an unparalleled vantage point, Strzelecki Peak (756m) was named after Polish

A rainbow arches over Fotheringate Beach and Trousers Point

geologist Sir Paul Edmund de Strzelecki, who climbed several island mountains during his Tasmanian explorations from 1840 to 1842.

Captain Cook named the island group after British navigator Tobias Furneaux, who recorded it in 1773, and the largest island was named for Matthew Flinders, who charted it in 1798. (With George Bass, as in Bass Strait, Flinders went on to circumnavigate Tasmania, proving it an island.) So a who's-who of mariners – and the sealers, mutton birders, farmers and tourists who followed in their wake – wrote Flinders' Island's European history.

Aboriginal people occupied the Furneaux Group of Islands from about 6,000 years ago, but the indigenous history of Flinders Island includes a tragic chapter. For here, in 1833, missionary George Augustus Robinson established 'a sanctuary for remnants of the Tasmanian Aboriginal tribes', to save mainland Tasmania's Aborigines from violent clashes with settlers. Diseases and despair claimed most of the nearly 200 Aboriginal men, women and children brought to the island and in 1847 the survivors were transferred to Oyster Bay, near Hobart. The only physical reminders of the Aboriginal 'sanctuary' at Wybalenna, on Flinders' west coast, are a cemetery and restored stone chapel.

The view from the top reaches north up the island

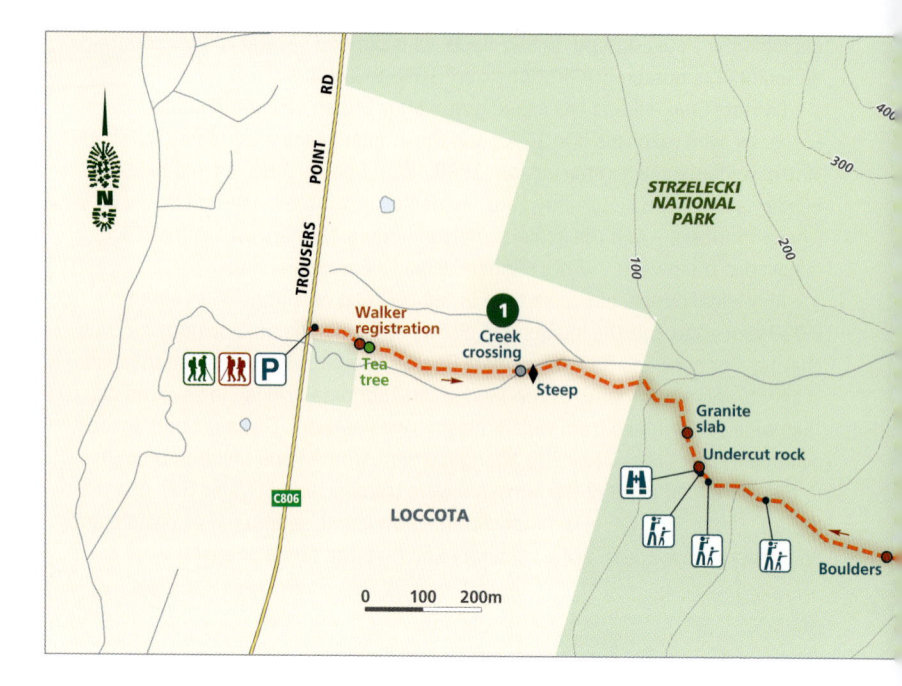

Dozens of walks explore the island's history, coast (see The Docks to Killiecrankie page 182) and lagoons (see Camerons Inlet page 178), but scaling Strzelecki Peak packs the most visual and aerobic punch.

The ascent starts from a stile beside Trousers Point Rd, 12.5km from Whitemark. Drive south from Whitemark towards Lady Barron on Palana Rd (B85) for about 6km, turning right into Trousers Point Rd (C806), along the foot of the Strzelecki range. If the peaks have their heads in the clouds postpone the walk because it is unsafe in severe conditions. If not, clamber over the stile and walk 100m across flat grassland to a walker registration hutch.

The climbing now starts through tea tree into bracken forest strewn with granite boulders embellished with lichen. Cross a creek on stepping stones (see point 1 on map) and continue uphill beside a cascade washing down a granite slide. In the mid-2010s, the island suffered such severe drought that little water ran here and moss fell off the trees and rocks.

Strzelecki National Park is significant because the geographical ranges of mainland and Tasmanian plants and animals overlap here. Orange arrows show the way within earshot of the creek, up through tea tree and bushy needlewood, a white-flowering hakea.

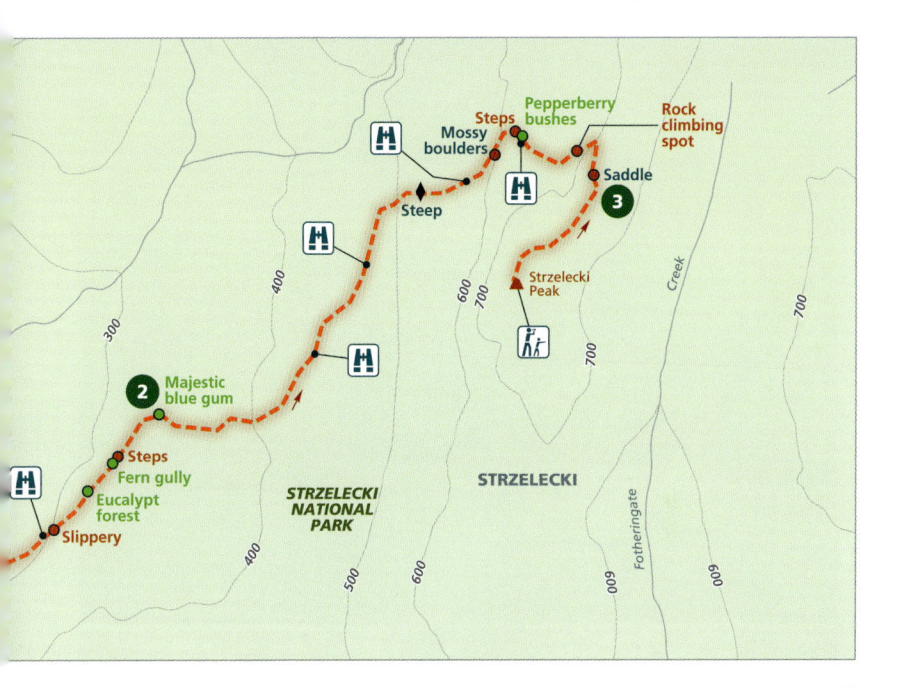

Looking back you start to glimpse ocean and coastal plains, and soon after skirting a massive granite slab about 900m into the walk, an undercut rock presents a coastal vista painted in yellow, green, grey and a colour card of blues. From another boulder you can see south-west Trousers Point and out to conical Mt Chappell Island beyond Fotheringate Beach's ribbon of sand.

Having zigzagged steeply uphill, the track flattens out so you can catch your breath taking in another fabulous vista, over neighbouring granite domes and up the island's west coast – and watching yellow-tailed black cockatoos fly overhead! Fallen leaves muffle your footsteps among eucalypts with course lower trunks peeling to smooth grey and yellow stripes up top. These beautiful trees are one of a handful of eucalypt species that grow on Flinders Island (compared with more than 800 across mainland Australia).

The track scales a treed ridge, with a ferny creek gully to the right, hillside dropping away to the left and granite pyramids thrust skywards ahead. A majestic multi-limbed blue gum (*see* point 2 on map) about 1.8km up frames the top of Strzelecki Peak.

Eucalypts give way to more open forest with fewer tall trees rooted in cutting grass, bracken and drifts of paper daisies. It's beautiful here in cloud

TOP: *The view from the top is worth every steep step up;* **BOTTOM:** *A majestic, multi-limbed gum frames the misted top of Strzelecki Peak*

and mist but dangerous, so if you're engulfed – it can happen without notice – stay put or retreat. Don't push on.

The track now traverses Strzelecki's western flank, gifting full-frontals of the two closest, conical peaks, the left one's granite flank like elephant hide. Lumpy with rocks and roots, the track steps up among age-twisted tea tree and massive mossy boulders that can drip with water. A natural chicane leads to an exposed saddle where you have Flinders Island at your feet. You've got a 75m descent before making the final rocky pitch (see point 3 on map); take care as the track can be boggy at its low point and slippery on the climb out.

Standing on top of Strzelecki Peak on a clear day, you are surrounded by crescent beaches, turquoise bays, blue sea, green-and-yellow coastal plains and grey ranges running north. You can sometimes see mainland Tasmania and Wilsons Promontory (Victoria's southernmost point, across Bass Strait) but this aerie is the plaything of capricious Bass-Strait weather gods who can envelop it in cloud without notice, shrouding even the brightest sun. Revel in the spectacle but stay alert to conditions and retreat if the weather closes in.

Enjoy the mountain and the views from the reverse perspectives as you retrace your steps to your car.

Cape Barren Island is often visible to the south from the summit

FLINDERS ISLAND

31 CAMERON INLET

Walk:	9.4km out-and-back
Time required:	2–3 hours
Best time:	Year-round
Grade:	Easy
Environment:	Ocean beach, dunes, bird sanctuary, lagoons, shipwreck timbers
Best map:	This one
Toilets:	No toilets
Food:	Furneaux Tavern in Lady Barron, 15km south, serves tasty lunches and dinners; tuck into pub grub at the Interstate Hotel, grab something lighter from a café or bakery, and shop at an excellent butcher (for Flinders Island wallaby and more), produce store and small supermarket in Whitemark, the island's commercial centre, 25km west.
Tips:	Carry binoculars and a zoom lens for watching and photographing birds on the lagoon and beach.

Take a walk on the milder side of Flinders Island, from bird-dotted east-coast lagoon to 19th century shipwreck.

Flinders Island's east coast is different from its much-photographed west. Instead of mountains dropping to headlands and bays framed in orange granite, here coastal plains end in bird-friendly lagoons, dunes, and expanses of white

The beach is littered with pretty shells

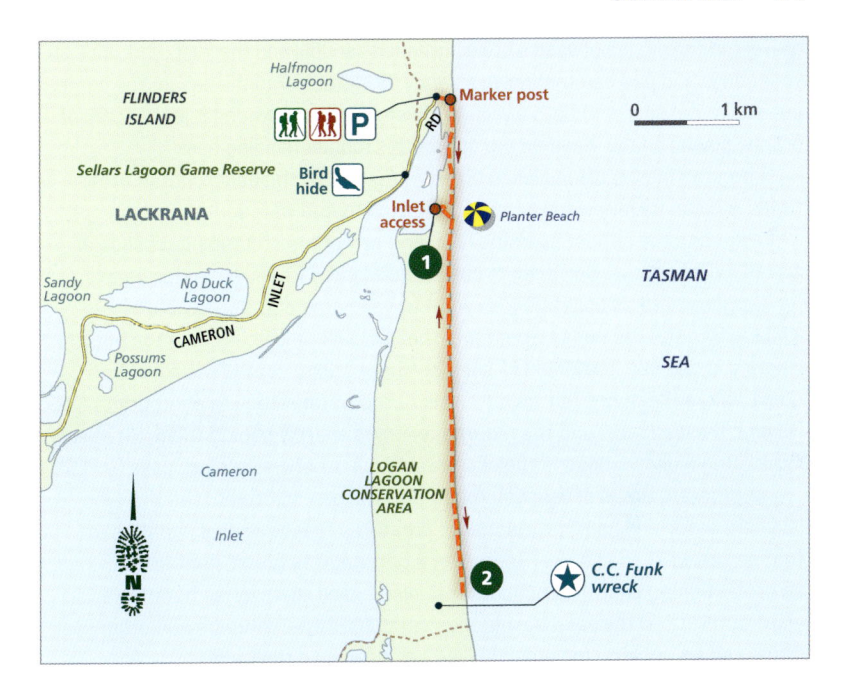

sand washed by blue sea. An easy beach ramble, like this one south from Cameron Inlet, reveals the Bass Strait island's other, often kindlier face.

Cameron Inlet Rd, 10km of unsealed road that's usually fit for conventional vehicles to travel with care, runs east off Lackrana Rd 15km north of Lady Barron and 25km east of Whitehaven. It follows the shoreline of Cameron Inlet, an often landlocked breeding ground for resident waders and shorebirds and a feeding and resting ground for visiting terns, snipes and shearwaters on their annual migrations. (The best months to witness this are November and March.) Logan Lagoon, to the south, is an internationally recognised significant wetland listed under the Ramsar Convention. (Signed in 1971, the Ramsar Convention is an international treaty of nations aimed at halting the worldwide loss of wetlands and conserving those that remain.)

Cameron Inlet is dotted with elegant black swans and fluffy cygnets in early autumn – and a bird hide part-way along the access road enables you to watch their goings-on unobserved. The sliver of sand on the inlet's opposite shore is an entry point to the lagoon from the beach.

Having passed through fire-browned and blackened trees that frame views across the inlet and inland to Strzelecki Peak (see page 172), the road ends at a gravel turning circle between a steep, greened sandhill and the inlet. Park, kick off your shoes and pad barefoot down a sandy 4WD track onto the beach. You come out at a metal post with both a yellow reflector wrapped around it and a scrap of orange plastic on top. Keep an eye out for this marker heading back.

Cameron Inlet is often closed off from the sea by the beach, but at other times you can usually wade across. So turn right and walk south down the white sand to the almost hypnotic hum and sometimes thumping crashes of waves rolling ashore. Surf fishers catch shark and flathead from this beach.

Cameron Inlet is accessible as soon as you come onto the beach, by walking through the dunes. There are, though, several places along the beach where you can gain easier entry, such as about 1.2km south (*see point 1 on map*), where the dunes flatten out. Walk to the water's edge to photograph wildlife, the wetlands, and the mountains rising sharply behind them. Strzelecki Peak often hides its head in the clouds, even on otherwise perfect days.

At different times of year you might find the beach littered with tiny blue jellyfish; assorted shells; all manner of creatures that have died and flotsam that's been washed ashore. (Once even a hardhat was found, perhaps provided as protection against the coconuts that also beach themselves here!) Leave your footprints in the sand beside those of gulls, oystercatchers and other sea birds, and keep watch for white-bellied sea eagles on the wing.

Strzelecki Peak rises behind Cameron Inlet

LEFT: *Kick off your shoes and head down the beach;* **TOP RIGHT:** *A red-capped plover strolls the inlet shore;* **BOTTOM RIGHT:** *Resident black swans dot the inlet*

About 3km down the beach, through a break in the dunes, you should see the keel of *C.C.Funk* (*see* point 2 on map), an American barquentine bound for Melbourne with a cargo of 600,000 feet of timber, wrecked in rough seas in 1898. All but two of the 13 crew and passengers, including the captain's wife and two young children, drowned. Apparently, members of Gunns Limited came to Flinders to salvage the cargo. (A building-then-timber production company founded by brothers in 1875, Gunns Limited was felled in 2013 by a controversial plan to build a pulp mill in the Tamar Valley.) There are still houses in Launceston with timbers off the *Funk*.

The ship's few remains rest well above the high-tide mark in soft sand where colonies of endangered, migratory fairy terns nest in spring. View the wreck timbers from below the high-tide mark at this time of year; don't venture into the soft sand beyond!

This is as good a place as any to turn back, unless you are in the groove and happy to walk further. So amble back up the beach, looking out for the post marking the 4WD track back to your car. Alternatively, you could turn left before then, and follow the inlet's shore.

FLINDERS ISLAND
32 THE DOCKS TO KILLIECRANKIE

Walk:	8.2km A to B
Time required:	4 hours
Best time:	Mild-to-warm, dry day year-round (exposed to wind and rain)
Grade:	Easy-moderate (lots of rock-hopping)
Environment:	Headlands, coastal scrub, rocky bays, beaches
Best map:	This one
Toilets:	Flush toilets at Killiecrankie
Food:	None
Tips:	There are no taxis on Flinders Island so you need to car shuffle or arrange a drop-off at The Docks, and collection from Killiecrankie (ask your accommodation provider).
	Leave food in your car at Killiecrankie and use the free barbecues for a post-walk beach feast.
	For the best chance of finding Killiecrankie diamonds (actually a type of topaz commonly found with tin, feldspar and quartz), chat to the experts at Killiecrankie Enterprises in Whitemark about how and where to find them.

Prepare for astonishing natural stonemasonry and boundless photographic opportunities on this fun coastal walk and rock-hop.

Prepare for astonishing natural stonemasonry

THE DOCKS TO KILLIECRANKIE   183

Most photographs of Flinders Island focus on the orange, lichen-washed granite decorating its coast. The prospect of unearthing Killiecrankie diamonds also attracts many visitors. This walk combines rugged, photogenic coastal geology with the outside chance of a 'diamond' strike. (You really need to dig and sift for these stones rather than just pick one up but you never know your luck outside the big city!)

Your geological jaunt starts at the Docks (a remote collection of handsome bays) off Palana Rd (B85), half an hour's drive (about 48km) north-west of Whitemark. The turnoff was unsigned at the time of writing, so ask a local for directions if unsure. Initially okay, the 3km access road ends as a designated 4WD track. You might navigate it in a conventional vehicle but may need to walk in. The road ends at a turnaround below Mt Killiecrankie (278m), a massive granite crag popular with rock climbers; 'B.O.O.B.' and 'Toblerone' are two of the 200 or so routes up its craggy, seaward face. There's also a walking track to the top.

Walk south, on a vehicle-wide track marked with a blue sign and distinctive boot-tread logo, into Killiecrankie Nature Recreation Area. Beyond a barrage of age-twisted tea tree, the track approaches and then skirts a rocky bay. You could clamber down and walk along the beach from here but there's plenty of rock-hopping to come and staying on the track is the easier option. Narrowing to walker-wide, the track then cuts through more old tea tree before presenting a view (left) of a wall with a twin-rock topknot (look for rock climbers) and of beach strewn with iconic Flinders Island boulders, blushed orange with lichen.

Having followed the track to another rocky beach, you skirt spines of granite eroded into crazed blocks. Weather and time have also cut caves in the cliffs behind. Tread the 'beach' from here or stay on the track immediately above it (there are cairns); either way, you'll see geological layers in close-up.

Rock (sculpted and daubed with orange lichen, in the water and ashore) and plants (banksias, she-oaks, spiky grasses, grey-green shrubs, and wind-bonsaied heath) create a kaleidoscope of colours and textures. Some of the boulders look like abstract artworks, some like wrinkled faces above distorted bodies. There's endless artistry along this walk and appreciating and photographing it slows you down as much as the rock-hopping.

As you round a cove (with all boulders and no sand) about 1.3km into the walk, note the zipper-like seam of intruded rock running through the granite you're crossing, and the stone sharks' fins on the promontory. Walk through cracked boulders, over granite ramps sloping down from the cliffs, past a rock shaped like a giant ice cream cone (*see* point 1 on map), to a promontory appliquéd with multiple shades of sea greenery.

This walk showcases the remarkable shapes, colours and textures found in nature

TOP: *Stackeys Bite frames Killicrankie Bay waters with compacted, layered rock;* **BOTTOM LEFT:** *Old Mans Head overlooks the rocky shore;* **BOTTOM RIGHT:** *Lichens splash colours across the rocks*

About 1.75km into the walk you come to an old driftwood climbers' hut with no roof and rickety walls. The track going left here leads to a cliff with several pitches including one called 'Trust Me I'm An Idiot'. Head right and continue above beach rock, enjoying a full-face view of the cliff (left) with its fingerholds and toeholds.

Water, exposure and lichen have fashioned the rock here into terrazzo flooring. Tread it towards the next headland, essentially keeping to the shoreline. It is fun but slow-going and it's easy to lose time admiring the rocks and discovering what grows on them and in the pools between. Around another headland you pass under a massive balancing rock like an elongated dog's snout pointing uphill.

As you round Old Mans Head, a landmark granite point about 3km into the walk, you get an uninterrupted view up Mt Killiecrankie (left) and, at sea level, a remarkable natural sculpture suggestive of Hollywood's *Alien* (see point 2 on map), with head lowered over knees. Then, out of the blue, among the relatively smooth granite you come upon chunks of jagged calcarenite (limestone sculpted by wave action, carbonic acid and the sandpaper-like tongues of feeding shellfish).

Roughly 3.8km into the walk you land on a tiny beach. If the tide allows, walk/wade to the end and look through an extraordinary sandstone arch. The track climbs over a rocky divide to Stacky's Bight beach for the best view of the sea arch. At mid to low tide, this sheltered bay is a lovely spot for a swim.

Refreshed, ascend the steep steps at the bay's end onto a sandy track that cuts through wind-pruned tea tree and banksias. A small cairn marks a good spot to return to the rocks if you haven't had enough yet; alternately remain on the track, towards a house.

The track deposits you on the beach beyond massed rocks, from where you amble clockwise to Killiecrankie. A short way along, calcarenite has formed a small arch over two pieces of granite; exposed sandstone at the top of the beach reveals different eras of sedimentation, compaction and uplift. But then there is just sand.

Five hundred metres short of Killiecrankie village you'll see a gully opening onto the beach. This is Killiecrankie Creek; it doesn't often flow down the beach but the tide sometimes comes up to meet it. Anchored fishing boats and cray-trap floats bob to your right as you walk on to Killiecrankie and a barbecue.

Cotton-wool cloud rests in the Upper Esk Valley below Ben Lomond

LAUNCESTON REGION

Whether you prefer pressing feet into sand dunes or treading alpine tracks, hanging out with kangaroos on coastal plains or getting down and dirty with fungi in lush rainforests watered by cascades, there's a walk for you near Launceston. You can spend an hour, half a day or from dawn to dusk checking out these northern delights.

33	**Bridport Walking Track**	190
34	**Cataract Gorge**	196
35	**Tamar Island**	202
36	**Liffey Falls**	206
37	**Higgs Track to Lady Lake**	210
38	**Meander Falls**	215
39	**Quamby Bluff**	220
40	**Ben Lomond Snow Pole**	225
41	**Narawntapu National Park**	231

LAUNCESTON REGION

33 BRIDPORT WALKING TRACK

Walk:	12.5km loop
Time required:	3-4 hours
Best time:	Mid-October to late-November for the wildflowers but the track is walkable year-round
Grade:	Easy
Environment:	Riparian bush, eucalypt and banksia scrub, town foreshore
Best map:	This one
Toilets:	Flushing toilets under Bridport Visitor Centre and along the foreshore.
Food:	Pub, cafes and takeaways in Bridport's main street.
Tips:	There's no drinking water until you get back to the foreshore.

This lovely loop through historic Bridport proves you don't have to go bush to go bushwalking.

Broad beaches and opportunities to hook fish from ocean and river attract summer and long-weekend crowds to Bridport, on Tasmania's north-east coast, dramatically increasing the resident population of about twelve-hundred. But Bridport Walking Track (www.bridportwalkingtrack.com.au) reveals that there's more to the 1860s port town than sand and sea life. Multiple access points

The remains of the Granite Point Jetty thrust from Anderson Bay

BRIDPORT WALKING TRACK 191

facilitate nibbling at it or you can tread the entire loop, a lovely way to experience the Brid River and inland wildflower scrub, which might otherwise remain overshadowed by the attention-grabbing coast.

Bridport Walking Track is divided into three legs: River–Forest, Wildflower Reserve and History Foreshore. You could start at Bridport Visitor Centre, in town, part-way along the foreshore, but the walk described keeps the sections distinct by kicking off with River–Forest.

An hour's drive from Launceston via the East Tamar Hwy (A8) and Bridport Rd (B82) – there are several alternative routes – Bridport and surrounds were, for millennia, a gathering place for Leenerrerter Aboriginal people, who feasted on local waterfowl, fish and plains animals. Nowadays the town has scallop, trout (farmed) and lobster industries. It's also the departure point for ferries (with limited passenger capacity) to Flinders Island in the Furneaux Group.

Park opposite the port (and a seafood takeaway) on the Brid River's west bank, cross the road bridge, and turn right, treading a formed track into riverside swamp paper barks. Emerging from these melaleucas, the track ducks under power lines and presents a river view, the water mirroring rocks and tall white gums on calm days. You then pass the back gate of Torrington House, Bridport's oldest original dwelling.

Early on you can hear traffic and port activity. The riverbank is also infested with blackberries but replanting works are underway and it's still pretty. Having almost touched Ada Rd, the track returns to riparian scrub and continues along a fence as Conrod Straight (sections of track are named after people involved in its creation). This brings you to a footbridge over Brid River (*see* point 1 on map) beyond which, steps climb the opposite bank. Platypus can show themselves any time of day so watch here for the tell-tale bubbles and water rings of these remarkable duck-billed, egg-laying mammals feeding and surfacing.

Cross a concrete water race and continue, with houses atop the slope to your right. Boardwalks cut through tree fern pockets to a reedy pond, soon after which a short side track visits a miniature waterfall over a low dam wall. The dam and weir were integral to Bridport's first modern water supply, opened in 1938, and the race, crossed earlier, now waters the fish farm at the town's entrance.

Beyond the dam, turn left onto a dirt road under more powerlines and descend to the old turbine station. The walking track resumes right of the turbines (ignore the vehicular track going uphill). Moss-edged, it snakes through bracken, paper barks, black peppermints (rough-barked eucalypts) and the semi-parasitic native cherry trees that feed on them. Farmland climbs the slopes across the river.

The track snakes through eucalypts and grasstrees

Dip into fern gullies, bisect a rough vehicular track, and enter a world of immature she-oaks, Tasmania's most drought-resistant tree species, rising from a wash of cutting grass as sharp as its name suggests. This is gorgeous forest despite the growl of trucks. Bridport Rd appears left as you continue through more mature she-oaks, their fallen needles muffling your footfalls.

Watch for green rosellas as you pull away from the river, cross vehicular tracks and climb to a bench (see point 2 on map) with a view of farmland and Mt Arthur (1188m), to the south-west.

You may have seen bell-shaped common heath flowers already on the walk but the spring spectacular begins in earnest beyond sealed Maxwells Street.

TOP: *One of many rocky coves along Bridport's foreshore;* **BOTTOM LEFT:** *Fungi thrive in she-oak forest;* **BOTTOM RIGHT:** *Wattle blossoms daub yellow across the inland scrub*

Cross towards Bridport Golf Club (looking right you'll get a good view of how far you've climbed) and pick up the track again several metres to the right. Walk towards Adams Beach, initially along a banksia corridor between golf course and houses.

Even outside peak wildflower season, spherical grass trees and shapely eucalypts make this delightful bush. From mid-October to late-November, however, this short leg can take hours due to the distraction of show-off blooms such as waxlip orchids, tapered leek orchids, running postman, pimelea, cushy bush pea and trigger plants.

When manicured greens give way to vistas reaching to the next-west headland, a wider track descends through grasslands, crosses another vehicular track (gated right), and traverses heathland towards bays, beaches and headlands. Part-way down there's a bench sited for watching sunrise and sunset (see point 3 on map).

Veer left at the next junction, through a chicane to Adams Beach. You could explore the beach before rock-hopping east around the headland at low tide to rejoin the walking track. Otherwise return to the main track and descend to the foreshore, swinging east at a vehicle turning circle onto a gravel road that runs along the shore, passing footpads into rocky coves.

About 150m along, turn left at a parking area onto Old Pier Beach for the best views of what's left of Granite Point Jetty, built in 1916 and mysteriously burnt down in 1938. Seabirds perch on the palisade of pylons. The saw-tooth peaks on the horizon are the Strzelecki Range on Flinders Island (see Strzelecki Peak page 172).

You're now on the History Foreshore walk. Dating back to a 1920s promenade, it is studded with storyboards, such as at Croquet Lawn Beach. The thwack of mallets on balls has quieted but the Croquet Club shed lives on as storage for Bridport Sailing Club.

Skirt grassy Bridport Seaside Caravan Park, Tasmania's largest campground according to the coordinator of Bridport Visitor Centre; facilities include a help-yourself herb garden beside the camp kitchen. Then pass the 'village green' lawns (see point 4 on map) rolling from the main street down to a playground above Gottons Beach, at the river mouth.

The walk follows the river inland now but low tide exposes a broad, flat, river beach – the Flinders Island ferry can depart only at high tide – which you can tread back to the car. Stay on wet sand to protect birds' nests above the high-tide mark and watch out for romping dogs.

LAUNCESTON REGION
34 CATARACT GORGE

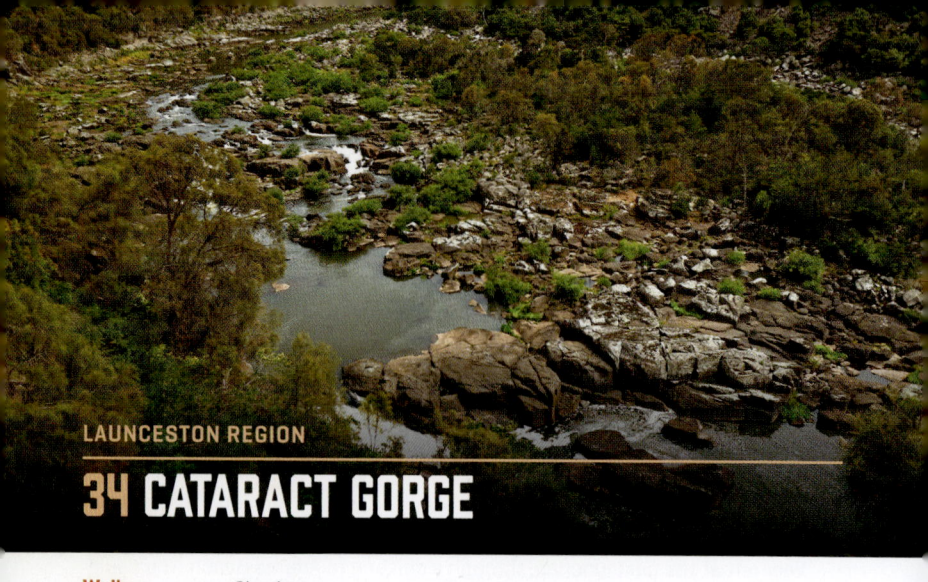

Walk:	9km loop
Time required:	3–4 hours
Best time:	Mild, sunny day year-round
Grade:	Easy–moderate (there are several steep and stepped sections)
Environment:	Dolerite gorge, river, eucalypt forest, historic power station
Best map:	This one
Toilets:	Toilets in First Basin picnic area
Food:	The First Basin kiosk sells fried foods, snacks, ice creams and drinks. Meals, Devonshire teas and drinks are available from the Gorge Restaurant and Gorge Kiosk, in the Cliff Grounds on the opposite side of the gorge at the base of the chairlift. There are free barbecues in the lawn area so bring the makings of a feast to cook up after your walk.
Tips:	Don't rely on the map boards around the gorge area for this walk. They do not show enough or consistent track names to easily follow this route. Bring your bathers/togs/swimmers for a dip in the pool.

Venture beyond the lawns and screeching peacocks and discover the bigger picture of a Launceston landmark.

Over time, the South Esk River has fashioned many holes in the floor of Cataract Gorge, where it forms eddies and little rapids

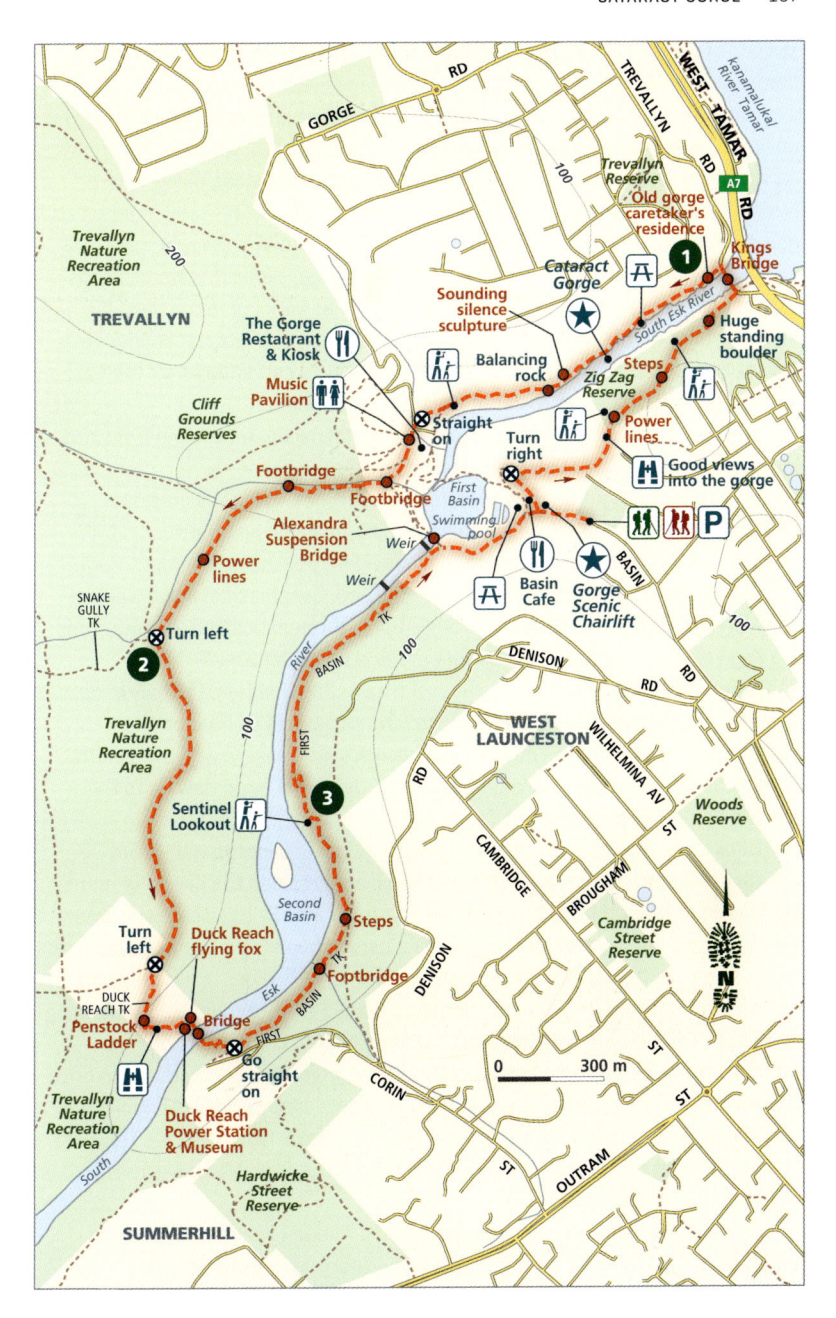

CATARACT GORGE 197

Millions of years in the making, Cataract Gorge is a fault line, formed by the final breakup of the Gondwana supercontinent, widened and deepened by water, and excavated by ice. Alternatively, it's the handiwork of an ancestral being who came down to Tasmania and cut *Mangana lieta* (South Esk River). Whatever its origins, geological or mythical, Cataract Gorge has long been a meeting place, where First Australians gathered over millennia to hunt, trade and perform ceremonies, and modern Australians have picnicked and played for over a century.

Two minutes' drive from the CBD, Cataract Gorge is one of Tasmania's major tourist attractions. Many Launceston locals visit to work out in the open air. Visitors come to ride the world's longest single-span chairlift, eat scones with cream and jam, and take peacock selfies. This loop walk ventures off the best beaten paths to reveal more about the geological wonder.

The walk starts at the First Basin car park (follow the road signs from York or Frederick streets). Parking is cheap so pay for the day.

Stay high and right on the paved footpath beyond the stone entrance shelter, with the chairlift, free gorge swimming pool and historic Alexandra Suspension Bridge to your left, and the screech of peacocks cutting through the voices and laughter from the lawns. Footpath becomes unsealed walking track and you turn hard right and steeply uphill through bush on the unformed Zig Zag Track, reaching the top almost under a house balcony.

Before the Zig Zag Track was cut in the early 20th century, the only access from Kings Bridge, at the river mouth, to First Basin was by boat up the Cataracts. Now the track is popular with walkers and joggers who bypass the small lookout on the left but you shouldn't; it delivers a good view up to the suspension bridge and chairlift.

Duck under power lines before zigzagging down the gorge wall. From another lookout you can see water, industrial suburbs and the beautiful houses that watch the world from the opposite cliff top. Kings Bridge comes into view as you pass a huge standing boulder like a carved head from Easter Island and steps bring you down onto the bridge.

Officially opened in 1864, the elegantly arched steel-girder bridge spanning the South Esk's mouth was fabricated in Manchester, England, shipped to Launceston, and assembled on a pontoon from which it was lowered onto brick abutments on an outgoing tide. The original single-lane bridge was duplicated forty years later and now, bypassed by the West Tamar Hwy, it carries Trevallyn traffic. Downstream from Kings Bridge, the South Esk and North Esk rivers become the Tamar.

Cross the bridge and turn left past a small wooden shelter – a fee was initially charged to enter Cataract Gorge and there were turnstiles here – and

The gorge caretakers' cottage at the mouth of the South Esk River is now a base for Launceston City Council's Artist in Residence program

the gorge caretaker's residence (see point 1 on map), built in 1890, and now a base for Launceston City Council's Artist in Residence program.

Admire the remarkable columnar dolerite structure of the opposite cliff as you promenade along the north side of the gorge, past a huge, horizontal balancing rock and the cataracts that give the gorge its name. Keep to the footpath past the beautiful timber Music Pavilion, presented to the Cataract Cliff Grounds in 1896 by the Ladies of Launceston. (The Gorge Restaurant and Kiosk are down to the left and toilets are beneath the pavilion.) Look for peacocks on the lawns and up the trees as asphalt becomes gravel track.

Turn right immediately over a footbridge onto the Trevallyn Walk, a narrow unformed track heading up a creek shaded by ferns. Ignore another track going right over the creek and back down the other side. Still climbing, the track pulls away from the creek into towering eucalypts, native cherry trees and cutting grass, Launceston again becoming visible behind you. Wallabies like to graze these slopes; watch for echidnas too.

Having walked under more power lines you reach a four-way junction with Snake Gully Track ahead (for a longer walk, keep straight on to Trevallyn Dam) and Reedy Gully (north and south) running left and right. Turn left for Duck

TOP: One of the manmade weirs built as part of the city's early hydro-electric scheme; **LEFT:** Crossing the Duck Reach suspension bridge; **MIDDLE RIGHT:** Look out for colourful bugs on the walking tracks; **BOTTOM RIGHT:** Paper daisies thrive along the gorge

Reach Power Station. Here you are treading a two-metre-wide track bordered with bracken and gums but you can't long forget that you're in a city, because Launceston's town clock, installed in 1909 above the General Post Office, chimes every 15 minutes (hourly at night).

About 1km from the Reedy Gully junction (see point 2 on map), cream-on-green signs direct you left to Duck Reach Power Station (www.duckreach.com.au). Another sign warns that descending the Penstock Ladder involves many steep steps but they are not very steep, and offer a good view of the opposite dolerite gorge wall and the five stone cottages built atop the cliff in 1895–1897 for engineers and workers.

One of the world's earliest publicly-owned hydro-electric power stations and Australia's first, Duck Reach Power Station generated electricity near-continuously from 1895 to 1955, interrupted only by the devastating 1929 Trevallyn flood.

One controversial aspect of constructing it was tunnelling 850m through a dolerite hill to provide more pressure from the water feeding the turbines. After 16 months of near non-stop drilling from opposing ends, the tunnel met within an inch of accuracy. From the tunnel mouth, wooden steps follow one of the two rusty penstocks (pipes) down the gorge wall. You have to duck under the pipe twice before reaching the turbine hall, now an interpretive centre.

Power station equipment and personnel were initially transported across the river by flying fox. Pass the flying fox winch house on the left (the flying fox is being restored – for show) and cross the suspension bridge that superseded it.

Having looked back at the power station and penstocks, step up from the bridge and follow the signs to First Basin, along the gorge. This last leg of the walk fords tributary creeks, and climbs and descends the gorge wall, revealing fine examples of dolerite geology on route to Sentinel Lookout, a mesh walkway projecting over the gorge (see point 3 on map).

Ignore the side track to Denson Rd car park beside this lookout and keep to the cliff, cutting a switchback almost to the gorge floor. Down below you, the river forms eddies and little rapids, its passage over time having fashioned holes in the rocks.

As you cross a gully beside a man-made weir you'll again see Alexandra Suspension Bridge and the First Basin. On reaching the bridge you can cross for another gander at the gorge or head straight for the kiosk and ice cream.

LAUNCESTON REGION

35 TAMAR ISLAND

Walk:	4.6km out-and-back
Time required:	1.5 hours
Best time:	A fine, mild day (there is no shelter from valley winds and sun)
Grade:	Easy
Environment:	Estuary, river island, wetlands
Best map:	This one
Toilets:	Flushing toilets at the Tamar Island Interpretation Centre and in the island picnic area
Food:	None
Tips:	Take binoculars for birdwatching. The boardwalk is suitable for wheelchairs and prams; the gravel tracks on Tamar Island suit sturdier prams only.

Tick off multiple bird species and catch a north Tasmanian sunset while strolling on the River Tamar.

Australia's island state lays claim to more than its fair share of spectacular smaller islands. They are, however, not all like Flinders (*see* page 170) and Maria (*see* page 124) islands. Tamar Island, north of Launceston, is neither mountainous nor subject to violent strait or ocean weather.

Tamar Island is perfect for a family stroll

TAMAR ISLAND

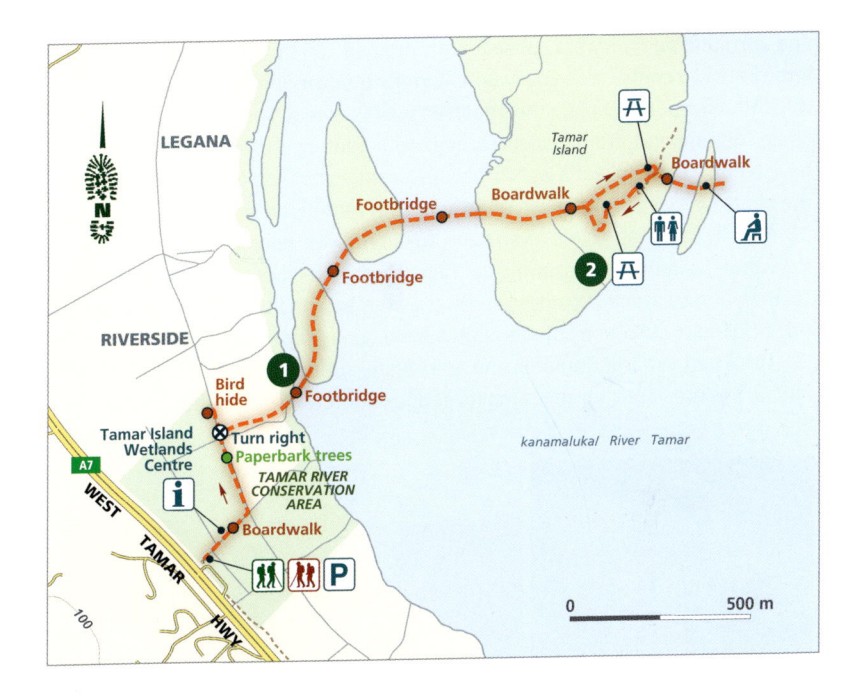

Even when wind whistling down the River Tamar rattles its fringing reeds, Tamar Island is more restful than most of the land fragments off Tasmania's coast; and the bird haven is a perfect place to stroll on a mild, sunny day.

Born of the confluence of the North and South Esk rivers at Launceston, the Tamar is Australia's longest navigable tidal estuary (70km) rather than a river proper, and it empties into Bass Strait through Port Dalrymple. Tamar Island is about 8km (10 minutes' drive) north of Launceston, via the Tamar Hwy (A7). Access is from a gravel parking area on the river's west bank.

A gate unlocked daily between 6.30am (summer) or 7am (other seasons) and sunset opens onto a boardwalk that leads through wetlands to the interpretation centre (*see* the multiple finely spun spiders' webs on its wooden exterior). Note also the sign warning that the copperhead snake seen in this vicinity is real and not rubber so leave it in peace! The interpretation centre sits on the only freshwater lagoon in this system and you may see small fish in the water, or a rare green and gold frog (*Litoria raniformis*). Dragonflies often dart about the water's surface.

In the late 19th century, seven-hectare Tamar Island was a base for dredging the river to support increased shipping to Launceston. The island

and surrounding flats were subsequently drained and farmed but staff at the interpretation centre, open daily until 4pm (winter) or 5pm (other seasons), will enthusiastically explain the importance of wetlands and the complex food chain they support, from insects through to predating raptors. Look around and have a chat. Then collect a walk brochure (from an outside pigeonhole when the centre is closed) and move on, stopping at numbered sites.

Initially following an old levee bank, the boardwalk doglegs among reeds; the white-flowering vine growing up them is native bindweed, which is on the Tasmanian threatened species list. River water lapping at its uprights at high tide, the boardwalk then cuts through a melaleuca (paper bark) thicket.

Turn right towards Tamar Island at a junction, leaving the bird hide, straight ahead, for later. Look for the remains of duck hunters' hides in the reeds as

TOP LEFT: *Handsome black swans often dot the land and estuary waters;* **RIGHT:** *Boardwalk meanders through the reeds;* **BOTTOM LEFT:** *Native bindweed is on The Tasmanian Threatened Species list*

you approach a footbridge crossing to an islet (see point 1 on map). To the left, down the Tamar, you can see the remains of barges, ships, and floating docks scuttled in the river's western channels to redirect the river's flow to the main channel; they are now a popular perch for birds. Pelicans cruise the water and perch on the uprights, black swans often dot the land and estuary, and purple swamphens stroll the silty shore. About 60 bird species have been identified in the reserve.

Rattling reeds provide background music as you walk to the end of the boardwalk, on Tamar Island proper. Treading compacted gravel now, ignore a track coming in on the right from the top of the island (you will come out that way). Instead continue straight, past an old ground well. It's been capped but the fine brickwork lining is visible.

The track leads to a picnic area with free gas barbecues where superb fairy-wrens let people quite close. Just to the right, a final length of boardwalk and pontoon put you on a sliver of island in the river current. Here you've got a lovely Tamar Valley view, taking in the metropolis of Launceston, upstream and right, and rounded hills rising from the river's east bank. To your left the river disappears towards Bass Strait. There's a bench seat so you can just sit and watch and listen. A river-facing sign reminds anyone landing by boat that camping and dogs are prohibited on Tamar Island.

Retrace your steps to the picnic area and swing left and uphill, keeping right when a side track branches left to the toilets.

Up top are leafy old oak trees, gnarled pines, elms, and fruit trees in need of a prune; these were planted when the island started to become a popular picnic spot (see point 2 on map). One of the oaks, marked with a number 13 (on the walk brochure) has grown around a rusty plough. The slight gain in elevation gives you a surprisingly broader view, albeit broken up by tree trunks, of river and wetlands, and Launceston in the distance.

The track loops clockwise and then descends the hill, passing under a cathedral-like oak tree whose branches touch the ground before depositing you on the main track, where you turn left. The reed beds, the hills behind (thick with eucalypts and European trees), and the paperbarks sheltering the bird hide paint distinct stripes of different greens as you head back towards the boardwalk junction.

Turn right and tread a compacted earthen bank between lagoons and through shadowy melaleucas to the bird hide for some avian voyeurism. Look for egrets, swans, cormorants, swamphens, gulls and more here, and as you head back along the boardwalk to your car.

LAUNCESTON REGION

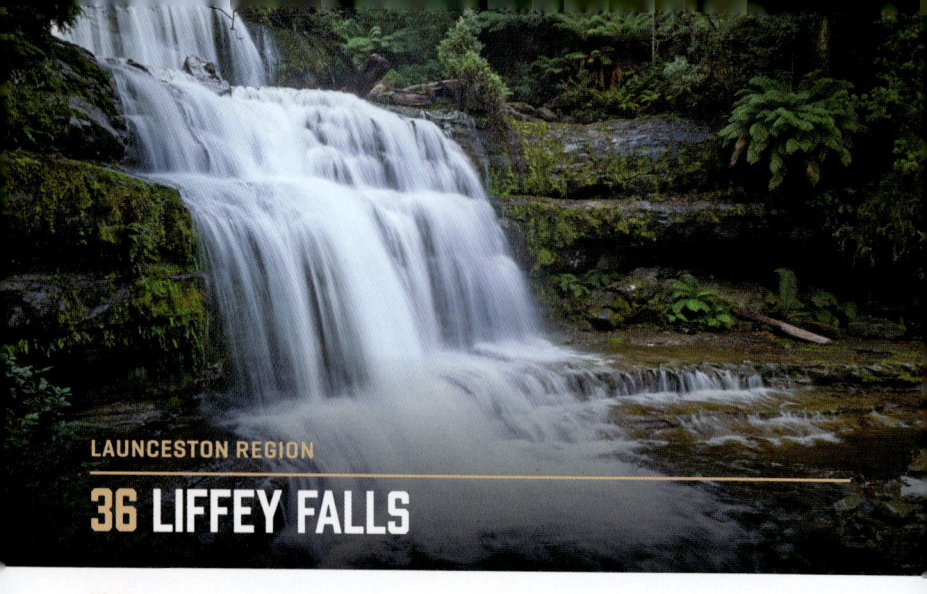

36 LIFFEY FALLS

Walk:	8.5km out-and-back
Time required:	3–4 hours
Best time:	Any time – the falls flow year-round but are most spectacular in late winter
Grade:	Easy but with a few short climbs
Environment:	Riparian rainforest, plunging waterfall, mountain creek
Best map:	This one
Toilets:	Pit toilets in the lower and upper Liffey Falls car parks
Food:	The closest food is in Deloraine, 30 minutes' drive north, where there are a pub, cafes, bakeries and huge, plump local cherries in summer.
Tips:	Take your time; look at the fabulous assortment of fungi, ferns and moss and enjoy the walk to the falls as much as the cascade.

Stroll upstream through verdant myrtle beech forest to one of Tasmania's most reliable and spectacular waterfalls.

Asked to nominate their state's prettiest waterfall, most Tasmanians would name Liffey Falls or Russell Falls (in Mt Field National Park – see Lady Barron Falls page 34), a fine duo in a state blessed with gorgeous cascades. The namesake of Liffey Falls State Reserve, included in the Tasmanian Wilderness World Heritage Area in

Liffey Falls cascades over three broad, fractured sandstone steps dripping with ferns

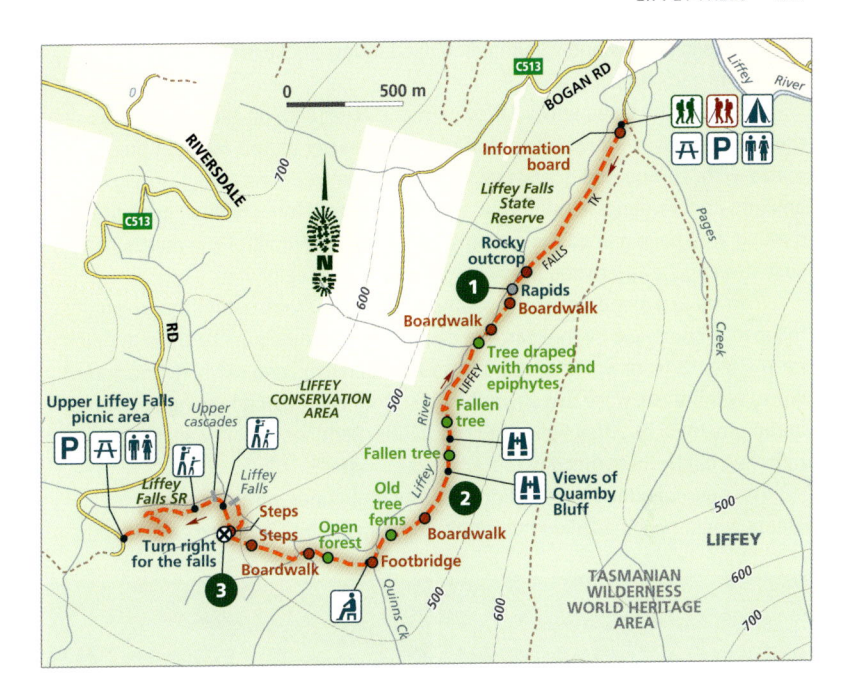

1989, rainforest-wrapped Liffey Falls tumble down sandstone steps at the north-east foot of the Great Western Tiers.

When 1.4 hectares of forest enfolding Liffey Falls were marketed for sale in 1990 as 'ideal for woodchipping', politician and local resident Bob Brown bought the block at huge personal financial risk. His actions saved the forest, and Bush Heritage Australia, to which Bob left the property, was born of the fundraising campaign to cover his debts. Bush Heritage now protects more than 6 million hectares across Australia.

If seeing Liffey Falls is your sole objective, a 2km return walk from the upper picnic area puts you in touch with the spray, but then you miss the beautiful approach up the Meander River – a slow and gentle build-up to the main event.

The longer option starts from the southern end of the Lower Liffey campground and Gulf Rd picnic area, 45 minutes' drive from Launceston. Head south out of the city towards Carrick on Hwy 1 and continue south on the C511 (Oaks Road). From Bracknell, dogleg south-west on the C513 (Bracknell Rd and then narrow gravel Gulf Road). The camping area but not the falls are signed at the turnoff, on a sharp left bend. The main road beyond here to the Upper Falls picnic area is narrow and winding, and used by log trucks, so is unsuitable for buses and caravans.

Access to the treed Lower Liffey camping area (with pit toilets) crosses the Meander River. You can hear but not see the river as you step out on a metre-wide compacted gravel track through pine trees festooned with lichen and into cool temperate rainforest. Some of the tree ferns within cooee of the parking area have gained many metres in height and most of the myrtle beech, sassafras and leatherwood drip with chandelier-like epiphytes.

Traversing a slope above the Meander River, the track cuts through long-fallen logs colonised by mosses and passes tree stumps punctured with holes for the planks from which timber cutters wielded axes and saws. By the end of World War II there were two sawmills active in this area and logging continued in the proximity of Liffey Falls until the 1960s. Sections of this walking track follow an old timber tramway route.

The now-luxurious, moist regrowth forest abounds with mosses that steam when the sun strikes them through the canopy. Conditions are perfect

LEFT: *Some of the tree ferns have gained many metres in height;* **TOP RIGHT:** *The Meander River rushes over rocks below the falls;* **BOTTOM RIGHT:** *Bushwalkers interested in fungi risk taking considerably longer than three hours*

for fungi too, and bushwalkers interested in the mushroom family risk taking considerably longer than a few hours. Damp means mud and leeches as well, although most of the track is in excellent condition and boardwalks keep boots off particularly soft or vulnerable ground.

The now extinct thylacine, or Tasmanian tiger, once roamed this forest (although some believe it roams here still) and nocturnal marsupials such as quolls and bandicoots leave evidence of their after-dark perambulations in soft ground. By day, you might see pink robins and superb fairy-wrens.

The track skirts a rocky outcrop green with ferns and moss on the river flats and passes gentle rapids (*see* point 1 on map). About 1.5km into the walk, stop and look up into the leafy canopy of an especially beautiful tree (among many beautiful trees) draped with moss and epiphytes.

The track now pulls away from the river and zigzags uphill, passing a massive fallen tree, skirting a root ball ripped from the soft soil and briefly entering drier forest before starting down again. Old tree ferns with thickly padded trunks, wearing grass skirts of dead fronds beneath green tops, populate this section. The ridgelines of surrounding hills show through the trees and to the right you'll see the august head of Quamby Bluff (*see* point 2 on map) (*see* page 220).

Back by the river, cross a new timber footbridge with the river rushing through rocks below. (Sections of this track were repaired and rerouted after record-breaking mid-2016 rain and flooding across Tasmania.) Across the bridge, new track ascends among massed tree ferns and re-crosses the river beneath a parasol-spread of fronds.

On reaching a junction, turn right for Liffey Falls – the Upper Cascades (left) are worth seeing after the main event – and step down into a rocky gully. Close to the water's edge, walk upriver to the falls, which cascade over three broad, fractured sandstone steps dripping with ferns (*see* point 3 on map).

Back at the junction, head uphill and walk as far as you want along good track, stopping at platforms overlooking the smaller cascades above the main fall. It's so beautiful here it is understandable why some people opt for just this short walk to the falls.

It's an easy 1km to the top parking and picnic area for a loo stop or you could just visit a couple of the lookout platforms before turning around and heading back to your car.

LAUNCESTON REGION

37 HIGGS TRACK TO LADY LAKE

Walk:	7.2km out-and-back
Time required:	3-5 hours
Best time:	Clear, mild spring or autumn day. The rainforest doesn't look its best in a dry summer and snow is common in winter.
Grade:	Moderate
Environment:	Wet forest, sub-alpine rainforest, heath, plateau, dolerite cliffs, alpine lake
Best map:	This one
Toilets:	Composting toilet on the plateau
Food:	None
Tips:	The walking tracks beyond Lady Lake hut can be very difficult to follow in snow; only experienced hikers with navigational skills should hike in these conditions.

Scale the Great Western Tiers and hang out beside an alpine lake undisturbed by Earth's upheavals.

Way back down Tasmania's geological time line, when the island was still part of the Gondwana supercontinent, the Central Highlands Plateau uplifted from the Meander Valley. Subsequent erosion sculpted the plateau's northern escarpment into the Great Western Tiers, a series of bluffs strung 100km across Tasmania,

Clear sky colours Lady Lake a beautiful blue

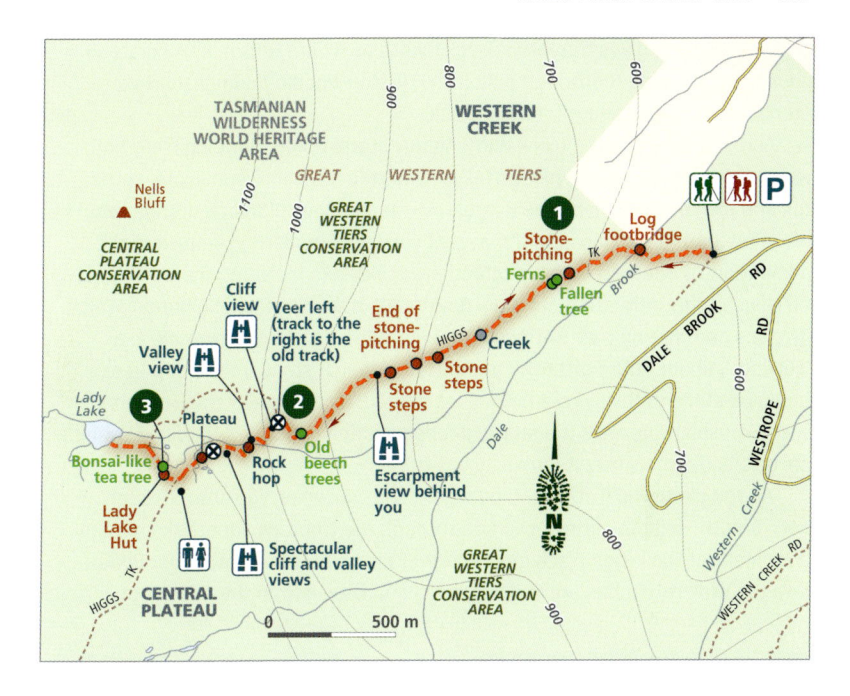

and pushed the escarpment south, about 6km (so far), marooning Quamby Bluff (see page 220).

An old stock route forged in 1879 by Sydney Higgs to graze cattle on the plateau in summer, Higgs Track (also used by fishers and snarers) gives you a taste of the Plateau which often stimulates appetites for return trips and longer explorations.

Higgs Track starts off Westrope Rd, near Western Creek, 28km from Deloraine. Enjoying the window-framed Great Western Tiers, take Mole Creek Rd (B12) west out of Deloraine and turn left (south) onto Dairy Plains Rd (C168) after about eight kilometres. Dairy Plains Rd doglegs south for about 13km before T-boning Western Creek Road (C168). Turn right and then left about 800m north-west onto Westrope Road. From here you've got 4km of good but single-lane gravel off which lead logging roads; follow the Higgs Track signs to Dale Brook Rd which ends in a gravel turnaround ringed by rainforest.

Step into the trees on gravel that shortly becomes leaf-littered track. Wind downhill through myrtle beech and sassafras, identifiable by their distinctive serrated leaves (and eight-petalled white flowers from September till October) and fallen trees greened with moss. A sign about 350m into the walk erroneously gives the Higgs Track length as 4.5km return. Immediately past this sign, a log footbridge built in 2014 after flooding demolished its predecessor, spans beautiful Dale Brook.

Across the bridge the track immediately starts uphill, climbing from hard water ferns (they look like plastic fakes) and tree ferns into eucalypts, some tall and elegant, and myrtle beech; grape-like bunches of beech orange fungi often festoon these trees. On the ascent you tread modern examples of the ancient art of Scottish stone-pitching: track workers restoring the track in 2014 used this intricate technique, developed in the Scottish highlands, which involves hammering rock wedges into the ground. The finest example is a 'corridor', about 300m after the bridge, along which stone-reinforced banks bookend stone pathway (*see* point 1 on map). Naturally rocky track roughened with exposed roots links the stone-pitched sections and it's difficult to imagine cattle treading this forest path.

As you climb you'll start glimpsing, behind you, when you stop to catch your breath, dolerite cliffs above and through the treetops. Ignore the original alignment of the Higgs Track forking right (*see* point 2 on map) about 2.4km into the walk (branches are laid across it) and keep left on the new route,

A valley view opens on your right as you climb

still climbing. Three hundred metres after the junction you rock-hop across a narrow gully. Immediately beyond, the track roughens and steepens and pushes uphill beside the gully, elevating you to more open beech forest with a ground storey of mountain berries, white-flowering heath shrubs, and tea tree.

The climbing ends at a cairn-marked track junction among summer-flowering mountain rocket (the red 'petals' are actually fruit, the flowers are white-to-pale-pink) and other alpine heath shrubs. Leaving the left-hand lookout track until your return, head for Lady Lake Hut, its back to a rocky rise, about 300m across a sponge-like moor, subject to winter snow and laced with pooling streams frequented by dragonflies. First, though, note the position of the cairn; the only marker for the start of your return descent, it is not obvious from a distance, even on sunny days, and hard to find in low-cloud conditions.

A faint footpad leads to the hut but there's minimal damage to the patchwork of coral fern, moss and pineapple grass, indicating that far fewer hikers come this way than tread Tasmania's more popular alpine tracks. For thousands of years the Great Western Tiers were a summer hunting ground for northern Aboriginal people but you might not see another human being.

As you approach Lady Lake Hut you'll see three unmarked footpads. The first goes hard-left to the toilet, its roof visible among the trees. The middle one heads left of the hut, and is an extension of the Higgs Track; it crests the hill and continues south across the Tiers plateau and exposed plain to Ironstones Hut and the imaginatively called Lake Nameless. The third footpad, and the one we're following, leads to Lady Lake Hut, which sleeps eight hikers on bunks. A handmade map and notes inside the hut describe this and other walks, many off-track, that you can do as day walks if you overnight here.

This is the second incarnation of Lady Lake Hut. The first, destroyed by a bushfire in the 1960s, was contracted in 1911 to Sydney Higgs. Men and packhorses carted the materials and equipment for the original hut's construction. Helicopters did the heavy lifting for its reincarnation in 2003–04 and an information board on the verandah tells the heroic tale of a helicopter crash on the mountain during construction and the miraculous survival and recovery of the four men on board.

Follow the third footpad, across the front of the hut and anticlockwise around the treed hill, to Lady Lake. You'll pass solo pencil pines, a bonsai-like tea tree (see point 3 on map) and snow gums on the flat, 300m walk. Avoid stepping on the vivid-green cushion plants along this short last leg, because these intriguing plant colonies are extremely fragile and take many years to recover from footfalls.

TOP LEFT: *Ferns colonise fallen trees;* **TOP RIGHT:** *Track restorers used the ancient art of Scottish stone pitching;* **BOTTOM LEFT:** *In places the track is a mix of laid and loose stone;* **BOTTOM RIGHT:** *Fagus (deciduous beech) leaves turn red before falling*

Roughly 100m in diameter, Lady Lake reflects expansive sky and in good weather the rocks around the shoreline make irresistible alternative picnic spots to the sheltered hut verandah.

Replete with food and alpine vistas, and amazed (perhaps even awed) by the sense of space and your smallness and vulnerability on the planet, retrace your steps. But before starting down off the escarpment, follow the short right-hand track at the cairn junction. This footpad leads through snow gums and flowering shrubs to the edge of the Great Western Tiers for a breathtaking view of their sheer, columnar dolerite cliffs and the Meander Valley plains spread out below.

Now you can start back to your car.

LAUNCESTON REGION

38 MEANDER FALLS

Walk:	10km out-and-back
Time required:	4.5–6 hours
Best time:	Autumn, late spring and early summer. The falls' geology makes them impressive year-round but the flow lessens greatly by late summer. In winter and early spring, the cascade can partly freeze and icicles drip from the pines, an unforgettable sight; these conditions raise the grade of the walk to challenging, suitable for only experienced hikers.
Grade:	Moderate–hard
Environment:	Rooty and rocky rainforest, eucalypt forest, boulder slopes, waterfall, dolerite cliff, river
Best map:	This one
Toilets:	At the time of writing, the only toilet was a grim one downhill to the right of the car park beyond a rustic Apex hut however by publication there should be a new loo in the car park.
Food:	None
Tips:	Snow can fall year-round and walkers should to be prepared for sudden, unpredicted deterioration in the weather including footwear with good grip and ankle support. Walking poles can be invaluable.

Tread an ankle-threatening track along a mountain river to one of Tasmania's most spectacular waterfalls.

The top of the Great Western Tiers as seen from the base of Meander Falls

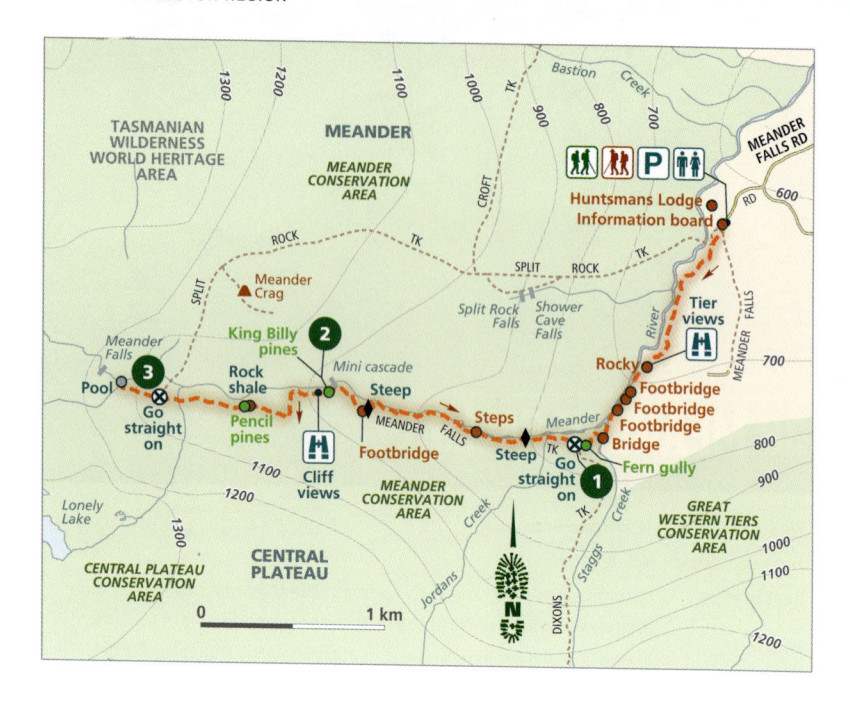

Early in its 112km journey from the Great Western Tiers to the South Esk River, near Hadspen, the Meander River drops down a chasm in the dolerite escarpment as spectacular Meander Falls. One of Tasmania's outrageous bounty of cascades (https://waterfallsoftasmania.com.au), Meander Falls is accessed by a continuous – and, in places, steep – climb on a rough track that necessitates watching every foot placement. It's worth the physical and mental effort.

Meander Falls takes the plunge about 29km south of Deloraine in the Meander Conservation Area, part of the Tasmanian Wilderness World Heritage Area. Head south-west from Deloraine on the A5 (East Pde becomes Highland Lakes Road). After 11km turn right onto the C167 (Meander Rd) and continue for 10.5km through Meander township. About 700m beyond Whiteleys Rd (left), turn left onto (here unsigned) Meander Falls Rd, which runs all the way to the falls car park (ignore Bessells Rd, branching left), and crossing Mother Cummings Rivulet and the Meander River. The walking track starts from a parking area at the end of several kilometres of sometimes-potholed gravel, generally navigable by conventional vehicles but muddy and slippery when wet.

Forest giants thrust through the canopy

Official estimates of time for this walk vary and the Tasmania Parks and Wildlife Service Great Short Walk sign, a few metres along the track, gives the return distance as 7.5km compared with online and GPS measurements of ten kilometres. There's no doubt, however, that the alternative loop walk, returning from the falls via Split Rock (five to seven hours), is tougher than the out-and-back option described here. Many challenging obstacles, including very steep sections, extensive boulder fields difficult to navigate in poor weather, and river crossings that shouldn't be attempted when in flood, make the loop suitable for only skilful bushwalkers.

The Meander Falls walking track heads south-west off the parking area. Crazy paved with protruding rocks and roots, it climbs marginally through regrowth forest of tall eucalypts, tea tree and myrtle beech, passing fallen trees and the stumps of axe-felled giants. The Meander River is audible but not yet visible on the right.

Continuing through more open eucalypt and beech forest you glimpse a flotilla of silver-grey dead eucalypts scaling the valley's steep far wall, and the river shows below. The track narrows and traverses a hillside dropping into a tree fern gully parallel to the river.

The walking track is marked with red arrows (the return with yellow ones) but the network of footpads a kilometre in, indicates how easy it is to lose your way hereabouts. Fallen trees and landslips can force diversions too. Watch for markers ahead as keenly as you watch your footwork on the rough track. As you come through here the forest opens enough for a good look at the precipitous cliff of the Great Western Tiers. Impregnable cliffs show through the trees on

LEFT: *Lichen augments the weathered Split Rock Track sign;* **RIGHT:** *The Meander River burbles through rocks below the waterfall*

the right as you cross an area of scree. Almost back at river level, with water gurgling through rocks to your right in leafy riparian forest, look closely at the exquisite mosses, plushest in cooler, damper months.

Having passed the Dixons Track and Wood-Maynard Loop (left) (see point 1 on map), 1.3km into the walk, the track hugs the river, crossing and following mini-tributaries and passing tempting waterholes beneath a thick, almost tangled canopy. Marginally less rocky track littered with beech leaves brings you to Wood-Maynard Memorial Bridge.

Over the bridge, cross and then follow a gully through beech forest adorned with fungi in wetter months, keeping straight on again beneath parasol-like tree ferns where the Dixons Track and Wood-Maynard Loop comes back in on the left.

The Meander Falls walking track is a blend of roller-coaster and tight-rope: up and down, loose underfoot and rocky, away from and towards the river, which here is piled with fallen trees washed down by rain, there cascading into pristine pools, most inaccessible from the track. Opposite one pretty miniature fall, wooden and stone steps, and uneven track scale the gorge wall, only to drop down again and work between river and scree slope.

Amid King Billy pines (see point 2 on map), about 3km into the walk, the track turns hard left and starts steeply uphill beside another scree slope (left), climbing into drier forest of myrtle beech, gum trees, mountain berries and spring- and summer-flowering mint bush (the throats of their distinctive tubular white flowers are spotted purple). This ascent deposits you on a cliff edge with pencil pines, jagged balancing rocks above and rugged cliffs and a huge scree slope with a reptilian texture opposite.

The track pushes on into beech forest, robbing you of the view but providing welcome shade on a warm day. A weathered wooden sign marks the Split Rock loop junction (see point 3 on map), shortly after which you'll see falling water through the trees. From a sun-trap opening in the forest, head right and continue about 30m down a ribboned route to Meander Falls' pencil pine-fringed plunge pool for some well-deserved lunch.

Even with a light summer flow, these falls are spectacular, plunging from the lip of the Great Western Tiers escarpment, way overhead, down the dolerite rock face in two tiers, into a natural bowl with blocky, sharp-edged walls. The promise of winter water volumes and seeing the falls frozen might have you planning a return visit before you test your surefootedness again returning to the car park.

LAUNCESTON REGION

39 QUAMBY BLUFF

Walk:	7.5km out-and-back
Time required:	3–5 hours
Best time:	Mild, clear day. Spring or summer is best for wildflowers; the sky is often clearest in winter but the plateau can be snowbound.
Grade:	Moderate (with a short, steep clamber)
Environment:	Farmland, rainforest, boulder field, alpine heath, mountain plateau
Best map:	This one
Toilets:	None
Food:	None – the nearest food (pubs, cafes, restaurants) is in Deloraine, 21km north.
Tips:	If spending a few days in the area there's no better place to camp than Quamby Corner (www.quambycorner.com) in Golden Valley, at the foot of Quamby Bluff. This country caravan park has everything you need but no superfluous luxuries.

Bag a local landmark for panoramic views over northern Tasmania.

A northern Tasmanian landmark visible from multiple compass points, Quamby Bluff is a solitary northern outlier of the Great Western Tiers, stranded (by about six kilometres) by the mountain range's erosion and retreat over time. Dolerite,

Quamby Bluff rewards climbers with a grandstand view

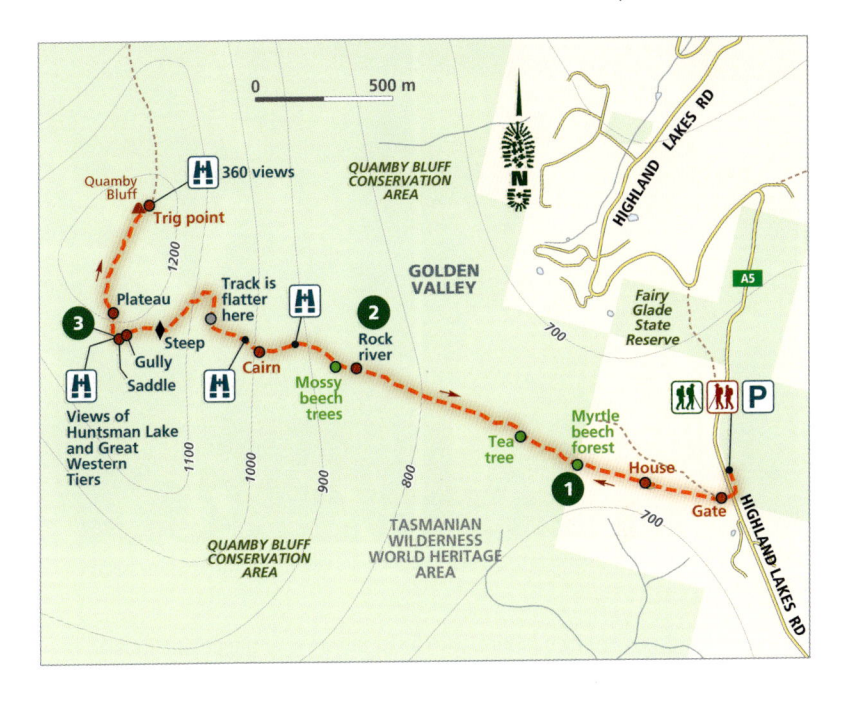

intruding through a base of sandstone and mudstone, and eroded to columnar cliffs, forms a largely-flat 'peak' at 1227m above sea level, which promises – and on clear days delivers – sweeping views of mountains, valleys and the north coast.

Reaching the top involves some fun rock-clambering but starts innocuously in farmland 21km south of Deloraine; follow the A5 out of town and through Golden Valley. The gravel Quamby Bluff Conservation Area parking area (with no facilities) is on the left/east of the road. There is room for a couple of cars at the start of the walk (the Fairy Glade route), 50m further along the road, but don't block the farm gates!

Marked with a yellow arrow on a blue pole, the track begins vehicle-wide and runs between fenced paddocks towards Quamby Bluff with the Great Western Tiers cliff line dominating the pastoral view to your left. A short way beyond a house that enjoys that view year-round, the track narrows into myrtle beech forest (see point 1 on map) blanketed with ground ferns and bracken. Climb gently through beech and tree ferns and a palisade of slender tea tree about 15m high.

Ignoring footpads other walkers have cut, keep to the arrowed track (red arrows lead up the mountain and yellow ones down it), ascending into tall

LEFT: Clambering up broken dolerite to Quamby's flat summit; **RIGHT:** Bark peels from a eucalypt like paper

eucalypts, many killed by bushfire, with an understory of beech and mossy rocks. Fallen trees can block the track on Quamby's lower slopes so you may need to work around a recent casualty.

The track then emerges from forest to work across and up a river of rocks (*see* point 2 on map) running down the mountain, the going becoming more and more uneven as you climb. Back in trees adorned with moss and epiphytes (stop and look up at these natural chandeliers) continue uphill, skirting a pile of rocks behind which looms Quamby's ridgeline. This rock pile is part of an imposing boulder field spilled down from a V-shaped saddle. Arrows and cairns mark the recommended route part-way up and across the boulder field. You may find an alternate route you prefer, but don't venture far from the markers.

More forest awaits and from among the branches you get a view over the scree and the treed hillside below, down the valley to the Great Western Tiers and up the boulder field to Quamby plateau. The rocks underfoot demand your attention for the remainder of the ascent.

Having climbed steeply through old beech trees whiskered with mosses and lichens, the track gradient eases slightly to traverse the face of the Bluff. Steps fashioned from lumps of local stone then climb, steeply again, between boulders and trees and up a gully to a saddle between outcrops. A rock atop the right-hand one looks like Shrek.

The track works across and up a river of rocks

On the saddle the track pushes through mountain berries and prickly heath plants and another stand of beech, passing a bristling scoparia bush with multiple trunks below a wall of vertically cracked rocks wallpapered with orange, grey and black lichen. If you brought walking poles, leave them on the saddle because hands are more helpful from here. The view opens up, taking in the Great Western Tiers and man-made Huntsman Lake (a wild brown trout fishery), to the south-west, as you clamber up broken dolerite (see point 3 on map) onto Quamby's flat summit.

With a barricade of dolerite cliffs at your back, walk 500m north-east across the plateau, following red arrows and then high-vis yellow ones through weather-pruned scoparia, mountain-berry bushes and tea tree gnarled with age but only a metre tall. The track is unformed with stepping stones fording patches that become boggy in the wet.

From the trig point (1227m above sea level) you get a panoramic 360° view across the plateau to the Great Western Tiers and over the plains. On a perfect day you can see Strzelecki Peak (see page 172) on Flinders Island, in Bass Straight, about 200km to the north-east.

If it's not too windy, you can lunch-with-a-view at the trig point before heading back the way you've come.

As you retrace your steps think about the geological forces that uplifted the Great Western Tiers and then separated this Bluff. Think too about the formation of the rock beneath your feet. Outcrops of metamorphosed sediments on Quamby Bluff are some of the oldest rock in Tasmania.

LEFT: *Moss grows velvet-thick on an old tree;* **RIGHT:** *Erect a sign and the lichen will come!*

LAUNCESTON REGION

40 BEN LOMOND SNOW POLE

Walk:	11.5km out-and-back
Time required:	3–5 hours
Best time:	Mild, clear day; snow can fall at any time of year. The alpine heath is prettiest when in flower, during spring and early summer.
Grade:	Moderate
Environment:	Eucalypt forest, boulder fields, alpine plains, ski village
Best map:	This one or TASMAP's *Ben Lomond 1:50,000*
Toilets:	Toilets in the Ben Lomond ski village
Food:	None
Tips:	After your walk, if you are confident on gravel roads and conditions are dry, drive 5km further up Ben Lomond Rd and navigate remarkable Jacobs Ladder, a steep switchback onto the plateau. For safety reasons, stopping is prohibited (as are pedestrians) so check out the view of this remarkable road and its dolerite-cliff frame from Watchtower Lookout at the top before coming down.

Tread the Plains of Heaven and climb Tasmania's second-tallest mountain on a great day out in the north-east.

The track traverses a field of red-hued rocks

226 LAUNCESTON REGION

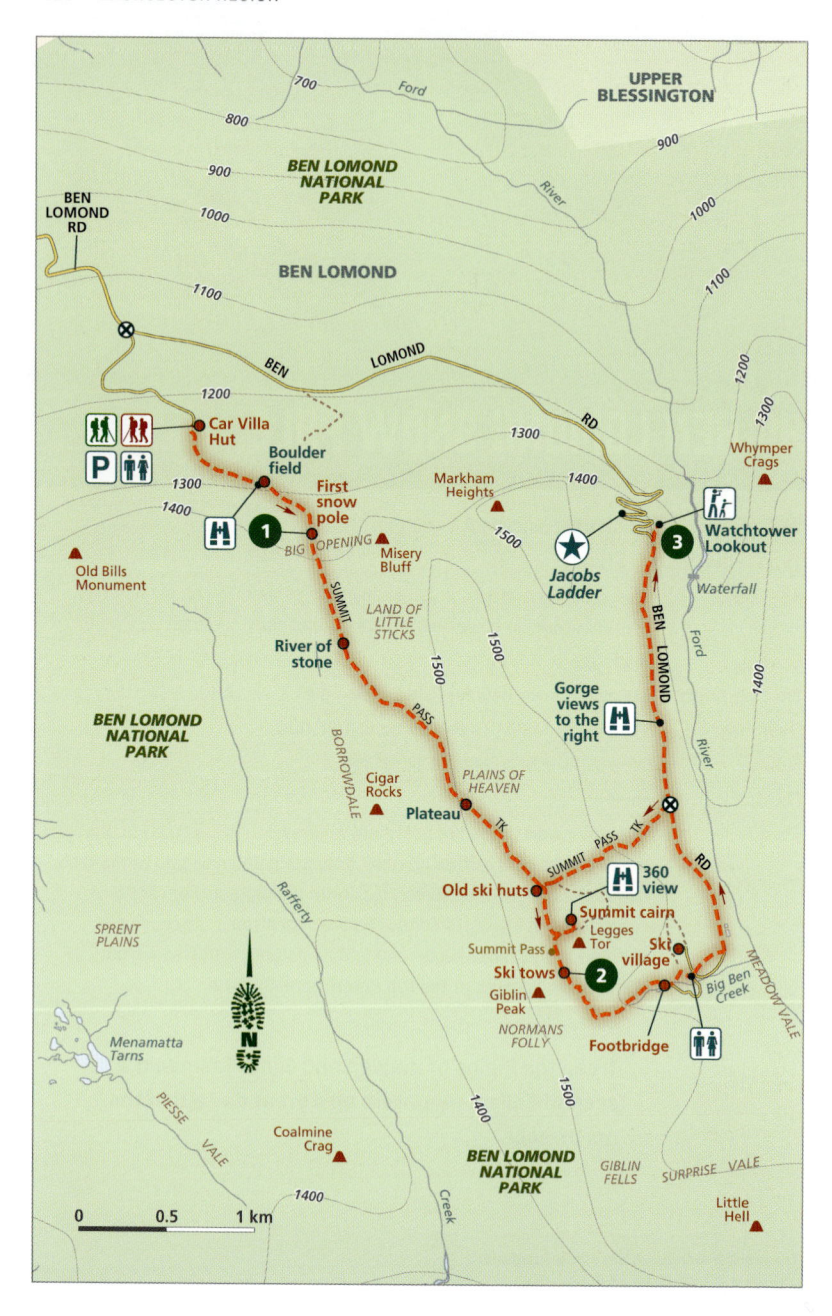

Crowning Tasmania's north-east, and towering over its namesake in the Scottish Highlands, Ben Lomond is an adventure playground suited to lovers of alpine summers as much as it is to snow-play enthusiasts. This lasso-shaped half-day return walk catches the top of the state's second-highest peak (after Mt Ossa, on the Overland Track see page 303).

Some hiking guides describe a loop walk that follows the road from Ben Lomond ski village back to your car. Many bushwalkers do this but the Tasmania Parks & Wildlife Service prohibits pedestrians on Jacobs Ladder for safety reasons and if rangers are on duty there they will stop you proceeding, leaving you no option but to retreat up the road and return via the Car Villa track. (Wire-meshed slopes, wired rocks and metal bands around cracked dolerite columns are some of the safety measures in place on the slopes of Jacobs Ladder but sometimes there is no stopping nature doing what it wants and pedestrians are too slow to escape a landslide or rock fall.)

By shuffling cars or arranging for a drop-off (sensibly at Ben Lomond ski village so you can walk down the mountain) and pick-up, you could walk only one way; otherwise you'll need to tread the route described.

The walk starts at Car Villa Scout hut and car park, on the tree line, 3km into Ben Lomond National Park and an hour's drive (47km) south-east of Launceston. The park is accessible from White Hills or Evandale via Blessington Rd (C401) (and other backroads). About 3.5km before Upper Blessington,

The walk starts at the treeline

turn right onto unsealed Ben Lomond Rd, the park's only road and subject to ice and snow from June until September. The Car Villa junction is 11km up the mountain and as you drive the next looping kilometre to the scout hut a dolerite ridge appears through the alpine gums.

The walking track starts to the right of Car Villa hut, available for private bookings through the Northern Area Rover Crew (NARC). But before starting up Ben Lomond, crest the low, rocky rise beyond the track signs for views and photos of Ben Nevis (1367m) and the Upper Esk valley, often filled with cotton-wool cloud. The mountain west/left of Ben Nevis, topped with towers, is Mt Barrow (1413m), which you can summit via unsealed road.

Well-formed and easy to follow, the walking track climbs immediately, traversing a rocky slope and then dissecting a field of red-hued boulders embellished with rosettes of grey, black and white lichen at the foot of dolerite parapets. It's a good track, with areas of compacted earth and jigsaw stonework, and you climb quickly towards the first snow poles (*see* point 1 on map), on a saddle (called Big Opening) in the dolerite ridge.

The snow poles are old, weathered, wooden ones poking from piles of rocks, most lacking the all-important red arrow or reflector, and shaggy with old man's beard. Follow the snow pole line for the next two kilometres or so, through the Plains of Heaven, an exposed, rocky plateau subject to whatever the weather gods unleash and carpeted with tough groundcovers. Here grows pineapple grass, mountain rocket, scoparia, yellow-centred white daisies and snow gentians. There isn't a tree in sight; occasional small rocks and boulders, some performing balancing acts, provide the only height. The overall effect is of unfurled tweed, woven from greens and browns and seasonally shot through with red, white and yellow flowers and fruits.

About 700m from the first snow pole you cross a 50m-wide river of stone; note the interesting fracturing underfoot as you step from rock to rock. Continue on unformed footpads in places worn through to base rock but otherwise spongy underfoot. Scoparia has formed prickly domes and great rafts, some of which have been opened up, exposing gnarled trunks indicative of long life. The going can be boggy but wherever possible avoid footfalls on plants, in particular the fragile cushion plants further on. Small-scale, ski-tow infrastructure comes into view ahead as the track climbs slightly left; follow the snow poles to locked old ski huts.

The track (and the snow-pole line) forks here. This walk will bring you back up the left-hand side so keep right for now, uphill across the foot of dolerite Legges Tor, high point of the Ben Lomond range. When the snow-pole line

Snow poles mark the route across the Plains of Heaven

branches again, follow the left line along the foot of the mountain ridge and then hard left about 80m up a gully of sorts piled with fabulously cracked and fractured rocks. The summit cairn is a few metres more hard left from the saddle.

The 360° view from the second highest point in Tasmania (1572m) is a visual feast over the ski field, Plains of Heaven and ridgelines beyond. In a gentle wind, there's no better lunch spot.

When you're fed, retrace your steps down the last rocky climb, swing left and walk cross-country to the main snow-pole line. Continue towards the ski tows (*see* point 2 on map) and walk down a tow line to a row of shiny new, high-vis red-and-white snow poles and follow them left (north-west). Initially there is no formed track, only footpads through spongy groundcovers, but they lead downhill into the Ben Lomond ski village (about a dozen chalets).

From here, tread the road down the Ford River Valley (the river is not visible but it runs along the base of the dolerite cliffs on your right). About 1km down you'll see a walking track on the left. This track takes you about 800m uphill back to the Summit Hut area so you can retrace your steps to the car.

If you are up for an additional 3km, continue another 1.5km down the valley road to Watchtower Lookout (*see* point 3 on map) for an aerial view of the Ford River gorge, Ben Nevis (a sign identifies the landmarks, including Flinders Island, which is visible on clear days), and Jacobs Ladder snaking down the face of Ben Lomond plateau.

From the lookout, walk back up the road to the walking track junction, climb the hill, and retrace your steps through the Plains of Heaven to Car Villa.

LEFT: *Posies of snow gentians sprout from among the rocks;* **RIGHT:** *Note the interesting fracturing as you step from rock to rock*

LAUNCESTON REGION

41 NARAWNTAPU NATIONAL PARK

Walk:	12km loop
Time required:	3–4 hours
Best time:	Mild, sunny day, but walkable year-round
Grade:	Easy (with one climb)
Environment:	Sand dunes, coastal scrub, Bass Strait beach, swamplands, hills, historic farm site, lagoons
Best map:	This one
Toilets:	Flushing toilets in main car park
Food:	None
Tips:	Walking sandals are all you need for this walk, so leave your boots at home. Much of the walk is in the open so wear a sun hat and sunscreen in warm weather; carry a jacket for wind protection in cooler temperatures.

Come all ye lovers of wildlife, sand dunes, lagoons, sweeping vistas, and beach combing: this is for you!

A zigzag climb up Archers Knob leads to an expansive view west to Port Sorrell (town and water)

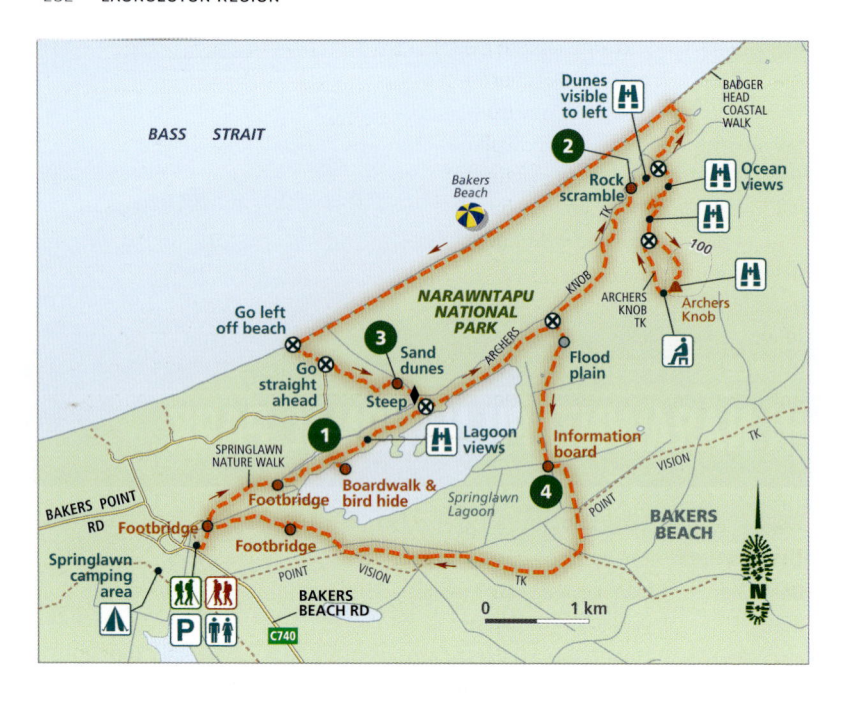

Incorporating the disconcertingly named Asbestos Range, and initially called Asbestos Range National Park, Narawntapu National Park protects a stretch of central north coast between Devonport and the Tamar River. The name change, in 1999, reflected that the park was safe (the small amount of asbestos mined locally was won beyond the range) and that it had traditional names. Narawntapu is what the Punnilerpanner Aboriginal people called the twin bluffs of Badgers Head and West Head.

For millennia the plants, lagoons, ocean beach and abundant birds and animals that now bring visitors to the park provided winter food and fibres for First Australians. Narawntapu was the equivalent of a well-stocked supermarket so they didn't need to travel far for good tucker. Their diet included native currants, boiled she-oak apples, swans' eggs and shellfish, as evidenced by middens within the park.

This figure-eight outing, combining several shorter walks, starts from Narawntapu's western Springlawn and Bakers Beach area, 30 minutes' drive east of Devonport on the B71 and an hour's drive north-west of Launceston.

From Launceston take the A7 to Exeter and then the B71, looking for the marked park turnoff (B740) short of Harford.

Star pickets mark the way from the visitor centre ramp across lawn, between the camping area and plains rolled flat to the low-rise Asbestos Range. Where lawn meets coastal scrub, swing left over a footbridge and creek, and stroll among bracken and banksias towards Badger Head (six to eight hours return). Another footbridge fords a tranquil wetland of tall, immature paper barks (melaleucas).

Pademelons and Bennett's wallabies are often seen. Also watch out for snakes, crossing the track or coiled in the sun. The three snakes found in Tasmania, the Tiger, the Lowland Copperhead and the White-lipped, are poisonous, so if you spot one, note its appearance and position and report it to visitor centre staff on your return. You may also glimpse a Tasmanian devil.

Over the 20 years since contagious devil facial tumour disease (DFTD) was discovered in wukalina/Mt William National Park (see page 165), wild populations of Tasmania's white-spotted black carnivores have plummeted by 80 per cent. Recent promising results with immunotherapy prompted Wild Devil Recovery (WDR) trials, with the release of disease-free animals into Narwantapu National Park in September 2015.

Look for animal tracks and droppings, and listen for rustling as you tread a sandy track through tea tree and melaleucas. Honeyeaters and other birds feast on the silver banksias' yellow wire-wool flowers.

About 800m in, a boardwalk branches right, to a bird hide (see point 1 on map) on Springlawn Lagoon where you can see cormorants, bitterns, grey teals, black swans, herons and many more birds. Beyond the hide, the main track climbs marginally, giving a widening view of the lagoon and the hills behind.

Ignore the Bakers Beach track on the left, about 600m after the bird hide, and another track going right to Springlawn and the visitor centre 700m further on (you'll go that way later). Alternately sandy, rocky, and leaf-littered, the track now wanders through banksias, rounds a rocky outcrop (see point 2 on map), and passes another palisade of slender, peeling melaleucas rooted in a swampy creek. Walkers have cut alternate dry- and wet-weather tracks here and occasional orange ribbons keep you on-route.

In addition to the 'disappointed' cries of crows you'll probably also hear the plaintiff calls of yellow-tailed black cockatoos – look up! Another slight climb gifts your first view of dunes and a sliver of ocean.

Head right for Archers Knob, at the next junction, on a narrow track that roughens as it heads inland and uphill. Keep to the ribboned track, which zigzags

TOP: *A big kangaroo buck lazes the afternoon away;* **BOTTOM LEFT AND RIGHT:** *Check out the sea life (and death) on the beach*

steeply for about 900m, rewarding with an expanding view west along the beach to Port Sorrell (town and water) and the distant Dial Range, and across the lagoon and swamplands. The impressive inland massive to the south-west is Mt Roland (*see page 238*).

Lower your gaze to the curly white hakeas, she-oaks, common heath and (in summer) pretty stalks of spotted pink-to-mauve hyacinth orchids. The summit is crowned with grass trees sometimes armed with flower spears.

The track loops clockwise around the top of Archers Knob (114m) and pops you out on the main track. Turn left and backtrack to the junction below at the foot of the hill. Turn right and pad about 400m along lagoons, through melaleucas, tea tree and banksias, over dunes and onto Bakers Beach – wide, flat, and firm at low tide. Hooded plovers and other shorebirds nest in the soft sand so stay below the high-tide mark.

For a longer leg stretch, you could amble east along the sand and climb over Little Badger Head. Otherwise, go west along Bakers Beach, stopping to look at the driftwood, shells, and odd exposed rock.

A blue-and-white post with a number one and a sign 'track' about two kilometres along marks your exit from the beach into the dunes. The first 10m is steep and soft; then you're back in thick coastal scrub that feels airless after the beach breeze.

Cross a vehicle turning area (the visitor centre is signed right, along the road) to a track signed for Archers Knob and follow orange arrows on a short, fun run through wind-rippled dunes (see point 3 on map) with sandy descents and views from the crests. Through a tree tunnel you're back at the Bakers Beach track junction passed earlier. Turn left and re-tread about 700m of track to the Springlawn junction. Turn right this time and cut through tea tree to grassed flats where Forester (eastern grey) kangaroos graze and laze.

With Archer's Knob behind, plain and sand hills to your left, and the lagoon ahead, follow yellow-topped star pickets about 500m to an information board (see point 4 on map). This is Springlawn, where settler George Hall drained marshy land in 1833 and planted potatoes, which he was soon selling for a handsome profit to the infant colony of Port Phillip Bay (Victoria) across Bass Strait. Hall also helped cut the first track across the Asbestos Range.

Springlawn changed hands several times but potatoes and beef were farmed here up until 1974 when the farm was bought to create Asbestos Range National Park; the shadows of old ploughing furrows are still visible in the adjacent paddock.

Turn left (east); the next marker post is about 100m away. Follow the markers across the flats to the edge of Springlawn Lagoon opposite the bird hide. The lagoon is a sanctuary for native wildlife and a refuge for ducks in hunting season. Watch for cute native water rats and platypus.

It's an easy and obvious 800m walk from here to the visitor centre car park.

The Nut rises to a flat top above the town of Stanley

NORTH-WEST

Whether you want to crack a volcanic 'nut', explore cracks in Earth's surface, climb a mountain or rock-hop along wild beaches, you'll find a walk to suit on Tasmania's rugged north-west coast.

42	**Mount Roland**	238
43	**Leven Canyon**	243
44	**Rocky Cape**	248
45	**The Nut**	254

NORTH-WEST
42 MOUNT ROLAND

Walk:	17km out-and-back
Time required:	5–6 hours
Best time:	Clear, mild day (the summit is exposed and can experience snow)
Grade:	Moderate
Environment:	Eucalypt forest, heathlands, fern gullies, sub-alpine plateau
Best map:	This one
Toilets:	None
Food:	Take your pick from cafes, restaurants and pubs in Sheffield.
Tips:	The forest track and the plateau boardwalk can be slippery when wet. Allow time to check out Sheffield's 85 famous street murals depicting regional history (www.sheffieldmurals.com).

Bag a Tasmanian massif on a leg-stretching day out to a sub-alpine plateau with 360° views.

'Because it's there' is as good a reason as any to climb Mt Roland, on the northern edge of Tasmania's Great Western Tiers. For although it has little else in common with Everest, which George Mallory famously said he wanted to summit 'because it's there' and died trying to in 1924, Mt Roland has presence. With mounts Van Dyke and Claude, Mt Roland is an impressive landmark.

Standing atop Mt Roland offers an all-points-of-the-compass view

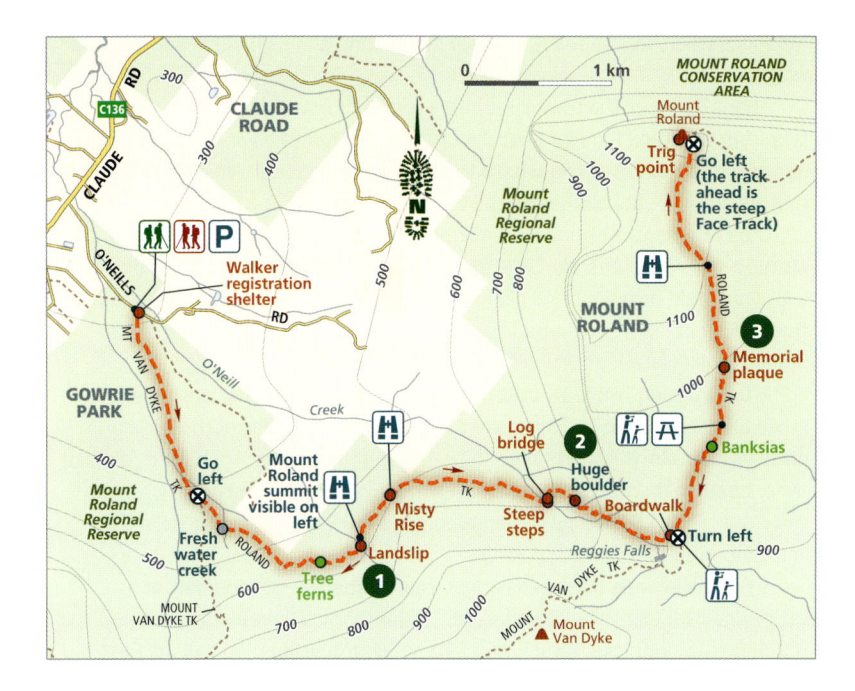

From far and near, its dolerite cliffs appear impregnable but there are several permutations and combinations of routes to the top. A tough, day-long through-walk from the Mt Claude (south-west) end of the range bags all three peaks. The shortest way up Mt Roland is a challenging climb-and-clamber up the vertiginous Face Track from Kings Rd in Claude Road village. The walk described here is an easier but longer out-and-back with kilometres in forest.

The track starts off O'Neills Rd in Gowrie Park, 15km from Sheffield and 75 minutes' drive from Launceston. Take the A1 out of Launceston to Elizabeth Town, then the B13 to Railton and B14 to Sheffield, from where you follow the C136 to Gowrie Park via Claude Rd, departure point for the Face Track. Turn left immediately after Gowrie Park campground into O'Neills Road. The trailhead and parking are 1km up.

Fill in your trip intentions at the walker registration shelter, beyond the white-on-blue Mt Roland Regional Reserve walking tracks sign, and set off on a disused, sealed vehicular track towards Mt Van Dyke, immediately to the right of taller, broader, flatter Mt Roland. To Van Dyke's right is Mt Claude. Note how much greener it is than the others, with foliage reaching all the way up its cliffs and only small patches of bare rock. Mount Van Dyke shows more rock and Mt

Roland is treed only half-way, the rest suggesting a huge, bald head – albeit a wrinkled one.

About 300m in, the track runs into a gravel forest road; turn left and follow this from tea treed flats into eucalypt forest with banksias and bracken, the gentle climb a warm-up for what's to come. A magnificent, old gum – multiple metres around – stands beside the track.

Cross Fossey Creek and continue uphill to a junction, at about 940m altitude, where mounts Van Dyke and Claude are signed right. (To spice up this walk you could turn right and climb Mt Van Dyke before Mt Roland, extending the walk by at least two hours.) Keep left and keep climbing; the top of Mt Roland still looks a long way off.

After crossing two ferny creeks, guarded by tall eucalypts, you pass a small landslip (see point 1 on map) revealing the looseness of the soil's grip on the mountain. Hills and valley show through the trees at Misty Rise (almost every bend on the walk is named – presumably it's often misty here); and as you traverse Van Dyke's lower slope you get a full-face view of Mt Roland's vertiginous cliff face.

The vehicle-wide track ends about four kilometres into the walk at a log bridge over fern-filled O'Neill Creek, beyond which, steep steps start up rougher track in thicker forest, with Mt Van Dyke now looming behind. Past

A farm dam reflects the Mt Roland masif, a local landmark

TOP: *A lookout is the perfect spot for lunch with a view;* **MIDDLE LEFT:** *The heath is awash with colour in spring;* **RIGHT:** *Old man's beard bristles on a track marker;* **BOTTOM LEFT:** *Boronias bloom across the plateau*

a huge boulder with a ferny mop-top (see point 2 on map), and over a creek flowing through a fern grove laced with shadows, it's up a rocky creek gully to a platform where the Mt Van Dyke track comes in on the right.

A less steep climb puts you on a high plateau carpeted with tea tree and button grass that unrolls north to Mt Roland. Mount Van Dyke is behind you, with valley and mountain ranges to your right; and a string of mini peaks, high points of the seeming impassable dolerite ramparts seen earlier, on your left. Star pickets with red reflectors and/or orange arrows mark the track. If bad weather or cloud rolls in, ensure you can see the next post before proceeding or retreating.

Boardwalk and track cross the plateau, climbing steadily but not enough to leave you puffing. Watch out for coppery skinks sunning themselves on the boardwalk; don't tread on them. Part-way across is a lookout deck with picnic table and bench seats, a perfect lunch spot with a view reaching from Mole Creek to the Great Western Tiers.

Continue uphill and skirt a rise, passing a memorial plaque for Matthew Lee Bell (died 2006) and Brock Bell (died 2010) that gives no curiosity-satisfying details (see point 3 on map). When a scree slope comes into view ahead, look left along and up the ridgeline behind to the Mt Roland trig point. Reaching it takes you across a saddle above the scree slope; wind can whip up and over here so you might be glad you brought a jacket!

About 2.5km across the plateau you reach a junction where the steep Face Track comes towards you from the north. Note the position of this junction among pink-and-white-flowering boronia and weather-pruned tea tree, so you can head for it coming down. Turn left and clamber to the top (1234m).

If you've got any breath left when you summit you'll probably lose it to the view: an all-points-of-the-compass spectacle, with Cradle Mountain and Barn Bluff (see the Overland Track page 303) to the south-west; the Great Western Tiers to the south; Sheffield, Devonport and Bass Strait to the north; and Launceston and, on those perfect blue-sky days, the impressive Ben Lomond plateau (see page 225) to the east.

Wind permitting (it can blow a gale up top), spend some time on the summit before backtracking down the mountain, because you're a long time in forest on the descent. Unless, that is, you are up for some adventurous climbing and descend the steep Face Track. You need to plan for this shorter harder option, to ensure safety and to avoid several kilometres of road walking back to your car; don't do it on the spur of the moment!

NORTH-WEST
43 LEVEN CANYON

Walk:	6.5km (with short link drive) or 10km return without
Time required:	2-3 hours
Best time:	Mild weather (can be bleak in winter)
Grade:	Moderate
Environment:	Fern forest, eucalypts, river gorge, cliffs
Best map:	This one
Toilets:	Flushing toilets in the picnic area
Food:	None
Tips:	Bring a picnic lunch to enjoy after the walk.

In a state famous for mountains, walk to the edge of a primeval gorge and down into its bowels where the water continues to chisel, chip and smooth.

Think 'bushwalking' and 'Tasmania' and you probably envisage mountains and alpine moors, sheer coastal cliffs and white beaches. Too few visitors dip into the island state's deepest limestone gorge!

Fed by run-off from the north–south Black Bluff ranges (the first place in north-west Tasmania to get winter snow) the Leven River is an integral part of a wildlife corridor between Cradle Mountain and Bass Strait. Over time the river has cut an astonishing zigzag gorge hundreds of metres down into the

Griffiths Ridge is a limestone blade slicing up and away from the riverbed

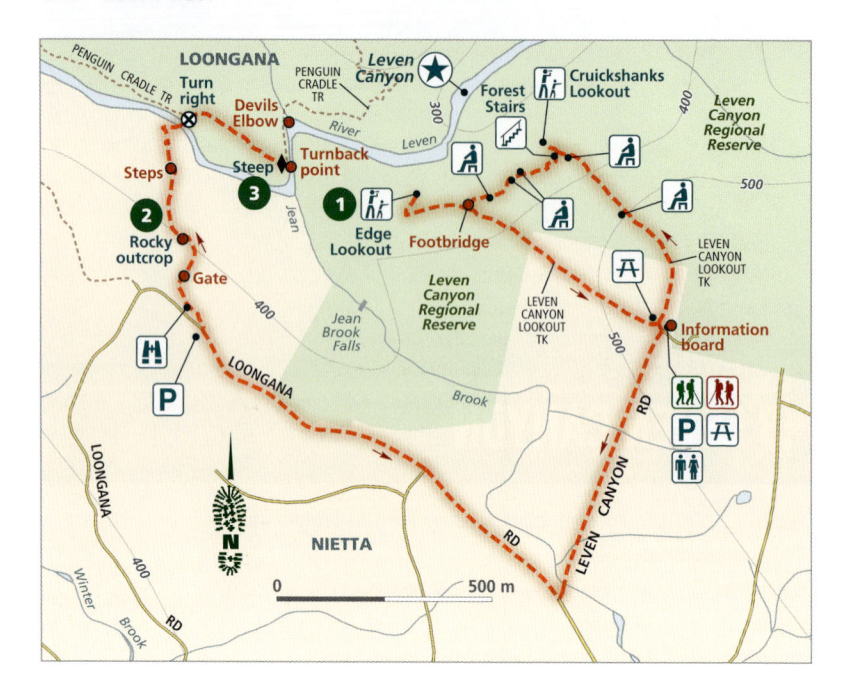

Loongana Range's layered, buckled and tilted limestone. This walk takes you to the gorge's lip and floor and offers dramatically different perspectives of the river and the geology it has exposed.

The fun kicks off from Leven Canyon Regional Reserve picnic and parking area, 42km from the coastal town of Ulverstone. Take the B15 (Main St then Castra Rd) south to Nietta, continuing on the C128 (Loongana Rd) to Leven Canyon Rd, which climbs about 800m through eucalypt forest to the car park.

A wide, flat walking track disappears into trees from the grassy reserve's north-east corner, just beyond the toilets, instantly surrounding you with eucalypts and tree ferns and mossy logs that testify to the area's high rainfall.

After a slight 300m climb with a bench at the top, an almost flat stroll to the soundtrack of running water puts you on Cruikshanks Lookout among Smithton peppermints (smooth-branched eucalypts) that tower over orchids thrust from the poor cliff-top soils from winter to spring. You are now on the lip of Leven Gorge, 275m above a spectacular V-bend. To your right the river snakes along the base of treed slopes and into the distance. Down to your left it cuts along a massive cliff with the Black Bluff range behind. In front is Griffiths

Leven Gorge in all its splendour

Ridge, a limestone blade slicing up and away from the riverbed. 'It's not a bad little view,' is an Australian understatement that could be expressed here.

Tear yourself away from this geology-in-the-raw and retreat to the Forest Stairs, on your right coming off the lookout, and start downhill. Six-hundred-and-ninety-seven steps (you could count them!) nose-dive through lush mossy forest, with regularly spaced benches for catching your breath or just watching and listening to the forest. The reserve is home to all but one of Tasmania's 12 endemic birds and while many are camouflaged, you might spot blue-cheeked green rosellas or a yellow-throated honeyeater.

The steps end at a footbridge over a creek tangled with ferns and fallen trees through which the water pours after heavy rain. Turn right across the bridge towards Edge Lookout and walk downhill, passing a huge-girthed tree, the root ball of another fallen giant, and a rock with a fern mop-top.

Clinging to the gorge wall about 140m above the river, Edge Lookout (see point 1 on map) gives another great view of Griffiths Ridge. Cruikshanks Lookout is up to your right and the river has drilled multiple holes in its rocky bank down to your left.

Back at the track junction and footbridge, walk straight on, up the creek's west bank through tree ferns grown to 5m tall over 150 years. Benches are positioned for resting and enjoying the sounds, smells, hues and textures of this exquisite fern forest.

TOP LEFT: *The track follows the creek back to the car park through tall tree ferns;* **RIGHT:** *Steps lead to a natural rock chicane through which water foams and eddies;* **BOTTOM LEFT:** *Young fern fronds unfold*

Most people are content with the lookout loop but venturing down to the bottom of the canyon completes the experience. If time's no issue and you're happy treading an additional 3.4km on gravel road through tall trees, walk down the entry road and a kilometre north-west on Loongana Rd to a gravel parking area backing onto forestry plantation. Otherwise drive, but don't leave valuables in your car.

A wide, gravel walking track starts gently enough from across the road, offering views through the trees, of Griffiths Ridge as you descend cleared ground, passing a gate and a rocky outcrop (see point 2 on map). Narrower track then steps more steeply downhill, gifting glimpses of gorge floor. The sound of rushing water accompanies you down a roped section and under a ferny overhang that looks like it's made of sandwiched clay and coal. Clearly visible below are the hollows carved into the river's rocky bank by years of swirling and pummelling water.

Steps lead to a metal footbridge spanning the gorge and a natural rock chicane through which water roars and foams and eddies; 45-70 gigalitres of water barrel through the gorge daily. This is the turn-back point for most walkers.

But park maps and notes describe a one-hour-return walk downstream (right) to the Devils Elbow, the first white-water rafting rapid (Grade 4) below the footbridge, where the Leven River turns hard-right around an ancient landslip that rerouted the river. Two attempts ten months apart brought me to a stop at the same spot, about 75m short of the Elbow, but it's worth venturing even this far and you might be surefooted enough to continue.

Across the bridge you are on the Penguin Cradle Trail, a 76km walk from the north-coast town of Penguin to Cradle Mountain–Lake St Clair National Park. It's most spectacular section (experienced hikers only) is the seven-kilometres-in-seven-hours leg between Blackwood Camp (to your right – the sign directs you to Gunns Plains, beyond Blackwood Camp) and Loongana (to your left).

The walking this side of the river is rougher and marked with orange arrows. It meanders through bracken forest on a steep slope above the river, passing huge rock slabs that presumably crashed down from the cliff. A short but steep descent on root steps lands you on the gorge rim above the river (see point 3 on map).

A faded scrap nailed to a tree, the only visible track marker, and scuff marks from other walkers' feet, suggest you squeeze behind some trees and traverse a loose, steep, crumbly slope to continue. (I did not.)

Or you could turn back from here and retrace your steps to finish.

NORTH-WEST

44 ROCKY CAPE

Walk:	19km loop
Time required:	5–6 hours
Best time:	Mild, sunny day, year-round
Grade:	Moderate (long with lots of beach rock-hopping)
Environment:	Exposed coastal hills, rocky beaches
Best map:	This one
Toilets:	Flushing toilets at Mary Ann Cove and Burgess Cove, either side of the cape, and at Sisters Beach
Food:	None
Tips:	Bring drinking water; there's none in the national park. Much of this walk is exposed to Bass Strait weather; be prepared for changes in conditions. Clean your footwear before walking to limit the spread of the deadly plant disease *Phytophthora*.

Aboriginal rock shelters, fantastic geology, abundant flowering plants, wind-swept beaches, protected coves and Bass Strait views – who could ask for more of a day walk?

Morning sun reflects in the waters off Rocky Cape

ROCKY CAPE 249

Rocky Cape's rugged shoreline awaits you

Human history in the Rocky Cape environs on Tasmania's north-west coast dates back millennia, to when rising sea levels last separated the island state from mainland Australia. Cave middens testify to 8000 years of continuous occupation by Aboriginal people who fished and hunted the bounteous sea and land.

Aboriginal Tasmanians still regularly visit and are involved in managing Rocky Cape National Park but their ongoing connection to this country is a blip on the geological timeline of one of Tasmania's smallest national parks. This all-day walk visits Aboriginal shelters and brings you face-to-face with hundreds of millions of years of sedimentation and overlaying; uplift, tilting and buckling caused by extreme pressures and temperatures; and erosion by wind and water.

Rocky Cape National Park is about two hours' drive from Launceston and 75 minutes from Devonport. Follow the Bass Hwy north-west (Hwy 1 to Burnie, then A2). Turn onto Rocky Cape Rd (C227), 30km beyond Wynyard, and stop where it swings left to Rocky Cape lighthouse and Mary Ann Cove (where there are holiday 'shacks', toilets and picnic tables). The other road runs 400m right to Burgess Cove (where there are toilets).

At the junction there's a small parking area (no facilities) and information shelter. Picture boards introduce Aboriginal names for the plants and animals of Tangdimmaa (Rocky Cape) and local landmarks. Martula, the distinctive flat-topped upthrust visible to the west is also known as The Nut (*see* page 254).

The walk starts 50m back along the access road: look for a blue sign on the right driving in. Initially climbing towards exposed rock, you traverse a slope, rough-stitched with green-and-red grasses and flowering coastal heath. Tabelak (banksias), stunted by salt, wind and poor soil, hug the ground, making the metre-high tea tree you pass seem tall. As you go, a string of coves and headlands unfurls to the east.

Cathedral Hill (112m), to the left early in the walk, is a rewarding short detour on a blue-sky day. Rocky Cape lighthouse is visible below and behind.

About 1.5km into the walk you reach Postmans Pass. Turning left here would take you down to Cathedral Rocks (about 30 minutes) but you will walk up from there on this track to finish – so walk straight on for now.

The easterly view drops behind a hill and a vista taking in the Nut opens up to the west as you continue on the high track, rockier now, across hillside bristling with yamana (grass trees) (*see* point 1 on map) and past occasional stunted eucalypts. Cathedral Rocks, the red promontory below, looks like a twin-humped camel from here.

An hour or so into the walk a footpad leads inland to Tinkers Lookout. This 600m-return add-on rewards with even broader views than the rolling hills

Any interest in geology and/or photography will slow your progress along the beach

and farmland seen walking the 200m to the next junction; turn left here to Cathedral Rocks via Blandifordia Hill for a shorter loop back to your car.

Staying high, traverse a button-grass plain; cut through eucalypts and snowdrifts of tea tree; descend into a valley boggy (see point 2 on map) with rivulets and climb out through coral fern, bush pea, banksias, boronia and fringe myrtle. Hundreds of plants have been recorded in the park, including more than 40 orchid varieties; watch for delicate blooms and look-at-me red Christmas bells. Ignore the Doons Falls track (left) but, in good weather, detour up Broadview Hill at the next side track for another overview.

In early summer you might meet people training for the annual 101km Gone Nuts 'fun' run from Stanley to Wyndham as you snake through the button grass on Broadview's flank. Don't feel inadequate: they don't have time to enjoy the wildflowers or the views – such as Sisters Beach as you round the hill. Descend into taller eucalypts (all of eight metres) with the same-named village curling around the beach below.

Turn left for Anniversary Bay (or right for a dash to the foreshore toilets) at a wooden-signed junction and walk through massed grass trees into gnarled, wrinkly banksias (see point 3 on map). Distinguishable by their shiny, serrated leaves and large, yellow summer flower spikes, these saw banksias (*B. serrata*) are one of the four original banksia species Sir Joseph Banks collected in 1770. Saw banksias are common on mainland Australia but are found in Tasmania only in Rocky Cape.

LEFT: *Show-off pea flowers are one of the hundreds of plants recorded in the park;* **RIGHT:** *Fingers of layered rock reach into the sea and back in time*

Lee Archer Cave, one of numerous caves in the park, is a must-see detour. Stepping off the main track among banksias, tread sandy track to another junction. Turn right for Wet Cave, descending to where another track climbs up from the beach (the best route if you ventured down to the toilets earlier). Wet Cave opens under overhanging rock a few metres further on. The local Aboriginal people request that you not enter.

Back at the last cave junction, follow Lee Archer Cave track to the lip of a rocky cove and – with stratified, uplifted stonework either side – step down towards a massive slab of slanted, layered rock thrust out of the sea. Clamber uphill below the projection to Lee Archer Cave. Formed by the fracturing and neat breaking-away of several rock layers, this angled slot is only a few metres wide and looks as though it were precision-cut. Several thousand years of Aboriginal use have been recorded here. It may be possible to rock-hop around to Anniversary Bay from here but there is no trail or markers so return to the main track and head right along the cave cove's rim.

A steep zigzag down a headland lands you on Anniversary Bay beach, where fingers of grey, black, yellow, brown and white-layered rock reach out into the sea and back in time. Any interest in geology and/or photography will slow your progress along the next kilometre of sand and stone. Two wooden poles just shy of the end of the beach mark the resumption of the walking track, over Anniversary Point to another bay.

The next 1.7km (*see* point 4 on map) or so is designated 'route only' because there is no track. Walk over, between, along, and around rock running down the beach, stepping carefully to limit damage to protruding paper-thin layers. The going is slow and tiring, and walking poles come in handy. It's also fascinating and fabulously beautiful.

Two posts, one with a yellow marker, mark where you leave the beach, just before sand runs into an outcrop like a huge crocodile's snout. You immediately climb, through dense tea tree, sometimes pushing through prickly branches, with the beaches and bays you've just trod now behind you.

Keep right and inland at a junction with a collapsed wooden sign where the shorter loop via Blandifordia Hill comes in left. At the next junction you can detour down to Cathedral Rocks (allow more than the suggested 10 minutes return) or continue towards Rocky Cape Rd (50 minutes), crossing a series of rivulets as you climb back up to Postmans Pass.

Turn right and retrace your steps to the car park, high above the rugged cliffs that forced the track inland.

NORTH-WEST

45 THE NUT

Walk:	5.5km loop
Time required:	2 hours
Best time:	Any time
Grade:	Easy (one short, sharp climb)
Environment:	Volcanic plug, cliffs, beach, foreshore, pioneer cemetery, historic town and fishing port
Best map:	This one
Toilets:	Flushing toilets at the beach car park
Food:	Lots of options along Stanley's main street
Tips:	The Nut is the perfect vantage point for viewing sunset and sunrise over Stanley; if you can't time your walk for either, make a second ascent for the light show. Don't leave Stanley without visiting the National Trust site, Highfield (www.historic-highfield.com.au), a 10-minute drive from town. A tour of the restored house, grounds and outbuildings provides insight into the expectation and optimism, disillusionment and disaster that shaped early European Tasmanian life.

Colonial history and a geological oddity make for a fun and fascinating walk on Tasmania's north-west coast.

There's no better view of The Nut than from historic Highfield

THE NUT 255

This walk is about cracking the Nut in Stanley, 130km north-west of Devonport. Name not ring a bell? It's the unique flat-topped formation seen so often in Tasmanian travel promotions.

The unmistakable landmark was officially named Circular Head by English navigator Matthew Flinders but is better known as 'The Nut.' One story suggests this nickname derives from its likeness to a walnut when viewed from the beach; another that onlookers declared it a hard nut to crack when large amounts of explosives failed to loosen the predicted amount of basalt from its cliffs during the construction of the town's breakwater.

Now a state reserve frequented by resident and migratory birds, The Nut was part of the original land grant to the Van Diemen's Land Company (VDL), founded in London in 1824 to produce merino wool in the convict colony. The arrival at Circular Head in October 1826 of an overland party of company personnel was the first European attempt to settle Tasmania's north-west.

Fine-wool production failed but the VDL Company found success selling land for agriculture and the settlement thrived. The Australian Handbook of 1875 described Stanley as an important 'port of entry and clearance' with frequent 'steam communication' with Melbourne. Modern-day Stanley's main industries are cray fishing and tourism.

This easy walk explores the town and its geological oddity. You can start anywhere along the route but the easiest parking is at Godfreys Beach (at the north end of town). From here, walk along the foreshore towards the Nut, passing playgrounds and barbecue facilities, and crossing another parking area towards the white picket-fenced cemetery. The pedestrian gate on the left opens onto The Nut State Reserve (no dogs or camping allowed) where, at dusk and early evening during spring and summer, you'll see little (fairy) penguins returning to their burrows to rest and feed chicks.

Wander around the cemetery beneath shading Norfolk Island pines, reading headstones dating back to 1828, then continue up the road. You'll shortly see the chairlift strung up The Nut; it operates daily, weather permitting, but that's too easy. Turn into the parking area and pass the weatherboard shop and café (the chairlift base is behind) to the sealed footpath that zigzags up to the plateau (430m). Look across the bay as you start; atop the next-north headland is the once-isolated Colonial outpost of Highfield, well worth a visit.

Pademelons graze the Nut's slopes and stopping to watch these cute, wallaby-like marsupials is a good excuse to catch your breath on the short, sharp climb (see point 1 on map). Up top, head left at the track junction immediately behind the chairlift station, and walk clockwise around the

Stone ruins at Highfield House frame a view of The Nut and Stanley

plateau. Stay on the broad gravel track to protect birds' nests in the coarse carpet of grasses and reeds.

You'll pass a seat looking across to Highfield and over the Southern Ocean. A trig point identifies the Nut's highpoint (143m above sea level), the altitude gain so minimal you would otherwise not realise you had climbed at all. Beyond it is a lookout, just shy of the Nut's easternmost point; this is the place for

TOP LEFT: *National Trust-listed Highfield overlooks The Nut;* **TOP RIGHT:** *Colonial-era ruins near Highfield;* **MIDDLE LEFT:** *Sunset silhouettes the chairlift that climbs The Nut;* **BOTTOM LEFT:** *Stanley from atop The Nut;* **BOTTOM RIGHT:** *Lobster pots crowd the decks of fishing boats in Stanley Harbour*

watching dawn over Stanley. The view opens up to include Stanley Harbour as you veer south along fenced cliff.

Step down to Fishermen's Wharf Lookout and then into the Nut's only stand of trees (see point 2 on map), a mix of American pines dating back to European settlement (planted as a wind break for a vegetable garden) and eucalypts, banksias, blackwoods, prickly wattle and more, part of an ongoing tree-planting program begun in the 1970s. The trees are full of birds – and pademelons hop across the track, which continues through a colonnade suggestive of a slightly neglected English garden. Highfield Lookout, passed as you complete the loop, presents a Southern Ocean panorama of Stanley, bay, Highfield and the chairlift.

Descend the Nut, exit the parking area and look right: the route into town starts at the white posts about 50m down on the left. Descend a bitumen track to Alexander Terrace and turn left.

Historic cottages line Alexander Terrace. At the time of writing, the attractive weatherboard at #48, with a huge palm tree out front, was home to Odd Job Bob. Exquisite iron lacework trims the Harbour Master's Cottage (c 1880) at #42. The stone Captain's Cottage with dormer windows in the roof (#30) was built in 1835. Bayview Guesthouse, at #16, dates from 1849 and is again providing heritage accommodation. The simple stone cottage at #14 (see point 3 on map) was the birthplace and childhood home of Joseph Lyons, former Tasmanian premier and the state's first Prime Minister of Australia, from 1932 until his death in 1939.

Continue down the road and U-turn right onto Lower Wharf Rd, passing the old lighthouse in the park. The two-storey bluestone building on the right was convict-built in 1843 as the VDL Company's wool warehouse. Having been a customs house, detention centre, fish processing factory and art gallery, it's now a boutique hotel.

When the road divides, take the right hand Upper Church St, just below Alexander Tce, with The Nut sitting high on your right. This is Stanley's main street. Walking along it, you pass galleries and restaurants and The Stanley Hotel, founded in 1847 (visitors are welcome to look around the pub's cellar, purportedly the oldest on the coast). The Plough Inn, further on, was established in 1840.

Pass the Anglican church, and just before the road swings left, turn right into the Godfrey's Beach car park to finish.

Cradle Mountain overlooks glaciated Dove Lake

CENTRAL HIGHLANDS

There's more to Tasmania's central highlands than Australia's most popular long-distance walk. In addition to hiking the Overland Track, you can tread low and high routes (or both) around the glacial lake guarded by Cradle Mountain; climb chains to cliff-edge lookouts and explore a valley whose beauty is of biblical proportions. Stick to the well-trodden routes or venture further: you'll soon appreciate why this part of Tasmania is world-famous.

46	Dove Lake	262
47	Dove Lake High	267
48	Dove Gorge	273
49	Lakes Loop	277
50	Cradle Mountain summit	282
51	Shadow Lake	289
52	The Labyrinth	294
53	Overland Track	303
54	Walls of Jerusalem	318

CENTRAL HIGHLANDS

46 DOVE LAKE

Walk:	6.5km loop
Time required:	2-3 hours
Best time:	Fine weather, although it can be dramatic in cloudy weather; don't proceed in wintry extremes.
Grade:	Easy
Environment:	Alpine lake and beaches, glaciated mountain slopes, heathland, rainforest
Best map:	This one
Toilets:	Flushing toilets in Dove Lake car park
Food:	Coffee, snacks and meals are available from the visitor centre café, 2km outside the park boundary; delicious bistro and restaurant meals are dished up at Cradle Mountain Lodge, within the park, opposite the ranger station and interpretive centre.
Tips:	For an eagle's-eye view of Cradle Mountain's glaciated splendour, splurge on a helicopter flight (www.cradlemountainhelicopters.com.au at Cradle Mountain Visitor Centre). A new visitor hub and contemporary viewing shelter at Dove Lake are due for completion early 2019.

With cute button grass, verdant rainforest, lake-side beaches and dramatic ice-carved mountains, this is the must-do walk in Cradle Mountain–Lake St Clair National Park.

Travelling clockwise around Dove Lake puts Cradle Mountain in your sights for longer

DOVE LAKE 263

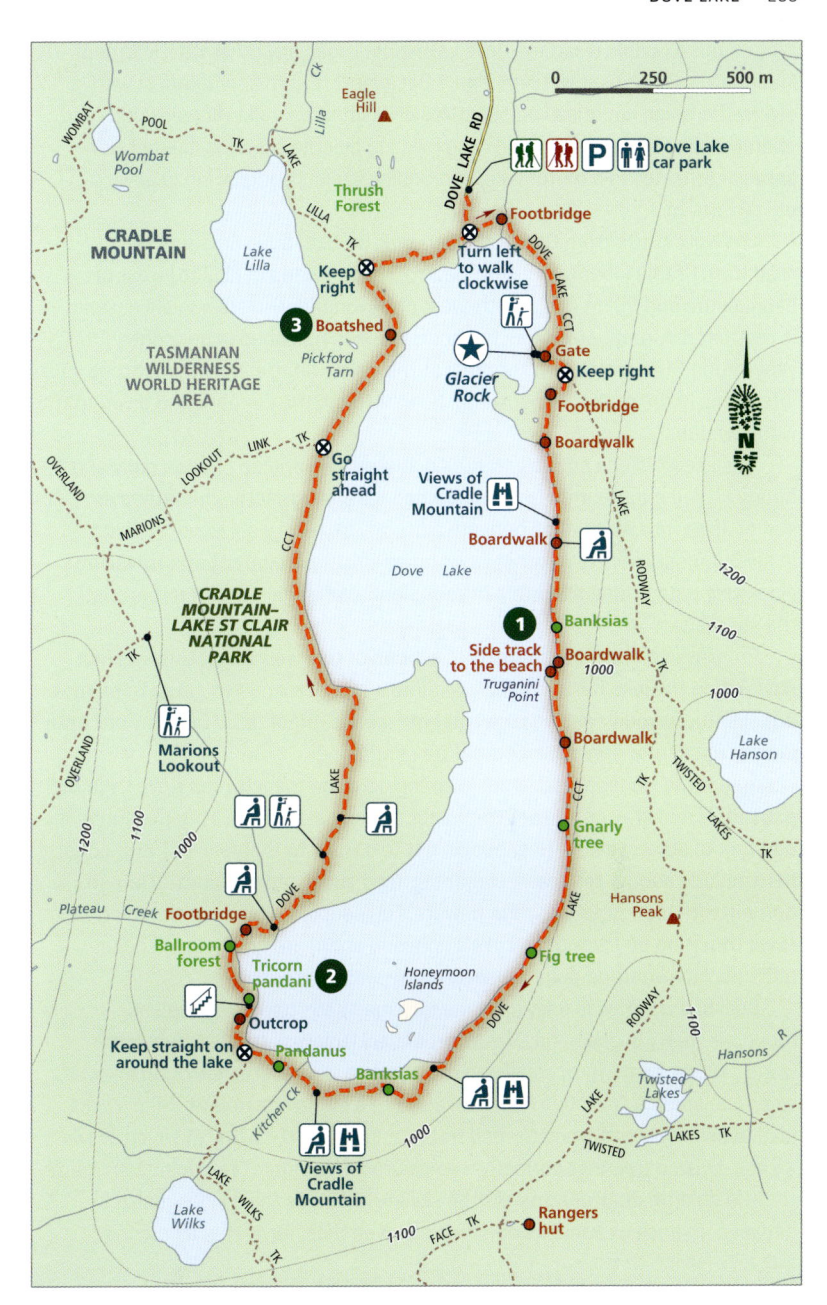

Why do more people tread the Dove Lake circuit than any other walk in Cradle Mountain–Lake St Clair National Park? Because it rewards minor effort with diverse flora and countless perspectives of Tasmania's most recognisable (and photographed) natural landmark: its crowning dolerite columns, dusted with snow, or reflected in a mirror lake, or brooding in cloud, or glowing in dawn's pastel hues or…

The walk starts from Dove Lake car park, an 8km drive on a narrow road from Cradle Mountain Visitor Centre, which is 142km (1.75h) west of Launceston and 80km (1h) south-west of Devonport. Private vehicle access is restricted during busy times but shuttle buses (included in park entry) run year-round from the transit terminal at the visitor centre. Having recorded your intentions in the walker registration, head through the car park and down to the water's edge.

This is capricious country where conditions can and do change daily and hourly so you might catch Dove Lake when it's silky smooth and bathed in sun or lifted into white caps beneath a stormy sky. The walk is worth doing in all-but-nasty-wintry weather (as long as you are prepared) and travelling clockwise puts Cradle Mountain in your sights for longer so turn left around the shoreline.

Progress can be slow on the first section of this walk on picture-perfect days, when the lake mirrors Cradle Mountain and demands you stop to enjoy it, but eventually you'll reach a side trail with a child-proof gate. Detour right onto Glacier Rock for a ring-side view before continuing.

Ignore the Hanson Peak track pushing uphill on the left (see Dove Lake High page 267) and stay on a lower track that only occasionally leaves the shore. In addition to other walkers (few people get this track to themselves) your cohorts here include august tea trees, elegant striped eucalypts and central lemon boronia with four-petalled white flowers. The people visible atop the main ridge thrusting up from Dove Lake's opposite shore are on Marions Lookout, a gobsmacking vantage point on several day-walk routes.

Duckboards provide easy passage through beech trees, pencil pines, mountain-berry bushes and Cousin It-pandani (run your hands through the world's tallest heath for a satisfying rattle) and a view of Cradle Mountain awaits when you emerge from this dense foliage into a stand of banksias. Side tracks lead to beaches (only tread formed tracks to the water), on one of which grows an age-twisted tree that perfectly frames Cradle Mountain (see point 1 on map).

The dolerite peak commands the skyline ahead as the track squeezes between an ancient conifer and steep exposed rock; navigates a colonnade of taller, greyer tea trees and banksias; and threads through button-grass mounds. Enjoy a fantastic view up Dove Lake from a bench on its southern shore, half-way through the walk.

Boardwalk slices through cutting grass towards Cradle Mountain but swings right at the last minute, putting the at-times-almost-menacing edifice on your left and then behind. If this low route is too tame and you have water, food, energy and time, turn left at the next junction and ascend to the Face Track via Lake Wilks and continue to the car park via Marions Lookout (this will extend the walk by up to two hours).

Otherwise stay on the lower track, treading raised boardwalk between rock outcrops and trees wrapped in lichen. The trees with mottled brown and white bark and glossy-green, tooth-edged leaves with a powdery underside are sassafras, a rainforest species that produces fragrant downward-facing white flowers in spring.

With the lake at your feet and Cradle Mountain now visible over your right shoulder, continue in the lee of a huge outcrop, its surface cracks holding enough nutrients for plants to grow. Note the distinctive, crinkle-cut leaves of the fagus, Australia's only deciduous native tree, which change from bright green to gold and even red in autumn before falling; and the creature-like tricorn pandani with three shaggy heads growing from a single trunk (see point 2 on map).

The lake circuit brings you to the much-photographed shingle boatshed

Step up and then down into the Ballroom Forest, so leafy and shadow-filled that only threads of sky are visible through the canopy and hints of water through the mossy tree trunks. But another commanding view of Cradle Mountain awaits on leaving the protection of the forest and starting on the walk's lone hill. There's a bench with a view, part-way up but a better one from the top.

Continue north: up and downhill, towards the water's edge and away, through tea tree, boronia and Tasmanian snow gums with hooked leaf tips. Beyond a signed side track to Marions Lookout, harsh weather has pruned all the plants to a maximum two metres. The track beaches you at the much-photographed shingle boatshed (see point 3 on map) on Dove Lake's shore. Many park visitors tread the few hundred metres from the car park to here so it's often busy with comings and goings.

You've got an easy run home from here: inland to a junction, right, and then along the shore to the car park.

LEFT: *Boardwalk hugs Dove Lake's shore;* **TOP RIGHT:** *Slender rice flowers add to the show;* **BOTTOM RIGHT:** *Crinkle-cut fagus (deciduous beech) leaves are everywhere*

CENTRAL HIGHLANDS
47 DOVE LAKE HIGH

Walk:	11km loop
Time required:	4–5 hours
Best time:	Clear mild day. Conditions can deteriorate severely even on sunny summer days; the visitor centre posts weather forecasts.
Grade:	Moderate (track rough in places, some steep sections)
Environment:	Alpine plains, tarns, dolerite formations, mountains, heathland
Best map:	This one or TASMAP's *Cradle Mountain Day Walk Map*
Toilets:	At Dove Lake car park, and a composting toilet at Kitchen Hut
Food:	The café adjoining Cradle Mountain Visitor Centre, 2km outside the park, is a good filling station; Cradle Mountain Lodge has bistro and restaurant meals.
Tips:	This walk passes the Cradle Mountain summit track, a 2–3 hour detour involving lots of clambering. There is no shelter so don't attempt in poor weather or if the top is clouded (often). A new village hub, including visitor centre, and new viewing shelter at Dove Lake are due for completion in early 2019.

Experience a natural high on this alternate Dove Lake loop, climbing to breathtaking lookouts and traversing Cradle Mountain's craggy north face.

Stony track zigzags across the plain towards Cradle Mountain

268 CENTRAL HIGHLANDS

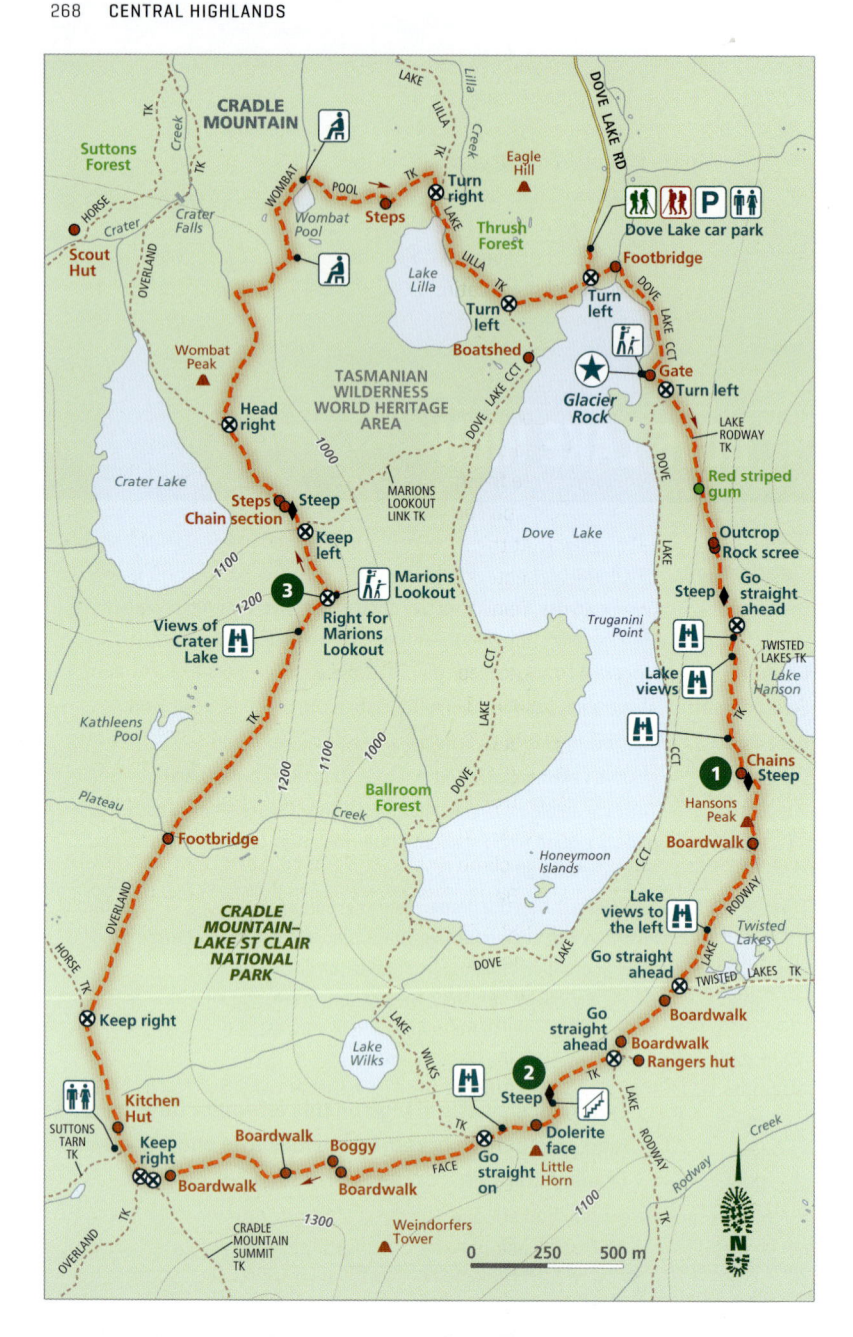

The Dove Lake circuit (see page 262) is the most popular walk in Cradle Mountain–Lake St Clair National park for good reason. This higher-altitude option offers more dramatic takes on the glaciated landscape and tougher terrain provides an escape route from the waves of walkers below.

Like the lower loop, this walk begins at Dove Lake car park, 8km from Cradle Mountain Visitor Centre, which is a 142km (1.75h) drive west of Launceston and 80km (1h) south-west of Devonport. Private-vehicle access to the lake is restricted during times of high visitation but shuttle buses (included in park entry) run year-round from the visitor centre.

Record your intentions in the walker registration shelter at Dove Lake, behind which you can fill your drink bottle with untreated rainwater. Then, forewarned that the whole day is one epic photo shoot, head downhill from the trailhead, on the east side of the car park and over a footbridge. About 600m clockwise around the lake, open a child-proof gate for the view from Glacier Rock. Then follow the pull of Cradle Mountain through button grass and tea tree.

Veer left for Lake Rodway at the next junction, onto an immediately rougher track up Mt Campbell. Red reflectors on poles show the way, through button grass, tea tree and eucalypts, none prettier than the red-striped alpine gum about 400m beyond the junction. Tasmanian Christmas bells splash red and yellow along here in summer. The people you'll probably spot on the cliff across Dove Lake are on Marions Lookout (1250m); that will be you in a few hours.

After skirting an outcrop and crossing a river of rocks the track steepens and becomes rockier but the footing remains sure, at least when dry.

Ignoring the Twisted Lakes track (a harder one-hour walk down to Lake Hanson and around Hansons Peak) you reach a saddle presenting views of Dove and Hanson lakes and the climb ahead up Hansons Peak (1185m). (The lake and peak are named after Bert Hanson, a 17-year old who died of exposure hereabouts in 1905 on a hunting trip.) From the saddle zigzag down into a gully and out again, to a cliff edge above Dove Lake.

Hauling on chains (see point 1 on map) gets you up the next short push to a stunning vista, Cradle Mountain looking even more impressive when wearing cloud. And the wow-factor only increases, with Barn Bluff, an Overland Track landmark (see page 308) appearing through the gap beyond Cradle Mountain. And still you're not at the walk's highest point!

Ignore the returning Twisted Lakes track and walk on in flowering heath that floods the mountains with colour in spring and early summer. Keep right at the next junction, onto the Face Track, passing a sign warning of 'geology at work' ahead. (The left-hand track goes to an emergency hut and Lake Rodway, an overnight hike.)

This is a stunning leg of the walk, across ground covered in scoparia, cushion plants and other heaths

Step and clamber steeply up Cradle Mountain to a protruding lip of rock (see point 2 on map). Then cross its north face, between dolerite fingers thrust upwards and Dove Lake below right. The tarn part-way down to Dove Lake is Lake Wilk and the track skirting it is a shortcut to the lower walk and car park (two hours). Stay high, with Cradle's dolerite crown on your left.

This is a stunning leg, with alternate boggy and rocky ground covered in button grass, spiky scoparia (that produces candle-like red, pink or cream flowers), green cushion plants and sculptural pandani, the world's tallest heath, whose strappy leaves are corkscrewed as if by a curling wand.

In good weather you'll start to see figures on the Cradle Mountain summit track to your left and soon after reach the track junction. Scaling Cradle Mountain (1545m) involves lots of clambering and takes an additional 2–3 hours (see Cradle Mountain Summit page 282).

Fifty metres beyond the junction, the Face Track runs into the Overland Track. Turn right towards Kitchen Hut, a stone-and-timber emergency and day-use shelter built in 1939 and extended in 1974. There's also a composting toilet.

Boarding and stone-slab steps enable you to stretch your legs beyond Kitchen Hut but don't rush it. Appreciate your inconsequence in this exposed environment. Even on warm days wind can howl here, knocking you off the boardwalk, and wintry conditions develop from nowhere. Plant life hugs the ground.

A lone button-grass seed head makes a perfect support for a spider's web

Keep right towards Dove Lake car park at the next junction; the alternative track, to Ronny Creek via Horse Track (2 hours), is described in the Cradle Mountain Summit walk (see page 282). Boardwalk, stepping-stone logs that rock in bogs, and rocky track lead to Marions Lookout (see point 3 on map), a natural grandstand looking over Dove Lake, Cradle Mountain and your route to here.

Ronny Creek parking area (the departure point for the Overland Track) comes into view as you leave Marions. Crater Lake then appears from deep, rocky folds.

Take in the view from the lookout at the next junction before heading left for all car parks. A steep ridge-top track brings you to a precipitous descent strung with chains that puts gravely beautiful Crater Lake directly below (ice, rather than fire, shaped its walls).

At the next junction you could take the steep, right-hand shortcut to Dove Lake and car park (a time-saver if you're late for a shuttle bus), but the more scenic left-hand option is recommended: down steps to taller scrub on a saddle between lakes and right at the next junction for Dove Lake via Wombat 'Poo' (some joker has blanked out the 'l').

Elevated boarding fringes Wombat Pool and twisted pines frame golden water and Cradle Mountain, peering over the hill behind. Tread timber steps away from this pool and down again through shapely pink-brown eucalypts to larger Lake Lilla.

Turn right for Dove Lake car park at the next junction, cross a creek exiting Lake Lilla, and follow a rooted track along a shore crowded with gnarled banksias. Another short climb and you're on the low Dove Lake loop. Turn left (or detour right to the much-photographed boatshed) and, with Cradle Mountain behind you, return to the car park.

LEFT: Mountain rocket shoots with pink and white flowers; **RIGHT:** A hardy paper daisy thrives in the harsh conditions on the plateau

CENTRAL HIGHLANDS

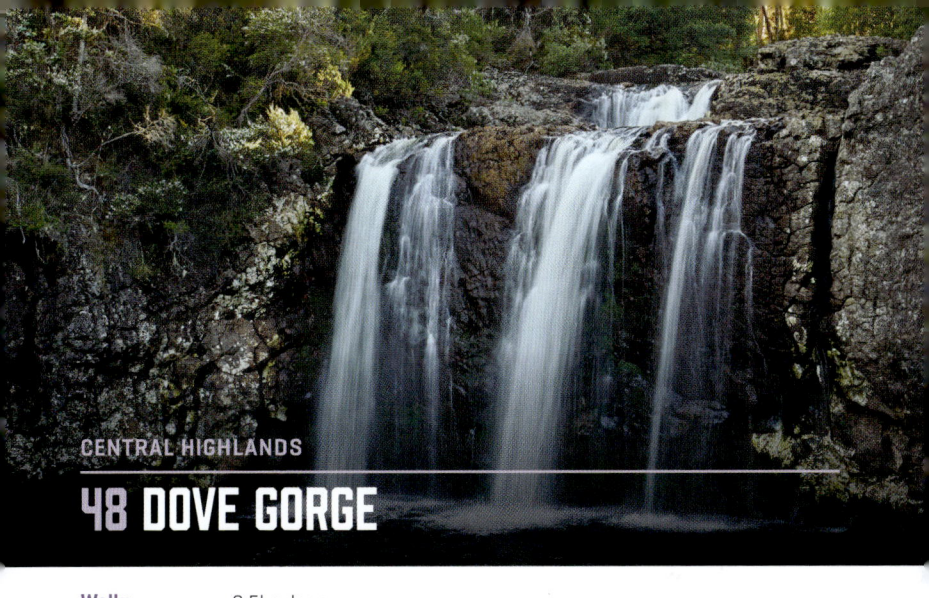

48 DOVE GORGE

Walk:	6.5km loop
Time required:	3 hours
Best time:	Any time except winter, when the park can be under snow
Grade:	Easy–moderate (the track becomes narrow and steep in places)
Environment:	Button-grass plains, rocky gorge, fern gullies
Best map:	This one
Toilets:	Flush toilets at the ranger station at beginning/end of the walk
Food:	Kick-start with a coffee and something to eat at the café at Cradle Mountain Visitor Centre, 2km outside the park boundary; Cradle Mountain Lodge, near the ranger station and interpretive centre, dishes up delicious bistro and restaurant fare.
Tips:	Wear footwear with good grip and ankle support. For a full-on Dove Gorge canyoning experience, book a place on a Dove Gorge adventure with Cradle Mountain Canyons (http://cradlemountaincanyons.com.au).

Lower your gaze from the above-ground wonders for a few hours and gorge yourself on this off-the-beaten-track walk.

Pencil Pine Falls drop into a wide pool

CENTRAL HIGHLANDS

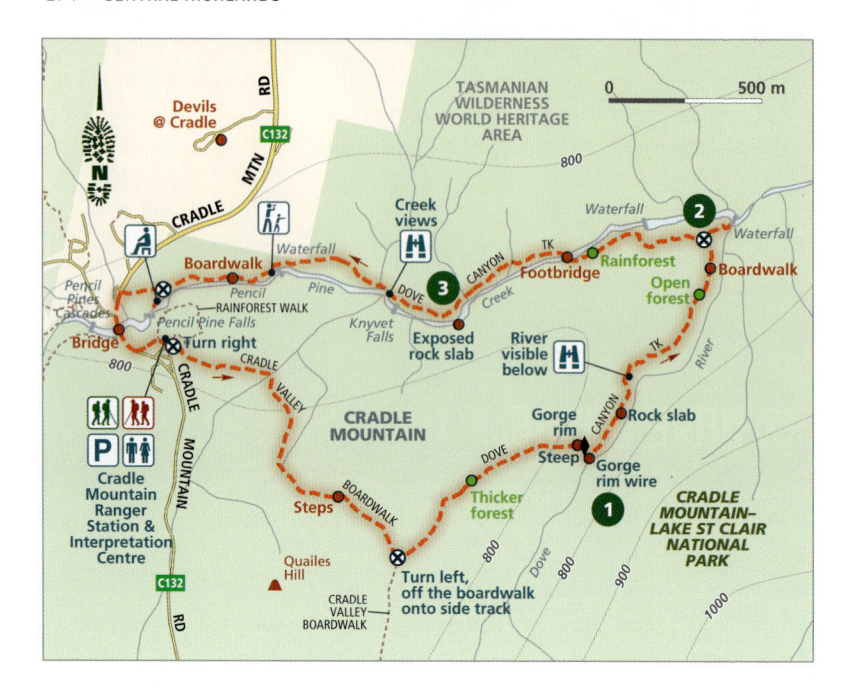

Cradle Mountain and the glaciated landscape over which the famous peak stands sentinel are the deserved stars of the show at the northern end of Cradle Mountain–Lake St Clair National Park. But not all the walks here involve rounding lakes and climbing mountains; you can delve into a different aspect of this dramatic country at Dove Gorge.

The Dove Gorge walk starts from the interpretive centre – it's well worth a visit – about 1.5km beyond the main car park and visitor centre. Head to the right of the buildings and pick up the Valley Boardwalk, following it right. You'll almost immediately enter lush myrtle forest strewn with mossy logs, emerging from that into drier eucalypts.

Having pushed through verdant button grass and tangled coral fern to a creek and climbed the other side, boardwalk approaches and then skirts left around rocky Quailes Hill, stepping up to a saddle; with the hill now on your right you come to a junction. Step off the boarding here onto a narrower unformed track signed for Dove Canyon (three hours) and marked with faded arrows on posts; keep an eye on the track markers ahead as you cross a rocky, scrubby patch.

(At the time of treading and writing, this walk was marked with a mix of arrows on posts, arrows on trees, and posts topped with orange paint. There were, though, more boards going in and the signage may also be upgraded.)

Walk on between button-grass plain and dense eucalypt scrub, passing elegant mature alpine gums with rough collars and smoother upper trunks striped grey, yellow and pink. The track can be boggy in places through here and there's parallel boarding in the open and rocky, rooty track through islands of trees. You may encounter canyoners along the way, adventurers headed for or returning from a more intense Dove Gorge experience. You enter taller, lusher forest where a track littered with tiny, papery beech leaves passes a lichen-covered rock wrapped in the roots of a tree growing atop it.

About 700m from the track junction you step from forest onto the rocky lip of a 50m-deep quartzite gorge cut by the Dove River, which is fed by Dove Lake (see page 262). You can't see the bottom but can hear the water below. A steep, rocky descent lands you on narrow track even closer to the edge with a wire strung across between you and danger (see point 1 on map). Staying this side of the wire but leaning out, you can see down the canyon's sheer walls, almost to the bottom. The water is loud but still hidden in shadow below.

The track continues along that wired lip before retreating from the brink and making a rough but reasonably flat passage through a patch of pretty rainforest, where the opposite gorge wall is barely visible through the trees. This part of the walk is a good sampler for the rougher forest sections of the Overland Track (see page 303).

Descending again, the track narrows across a steep slope, runs along a huge slab of damp rock fringed with dead foliage and traverses a rainforest-clad slope running down to the Dove River, now visible below. Climbing again, away from the water, the track disgorges you into light-flushed tea tree, and here the going flattens out for half an hour or so. Having worked through the edge of a patch of fagus (deciduous beech) forest, you find yourself on a hillside covered in tea tree, with rainforest below and button grass nodding its head against the skyline. Watch for skinks darting across the boardwalk.

Where the boarding swings left, about 200m out of the forest, look for a faint footpad on the right and a couple of old marker posts. This is an unmaintained and in-places overgrown 300m-return detour down to the confluence of the Dove River and Pencil Pine Creek (see point 2 on map). You'll need to push through coarse scrub but there's a small waterfall at the junction and it's a lovely place to soak your feet, paddle or just rest on the rocks.

After the detour, tread boardwalk and rocky track through scrubby heath to the sound of Pencil Pine Creek. Dropping downhill again, you'll see a small waterfall and a cliff through the trees to your right, with native pines bristling on the edge. The creek is heard more than seen as you wander through tea tree and occasional patches of rainforest, but then the track descends to a footbridge fording the creek between pretty rapids and a tranquil pool.

Clear of the bridge, stone-inlaid gravel track passes a monster wombat hole (left), steps up to boardwalk and follows the contours of a coral fern-covered hill tipping down to Pencil Pine Creek. Across the water there's a great slab of exposed rock (see point 3 on map) and above it an expanse of button grass edged with eucalypts.

Further on, rainforest closes around you again but beautiful Knyvet Falls shows through the trees, left, and soon after, you reach a lookout atop the cascade. Knyvet Falls is a popular short walk from the interpretation centre and boardwalk runs most of the way back to the car park from here, upstream through rainforest, past infant rapids and shallows where you can cool your feet or just sit and contemplate the leaf patterns.

Ignore stairs climbing right and follow the boardwalk to its end at Pencil Pine Falls, which drops six or seven metres into a wide plunge pool. Retreat, climb the stairs and tread boardwalk cutting through button grass towards Cradle Mountain Lodge.

At the main park road, cross and walk down the other side to the bridge. Across the bridge, which presents a full-frontal view of a set of cascades immediately upstream, re-cross the road at the pedestrian crossing to the interpretive centre car park to finish.

LEFT: *The walks snake through mossy forest;* **RIGHT:** *Follow the boardwalk and track markers*

CENTRAL HIGHLANDS
49 LAKES LOOP

Walk:	7.3km loop
Time required:	3 hours
Best time:	Mild, sunny day
Grade:	Easy
Environment:	Button-grass moor, waterfalls, eucalypts, alpine lakes
Best map:	This one
Toilets:	Flushing toilets at Dove Lake car park
Food:	The café at Cradle Mountain Visitor Centre, 2km outside the park boundary, serves coffee and snacks; for something more substantial check out the bistro and restaurant menus at Cradle Mountain Lodge, opposite the ranger station and interpretive centre.
Tips:	This walk offers great wombat-spotting, so if conditions allow, walk later in the afternoon so you finish at dusk, when the furry marsupials are at their most active.

You'll hardly raise a sweat on this lasso-shaped walk grouping several of the pretty lakes and tarns in Cradle Mountain's shadow.

Crater Lake reflects the glaciated cliffs enfolding it

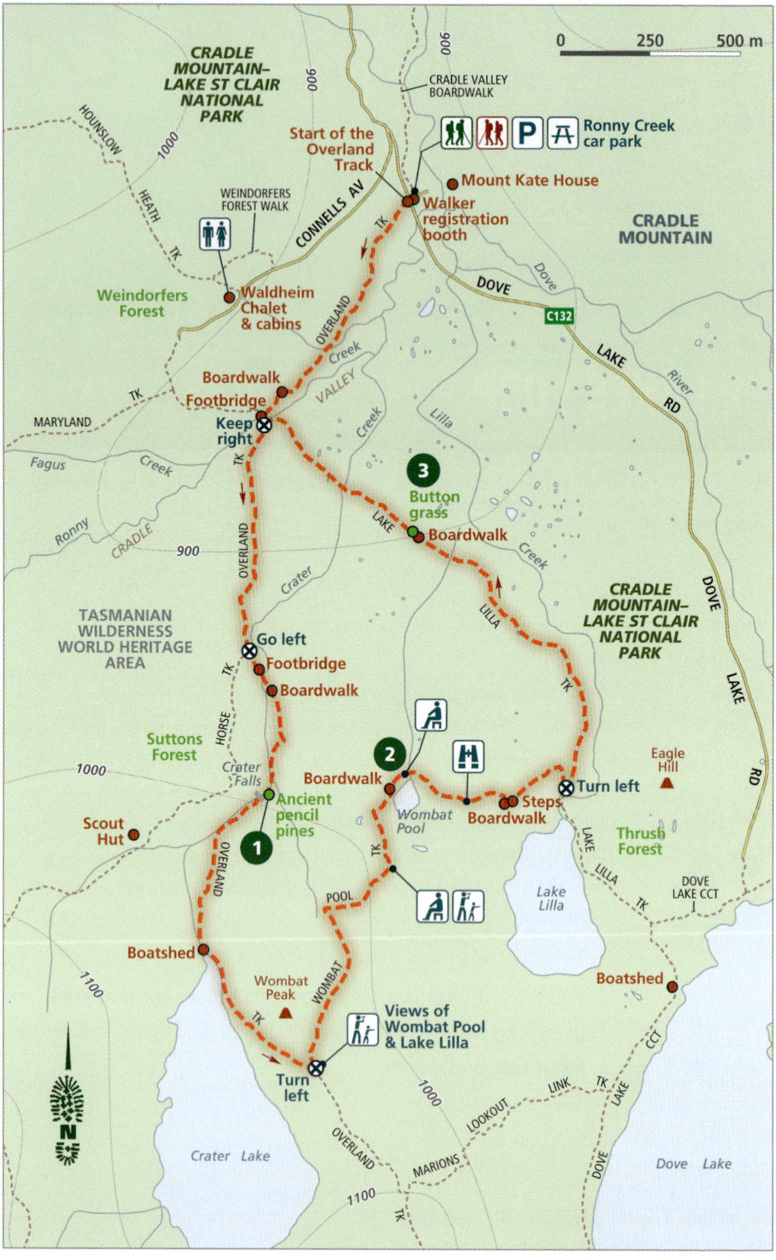
0 250 500 m
CRADLE MOUNTAIN–LAKE ST CLAIR NATIONAL PARK
CRADLE VALLEY BOARDWALK
Ronny Creek car park
Start of the Overland Track
Mount Kate House
Walker registration booth
CRADLE MOUNTAIN
WEINDORFERS FOREST WALK
CONNELLS AV
HOUNSLOW HEATH TK
Weindorfers Forest
Waldheim Chalet & cabins
DOVE RD
C132
LAKE RD
Dove River
OVERLAND TK
Creek
VALLEY
Boardwalk
Footbridge
Keep right
MARYLAND TK
Fagus Creek
Lilla Creek
3
Button grass
Boardwalk
LAKE LILLA TK
Ronny
CRADLE
900
1000
1100
Crater Creek
TASMANIAN WILDERNESS WORLD HERITAGE AREA
CRADLE MOUNTAIN–LAKE ST CLAIR NATIONAL PARK
DOVE LAKE RD
Go left
Footbridge
Boardwalk
HORSE TK
Suttons Forest
Crater Falls
Ancient pencil pines
1
Scout Hut
2
Boardwalk
Wombat Pool
Steps
Boardwalk
Turn left
Eagle Hill
Thrush Forest
LAKE LILLA TK
DOVE LAKE CCT
Lake Lilla
POOL TK
WOMBAT
Wombat Peak
Boatshed
Boatshed
Views of Wombat Pool & Lake Lilla
Turn left
Crater Lake
OVERLAND TK
MARIONS LOOKOUT LINK TK
LAKE CCT
DOVE LAKE
Dove Lake
N

Cradle Mountain–Lake St Clair National Park doesn't only reveal its treasures to those embarking on mountain climbs and multi-day walks. This lovely lakes loop gives you a taste of the park plus bragging rights that you've 'walked the Overland Track' – if only for three kilometres!

The fun kicks off at Ronny Creek car park, 6km from Cradle Mountain Visitor Centre and 148km (allow 1.75 hrs by car) west of Launceston via Deloraine and Sheffield. Private-vehicle access to the car parks is restricted at peak times so if in doubt ride a shuttle bus (included in park entry) which run year-round between the visitor centre and Ronny Creek.

Sign the walkers' register and cross the road to the boardwalk, perhaps stopping for a photo with the cut-out metal Overland Track sign. As you tread boardwalk to the bridge fording Ronny Creek, watch for wombats, which emerge from tunnels in the hillside and valley floor early morning and late afternoon to graze, chase one another and leave distinctive cuboid scat on the boardwalk. (These chunky marsupials have backward-facing pouches, so that they don't fill with soil when digging!)

Ignore the track coming down from the trees up to your right: this descends from Waldheim Chalet, a re-creation of the home and guesthouse built by Austrian-born, amateur botanist Gustar Weindorfer and his Australian wife, Kate, in the early 20th century to introduce people to the wonders of the Cradle Mountain region and champion its protection. Instead cross the bridge to another junction. The left-hand track will bring you back to here from Lake Lilla, so keep straight on towards Crater Lake on the Overland Track: uphill through

Mount Kate House overlooks Ronny Creek car park

Boardwalk cuts through button-grass moor back to Ronny Creek

button grass and a lacy carpet of coral fern into alpine gums, shrubby tea tree and bushes festooned with red and pink mountain berries. The going is fairly easy despite a steady climb.

Up gorgeous Crater Creek, which burbles to your left, you pass the Horse Track, on the right, one of several routes down from Cradle Plateau (see Cradle Mountain Summit page 282). Keep left, crossing the creek and continuing through eucalypts. The track then plunges into rainforest along Crater Creek, boardwalk stepping up the thickly treed gully through pandani and sassafras to Crater Falls. The three trees on the platform overlooking the falls are ancient pencil pines (see point 1 on map).

Further upstream, past another small cascade, the track swings left and out of the gully but continues beside the creek to a weathered boatshed on Crater Lake's shore. Despite its conical appearance, which earned the lake its name, Crater Lake is a deep glacial bowl rather than volcanic. Morning sun and calm weather gifts reflections of the 200m cliffs and their cloaking fagus whose concertina leaves turn yellow and red in autumn before dropping.

The track then pulls away from Crater Lake and climbs up onto a saddle. At the junction here, the Overland Track heads right to Marions Lookout and Cradle Mountain but we're going left. First though, cross to the lookout platform directly opposite for a panoramic view of Wombat Pool and larger Lake Lilla down to the left, and higher ridges that can be explored on other walks.

Now head down the saddle, past a smaller tarn and towards Wombat Pool (see point 2 on map). Elevated boardwalk wraps clockwise around this exquisite toffee-coloured tarn, gnarled pencil pines framing views of water and mountains. A platform projecting over the water is a perfect pitch for lunch or just a break. Boardwalk steps up from Wombat Pool into tea tree and down to larger Lake Lilla, through alpine gums with smooth pink-brown trunks; Cradle Mountain is watching from over a nearer hill.

Turn left at the next junction, beside Lake Lilla, towards Ronny Creek, and meander across a slight rise bottoming in a creek gully. Look back occasionally at Cradle Mountain as you skirt lumps of exposed rock, and pass another tarn filled with tannin-stained water and inhabited by what sounds like a full orchestra of frogs.

Having now almost circled Wombat Peak (1105m) on your left, you cut through a button-grass moor (see point 3 on map) toward trees and the Waldheim chalets and cabins, visible ahead. Watch for the peak's namesake as you tread the last boarded descent to Ronny Creek, cross the bridge, and retrace your steps to the car park.

CENTRAL HIGHLANDS

50 CRADLE MOUNTAIN SUMMIT

Walk:	15.4km loop
Time required:	7–9 hours
Best time:	Clear, mild weather (snow-bound in winter)
Grade:	Hard
Environment:	Button grass and alpine moors, dolerite mountain, rainforest, waterfalls, tarns
Best map:	This one and TASMAP's *Cradle Mountain Day Walk Map & Notes 1:50,000*
Toilets:	A composting toilet at Kitchen Hut
Food:	Grab a coffee and snack from the café at the visitor centre, 2km outside the park; Cradle Mountain Lodge dishes up bistro and restaurant meals.
Tips:	Cradle Mountain provides no protection from extreme weather and summiting involves extensive clambering, so don't attempt this walk when poor weather is forecast. Be prepared for bad weather even on good-weather days. Only very experienced, well-prepared hikers should tackle it in snow.

Windswept moors that accentuate your insignificance and lookouts that curl your toes bookend the hand-over-hand climb to the top of Cradle Mountain.

Cradle Mountain is a visual force

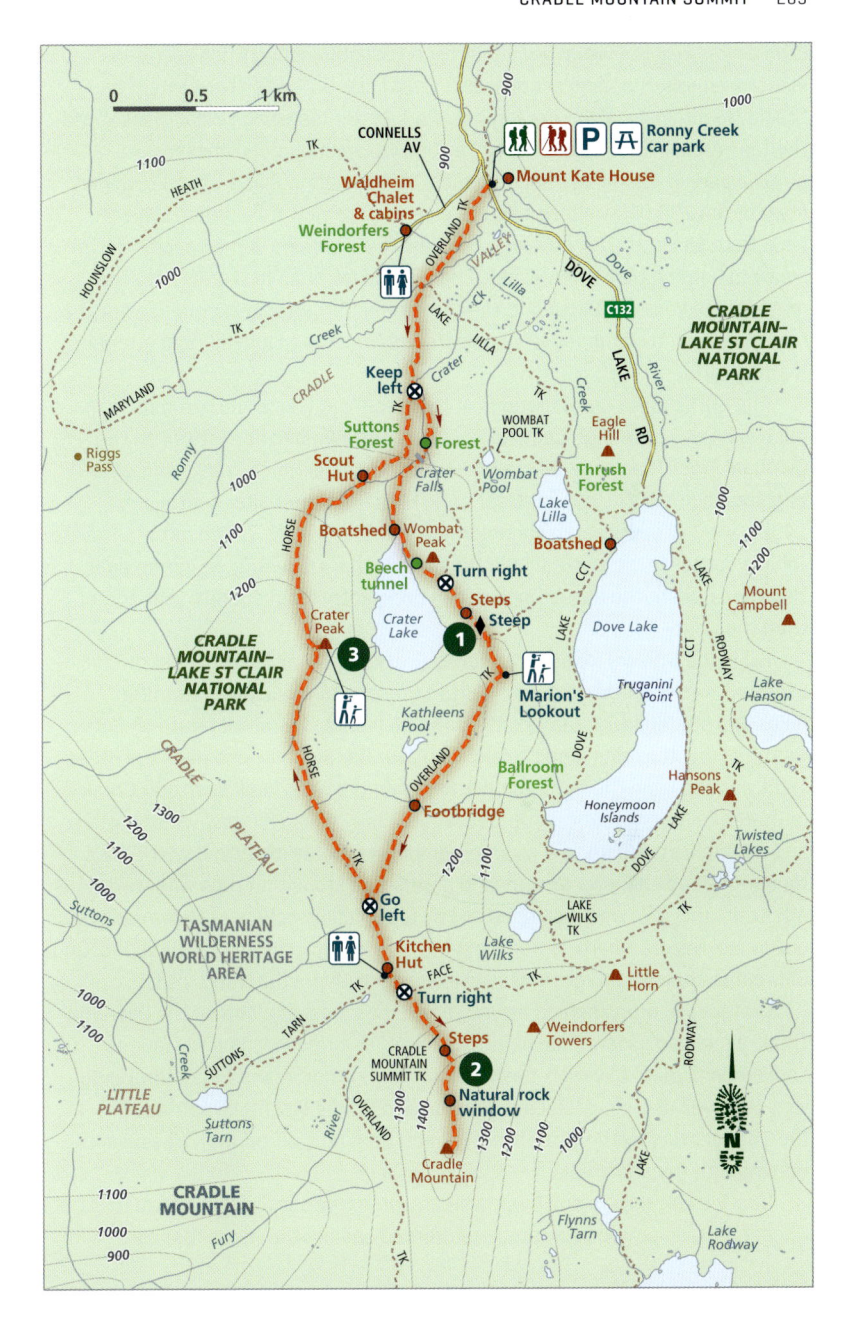

CRADLE MOUNTAIN SUMMIT 283

Cradle Mountain is a visual force that becomes intimidating when secreted in storm clouds. Standing sentinel over Dove Lake, at the northern extent of Cradle Mountain-Lake St Clair National Park, in the Tasmanian Wilderness World Heritage Area, it lures hikers like currawongs to an unguarded backpack.

The park is Tasmania's second-most visited national park after Freycinet. Most of the 200,000 visitors a year are content to view the Jurassic dolerite peak from easier tracks, however, considerable numbers come specifically or solely to bag the park's namesake, and in good weather you rarely have the mountain to yourself. Getting to the top is an unforgettable experience but the hand-over-hand clamber demands surefootedness and a head (and stomach) for drop-offs.

One of the many combinations of trails that get you to the summit track (also see Dove Lake High page 267), the route described here starts on the Overland Track (see page 303) and returns down the Horse Track. Your peak-bagging begins at Ronny Creek car park, 6km from the visitor centre and 148km west of Launceston via Deloraine and Sheffield (1.75 hrs by car). Private vehicle access to car parks within the national park is restricted during peak visitation but shuttle buses (included in park-entry fees) operate year-round from the visitor centre.

Fill in the walkers' register at Ronny Creek and set off south-west on the Overland Track boardwalk across button grass moor drilled with wombat holes and studded with remarkable pandani plants, the tallest heath on Earth, wearing curly topknots. Keep straight on over Ronny Creek and pass the Horse Track coming in on the right about 1.5km into the walk. Walk up Crater Creek to Crater Falls, in verdant rainforest, where many hikers fill their water bottles, and continue upstream to a weathered boatshed knee-deep in Crater Lake's tannin-stained shallows. Wrapped in prehistoric stone that runs with waterfalls after rain, this lake was fashioned not by the volcanic action its name suggests but by ice. Needle-sharp, leafed scoparia shrubs grow metres tall here and King Billy pines, their bright-green leaves like plastic, share the water's edge.

Crater Lake drops behind as you tackle the steepest climb on the Overland Track, a chained ascent (see point 1 on map) to a ridge leading to Marions Lookout. A popular day-walk destination, Marions commands a jaw-dropping view of Dove Lake, elevated Lake Hanson and Cradle Mountain, named in the 19th century by the Van Diemen's Land Company purportedly because it resembles a miner's cradle.

Rocky track, pavers and boardwalk traverse treeless Cradle Plateau to Kitchen Hut, an emergency refuge reinforced against the winds that can

CRADLE MOUNTAIN SUMMIT 285

Climbing Cradle Mountain gives you a natural high

roar through here, knocking hikers off the boarding. Having passed the other end of Horse Track about 400m before Kitchen Hut, turn left onto Face Track 150m after it. The Cradle Mountain climb starts 50m along. (For more detailed description of the walk to Kitchen Hut see the Overland Track, page 303.)

Don't be fooled: what appears to be the top of Cradle Mountain isn't. The 300m altitude gain over the next 1.5km involves much more clambering than is obvious from here and many people take longer than the two hours on the sign. But if the forecast is good and the summit is clear – let's go! (Pull out if not.)

Step out on old timbers interspersed with boggy areas, through cushion plants, pineapple grass and scoparia. As you gently ascend, enjoy the expansive view (left) of Dove Lake and encircling ridges – and (right) over plunging valleys, cliffs, and ranges. Several other walking tracks are now visible.

Follow marker poles right from a Summit Track sign, across rock and scree and slate-like layers. The full-body workout starts about 100m into this traverse: clambering up past a natural window (right) (*see* point 2 on map) and through classic dolerite columns, standing, toppled and camouflaged in orange, grey, black and brown lichens. There are numerous big step-ups

You can't help but feel insignificant in this country – and completely at the mercy of its whims

and places where it can be easier to crab walk and/or slide on your backside. Columnar cliffs and rock-framed views from a narrow saddle still your feet before the track descends and makes the final push onto the summit plateau.

As you walk, you will come to appreciate Gustav Weindorfer's thinking, when he said, after scaling Cradle Mountain with his wife, Kate, in 1910: 'This must be a national park for the people for all time.' The natural stonemasonry and glaciated setting (which you'll traverse for about an hour) inspired the pair to champion this part of Tasmania. A toposcope (orientation table) on Cradle Mountain's highest point (hard right as you reach the plateau) identifies natural landmarks.

What goes up must come down – so when time dictates, retrace your steps to the Horse Track, beyond Kitchen Hut, and veer left, on honeycomb-like moulded walkways that are hard on the eye but forgiving underfoot. Beneath, you can see old, rotted boards.

Barn Bluff sits to your left as the track crosses treeless moorland dotted with tarns; you can't help but feel insignificant in this country and completely at the mercy of its whims. Cradle Mountain disappears behind and then reappears as you navigate a broad creek gully. From this rise it's downhill through tarns, skirting rocky rises and following a creek gully that carries your gaze across range upon range.

The Horse Track passes by a grove of remarkable trees whose stunted stature – none are more than 1.2m high – belie their age-twisted trunks. Walk on, noting the swirled and linearly cracked rock underfoot.

About 1.5km after leaving the Overland Track you come to a sign facing away from you (most people walk the Horse Track in the reverse direction). Take the five-minute detour right to Crater Peak (see point 3 on map) for a gobsmacking cliff-edge view over Crater Lake, the Marions Lookout track and Cradle Mountain, peeking over the grey cliff immediately right.

The walk is all downhill now, and Ronny Creek Valley and car park appear. Waldheim Hut shelters in the pine forest on the valley's north-west slope. Dove Lake comes into frame on the right as you descend – through rafts of scoparia and wildflowers (in spring). The dense heath shrubs here shield wildlife from weather and aerial predators and you will probably walk along to the chatter of hidden birds.

Wind has fashioned topiary here too, inhibiting growth on the windward side of lone pines and sweeping their remaining branches into horizontal mohawks. Moving on, you'll see the first sizable trees since Crater Lake, then skirt a grove of fagus (deciduous beech) trees and King Billy pines.

Descending a creek gully into button grass you pass the Baden Powell Scout Lodge (http://thescouthut.com.au), built to commemorate the 50th anniversary of the Scout movement and the centenary of the birth of its founder, Lord Baden-Powell; Scout groups, Scout families and the public can book beds here. Ignoring a footpad going right, continue towards Waldheim and Ronny Creek, following marker posts steeply through swathes of honey myrtle awash with fluffy pink flowers in spring and summer and down into striped snow gums.

Flatter track cuts through open eucalypt forest and button grass to the Overland Track. Turn left and watch for echidnas and wombats (particularly late in the day) as you re-enter Ronny Creek Valley. Having crossed the creek, tread the boardwalk back to your car.

LEFT: *Snow can fall at any time on Cradle Mountain;* **TOP RIGHT:** *A rock window gives you a breathtaking view over the glaciated park;* **BOTTOM RIGHT:** *Look out for wombats feeding around Ronny Creek valley*

CENTRAL HIGHLANDS
51 SHADOW LAKE

Walk:	14km loop
Time required:	4–5 hours
Best time:	Mild, sunny day
Grade:	Easy–moderate
Environment:	Eucalypt forest, cool temperate rainforest, button-grass moor, sub-alpine lake
Best map:	This one or TASMAP's *Lake St Clair Day Walk Map*
Toilets:	Flushing toilets at Lake St Clair Visitor Centre
Food:	Variety of snacks, food and beverages in the visitor centre café; scrumptious burgers at the Hungry Wombat Café at Derwent Bridge, 5km back, on the Lyell Hwy
Tips:	This is a great family walk, which climbs only 270m. Be alert for snakes, particularly in warm weather when they may curl up on the track to catch the sun.

This half-day loop to a beautiful sub-alpine lake is a feast of forests, mountains and moors.

Mt Rufus is the backdrop for this lazy loop from Lake St Clair

CENTRAL HIGHLANDS

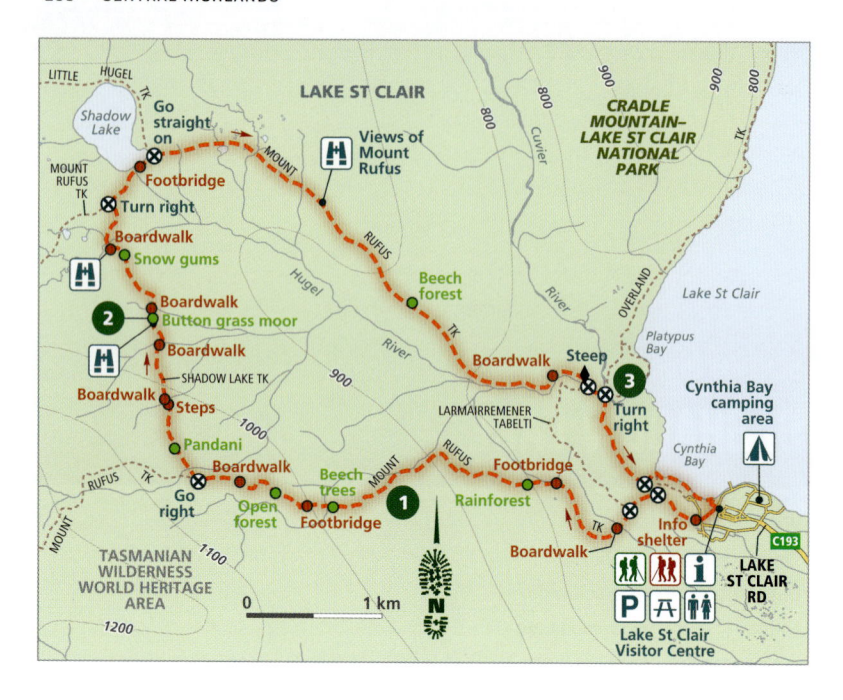

Many people know Lake St Clair as the southern end of the Overland Track (see page 303), but Australia's deepest lake (maximum 160m), in Tasmania's Central Highlands, is a walking destination in its own right. It's a trailhead for pedestrian outings from an hour-long lakeside stroll to overnight hikes in the rugged Du Cane Range, such as The Labyrinth (see page 294).

The half-day Shadow Lake loop introduces three distinct habitats: highland eucalypt forest, cool temperate rainforest and moorland. You can tread it in either direction but clockwise gives you the steepest climbs early and an easy run home.

The park is two hours' drive from Hobart via the sometimes-windy Lyell Hwy. Turn north for the lake at Derwent Bridge. Walk through the visitor centre to where all the walks are signed left and the lake ferry (Ida Clair) to the right. Swing left and walk past huts and staff quarters to an information shelter.

Initially following the Mt Rufus route, tread wide, flat track to a junction. Turn left for Shadow Lake (five hours), following track and boardwalk through eucalypt forest, button grass and tea tree. A marginal climb brings you to the Leeawuleena 'tabelti', a one-hour Aboriginal cultural loop, coming in on the right, 600m into the walk. (The Larmairremener people, of the central Big River Nation, call the lake Leeawuleena, meaning 'sleeping water'.)

Continue straight on, treading good but narrower track among banksias and tea tree, and boardwalk through paperbarks (melaleucas). How many different bird calls can you hear? Eleven of Tasmania's 12 endemic bird species have been recorded in Cradle Mountain–Lake St Clair National Park; it's also habitat for flame robins, pink robins and striated fieldwrens. The loud, swallowing noise often heard on this walk is the yellow-cheeked wattlebird, unique to Tasmania. Watch for green parrots too.

Obvious but also marked with occasional arrows and reflectors, the track dips into cool temperate rainforest gullies crammed with ground ferns, grey-and-white trunked sassafras trees and myrtle beech, which scatter confetti-like leaves in your path. In drier forest, look out for mountain berries (autumn and winter) and needle bush with creamy, curlicue flowers. The finger-like roots of a fallen giant about 2.5km into the walk reach out from a woody core embedded with clay and stones.

Fairly rocky in places, but still navigable, the track now makes several steep but short ascents. Watch for a magnificent eucalypt that splits into four trunks about a metre above the ground about 3.5km into the walk (see point 1 on map); the trunks appear scratched, its peeling bark revealing pink beneath.

Fallen trees line the approach to Shadow Lake

Soon after, orange arrows mark a short clamber up through rocks and trees shaggy with lichen and moss.

Having crossed a creek and climbed natural root steps that are slippery when wet, arrows keep you on the main track through a beech gully littered with fallen logs. Open forest then shows you a ridge through branches.

This forested ridgeline ends ahead as Mt Rufus and a more energetic extension to this walk puts you up top for views over mountains and lakes and into Franklin–Gordon Wild Rivers National Park. Turn right at the Mt Rufus track junction, almost 5km into the walk, and continue among heath shrubs and eucalypts, including stylish, striped snow gums. Beyond a creek you cross on stepping stones you'll find yourself among pandani (the world's tallest heath), with leathery leaves ending in curls, and scoparia, a spiky shrub which produces profuse candle-like summer flower spikes in every shade from white to red. Slender rice flower shrubs produce pretty heads of pink-tinged white flowers most of the year.

The track navigates gullies, boardwalks, boggy areas, and more beech forest before offering another look at Mt Rufus and, clockwise, Mt Hugel's indented dolerite profile. Heading towards Hugel, tread boardwalk across a button-grass moor (*see point 2 on map*) and then walk along its edge. The track briefly pulls away from the moor and through snow gums before cutting another corner of moor.

Climb slightly now, water showing between native pines, beech and gum trees, and pass the Mt Rufus extension returning on the left. Rooty track through beech forest leads to Shadow Lake, its bank and shallows strewn with fallen trees. The track heads east along the lake, footpads leading to waterside rocks on which you can sit and lunch looking at a cinematic dolerite-peak backdrop.

Having crossed a creek emptying out of the lake you come to another junction. If you have time, turn left for Forgotten Lake, 30 minutes west of Shadow Lake. Or walk on.

Visitor centre-bound now, the track is rocky in places but fairly flat. It passes through banksias, juvenile tea tree, moor and clusters of snow gums. Just past one magnificent specimen, on the right, and opposite a lumpy dead tree, there's a pretty wetland, behind which rises Mt Rufus.

A gentle descent takes you from snow gums to beech forest where there's no alternative to getting your boots muddy (or at least none that won't increase track damage). These damper conditions promote the growth of fungi, including beautiful, pink, coral fungus.

Still descending, you find yourself walking in more open eucalypts to the burble of running water – the Hugel River, down to your right. The track veers away from the river but descends steeply back into beech forest above the water with a footbridge visible below. Stop on the bridge and watch the river run over the rocky bed.

Continue along the other side to where the Leeawuleena tabelti (Aboriginal Cultural walk) comes in and keep left towards Watersmeet, where the Hugel and Cuvier rivers converge (*see* point 3 on map). Crossing the bridge below the confluence would start you on the Overland Track. It's also the way to Platypus Bay, on Lake St Clair. (The Platypus Bay walk circuit adds 30 minutes to this walk but it will be worth it if you spot one of these remarkable monotremes.)

Remaining this side of the Hugel, which runs into Lake St Clair, gives you an easy walk back to the visitor centre via the lake. A vehicle-wide compacted gravel track climbs through sassafras, beech, silver wattles and tall eucalypts, some metres in diameter. Here too are Tasmanian waratahs, with elongated leaves, and red spider flowers in spring.

Turn left at the next junction, for the visitor centre via the lake, and walk through a camping area to the lake. Built in 1940 as part of the state's hydroelectricity scheme, the lone industrial building seeming to float 300m offshore across the water is now the luxury Pumphouse Point accommodation.

Stroll along the water's edge, towards the ferry jetty, with the lake lapping metres from your feet. Steps at the end of the beach lead up to the visitor centre.

TOP LEFT: *Mountain-berry bushes in fruit;* **RIGHT:** *A splendid old eucalypt;* **BOTTOM LEFT:** *Myrtle beech leaves create lacy patterns*

CENTRAL HIGHLANDS
52 THE LABYRINTH

Walk:	30km out-and-back
Time required:	3 days
Best time:	Mild, clear weather (snow bound in winter)
Grade:	Moderate
Environment:	Lakes, tarns, rainforest, eucalypt forest, glacial valleys, alpine plains, dolerite mountains, wildflowers
Best map:	TASMAP's *St Clair 1:50,000*
Toilets:	Flush toilets at Lake St Clair Visitor Centre; composting toilets at Narcissus Hut and Pine Valley Hut.
Food:	Café and restaurant food and drinks are available from the café within the Lake St Clair Visitor Centre; head to Derwent Bridge, on the main road outside the park, for a burger at the Hungry Wombat café.
Tips:	Track markings beyond Pine Valley are limited and within the Labyrinth proper there are only occasional cairns. You should be comfortable following unsigned tracks to do this walk safely. At a push, Pine Valley Hut can accommodate 24 friendly people. Hut space cannot be booked, however, and can fill fast.

Explore and escape the Labyrinth on a hike into the heart of glaciated mountain country.

The conical Minotaur dominates the Lake St Clair view from the Gap

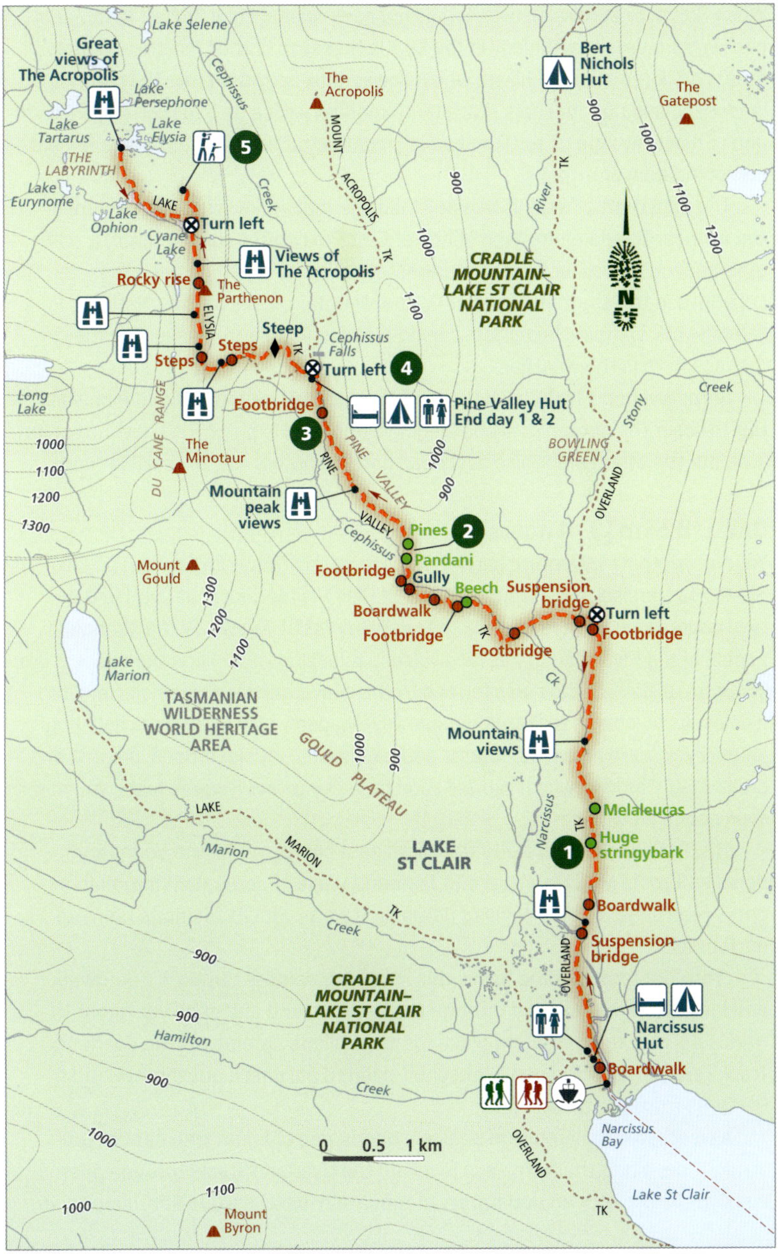
Great views of The Acropolis
Lake Selene
Lake Persephone
Lake Tartarus
Lake Elysia
THE LABYRINTH
Lake Eurynome
Lake Ophion
Cyane Lake
LAKE
Turn left
5
Cephissus
Creek
The Acropolis
MOUNT ACROPOLIS TK
Views of The Acropolis
Rocky rise
The Parthenon
ELYSIA
Steep
Steps
Steps
Cephissus Falls
Turn left
4
Long Lake
Footbridge
Pine Valley Hut
End day 1 & 2
3
DU CANE RANGE
The Minotaur
PINE VALLEY
Mountain peak views
Pines
2
Pandani
Gully
Footbridge
Beech
Suspension bridge
Boardwalk
Footbridge
Footbridge
Turn left
Footbridge
Mount Gould
Lake Marion
TASMANIAN WILDERNESS WORLD HERITAGE AREA
GOULD PLATEAU
Mountain views
LAKE MARION TK
LAKE ST CLAIR
Melaleucas
Huge stringybark
1
Boardwalk
Suspension bridge
Narcissus
OVERLAND TK
Narcissus Hut
Boardwalk
CRADLE MOUNTAIN–LAKE ST CLAIR NATIONAL PARK
Hamilton Creek
Narcissus Bay
Lake St Clair
Mount Byron
0 0.5 1 km
Bert Nichols Hut
The Gatepost
River
CRADLE MOUNTAIN–LAKE ST CLAIR NATIONAL PARK
N
Creek
Stony
BOWLING GREEN
OVERLAND
Ck

When Surveyor General George Frankland gave several Lake St Clair landmarks names from Greek mythology in the 1830s (because of their 'classical beauty') other cartographers and hikers who followed took up the theme. The result is a landscape and national park dotted with monikers such as Hyperion (the Titan god of heavenly light), Eros (the god of sexual attraction) and Ossa (the female personification of rumour).

The Labyrinth of legend was an elaborate maze-like structure designed by the artificer Daedalus for King Minos of Crete to confine the Minotaur, a half-man half-bull monster, who was ultimately killed by Athenian hero Theseus. The Labyrinth in the southern folds of Cradle Mountain–Lake St Clair National Park is a network of alpine lakes, ice-carved plains and dolerite peaks. The major menace here is the weather.

Some Overland Track hikers extend their journey by detouring to Pine Valley Hut to scale The Acropolis (a challenging climb) and explore The Labyrinth at its foot, but the three-night hike described here is another way of tackling them.

DAY 1: 9.5km (3–4 hours)

Your labyrinthine adventure begins with a ferry ride (must be booked) up Lake St Clair to Narcissus Hut from the Lake St Clair Visitor Centre at Cynthia Bay, two-hours' drive from Hobart via the Lyell Hwy (A10). Known by the Aboriginal people of Big River Country as leeawuleena (sleeping water) and the deepest lake in Australia, Lake St Clair was formed by the convergence of three glaciers into a colossus of ice and rock that gouged a U-shaped valley. During the half-hour journey you learn about the forests and mountains – table-topped, pointed and crenelated – among which you will soon be walking; and if you're lucky, you might even spot a platypus.

The Traveller Range, along the lake's east shore, marks the boundary between Cradle Mountain–Lake St Clair and Walls of Jerusalem national parks (see page 318 for Walls of Jerusalem walk). Mount Olympus rears up on your left.

From the ferry landing below this imposing dolerite rampart, boardwalk and leaf-littered track lead through boggy heathland and eucalypt forest to Narcissus Hut, the gathering place for most hikers coming off the Overland Track (see page 303). Even if you don't need to go, check out the view of Mt Olympus from the toilet here.

A weathered wooden sign beside a handsome old gum tree directs you straight on, along the Narcissus River, on the Overland Track, through open eucalypt forest with an understory of mountain-berry shrubs and Tasmanian

Stepping down rough track to Cyane Lake in the Labyrinth

waratahs. The track offers views downstream to Olympus and upstream to mossy banks and soaring gum trees before pulling away from the water. Boardwalk crosses a swampy flat to cabbage gum woodland – note the very different foliage on the understory she-oaks, silver banksias and mountain needlebush – through which you walk to a one-person suspension bridge.

Across the Narcissus, the track continues through button-grass moor patched with coral fern where you get a good look at extraordinary peaks. You'll feel the temperature drop as the track skirts and then snakes through beech rainforest inhabited by some substantial trees and the stumps of more. Back in eucalypt forest, about 2km into the walk, you'll pass a huge gum-topped stringybark (see point 1 on map) with a collar of thick, fibrous bark and bulbous roots reaching across the track and up into bush pea and berry scrub. As you walk through smooth-barked, striped cabbage gums a kilometre on, The Acropolis rises to your left, some of its dolerite columns like figures on the ridge; you may even see snowdrifts.

Continue north on an undulating track, crossing creeks (one on a log cross-scored for more secure footing) among Tasmanian waratahs, some seven metres tall, to a track junction marked with a wooden sign, 4.5km into the walk. Turn left off the Overland Track towards Pine Valley, passing a couple of fallen cabbage gums whose root balls reveal that there's only a shallow layer of soil over the rock here. Soon after you'll cross the Narcissus on another one-person suspension bridge.

The walk to Pine Valley Hut climbs slightly over much of its length but you'll hardly notice until you tread it downhill back to Narcissus Hut on Day Three! Through alpine heath myrtles, whose summer flowers are like dustings of snow, and across a button-grass moor you reach a sturdy footbridge over Cephissus Creek; hikers used to cross the caramel-coloured water via the old scored fallen tree to the left and you could too. Continue through beautiful creek-side woodland with wobbly wire-meshed half-logs fording some boggy sections, with eucalypts, scoparia and pandani (some five metres tall) (see point 2 on map) crafting a fabulously textured wall between you and the water. Eagle-eyed hikers might spot orchids beside the track.

Having crossed back over Cephissus, the track becomes more rooted as you follow the creek valley. Rough track and boardwalk lead through giant pandani, celery top pines and a flotilla of variegated sassafras trunks into beautiful cool temperate rainforest. This is a shadow-filled world of mossy roots and fallen trees, myrtle beech and alpine yellow gums; the older tan bark of these magnificent eucalypts peels to reveal vivid-yellow, skin-smooth bark

THE LABYRINTH 299

TOP: *Turn left for the Labyrinth;* **LEFT:** *Textures and colours abound;* **MIDDLE RIGHT:** *Tasmanian waratahs splash red across the mountains in spring;* **BOTTOM RIGHT:** *Lichen rosettes adorn granite*

beneath. Mud reminds you that this is high-rainfall country and through-tree glimpses remind you that the focus of this walk is mountains not forest!

Having crossed Cephissus one more time (see point 3 on map), the track hugs the creek's curvaceous mossed banks to a wooden sign directing you 30m uphill to Pine Valley Hut (and tent platforms) in the shelter of myrtle beech, King Billy pines and pandani.

Within the hut there's a walker registration book that should be completed by all visitors, day and overnight.

DAY 2: 10.7km return (5–7 hours)

A sign just metres behind and north of Pine Valley Hut warns of fall risks on The Acropolis and The Labyrinth's unmarked tracks and alpine environment. Infrequent small cairns are the only route markers through the Labyrinth and it's easy to become disorientated, particularly in poor weather, so you must be well-prepared and experienced to explore it safely. Adventurers who proceed further along the track shortly reach a lichen-laced wooden sign pointing straight on for The Acropolis and left for The Labyrinth.

Turn left and cross a creek, following a track marked with orange arrows through lush rainforest, past a massive gum-topped stringybark and another toppled tree colonised by moss and lichen. The track climbs slowly and then turns sharply up a gully and you've got rocks and an uneven lattice of pencil pine roots underfoot as you work across the side of a hill.

About 800m from the hut, the track turns hard right and climbs a rocky creek bed (see point 4 on map). About 30m up, and short of the top, look for a cairn and an arrow pointing left, and a post with an arrow a few metres into the stunted beech forest. Step up and walk on, climbing slowly through tangled roots up the lower south-east slope of the (hidden) Parthenon, another Lake St Clair mountain name with Greek connections.

The track flattens out and works clockwise around the Parthenon – a huge edifice beside and above you – through hardier, scrubbier forest of waratahs, berry bushes, striped gums, beech and needlebush, with flat-topped Mt Olympus and Lake St Clair showing themselves to your left. About one kilometre from the creek bed the track climbs steeply up uneven natural rock steps for about 250m to a gap; enjoy the southerly view of the lake and encircling mountains from the small foot-worn patch near the top, because you'll lose this perspective for the next few hours. The conical peak to the south, on the Du Cane Range, is the Minotaur – you can't have a Labyrinth without one!

The Gap (1160m) is almost crowded with waratah blooms in spring, their red flowers like beacons among the green foliage and against the grey rock and blue sky. Through that colourful show you emerge in the front row of a dress circle giving you an unrestricted view of the Parthenon on your right, Mt Geryon's finger-like summit on the horizon ahead, and rock tiers spiked with stags (dead trees) stepping down to the Murchison Valley off to the left, best in morning light.

Occasional cairns mark your route north along the Parthenon's west face, past tarns and fabulous pencil pines (alive and dead) and striped, twisted snow peppermints. This is the easiest section of today's walk, despite the rock slabs and stepping stones and slight climb to the north, but taking photographs will probably keep your speed down.

A kilometre from the gap, the ground drops away, delivering an eye-level view of The Acropolis to your right and the labyrinth of boulders, lakes and pencil pines over which the mighty bluff stands sentinel. For a shorter walk you could return to the hut from here. Otherwise, if the weather allows, clamber down this very rocky slope to the Labyrinth plateau, and follow cairns through

The Acropolis rears up behind Lake Elysia

a warren of pencil pines and slabs of dolerite splattered with lichen to the Lookout track junction at Cyane Lake's north-east corner.

The rocks at the water's edge to the left of you here, provide a lovely spot for less energetic party members to soak up the raw scenery while others climb to the Lookout, or for everyone to take a break and refuel before making the detour. Tucked in beside these rocks are bonsaied fagus with easily recognisable crinkle-cut leaves.

A reasonably steep detour of about 1.4km to the top of an unnamed peak in the Du Cane Range, the Lookout (1219m) (*see* point 5 on map) offers another angle on this severely beautiful plateau and elevated lake field. From the junction, the track winds east through alpine scrub before rounding a cluster of handsome rocks and starting seriously uphill, past a splendid pencil pine stag silhouetted against The Acropolis. The 360° view from the top takes in The Acropolis, Mt Geryon, the lakes strung across the plateau, the conical Minotaur, the Parthenon, and, just visible to the left of the Parthenon, Lake St Clair.

Back down from the Lookout, you could turn back for the hut, but it is recommended that you walk on to Lake Elysia (named after the heavenly fields of Elysia in Greek mythology). A footpad (with no markers or cairns) heads west from the Lookout junction along Lake Cyane's north shore, navigating roots and rock slabs and bogs (get your boots wet rather than damage more plants) beside gently lapping water. The footpad continues along Lake Ophion before veering right, cairns guiding you on a serpentine cross-country route to Lake Elysia. (Note the tightness of the curled ends of the pandani as you walk through here.) Lake Elysia is the largest of the three mountains here and the most spectacular, with mighty Mt Geryon and The Acropolis as its backdrop.

Boulders on the shore are ideal spots to contemplate the millions of years of geological craftsmanship that fashioned the mountains through which you've walked today – or just to dry off after a dip in the lake!

From Elysia retrace your steps to Pine Valley Hut, enjoying the different play of light on this remarkable part of Tasmania.

DAY 3: 9.5km (3 hours)

Retrace your walk from Day 1 in reverse. On reaching Narcissus Hut, ring the ferry on the radio to let them know you have arrived for your boat.

CENTRAL HIGHLANDS

53 OVERLAND TRACK

Walk:	65km A to B
Time required:	6 days (more with side trips)
Best time:	October to May (the track is snowbound in winter)
Grade:	Moderate (hard side trips)
Environment:	Alpine moors, temperate rainforest, Tasmania's highest mountain
Best map:	TASMAP's *Cradle Mountain-Lake St Clair National Park 1:100,000 Map & Notes*
Toilets:	Composting toilets at Kitchen Hut and all overnight stops
Food:	Snacks are available from the Cradle Mountain Visitor Centre cafe, and meals at Cradle Mountain Lodge. Refreshments and alcoholic beverages, can be purchased at Lake St Clair Visitor Centre restaurant.
Tips:	Bookings are required, and the Overland Track Fee paid, for the official walking season (1 Oct-31 May) at https://bookings.overlandtrack.com.au. A National Park Pass is also required. Children aged 17 and under must be accompanied by an adult.

With jaw-dropping ice-carved mountains, windswept moors, pristine alpine lakes and ancient forests, it's no wonder this Tasmanian classic is Australia's most popular long-distance walk.

Approaching Mt Pelion West on the Overland Track

304　CENTRAL HIGHLANDS

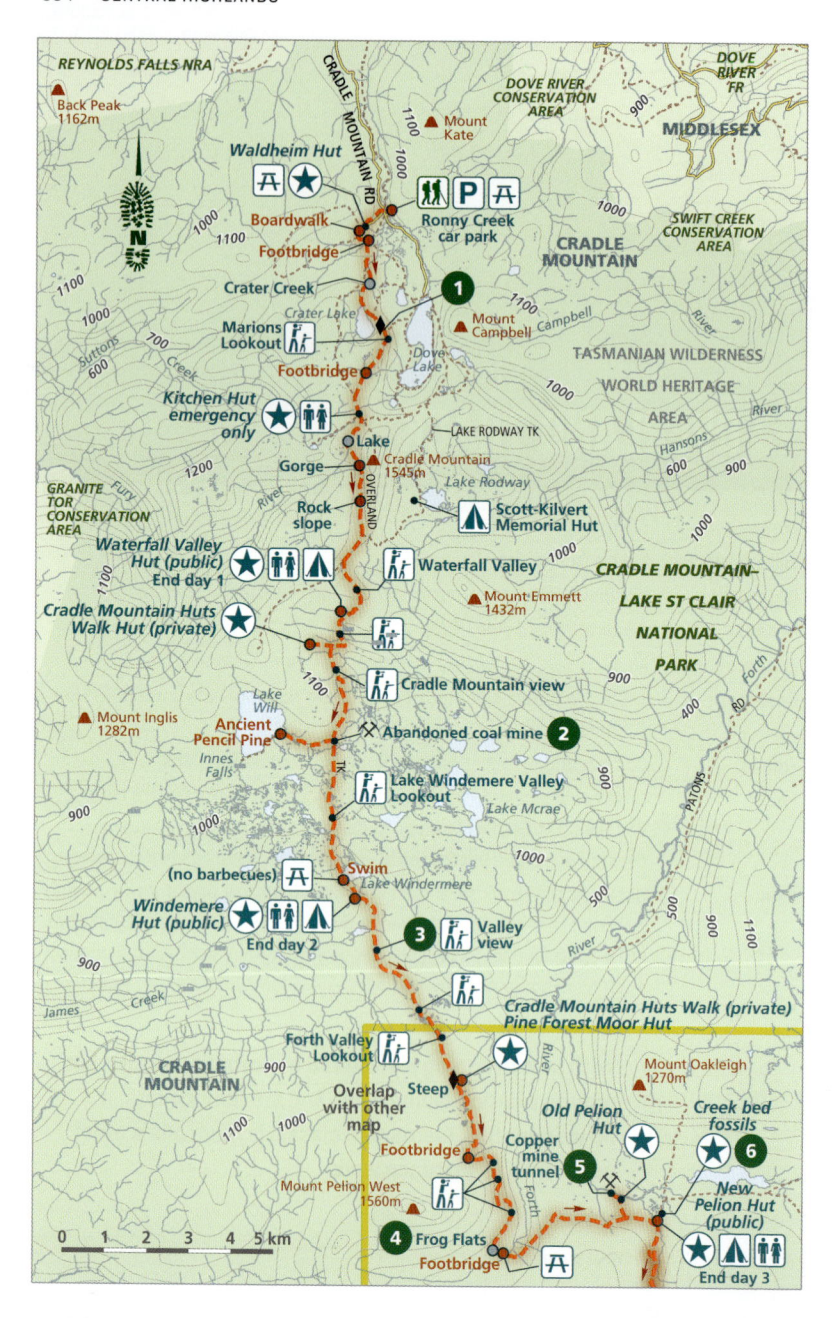

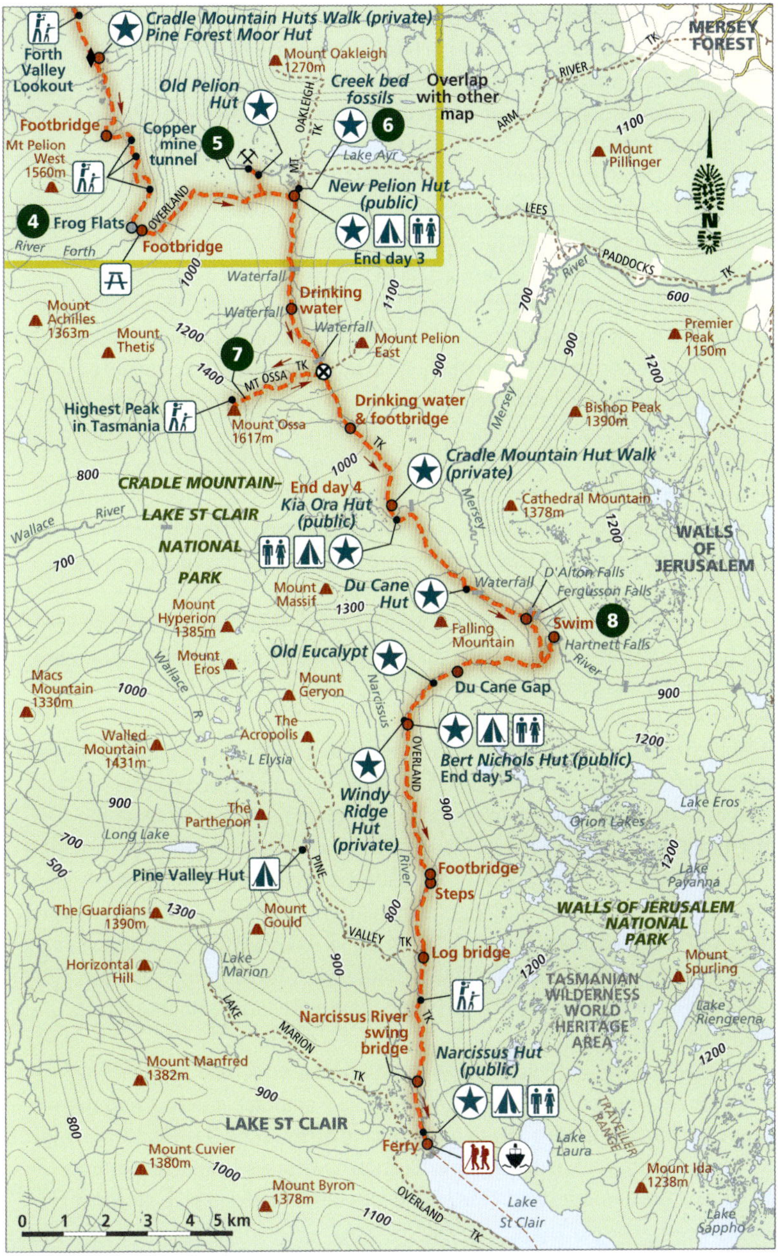
Cradle Mountain Huts Walk (private)
Pine Forest Moor Hut
Forth Valley Lookout
Mount Oakleigh 1270m
Old Pelion Hut
Creek bed fossils
Overlap with other map
MERSEY FOREST
Footbridge
Copper mine tunnel
Mt Pelion West 1560m
Lake Ayr
New Pelion Hut (public)
Mount Pillinger
Frog Flats
Footbridge
End day 3
Forth River
Drinking water
Waterfall
Mount Achilles 1363m
Mount Thetis
Mount Pelion East
Premier Peak 1150m
Highest Peak in Tasmania
Mount Ossa 1617m
Drinking water & footbridge
Bishop Peak 1390m
Cradle Mountain Hut Walk (private)
CRADLE MOUNTAIN–LAKE ST CLAIR NATIONAL PARK
End day 4
Kia Ora Hut (public)
Cathedral Mountain 1378m
WALLS OF JERUSALEM
Mount Massif
Du Cane Hut
D'Alton Falls
Fergusson Falls
Swim
Hartnett Falls
Mount Hyperion 1385m
Falling Mountain
Mount Eros
Old Eucalypt
Macs Mountain 1330m
Mount Geryon
Du Cane Gap
The Acropolis
Walled Mountain 1431m
Bert Nichols Hut (public)
End day 5
L Elysia
Windy Ridge Hut (private)
The Parthenon
Long Lake
Lake Eros
Orion Lakes
Pine Valley Hut
Footbridge
Steps
Lake Payanna
The Guardians 1390m
Mount Gould
WALLS OF JERUSALEM NATIONAL PARK
Horizontal Hill
Lake Marion
Log bridge
Mount Spurling
TASMANIAN WILDERNESS WORLD HERITAGE AREA
Lake Riengeena
Narcissus River swing bridge
Narcissus Hut (public)
Mount Manfred 1382m
LAKE ST CLAIR
Ferry
Lake Laura
Mount Cuvier 1380m
Mount Ida 1238m
Mount Byron 1378m
Lake St Clair
Lake Sappho
0 1 2 3 4 5 km

The awesome glaciated landscape of Cradle Mountain that won the heart of Gustav and Kate Weindorfer and which he championed until his death in 1932, was declared a scenic reserve in the 1920s and the much-expanded Cradle Mountain–Lake St Clair National Park was included in the Tasmanian Wilderness World Heritage Area in 1982.

Personal Locator Beacons (PLBs) for emergency assistance in life-threatening situations can be hired from Parks and Wildlife Service Tasmania and at the Cradle Mountain and Lake St Clair visitor centres; there is a helicopter pad at each hut. Unless you plan to walk the final 17km down Lake St Clair (not described here), you'll need to book passage on the *Ida Clair* ferry to finish the walk (phone (03) 6289 1137 or email sceniccruises@lakestclairlodge.com.au). You must check in at the Overland Track counter in the Cradle Mountain Visitor Centre to collect your Overland Track Pass; remember to also log out at Lake St Clair on completion.

Many of the national park's wonders can be experienced on day walks and overnight hikes, but those hiking the Overland Track get the full impact. Thousands walk this much-loved – some say overloved – track annually, and from 1 October to 31 May numbers are restricted, and you must walk north–south.

There are seven public huts (and two emergency-only refuges), each with bunk beds or bed shelves, a communal eating area, rainwater tank and heater, but no cooking equipment, lighting or toilet paper; pods of toilet waste are helicoptered out.

But extreme weather helped fashion this spectacular landscape and rain, ice and even snow can occur even at the height of summer, so you must carry a tent for emergency shelter. In any case, you might prefer camping on the timber tent decks at each hut to 'sleeping' indoors with snorers.

Guided Overland Track hikes with Wilderness Expeditions Tasmania (wildernessexpeditions.net.au) and Tasmanian Wilderness Experiences (www.twe.travel) are a safer option than walking alone. And if a 10kg pack, private huts with drying rooms and hot showers, and nightly three-course dinners with Tasmanian wine sound more like you, then there's the Cradle Mountain Huts Walk (cradlehuts.com.au).

However you go, you'll soon understand why this walk is so popular. You'll soon have wet and muddy feet, too. Accept this – embrace it even – and the journey will be even more enjoyable. Many kilometres of the Overland Track are boarded, but boggy areas still remain. Cutting new tracks to keep boots dry only widens the damage, so unless your depth-finder walking pole disappears into the mire, walk through it. Muddying your feet helps protect this fragile country – and it's fun!

Several side trails branch off the Overland Track. This walk takes several short detours and climbs Mt Ossa, Tasmania's tallest peak. It finishes with a ferry ride down Lake St Clair.

DAY 1: 12.7km – Ronny Creek to Waterfall Valley Hut

The Overland Track begins at Ronny Creek car park in Cradle Mountain–Lake St Clair National Park's north. A good alternative to car shuffling, which involves a 200km drive back to Cradle Mountain after the hike, is bussing into Cradle Mountain Visitor Centre and out of Lake St Clair (www.tassielink.com.au) and riding the shuttle bus to Ronny Creek to start.

After signing the walkers' registry at Ronny Creek, follow the boardwalk south through button grass moorland, where wombats trundle at dusk. Carpeted with tight-knit coral fern and central lemon boronia, this moorland bristles with spiky palm-like plants whose serrated leaves dry to papery ringlets. Found only in Tasmania, these are pandani, the world's tallest heath plant, which grow to 10m.

Cross Ronny Creek by footbridge and climb through tea tree and elegant eucalypts into gorgeous green rainforest, where Crater Creek foams around

Boarding keeps you out of the bog (much of the time) while crossing fragile moors

boulders and beneath moss-wrapped fallen trees. Crater Falls, upstream, is a good spot to fill your water bottle.

King Billy pine, an endemic Tasmanian conifer, grows only millimetres a year, so the three broad-girthed trees guarding this watering spot could be more than a thousand years old. Exit the creek gully but continue upstream, looking for red and yellow Christmas bells on the creek's steep bank.

The track lands you beside a weathered boatshed on the rocky shore of Crater Lake, which isn't actually a crater but rather a deep, bowl-shaped depression carved by a glacier. The ancient wall of rock wrapped around it, which runs with ribbon waterfalls after rain, dates from the breakup of the Gondwana supercontinent.

Now for the steepest leg of the Overland Track, up to Marions Lookout. Crater Lake drops behind and Dove Lake spreads out below as you haul yourself up bolted chains to an exposed ridge (see point 1 on map) leading to the lookout. Even in rain, the view from Marions will leave you slack-jawed. An almost palpable presence to your right, Cradle Mountain rears above Dove Lake like a giant chipped axe head (its name apparently comes from a perceived likeness to a miner's cradle). Opposite perches Lake Hanson, on the Dove Lake High loop walk (see page 267) below, the easier and shorter but no less spectacular Dove Lake circuit (see page 262).

Beyond Marions Lookout, rocky track, stone-paving and boardwalk traverse Cradle Plateau, cutting through small-leafed alpine plants hunkered down against the often fierce winds en route to Kitchen Hut, an emergency refuge whose timber shingles are greyed with age. This is the perfect spot to take a break, and for meeting other dripping hikers in wet weather.

Just past Kitchen Hut, the Cradle Mountain summit track (3 hrs return, clear weather only) breaks left. The Overland Track climbs through pandani and deciduous beech, Australia's only native winter-deciduous tree, whose tiny crinkle-cut leaves turn yellow in autumn and then festoon the ground. Here too are massed mountain rocket shrubs that produce long-stemmed white and pink flowers in summer and high-vis orange-red fruits in autumn. The now rocky and often muddy track skirts Cradle Mountain, its dolerite fingers thrusting skyward to your left, and rough-hewn Barn Bluff soon comes into view.

Wooden steps climb to a panorama of Waterfall Valley, prettiest when water streams down its cliffs. The track emerges from pandani and oh-so-fashionable black, white and grey beech trunks into a sea of prickly scoparia. When covered in white, yellow, orange, red and pink summer flower spikes, this spread looks like a feature garden in a flower show.

TOP: *On the track;* **BOTTOM LEFT:** *Mosses and lichens abound;* **BOTTOM RIGHT:** *Orange fungi forms extraordinary clusters on myrtle beech*

The Waterfall Valley public huts (1950s and 1994), your home for the night, are 150m off the track, on flats below Barn Bluff. A family of spotted-tailed quolls lives under the old hut.

DAY 2: 9.2km – Waterfall Valley to Windermere Hut via Lake Will

Back on track, head briefly downhill to the Waterfall Valley cliff-line and tread its edge, past pink and grey snow peppermints, twisted like wizards frozen mid-spell.

In all but the bleakest weather, when you can't see anything except your feet on the boardwalk, Barn Bluff (1559m) dominates this section of track, its lower slopes culminating in a wall of dolerite columns. On reaching the next rise, however, the track, snaking towards the horizon across water-pooled button grass, might lower your gaze, albeit briefly.

Just before Lake Holmes on your left, a side trail heads right (see point 2 on map). Leave your pack here and stroll 1.5km to Lake Will, crossing a seam of coal unprofitably prospected in the 19th century by Joseph Will, after whom the lake is named. If the weather gods are kind, you can see the remote Eldon Range, to the south, from this detour.

Lake Will's quartzite beach is a lovely spot for morning tea. The pencil pine leaning out over the tannin-stained water is estimated to be approximately 1500 years old.

From the lake junction, the Overland Track climbs through heathland striped hot pink in summer with grass trigger plants. Look closely: each flower is armed with a trigger that daubs pollen on unsuspecting insects.

A rocky pile topping the next hill offers a feet-stilling, breathtaking view over Lake Windermere and smaller tarns, with Mt Pelion West straight ahead and Mount Oakleigh's signature dolerite crown to the south-west. And there's no drop-off in wow factor as you descend to Windermere.

Rounding boulders and passing old pencil pines, the track follows the shoreline to picnic-perfect fallen trees and a paved path into the lake. Drop your pack here and take a refreshing dip or push on to the Windermere Hut (500m) to stash your things, then come back for a couple of lazy hours by the lake.

DAY 3: 16km – Windermere Hut to New Pelion Hut

The longest hut-to-hut section on the Overland Track begins by venturing from snow peppermint woodland to myrtle beech forest. A rocky trail then crosses moorland bristling with antennae-like button grass; this is the beginning of Pine Forest Moor.

An unmarked but obvious side trail on the left (see point 3 on map) about 1.5km along leads to a lookout that hands you Pelion West, Mt Ossa's torn-paper profile, and Mt Oakleigh on a plate. Clearly visible from here too are the flat paths of two glaciers and the moraine deposited between them, which, once back on the main trail, you cross on boardwalk and rocky track. Carved words on the boardwalk coming out of a patch of forest confirm this is Pine Forest Moor. The only things brave enough to stand tall here are lichen-bearded track marker posts.

Shortly after skirting a mossy tarn reflecting Mt Pelion West, there's another track junction. Turn left to the River Forth Gorge lookout and take a breather, watching the colour play as shadows drift across the treed mountain slopes reaching up from the river.

An ankle-threatening crazy paving of rocks, tangled roots and mud plunges into wet eucalypt forest, fording several creeks before climbing through woolly tea tree, myrtle beech and pandani. An equally rough track heads down the other side.

You are now on part of the 120km long Innes Track (officially the Mole Creek Track), surveyed in 1896 by Edward George Innes's party and cut by Public Works Department gangs for a rail line to Tasmania's west coast mining areas. The rail line was never built, but the track found favour with miners, drovers and hikers.

The prospective supply line lands you on Frog Flats (see point 4 on map), a grassy spread ringed by mountains and inhabited by leeches. Rest here, because after crossing the River Forth by footbridge you climb again: through damp forest and tree ferns. Fallen trees reveal how shallow roots are in this forest. Beech orange fungi grow like grape bunches on the myrtle trees.

The track tops out in open forest. Then it's down onto Pelion Plains, an Impressionist working of yellow, red, brown and green shrubs and grasses and elegant yellow gums below Mt Oakleigh. Leave your pack at the junction for Old Pelion Hut (you can see New Pelion Hut ahead) and walk unencumbered to the oldest building in the national park.

Button-grass flower heads poke skyward like antennae

Old Pelion is the sole survivor of two huts that were built by the Mt Pelion Mines No Liability Company in 1917 but soon after abandoned because the copper content of the plains was too low. The log-and-plank bunk beds date from the 1930s, but some of the King Billy pine roof and wall timbers are thought to be original. An unsigned track behind the hut leads 300m northwest along Douglas Creek to a mullock heap and copper mining tunnel (see point 5 on map) that burrows about 20m – take a head torch – into the hill.

With your pack back on, you've got another 800m to New Pelion Hut for the night.

The 8km return walk to Mt Oakleigh's summit ridge via some of the park's worst bogs (or best, if waist-deep mud rocks your boat) begins behind New Pelion Hut. It branches off Arm River Track, a popular shorter route from the east into New Pelion Hut to climb Mt Ossa (a three-day option) or Ossa and Oakleigh (four days). Much less taxing is an afternoon stroll about 200m along Arm River Track, to a footpad branching right (see point 6 on map) to a river beach awash with fossils.

DAY 4: 13.5km – New Pelion Hut to Kia Ora Hut via Mt Ossa

Day four begins with an easy walk through moors and forest and a short detour down an unsigned boarded track, about 1.5km in, to a pretty cascade at the confluence of two creeks. A smaller tiered waterfall about a kilometre further on is the last place to get drinking water for the climb to Pelion Gap (and Mt Ossa).

An unremitting 1.7km ascent through beech trees draped with lichens, liverworts and mosses ends beneath a spread of sky resting on the encircling mountains. If you can tear your gaze from Mt Ossa, turn around for a view north to Cradle Mountain.

At 1617m, Mt Ossa is Tasmania's tallest peak. Summiting it is a climb, not a walk, with exposed slopes, rock-hopping, steep drops and places where you'll wish your legs were longer. The view from the top on a clear day takes in much of Tasmania, but life-threatening weather can come in fast; don't climb in foul conditions or if cloud hides the summit.

Leave your pack with the others on the roomy boarded area at the Mt Ossa junction (you need to take water, a snack and a wind- and waterproof jacket), but remember to remove foodstuffs from zipped pockets. Overland Track currawongs, one of more than 80 bird species recorded in Cradle Mountain–Lake St Clair National Park, have learned to unzip packs in search of goodies.

The 6km return Ossa climb snakes through living and skeletal dead pencil pines as it works up and around Mt Doris, another impressive dolerite mountain

It's soon obvious why this is Australia's most popular long-distance walk

construction. Doris's flanks are carpeted with bright green cushion plants, colonies of plants that grow low and tight to protect their stems from the harsh conditions and produce tiny white flowers.

Coming around Doris, the view back across the gap disappears and another valley spectacle opens up to the north. And rearing up to your left are the Gates of Mordor, twin towers of fluted dolerite between which the Ossa trail is clearly visible, scaling a steep, rocky slope. About 1.5 hrs of climbing puts you through the 'gates' on a false summit (see point 7 on map), with a final push to the plateau and its crowning red boulders.

When George Frankland in 1835 gave several Lake St Clair landmarks names from Greek mythology he started a trend continued by other cartographers and the hikers who followed. The Titans stacked Mt Pelion atop Mt Ossa to ease ascent to heaven during their war against the gods, and there are certainly places on Ossa where you might pray for divine intervention.

The plateau is carpeted with cushion plants, snow gentians and tarns that pool blue sky on sunny days. And from the edge, the country plunges into valleys and rears again as columnar massifs. Distinctive Frenchmans Cap (see page 357), another famous Tasmanian walking destination, is visible on clear days.

Back down the mountain you've got roughly 4km, mostly downhill. Heathland makes way for grassland and red-striped gums that frame Ossa on the right and august Cathedral Mountain ahead. The descent and today's walk ends at Kia Ora Hut, among tea tree.

DAY 5: 14km – Kia Ora Hut to Bert Nicholls Hut (Windy Ridge)

Today is a celebration of waterfalls, beginning with an easy walk through eucalypts and button grass and lichen-covered beech to historic Du Cane Hut. Pioneer bushwalker, trapper, prospector and bowler hat-wearer Patrick (Paddy) Hartnett built this hut, from King Billy pine, in 1910 as a base for winter snaring of quolls, brushtail possums and wallabies for their pelts. Lucy Hartnett spent three winters here with her husband, cooking, caring for their son Billy, and treating the plush skins for sale in Europe.

The hut was extended in the 1930s to accommodate the increasing number of hikers (it is now an emergency-only refuge) and changed several more times, but it retains the huge, timber chimney in which the skins were dried. A Hartnett grandson helped repair the hut in 1992.

Beyond Du Cane is some of the oldest rainforest in the national park. The track is very rough and interlaced with roots, and slows your pace through shadow-filled forest of myrtle beech and ancient, fissured King Billy pines. Deep

Lunch stop below Mt Ossa, Tasmania's tallest peak

316   CENTRAL HIGHLANDS

in the forest is a track junction with lichen-patched wooden signs directing you deeper into the rainforest to D'Alton Falls, which pours down a rocky slope in a great curtain of white foam after good rains, and Fergusson Falls. A plaque on one of the trees at the junction remembers Albert 'Fergy' Fergusson, a long-time Lake St Clair ranger and 'bushwalker's friend'.

Another side trail, a kilometre on, visits Hartnett Falls (named after Paddy Hartnett). This detour breaks out of the shadows into eucalypt forest, flattening out among button grass and pandani, and brings you to a footworn area where the Mersey River falls to a rocky riverbed. There is a spider's web of footpads here; one follows the cliff-line downstream before descending steeply to a side stream (see point 8 on map); note where this lands you, because it is easy to overshoot when heading back. Across the stream and upriver is a pebbly river beach facing up the gorge to the falls.

This is a popular spot for an invigorating – that's Tasmanian for 'cold' – swim, but the rocks underfoot are slippery, so take water sandals. With care you can walk up the flow towards the cascade.

From the Hartnett Falls junction the Overland Track climbs to Du Cane Gap, sometimes steeply, sometimes on boardwalk, through rainforest, woodland,

TOP: *Look closely at a banksia to appreciate its remarkable structure;* **RIGHT:** *A stroll from Mt Pelion Hut brings you to a length of Arm River awash with fossils;* **BOTTOM LEFT:** *Every fern is different*

pine pockets and snow gums, with mountain ridges showing themselves above the treetops. At the gap (1070m) – small and treed, not open like Pelion Gap – look up to your right. The fantastic rise of dolerite columns is appropriately called Falling Mountain; this is the end of the rugged Du Cane Range. To your right stands the Traveller Range.

From Du Cane Gap you descend through arguably the most beautiful forest on the Overland Track, with magnificent, multi-coloured alpine yellow gums merging into almost luxuriantly mossy myrtle rainforest. Tree stumps with indentations from timber cutters' standing boards tell of a time when this forest was viewed very differently.

The track leads to the youngest public hut on the Overland Track, a large, hard-to-heat structure built to replace one destroyed by fire and named in honour of trapper, ranger and pioneer guide Bert Nicholls, who blazed the track in 1930.

DAY 6: 10.5km – Bert Nicholls Hut to Lake St Clair Jetty

While your last day is not all descent, it would be petty to call the few short, slight ascents 'hills'. Following a moraine left by a retreating glacier, and heading down the Narcissus Valley, it's the easiest section too, albeit with an occasional mud hole for old time's sake.

The track meanders through silver banksias and woolly tea tree beneath towering stringybarks and cabbage gums and passes a flat, grassy frost hollow on the right. Ridgelines peek through the trees, but after the attention-grabbing geology of previous days it is restful to focus on the forest, particularly when summer wildflowers are on show. Purple fairies' aprons, silver banksia and slender riceflowers are some you might see. And you could well hear more birds today than on the past five days combined; look out for yellow-tailed black cockatoos.

Boardwalks skirt rainforest and snake through heathland planted with gums towards the might of Mt Olympus and tiny Narcissus Hut, and a one-person-at-a-time swing suspension bridge takes you over Narcissus River.

The mosquitoes at the 1963 Narcissus Hut renovated in 2015, are voracious, but the composting loo behind has the best view of any on the track.

You're all but done now, with just 350 flat metres to the jetty near the mouth of the Narcissus River. Confirm your arrival for the ferry pickup on the hut radio and then head down to the jetty. If game, take a ceremonial plunge in the cold river before the 20-minute ride down Lake St Clair, Australia's deepest natural lake, to your journey's end.

CENTRAL HIGHLANDS

54 WALLS OF JERUSALEM

Walk:	28.6km out-and-back
Time required:	3 days
Best time:	Clear, mild weather (snow can fall any time of year)
Grade:	Moderate (mostly because of remote location)
Environment:	Eucalypt forest, alpine moors, pencil pine forest, mountains
Best map:	This one and TASMAP's *Walls of Jerusalem National Park Map & Notes*, 1:25,000
Toilets:	Composting toilets at Wild Dog Creek Camp & Dixon's Kingdom Hut
Food:	Bring your own. The nearest town of any size is Mole Creek, which has some cafes and a pub. You can get counter meals and scrumptious home-made lamb pies at Mole Creek Hotel's Tassie Tiger Bar.
Tips:	Be prepared for cold-weather walking and camping whatever the forecast; conditions can deteriorate unexpectedly and suddenly.

This three-day pilgrimage to the heart of Tasmania's Central Highlands will stay with you forever.

Walls of Jerusalem National Park is divine but its spirituality is borne of worldly forces: prehistoric ones that layered sediments, ruptured Earth's crust and spewed molten rock, creating Tasmania's Central Highlands; and more recent

Navigating boardwalks on the track into the Walls of Jerusalem

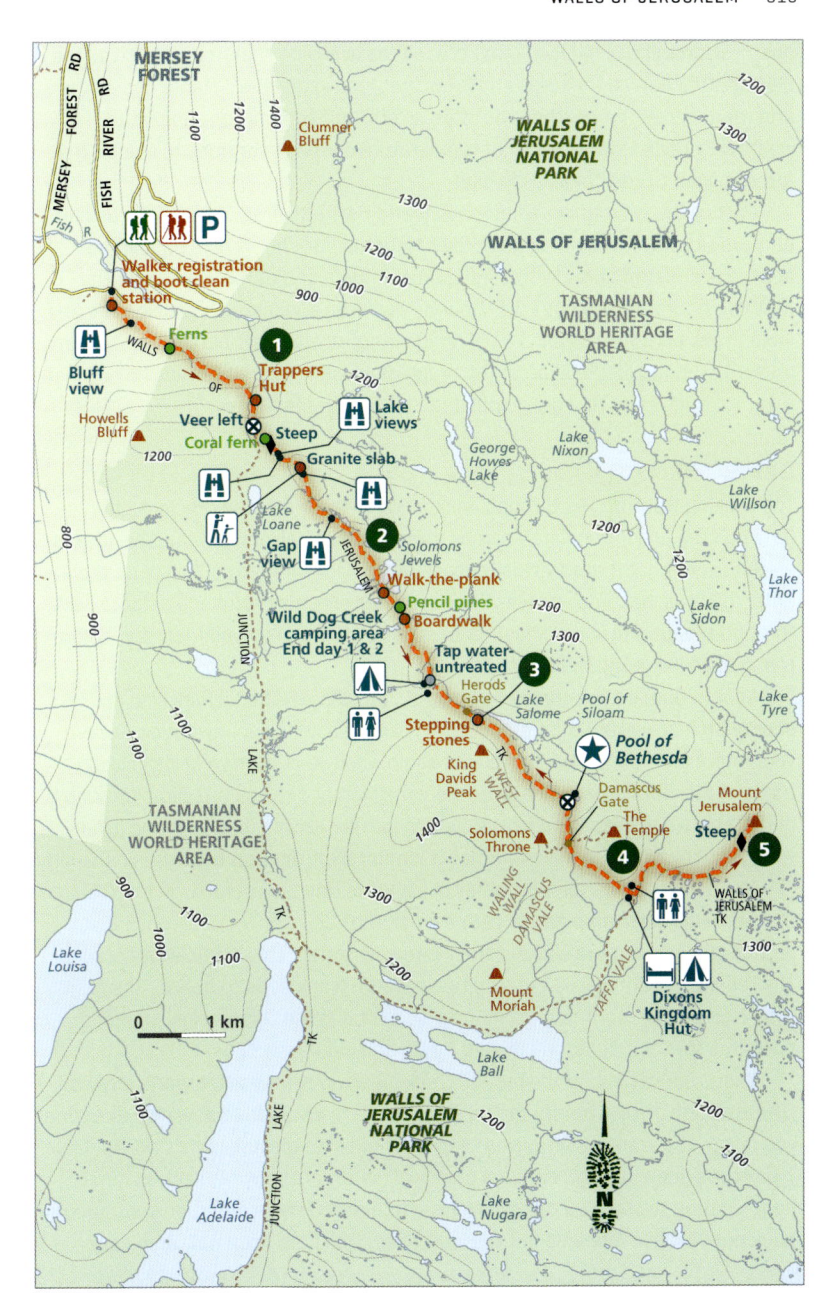

WALLS OF JERUSALEM 319

ones – everything is relative – that eroded the overlying rock, forces such as the glaciers that carved the tarns and lakes that feed specialised plants and animals. And then there's the weather: the often erratic and sometimes dangerous weather here can lower overnight temperatures, even in summer, to a point that forces hikers to wear beanies in bed!

Part of the Tasmanian Wilderness World Heritage Area, Walls of Jerusalem borders Cradle Mountain–Lake St Clair National Park but is less popular so access is a test of sorts, with inadequate signage and uphill walking for the first two hours. You've got a 1.5-hour drive from Launceston, via Deloraine and Mole Creek on the B12 (1hr 15m from Devonport, via Sheffield), the last 30km on south-bound Mersey Forest Rd, much of which is gravel. Turning left up Fish River Rd brings you to a gravel parking area with no facilities.

DAY 1: 7.6km (3–4 hours)

The walking track begins through an opening in the forest that encloses the parking area and immediately climbs through tall eucalypts and tea tree. It's not a killer ascent but there's virtually no let-up for four kilometres. And to up the ante, the track becomes a creek in places after rain; it's easier and safer to walk through the flowing water – leather boots and gaiters keep you fairly dry – than trying to walk around the wet stuff.

About 200m up you come to a Walls of Jerusalem National Park sign and shortly after, a walker registration booth beside a boot-cleaning station. Record your intentions (remember to sign out again when you return) and clean your boots. Watch for flame robins and other small forest birds as you climb through gum trees, white hakea and pink mountain berries, skirting boulders and fallen trees; you're unlikely to miss landmark Clumner Bluff through the trees on the left.

The perfect place for a breather is Trappers Hut (see point 1 on map), 3km into the walk and immediately past a creek that flows down to the Fish River, sometimes turning the walking track into a waterfall. This rustic weathered shelter was rebuilt in 1989 in traditional wood-plank style to honour the men who lived on the mountain for months at a time in the Depression, trapping possums for their pelts, which sold for 25 shillings each.

About 500m beyond the hut, on track clearly marked with orange arrows (there are no arrows before the hut) you come to a very blue new sign directing you left to the Walls of Jerusalem and right to Lake Adelaide. The Lake Adelaide Track runs deep into the national park, well south of the Walls section most people come to see. You can do a loop, through the Walls and then south and back out via Lake Adelaide but the walk described here is an out-and-back

TOP: *Although it seems impossible, the 'wow' factor ramps up as you climb Mt Jerusalem;*
BOTTOM: *An ancient pencil pine frames Solomons Throne*

route allowing a whole day to explore the Walls from a base camp. Keep left at this junction, over a rise and out of the valley.

Still climbing, through shorter trees and shrubs, you pass a hollow carpeted with coral fern and, about 4.5km into the walk, come to the first of a string of rock platforms looking south-west to the southern mountains of Cradle Mountain–Lake St Clair National Park. This scene is at its peak when the ranges are dusted with snow – sometimes in summer!

Look for a tree growing out of a boulder as you meander through tea tree and beautiful white-and-silver striped snow peppermint trees (eucalypts). Stepping stones and old boardwalk skirt a small tarn that often thrums with frogs.

Heading south-east towards King Davids Peak (1499m), which rears up behind Wild Dog Creek Campsite, the track crests rocky rises topped with peppermint trees as it works along a chain of exquisite glacial lakes (see point 2 on map). Launceston solicitor Reg Hall, who hiked here in the 1920s and '30s, suggested many of the park's biblical names, presumably calling these waters Solomon's Jewels because they are fit for a king.

About 6.5km into the walk the track skirts another lake, noisy with frogs, shortly after which you walk the plank over a wetland laced with coral fern. Beyond a row of pencil pines, across a creek-watered valley and over more rocky rises, Wild Dog Creek Campsite appears ahead, below King Davids Peak and Herods Gate, the saddle through which you enter the Walls proper. Boarding zigzags across well-watered flats to camp.

Wild Dog has twelve wooden tent platforms over three levels. The lowest are more exposed to weather – and the top two platforms, beside the toilet block, are reserved for commercial groups.

DAY 2: 13km return (allow all day)

Day 2 begins with a short climb, to the music of Wild Dog Creek, from sheltering trees to Herods Gate, which opens onto the plateau at the park's heart. Rocky track, stepping stones (see point 3 on map) and boardwalk (which can be slippery despite its wire netting) head south-east between monolithic grey King Davids Peak and Lake Salome and through prickly scoparia and bright-green cushion plant mounds.

About 700m from camp the view broadens, revealing the awesome West Wall, more than a kilometre of daunting natural fortification whose folds sometimes hold snow well into summer. Your next destination is Damascus Gate, the saddle at the wall's end.

Boardwalk cuts diagonally across the plateau towards a stand of conical pencil pines, fording a series of creeks that have cut deep paths through the delicate groundcover. Some of these pines are centuries-old, their trunks thick and gnarled by years in this unforgiving environment.

Beyond the trees you come to an unsigned track junction. A memorable short side trip to the Pools of Bethesda leaves from here, but it's best left till you are on your way back to camp and know how long you can linger. Ignore it now and instead continue up to the saddle between The Temple (left) and Solomons Throne (right).

The ascent to Solomons Throne is extremely steep, with sections that in poor conditions have gazumped even technical climbers. The way up The Temple (1446m) is an excellent, if coarse, crazy pavement of shaped and repositioned lichen-patterned stones sourced from the rock pile it crosses. The product of weeks of stonemasonry, the track leads to a blustery summit with 360° views including Mt Jerusalem and the thousands of tarns on Tasmania's Central Plateau. The Temple (see point 4 on map) is a great alternative to Mt Jerusalem, or an add-on if you have the time (and enthusiasm) on the way back.

As you mount the saddle you get a wonderful view to the right of the Wailing Wall (a continuation of the West Wall) running south down Damascus Vale and ahead you can see rigidness and valleys and pools of water to the horizon.

Wild Dog Creek camp

The groundcover changes over the saddle, with more alpine grasses than cushion plants. Stepping stones and boardwalk take you downhill through Tasmania's largest surviving tract of pencil pines, a remarkable forest of gnarled mossy trees with twisted, weathered limbs, some witness to a thousand years of alpine winters. Note how much taller the pines are lower down, in the relative protection of Jaffa Vale.

Track arrows lead to Dixons Kingdom Hut, built of pencil pine logs by Reg Dixon and family in 1949 as a base for his cattle-grazing lease in the Walls (grazing ceased in 1972). Tasmania's highest altitude grazing hut, Dixons is now a shelter for bushwalkers who also camp here (there is a toilet up the hill).

Turn north at the hut for signed Mt Jerusalem and tread boards up the vale, behind the Temple. Water has cut a network of tunnels into and below the peaty groundcover and you can hear creeks underfoot. Scat indicates where animals have drunk from hidden water sources. Here, too, there's scoparia again, after none among the pencil pines. Some grows in great mounds, forming rings with age that provide shelter from wind and snow for wildlife.

The boarding ends at a sharp-right turn – and a rocky, muddy track – worn down through the peat – climbs from the vale to another plateau of sorts. Snow poles show the way through a wonderland of hardy heath, miniature pencil pines and tarns crackling with croaky frog choruses. The markers on these snow poles are bleached to grey and far less visible, particularly in bad weather, than the orange ones followed earlier in the walk. The ground-hugging grass that looks like pineapple tops is, not surprisingly, called pineapple grass. The dead pencil pines punctuating the scene may be bushfire victims.

Although it seems impossible, the 'wow' factor ramps up as you climb Mt Jerusalem, with views broadening and deepening with each step up the rocky track: down the Wailing Wall, along the West Wall to Herods Gate, across to Cradle Mountain–Lake St Clairs mountains, and east, into the vast Central Plateau, Tasmania's largest area of high ground. Together with Walls of Jerusalem National Park, the Central Plateau Conservation Area protects about 4,000 alpine lakes scoured by ice flows 10–20,000 years ago, lakes that reflect blue sky, like scattered pieces of mirror.

The track steepens (see point 5 on map) and can be wet in places but you are soon on the top, trying to determine which of three cairns marks the actual summit. All share a 360° panorama of starkly beautiful alpine country sometimes appreciated from above by wedge-tailed eagles.

Eventually you will have to start back – few leave willingly – so retrace your steps to Dixons Kingdom Hut and keep right on the hillside as you start up through the pencil pines. It can be a little confusing here so pay close attention.

Walk up and over to the unmarked junction passed on your way up and turn right, treading boardwalk across a little gully and over a rise to the Pools of Bethesda. Named after the Bethesda Pool in Jerusalem, which is linked to a Roman temple to the god of medicine and is believed to be where Jesus healed a paralytic (John 5:1-15), this tarn is a balm to eye and soul. Follow the track to its far end for some quiet contemplation of your surroundings and an impressive view of the West Wall.

From there return to camp for the night.

DAY 3: 7.6km (3 hours)

Retrace your steps from Day 1 in reverse marvelling once more at the ice-carved landscape and the plants that thrive here and the majesty of the eucalypt on the forested descent to the car.

TOP LEFT: Moss forms fluffy mounds on fallen trees; **TOP RIGHT:** Highly visible track markers show the way; **BOTTOM:** Check out Dixons Kingdom Hut, built of pencil pine in 1949

Sunrise from the plateau at the foot of Frenchmans Cap is a grand spectacle

WEST & WILDERNESS

Setting your GPS for Tasmania's wild west opens up endless possibilities on foot, from easy forest ambles to challenging multi-day hikes deep into World Heritage wilderness. You can scale mountains with incomparable views into the south-west; feel the spray off plummeting waterfalls; dip your toes in toffee-coloured tarns trimmed with ancient pencil pines and swim in a river that was saved by a groundbreaking grassroots campaign that captured the imaginations of people worldwide.

55	Philosopher Falls	328
56	West Point to Black Rocks	333
57	Mount Donaldson to Corinna via Savage River	337
58	Montezuma Falls	342
59	Mount Farrell & Lake Herbert	346
60	Pillinger Point	352
61	Frenchmans Cap	357
62	Donaghys Hill	368
63	The Needles	371
64	Mount Eliza Plateau	375
65	Hartz Peak	380
66	Mystery Creek Cave	386
67	South Cape Bay	390

WEST & WILDERNESS

55 PHILOSOPHER FALLS

Walk:	3.6km return
Time required:	1.5 hours
Best time:	Overcast day after rain (for best forest colours)
Grade:	Easy–moderate
Environment:	Cool temperate rainforest, waterfall, historic water race
Best map:	This one
Toilets:	None
Food:	None
Tips:	Stop, look, listen. Appreciate the forest rather than boot-camp march to and from the falls.

Unearth a treasury of natural wonders on a short walk deep in prehistoric takayna/Tarkine rainforest to a fern-framed waterfall.

For decades, only 'greenies' campaigning against logging, mining and for the protection of Aboriginal cultural sites in north-west Tasmania used the name takayna/Tarkine. Now, takayna/Tarkine appears on maps and in tourism brochures and advertisements although only a fraction of it is safe from the threat of mining and forestry. Save The Tarkine continues to work, with other

The track is wide and the walking is easy; downhill through verdant forest

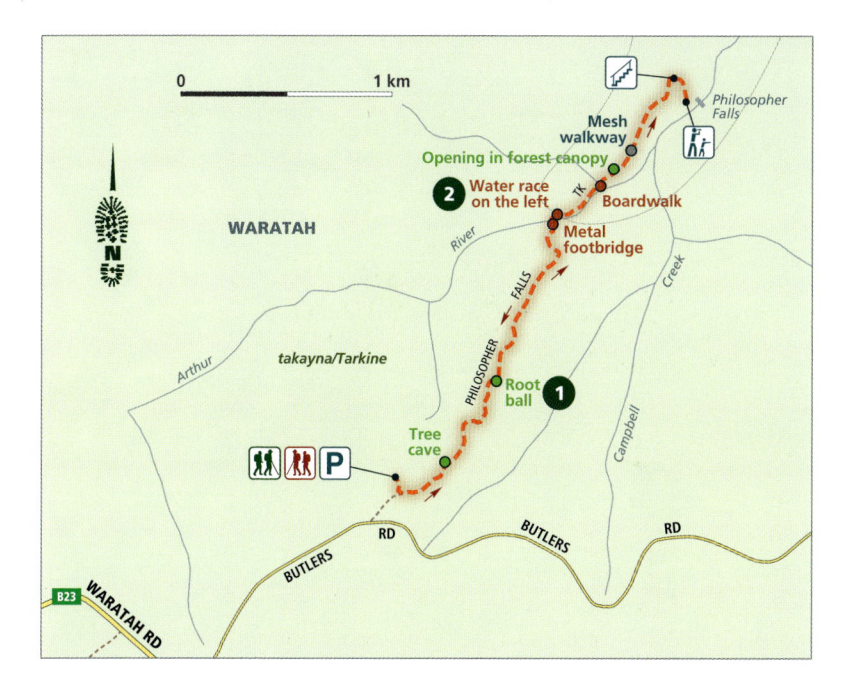

conservation groups, towards the area's protection as a World Heritage-listed national park.

Roughly defined by the Arthur and Pieman rivers north and south, and the Southern Ocean and Murchison Hwy west and east, the takayna/Tarkine encompasses almost half a million hectares. It's home to more than 60 species of rare, threatened and endangered fauna species and is one of the last places where the Tasmanian tiger was seen in the wild (and, some people believe, where the striped carnivore still hunts).

The shadowy world of trees and ferns in which you find Philosopher Falls – and perhaps the elusive tiger! – is the popular image of the takayna/Tarkine but the world's second largest tract of cool temperate rainforest, dating back to the breakup of the Gondwana supercontinent, is one of its other many facets. Others include sand dunes and wild beaches (see West Point to Black Rocks page 333), historic mining villages, free-flowing river systems and wind- and flame-sheared mountains (see Mt Donaldson to Corinna via the Savage River page 337).

A mesh walkway covers a water race cut in the 1920s

Philosopher Falls turnoff is on the B23 (Waratah Rd), just short of the Arthur River bridge, about 10km south-west of Waratah, an hour's drive south-west of Burnie via the B18 (Ridgley Hwy). From the turnoff it's 1km to a gravel turn-back loop, where Waratah–Wynyard Council signage directs you into a wall of forest and warns about snakes, possible tree falls, uneven ground, and steep walking. There's a more uplifting information board a short way further in.

TOP LEFT: *Philosopher Falls cascades in tiers between walls of greenery;* **TOP RIGHT:** *Plump snow berries grow in the forest;* **BOTTOM LEFT:** *Take a closer look at the different types of ferms;* **BOTTOM RIGHT:** *High-vis fungi grows on mossy tree trunks*

The track is wide and the walking easy: downhill through verdant tree ferns, native pines, sassafras, and centuries-old myrtle beech trees wrapped in moss. In late summer, leatherwoods, the source of Tasmania's own leatherwood honey, carpet the track with blousy white flowers with multiple purple-tipped stamens.

A short way into the walk, the track skirts a splendid tree covered in moss, several strands of its roots having been pulled from the ground and formed a small cave. Soon after you pass a toppled tree's huge root ball (see point 1 on map). The hole it ripped in the forest floor is long-since darned with greenery, the toppled trunk spongy with moss and lichen and decorated with caramel-coloured fungi (fungi are the forest's main agents of decay and nutrient recycling). Other trees have fallen too but many more stand tall, their roots buried in the moist soil and their crowns woven into a thick canopy.

Fifteen minutes of zigzag descent through rainforest ornamented with hard plate fungi and soft mushrooms, in brown, white and orange, brings you to a metal footbridge over the upper Arthur River, which runs clear beneath your feet and more than 150km west to the sea.

Philosopher Falls is named after local farmer, explorer and prospector James 'Philosopher' Smith, whose discovery of tin nearby in 1871 spawned Tasmania's mining industry and saved its struggling economy. On the other side of the Arthur River, the walking track runs along a race (see point 2 on map) cut by hand in the 1920s to carry water to Magnet Mine, in the hills west of Waratah. Opened in 1894, this mine produced nearly 40,000 tonnes of lead and more than 200 tonnes of silver before its closure in 1940.

A much flatter track of metre-wide compacted stone heads downstream from the bridge, beside and sometimes in the water race, between rock dripping with moss and lichen and a thickly greened slope dropping down to a hidden but burbling river. The track ducks under fallen trees and tangles of mossy branches and limbs and then suddenly you are in the open where a fallen tree has ripped opened the canopy; after the forest shadows you might feel spot-lit here on a sunny day.

Back under the canopy, you come upon an impressive staircase (the water race disappears into a tangle of fallen trees about 20m further on). Two hundred-plus timber-and-metal steps drop down the hillside to a viewing platform beside Philosopher Falls, a multi-tiered veil cascading between walls of greenery.

Watch the frothy falls. Inhale deeply the intoxicating smell of clean water and humusy forest. Feel the percussion of thumping, splashing water. Then return to your car.

WEST & WILDERNESS

56 WEST POINT TO BLACK ROCKS

Walk:	10km out-and-back
Time required:	3 hours
Best time:	Any weather, although the beach can be wild in westerlies
Grade:	Easy
Environment:	Remote beach, dunes, headlands, beach 'shacks'
Best map:	This one
Toilets:	None
Food:	None
Tips:	With a car shuffle you can do a through-walk continuing beyond Black Rocks to Bluff Hill Point (9km one-way). Carry drinking water because there's none along the walk.

More than a just a beach stroll, this walk reveals an untamed coastline shaped by rolling ocean and the Roaring Forties.

Bludgeoned and chiselled by the winds that whip around our planet between latitudes 40° and 50°, Tasmania's west coast is a place of rugged handsomeness: a string of beaches, dunes, headlands, coves, bays, rivers and harbours. Parts of the area are also of great historical and cultural significance to Tasmanian Aboriginal people.

Multicoloured, layered rocks reach out into the water

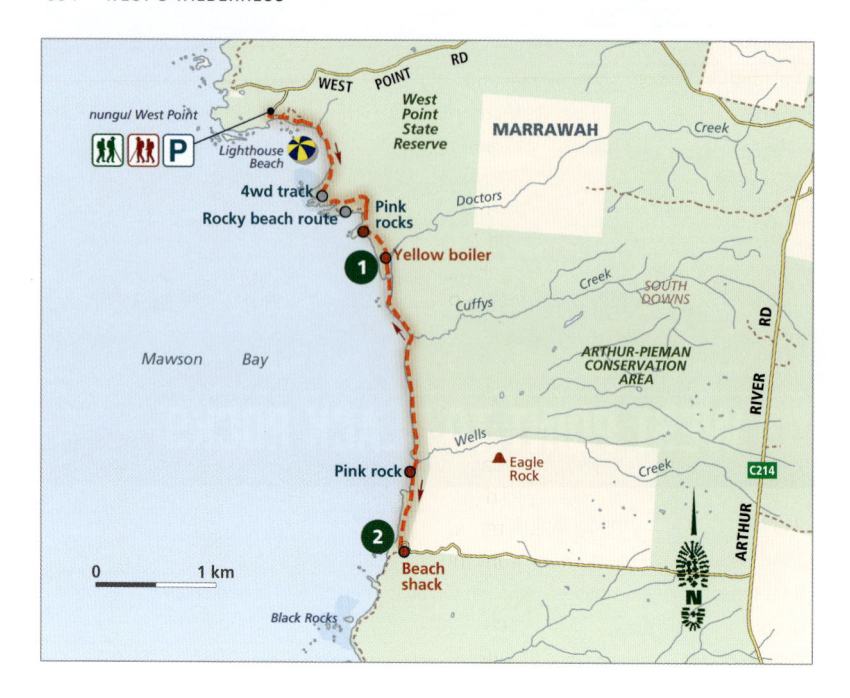

The Arthur–Pieman Conservation Area, which encompasses more than 1000 square kilometres of the takayna/Tarkine, has probably the greatest density of Aboriginal archaeological material in Australia; and West Point State Reserve, at its northern extreme, contains middens, stone artefacts and hut depressions.

Controversy continues regarding the closure of several 'traditional' coastal 4WD tracks to protect Aboriginal sites, with some parties lobbying for their reopening – but there are few restrictions on exploring by foot. Strolling – it's a different prospect in rough weather – along Mawson Bay, from West Point to Black Rocks and back (or through to Bluff Hill Point) gives you a taste of the wonders of Tasmania's west coast.

West Point is about 9km south-west of the tiny town of Marrawah, Tasmania's westernmost settlement, off West Point Rd, which runs through the Arthur–Pieman Protected Area to West Point State Reserve. After a kilometre of potholes, swap wheels for feet at a vehicle turnaround and tread a sandy 4WD track through sand hills to Lighthouse Beach (only the base of West Point Lighthouse, built in 1916, survives).

Sedgy grasses and succulent pig face flowers, which turn the dunes pink in spring and summer, have colonised these hills. Unfortunately sea spurge, a bright-green weed with disc-shaped leaves, thrives here too. About 200m from the parking area you'll see a footpad going right. This negotiates a rocky outcrop and is a more fun alternative to following the 4WD track to the beach. Both options deposit you on a sweep of pale sand between greened dunes and colourful rocks.

This beach attracts surfers, who revel in long rides in westerlies, and when they're out on the water you could sit and watch the board riders rather than walk anywhere! (Green Point Beach, north of West Point, is regarded as one of Australia's best surfing spots.) West Point's also a bird-breeding area so avoid soft sand above the high-tide mark, where hooded and red-capped plovers nest in shallow scrapes.

Walk south down the beach, watching for contrasting black-and-white pied and sooty oystercatchers among the grey gulls. During their late-spring and summer breeding season these cartoonish birds, with long red beaks and red legs, wheel above, squawking, to distract you from raiding their nests in the soft sand. Kelp stalks with wavy tentacles litter the beach like discarded cat o'nine tails. Red rocks project from the sand, some with sharp edges, others polished to a marble finish.

A stream runs down the beach from the rippled dunes, some of which are many metres tall and bear the footprints of people who have clambered up them. If the temptation to do likewise proves irresistible, turn back if you see any birds' nests or aboriginal shell middens.

You can probably round the next headland, about 1.25km south, on the rocks but a 4WD track detours inland; you can then either stay on the track for another loop to the next beach or make your way around the rocky shore.

Succulent pigface flowers turn the dunes pink

Watch for sooty oystercatchers among the silver gulls

A masterful piece of driftwood looks like it was placed on this headland rather than dumped by the sea and intriguing examples of conglomerate rock adorn the next, smaller headland about 100m beyond. It's as if a giant picked up assorted rocks and squeezed them together.

A yellow-coated rusting metal boiler (see point 1 on map), presumably washed ashore from a ship, rests on the southern bank of Doctors Creek, which exits the dunes just over 2km into the walk. It's encrusted with molluscs and worth a closer look although doing so might disturb the swarm of tiny insects it attracts.

From the next headland, about 400m on, you get a long view down the bay to Black Rocks and, sometimes, the lighthouse on Bluff Hill Point, the alternative finishing point. Continue south along beaches and over small headlands, splashing through Cuttys and Wells creeks. You'll know you've reached Black Rocks when you see a beach house, colloquially called a 'shack', in the dunes – 'mansion' is a more appropriate name for the 'shacks' at Bluff Hill Point, some of which are owned by cray fishermen. There's a huge striped and honeycombed boulder on the beach at its foot.

The beach ends in a mass of upended, layered, rock-painted orange with lichen. Walk around the seaward end of its first two upthrusts and head up the vehicular track disappearing into the dunes. A walking track branches right below the house, and climbs steeply over the headland before dropping into another cove (see point 2 on map). This is where out-and-back walkers turn around.

Through amblers continue south, over several more headlands, with Bluff Hill Point lighthouse disappearing from view with each step closer.

WEST & WILDERNESS

57 MOUNT DONALDSON TO CORINNA VIA SAVAGE RIVER

Walk:	14.5km, A to B with car shuffle
Time required:	4.5–6 hours
Best time:	Clear, mild weather (there's no protection on Mt Donaldson)
Grade:	Moderate
Environment:	Cool temperate rainforest, river, exposed hill, historic mining village
Best map:	This one
Toilets:	Flush toilets at Corinna
Food:	Delicious meals are available from the Tarkine Hotel in Corinna and a few staples from the adjoining General Store, which also sells recreational fishing licenses. There's tank rainwater for drinking behind the hotel.
Tips:	You need to car shuffle to do the described walk. Alternatively, make it a two-day return walk, tenting in the tiny parking/camping area below Mt Donaldson or on the mountain; or do two return walks: Corinna to Savage River and back, and up and down Mt Donaldson.

Walk from exposed mountain summit with uninterrupted Tarkine views to a historic mining town through verdant riparian rainforest.

The Savage River snakes through the Tarkine

338 WEST & WILDERNESS

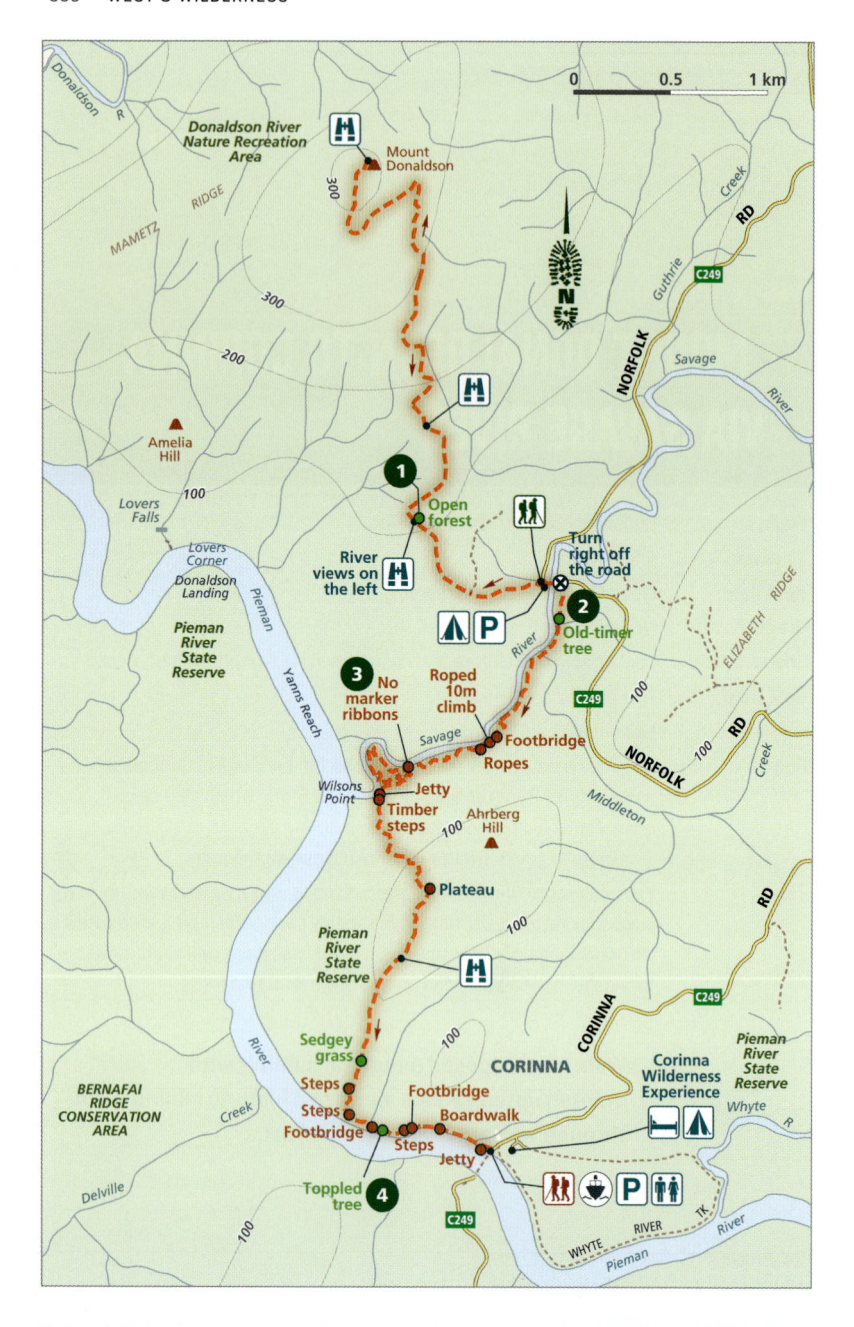

A rough, tough, boom town in the late 19th century, when gold mining swelled the regional population to 2500, Royenrine, as Corinna was once called, is enjoying a quieter second life as a wilderness retreat, deep in Tasmania's Tarkine. (Corinna is an Aboriginal word for a young Tasmanian tiger.)

With accommodation in restored miners' cottages and custom-made units, a camping area, and a hotel-restaurant-general store, Corinna is a base for exploring the Pieman River and its enfolding forest by boat and boot. It's also a popular stopover for travellers crossing the Pieman on the Fatman Ferry to continue journeying north or south.

'The Pieman' was Thomas Kent of Southampton, a baker transported to Van Diemen's Land (Tasmania) in 1816 and sent to the infamous Macquarie Harbour Penal Station in 1822. Kent escaped but was caught near the mouth of the river that now bears his nickname.

Corinna walks range from short and easy to overnight. Combining the Mt Donaldson climb and a one-way walk to Corinna down a Pieman tributary, this one begins about six gravelly kilometres north of the settlement. Take Corinna Rd out of the village for roughly 3km then Norfolk Rd north-west for the same distance to a one-lane bridge over the Savage River.

Starting on the left, over the bridge and opposite a pocket handkerchief-sized parking and camping area (with no facilities), the Mt Donaldson track plunges into shadowy forest. Cross a footbridge guarded by a splendid old tree and start uphill, through tree ferns and mixed eucalypts, the fallen ones cloaked in moss. On warm days it can be stuffy here and the steady climb seems steeper than the later pitch up the mountain.

Button-grass seed heads bristle like antennae on Mt Donaldson

About 1.4km up, you emerge into open forest (see point 1 on map) and swing right. Descending unexpectedly, you pass through dead eucalypts that appear like ships' masts, victims of a 2008 bushfire that burnt much of Mt Donaldson. Climbing again, you've a great view over the skeletal timbers and leafy new growth to the Norfolk Range. Then you're above the tree line on a hillside bristling with button grass, dwarf banksias and stunted tea tree.

Here feet have compacted Mt Donaldson's peaty covering. The track is still fairly soft but loose rocks can make the going slippery higher up. More loops of the Savage River come into view as you climb and the plants become shorter and stumpier, as if keeping their heads down.

Mt Donaldson feels the brunt of west-coast weather and while the summit breeze is welcome on warm days it can be full-force in colder weather so take a jacket. Up top, about 444m above sea level, are an upended trig point and a knockout 360° vista of the Norfolk Range, forest-clad Tarkine, serpentine Savage, and Southern Ocean coast. It is worth setting out early on this walk to catch sunrise from the top.

Back down the mountain, cross the bridge and step right into mossy riparian rainforest. Initially vehicle-wide, the track can be churned by wheels but it's flat and easy going. The route is marked with pink ribbons but essentially you keep the Savage River on your right.

Among predominantly walking-stick thin immature trees are some giants with branches thrusting out from mossy bases piled with years of leaf litter; plate fungi project from their trunks. One old-timer (see point 2 on map) has lost its top and its wide, undercut base is hollowed and drilled with holes yet its surviving branches are thick with epiphytes.

About 1km from the road a creek runs into the river. Depending on water level, you may be able to walk across or shuffle along a fallen log; look for ribbons marking the best places. A footbridge fords another creek 100m further on. Now look for pink ribbons marking a steep, roped 10m climb up and over a bluff about 1.25km from the road. It's far from mountaineering but the ropes provide welcome help for those not related to mountain goats. Back on the riverbank, follow the Savage 100m or so downstream to another roped clamber.

Continue downriver, noting the multiple mosses growing on the logs you step over. There are numerous marker ribbons, too, some of which would be more helpful beyond the next creek, where it's easy to lose the track (see point 3 on map). If you do, keep to the river, with the creek on your left.

Two more creek crossings (work your way upstream to find a spot) bring you to a jetty, to which kayaks are often tied. Paddling on the Savage and the Pieman River, visible 150m downriver, is s popular activity (Corinna hires

The view from the top of Mt Donaldson reaches to the sea

boats). One attraction is the hull of steamship *Croydon*, which rests in 10m of water here, having sunk early on 13 May 1919 while loading logs.

Now for the Savage River Walk, which starts steeply up Ahrberg Hill from the jetty on boardwalk and timber steps. The walk is officially rated moderate–hard and marked with white metal squares (yellow ones coming out of Corinna).

Up top are some big beech and Huon pines, the prized timber that brought 'piners' to this remote region before gold miners, and saw boats wrecked at Pieman Heads. Their branches creak against each other in wind. Fungi grow on the forest floor and fallen logs. Trackside holes ringed with dirt doughnuts are the handiwork of burrowing crayfish.

Watch for tripping roots in the track as you walk over the hill and start down the other side, in open forest through which you can see the Pieman's hilly opposite bank but not the river itself.

Back at water level, cross a creek, step up and duck under a toppled tree (*see* point 4 on map) (tall people might have to limbo), and then walk on with the Pieman lapping at roots and moss-covered rocks to your right. The unimpressive trees leaning over the water here are Huon pines. They are centurions but escaped the piners because the water made them grow in strange shapes that wouldn't yield usable timber. The Pieman River and tributaries mark the northernmost distribution of Huon pine in Tasmania.

The boarded Huon Pine Walk gives you an easy 300m warm-down into Corinna to finish.

WEST & WILDERNESS
58 MONTEZUMA FALLS

Walk:	11km return
Time required:	3 hours
Best time:	Year-round: damp, even misty days with no sun intensify the greens
Grade:	Easy
Environment:	Rainforest, waterfall, mining history
Best map:	This one
Toilets:	Pit toilets at the start of the walk, beyond the gate, and in the top picnic area.
Food:	The nearest available food is from the supermarket, cafes and pub in the mining town of Rosebery, 8km away.

Tips:	Wear closed shoes; most of the walk's on compacted gravel but even in summer there can be mud.
	     Take a torch (or use your phone) for exploring the adit (mine tunnel) on the track.
	     Leashed dogs and mountain bikes are permitted.

Time-travel through Tasmanian mining history on this easy walk in lush, leafy rainforest to one of Tasmania's tallest waterfalls.

The walking track passes an old timber bridge, all mossy timbers and rusty bolts

MONTEZUMA FALLS 343

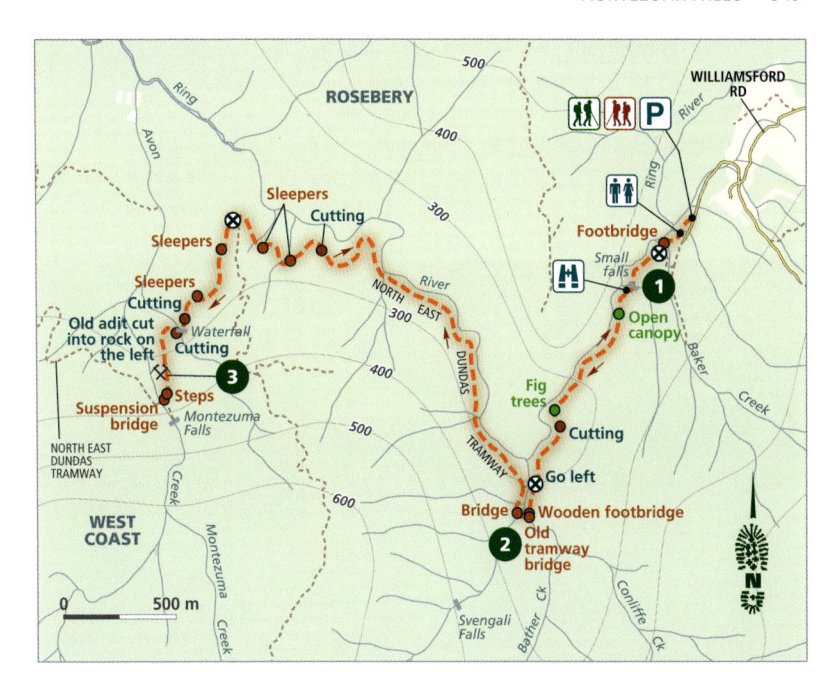

Why does Tasmania's highest single-drop cascade (104m) bear the name of Mexico's last Aztec emperor? Because it's named after the Montezuma Silver Mining Company, founded in 1891, which found gold and silver, the treasures of the Aztec empire, (as well as tin, lead and zinc) from leases in the surrounding hills. Local mining has ceased but the falls are another treasure worth unearthing.

The historical falls walk starts in a gravel car park 6km of winding bitumen and 2km of potholed gravel (called Williamsford Rd) off Murchison Hwy (A10). Branching south off the highway about 2km west of Rosebery and 27km east of Zeehan, the access road winds through the remains of the old mining community of Williamsford on the Ring River Goldfield.

The walk follows the route of the North East Dundas Tramway (a 61cm narrow-gauge railway) constructed in the 1890s between hills mining operations and smelters in Zeehan in Tasmania's west. One step past the green gate at the end of the car park and you're on a flat gravel track in a railway cutting.

Follow the tramway route past toilets (right), and keep left at a track junction, crossing rocky Ring River by a footbridge (the right-hand track enables cyclists to ride through the water). Keep left again at the next junction, and climb a narrow track through trees, or tread the wider one, watching and listening for bikes. Turn right at the top into another cutting whose hand-cut walls are a gateway into cool temperate rainforest.

Everything here – trees, rocks, forest floor – is plush with almost luminescent moss. With the Ring River frothing over rocks at the bottom of the steep bank to your right, you'll pass a gully down which runs a waterfall-fed

The further along the track you go, the more sleepers you'll see in the cuttings

creek (see point 1 on map). A pocket of fern-filled forest opened to the sky by a tree fall exposes the river's equally steep opposite bank.

A lush corridor of fig trees leads into another cutting. Standing here beneath a canopy of myrtle beech, sassafras, leatherwood and blackwoods, some clinging to the lip of the cutting with finger-like roots, it's hard to believe that much of this land was cleared between the 1890s and 1910s. The trees were felled to make sleepers, build bridges and houses, shore-up mine shafts, and fuel smelters and cooking fires. The smelters closed in 1914, after the outbreak of World War I, and the tramway was used only infrequently until its closure in 1932. You are walking through regrowth forest, aided in no small part by a staggering local average annual rainfall of three metres!

About 1km into the walk the track swings south up Bather Creek, crossed by a wooden footbridge beside the original tramway bridge (see point 2 on map), all mossy timbers and rusty bolts. Having crossed another creek, head back towards the river and walk on to a relaxing gurgle of water. About 3km into the walk, the track again pulls away from the river, and turns sharply south. Ignore the incoming vehicular track on a bend; there's a bench seat shortly after.

The further you go on this track the more railway sleepers you will see in the cuttings. These lovely old tramway timbers are very slippery when wet, but risking that can be a welcome alternative to getting muddy and in the largest cutting, on the final approach to the falls, additional walking planks have been laid. The ground is muddy here but also littered with small rocks loosened from the exposed, yellowish rock wall.

The sound of falling water is loud by the time you come to an adit (see point 3 on map) hand-cut into the hill. Go in and examine the tool marks by torchlight.

The last track junction is just beyond another footbridge. A track keeping left along the valley wall leads to the base of the falls but first, if you've got a head for it, step up right onto the very narrow, very high suspension bridge across Avon Creek (a Ring River tributary). Enjoy a view of the cascade and your only chance to fit the whole drop in a photo frame. The tramway crossed a 48m long timber trestle bridge built so close to the falls that spray hits the carriage windows but the few relics of this 19th century engineering feat are lost in foliage.

It's only a short walk from the far side of the replacement suspension bridge to another parking area but the 14km of 4WD track access to here is rough and driving it can take hours.

Back across the bridge, head to the base of the cascade and watch the water drop in a single veil from 100m above. Then retrace your steps to the car park.

WEST & WILDERNESS

59 MOUNT FARRELL & LAKE HERBERT

Walk:	10.5km return
Time required:	4–6 hours
Best time:	Clear, mild day
Grade:	Moderate
Environment:	Forest, sub-alpine button-grass plains, man-made and natural lakes, exposed hillsides and ridgelines
Best map:	This one
Toilets:	Public toilets in Tullah's main street
Food:	Drop in to Tullah Tavern for pub grub, including assorted chicken parmas. All meals at Tullah Lakeside Lodge come with a side serve of Lake Rosebery view.
Tips:	Wear trousers or gaiters as protection from the sharp shrubs on the overgrown last leg of this walk. Be prepared for changes in weather; take a water- and windproof jacket and turn back if conditions deteriorate.

Mix man-made lakes, tranquil tarns, panoramic mountain views and a bit of a bush bash and you've got a great half-day adventure.

From Mt Farrell you can see into the Cradle Mountain range

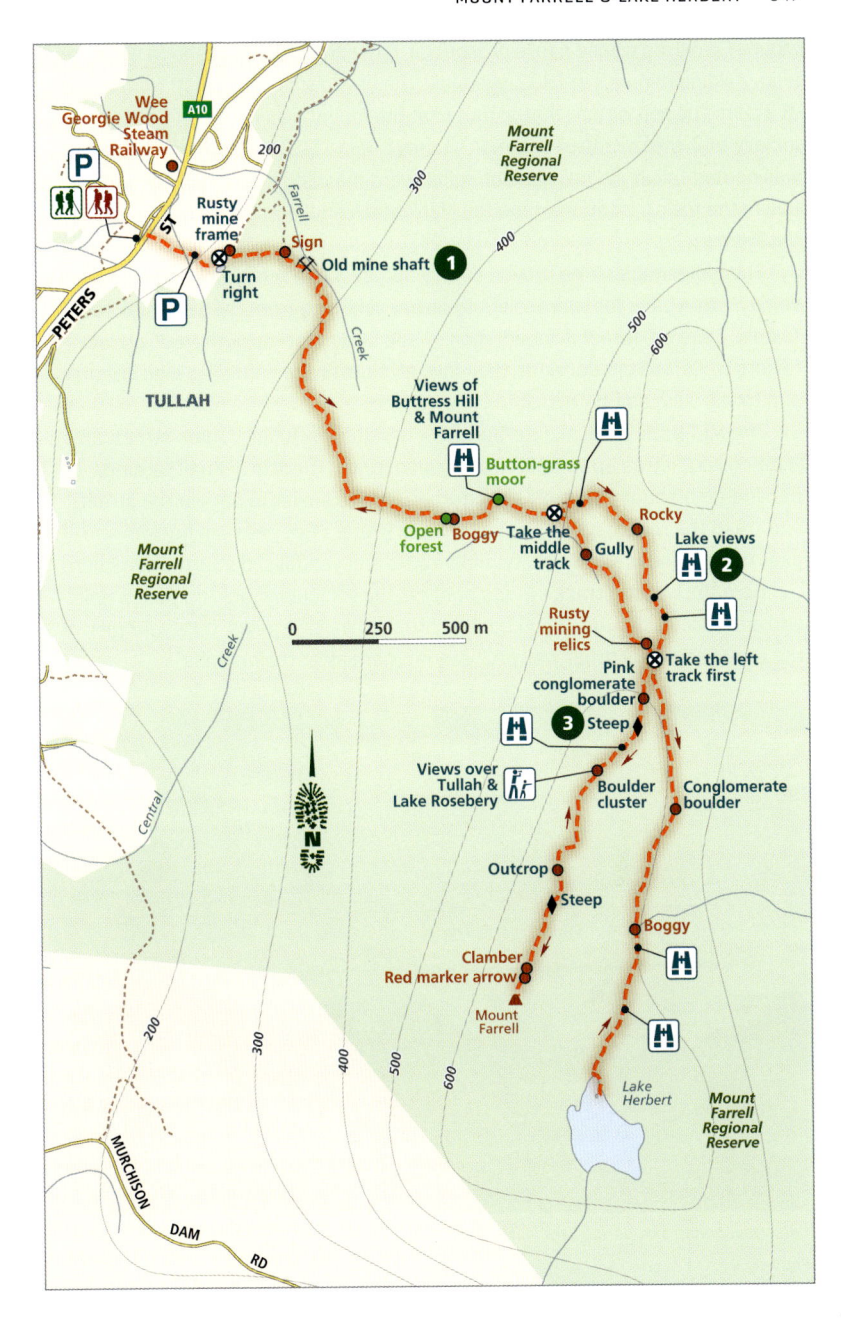

MOUNT FARRELL & LAKE HERBERT 347

Mount Farrell, on whose flanks prospector Tom Farrell found galena (a silver- and lead-yielding mineral) in 1892, overlooks the tiny township of Tullah from a height of 712m. The settlement that sprouted at the mountain's foot after Tom's strike initially took the mountain and man's name but in 1901 the town proclaimed it was named Tullah. Tullah is an Aboriginal word meaning meeting of the waters, due to the town's location where the Mackintosh and Murchison rivers become the Pieman.

The indigenous name proved doubly apt, because the ex-mining town was a construction base for hydro-electric power schemes from the 1970s to 1990s. Twenty years on, forest-fringed, man-made lakes stocked with trout attract fishers while walkers continue their love affair with the enfolding high country and tarns, such as tiny, elevated Lake Herbert.

The Mt Farrell and Lake Herbert walk is signed in Tullah's main street, 56km winding kilometres up the B28 from Queenstown. There is a small turning/parking area about 150m off the bitumen but it's easier to park in the street and tread the rough, gravel vehicular track (Peters Rd) between houses and past the parking area to a rusty mine frame and vandalised information board.

Here the walking track swings right off the vehicular track, up past a pole and a rustic 'track' sign. If you haven't brought walking poles, take your pick of the assorted sticks other walkers have left here after their climbs.

Catch your breath overlooking Lake Mackintosh

The track, obvious and marked with ribbons and red arrows, starts steeply enough to stretch your Achilles tendons. Ignore a track going left from a Mt Farrell Regional Reserve sign and keep climbing, past what looks like an old mine shaft (unsigned) (see point 1 on map). The going's reasonably easy despite the odd rock and root – and in any case, someone has placed a couple of plastic chairs on the track for rests!

About 1.7km from the start you step from shaggy eucalypts and occasional tree ferns into open forest of white-flowering bauera and button grass. The forest interchange can be boggy but full-frontals of Buttress Hill, ahead, and Mt Farrell to its right, make up for the mud.

Worn through 30cm of peaty soil, the track heads towards Buttress Hill before veering right and gifting a view along Mt Farrell to the craggy monolith of Mt Murchison. (A more challenging hike with a rock-clamber finish puts you atop Mt Murchison). Man-made Lake Rosebery appears behind as you continue up Mt Farrell.

At an unsigned three-way junction, take the middle track, ignoring the logs someone has laid across it. The right-hand track is the shortest route up Mt Farrell but we're visiting Lake Herbert before summiting and coming back that way. The left-hand track is a loop to nowhere that re-joins the middle one a few metres on.

In spring and summer, red Tasmanian Christmas bells and pink trigger plants decorate the slope up to a rocky saddle and on the climb Mt Murchison disappears behind Mt Farrell and man-made Lake Mackintosh appears left. The view encompasses more of that huge lake, and backdrop glaciated ranges, as you work right (see point 2 on map), around the back of the mountain. (Mt Farrell's quartzite spine blocks the worst westerlies, but this east-face traverse can still be windy.)

Mount Murchison reappears as you pass a conglomerate boulder, it's rugged visage dwarfing Lake Herbert, the exquisite tarn that comes into view below as you crest a pyramidal rise, but the mountain disappears again as you make the often boggy final approach to the tarn. Look for cute mauve-and-white fairies aprons and other wildflowers along the way.

Lake Herbert, 4km into the walk, is a gorgeous spot for a cooling swim in warm weather however it might stop your heart in wintry weather! Work clockwise around its shrubby shore to stepping stones leading to a tiny island for a close look at the rocky bed through liquid-toffee water.

Retrace your steps roughly a kilometre, turning left onto a faint footpad, usually marked with a ribbon, a shortcut to the summit track that saves you

TOP: *Rugged Mt Murchison rears up beyond Mt Farrell;* **BOTTOM LEFT:** *This way!;* **MIDDLE RIGHT:** *Keep an eye out for fungi in the forest;* **BOTTOM RIGHT:** *Lake Herbert comes back into view as you near the top of Mt Farrell*

more than 1km of backtracking. A short climb leads to a shoulder-wide, chin-high cutting. Immediately inside, clamber left onto the ridge, rather than push through the overgrown shrubbery.

The summit track heads left from here up the ridge, with the view behind broadening into a horseshoe of 'wow'! Note the pink conglomerate boulder and, uphill to its right, a natural rock arch. Topping this slope you'll see Mt Murchison again and Lake Herbert nestled down left.

A very steep pitch (see point 3 on map) puts you under a banksia in a conglomerate cluster. Tread the right-hand track a few metres out onto the boulders for an expansive view over Tullah and Lake Rosebery and the takayna/Tarkine. The track beyond here is less distinct and more exposed but navigable in clear conditions.

Enjoy the view before backtracking down the mountain or proceeding (weather permitting) through button grass. Having veered right around one outcrop, you've got a short, steep pitch onto another. Tullah and Lake Herbert now lay either side of you, range upon range fading into the distance behind the tarn.

Push, literally, through wiry heath along the ridge, following a faint track very occasionally marked by a pink ribbon. After several false summits, a major outcrop gives you your first look at the trig point 100m ahead. (A red arrow tied to a tree identifies the step-down point from these rocks for your return.) The summit is secured after one more climb and it's worth the effort, because the view beats everything that's come before. There's even a flattish rock on which to sit and enjoy it.

Back where the shortcut came up (it's easy to miss from this angle – keep to the most obvious track), follow the main summit track down over a grassy knoll, passing rusty metal scraps probably from the mining days. The track changes from boot-wide and sporadically boggy to rocky as it descends a scrubby gully (watch for snakes). The track then escapes the gully and crosses a hill to the junction passed earlier. Turn and retrace your earlier steps downhill.

The forest descent back to Tullah can tire legs weary from rock work. Take your time; appreciate the lichen, moss and fungi – even some purple ones – that you probably missed coming up.

WEST & WILDERNESS

60 PILLINGER POINT

Walk:	15km return with a 4WD car shuffle (25km return if you're doing it all on foot)
Time required:	3–4 hours (or 5–6 hours if all on foot)
Best time:	Overcast day for most intense rainforest greens.
Grade:	Easy (but long without an AWD/4WD)
Environment:	Rainforest, river, bay, historical mining town
Best map:	This one
Toilets:	In the townsite of Pillinger (on the shore of Kelly Basin)
Food:	You can tuck into tasty tucker at the Empire Hotel in Queenstown, 49km north, the closest town.
Tips:	Without at least an all-wheel-drive you may have to tread an extra 10km in/out from the road; and even with a 4WD, fallen trees can have you on foot earlier than planned. Don't leave Queenstown without visiting the Empire Hotel to see the terrazzo tiled hallway and National Trust-listed staircase.

Walk through a kaleidoscope of forest greens to the relics of a once-bustling mining port and township on the banks of Tasmania's most infamous waterway.

Forest is slowly reclaiming the mess hall chimney at Pillinger Pt

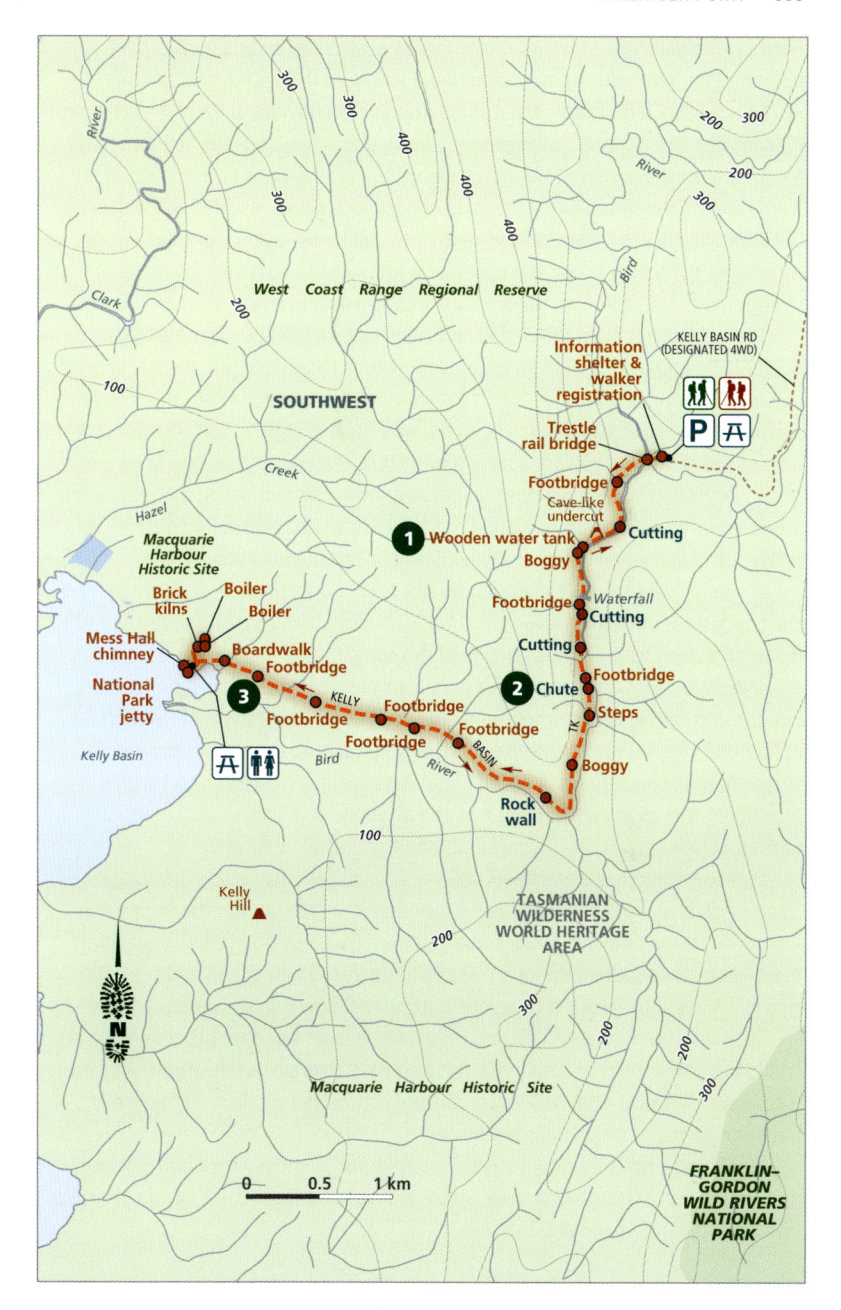

PILLINGER POINT 353

Home to Sarah Island, a remote hell-hole to which reoffending convicts were banished for harsh punishment and heavy labour in the 1820s, Macquarie Harbour earned a fearsome reputation among the convicts of Van Diemen's Land (Tasmania). But for late-19th century miners and piners (cutters of Huon pine) Macquarie Harbour was a hub for transporting minerals and timbers harvested from the forests and mountain ranges encircling the wild, west-coast waterway.

This walk follows the disused North Mt Lyell Railway line from deep in wet forest to the rusting relics and crumbling ruins of the port and township of East Pillinger, at Kelly Basin, on the harbour's south-east shore.

The walk starts from the Bird River Bridge parking and picnic area, 49km south of Queenstown. Head out of Queenstown on Lynchford Rd; this becomes Mt Jukes Rd which you follow for 29km until it becomes gravelled Kelly Basin Road. Another 11km on gravel brings you to the Bird River Bridge turnoff. The 5km from here to the official walk start is designated 4WD. The track has a firm base and is often navigable by all-wheel drive and even conventional vehicles; it is narrow and single-lane, however, with few places where you can pull over for an oncoming vehicle. And even a 4WD can be stymied by a fallen tree blocking the track.

If you get all the way by car, you've got a 15km return walk to Pillinger. From the road it's about 25km return. You walk, though, through stunningly beautiful forest, dripping with various shades of green.

The 4WD track ends at a small picnic and parking area with an information shelter and walker registration book. Record your plans and head through a chicane that prevents motorbikes proceeding further, to a sign and map of the Kelly Basin walk (as it is called in the Tasmania's 60 Great Short Walks brochure). The sign incorrectly gives the distance to Pillinger as 5.4km; it is actually 15km return, as indicated at the information shelter.

Walk on and cross beautiful Bird River on a handsome trestle rail bridge (clamber left or right down the river's west bank to photograph the bridge and its original Huon pine piles). Continue along a railway embankment, navigating boggy patches and the odd root. Pass through a tree tunnel and under trunks that fell, long ago, across the top of a cutting and now drip with moss and ferns.

Tree falls are common and you may have to clamber over others on the track, but otherwise the walking is flat and easy. And all the time you have the Bird River's treacle-coloured water on your left, working seaward musically between banks of moss and tree ferns.

You'll pass, on the right, a cave-like undercut of mossy rock and soil and, about 1km from the parking area, a rail-era wooden water tank sat up on the right-hand bank (see point 1 on map).

PILLINGER POINT 355

There are numerous cuttings along this walk; here men, working predominantly by hand, probably often in pouring rain, cleared passage for a train line. The ground within these cuttings is often very muddy so it's best to wear closed shoes that you don't mind getting dirty. Multiple varieties of moss and fern festoon the vertical walls of these cuttings, often so thickly that you cannot see the rock.

Shortly beyond a waterfall gully, the train bed has fallen away and the walking track narrows and climbs right. From there it descends to a footbridge presenting a good view of the river and enfolding greens. Narrow track, with

TOP LEFT: *High rainfall means lots of fungi;* **TOP RIGHT:** *The track loops through brick kiln ruins;*
BOTTOM LEFT: *Check out the rusty old boilers amid the greenery;* **BOTTOM RIGHT:** *Look out for natural treasures on the forest floor*

steps, returns you to flatter track in another cutting. Look down and you'll see the river working through chutes (see point 2 on map) and over rapids. Note how the water has undercut the cliff opposite.

About 2.5km from the information and walker registration, the track navigates a landslip that's brought down trees. The roots of other trees reach, finger-like, down the embankment and into the track. This is an ideal environment for fungi, too, on the trees and ground.

The valley now widens and the river branches, becoming estuary-like as it heads for Kelly Basin. The track fords multiple gullies, the raised train route keeping you out of boggy creeks. The forest then opens out and you can see further through the trees and more sky above. Crossing a footbridge, you've got a collapsed rail bridge immediately to your right (see point 3 on map), with rusty bolts poking from squared timbers. A longer boardwalk reveals another section of old track, to the left, some of its bolts 60cm long.

The water body soon visible through the trees is Kelly Basin and as you continue among ground ferns and eucalypts you reach an information sign. Welcome to Pillinger, built in 1898 for James Crotty's North Mount Lyell Mining Company. Copper and silver ores were transported via the North Mount Lyell Railway from the mine to smelters at the township of Crotty (to the north) and then to here for shipping. The smelters failed, though, when James Crotty died and in 1903 the company merged with a rival and Pillinger became redundant. The last train ran in 1925 and the last people left in 1943.

The government town of West Pillinger has long-since been consumed by the forest but walks here lead to remains of the company town of East Pillinger.

Turn right and tread boardwalk to the ruins of the brick kilns, red-brick shells with arched fire pits that contrast the forest's green leaves (there were also a sawmill and ore-crushing plant), and on to two rusty boilers. As you wander back through the forest to the junction, try to imagine East Pillinger in 1902 when it was home to 600 people and comprised 80 dwellings, two-dozen businesses, a Catholic church, three hotels and a coffee palace.

Turn right at the junction and walk a loop to the shore, where train tracks extend 100m into the water on stumps. Return along the shore, through paperbarks, passing the brick chimney of the Mess Hall (check out the old bottles) and the National Park jetty. Beyond this public landing place are toilets and a picnic table, although you often have to fight off ravenous mosquitoes to tuck into a sandwich.

Having explored the site, and perhaps dipped your feet in the once-infamous Macquarie Harbour, start back to your car.

WEST & WILDERNESS
61 FRENCHMANS CAP

Walk:	50km out-and-back
Time required:	3–5 days
Best time:	Daylight-saving months (December to April); but extreme weather can occur year-round. Often snowbound in winter
Grade:	Hard
Environment:	World Heritage wilderness, quartzite mountain, rainforest, button-grass moors, waterfalls, lakes
Best map:	TASMAP's *Frenchmans Cap Map & Notes 1:50,000*
Toilets:	Composting toilets at Lake Vera and Lake Tahune
Food:	The Hungry Wombat Café at Derwent Bridge, about 25km east of Frenchmans' parking area, offers satisfying post-hike food.
Tips:	Some people knock off Frenchmans Cap in three days, but allowing four or five opens more windows for summiting in clear weather. There are bunk huts at lakes Vera and Tahune but carry a tent for safety.

In-your-face mountain scapes and exquisite rainforest headline this classic multi-day adventure.

Afternoon light casts the mountains multiple shades of blue, grey and green

358 WEST & WILDERNESS

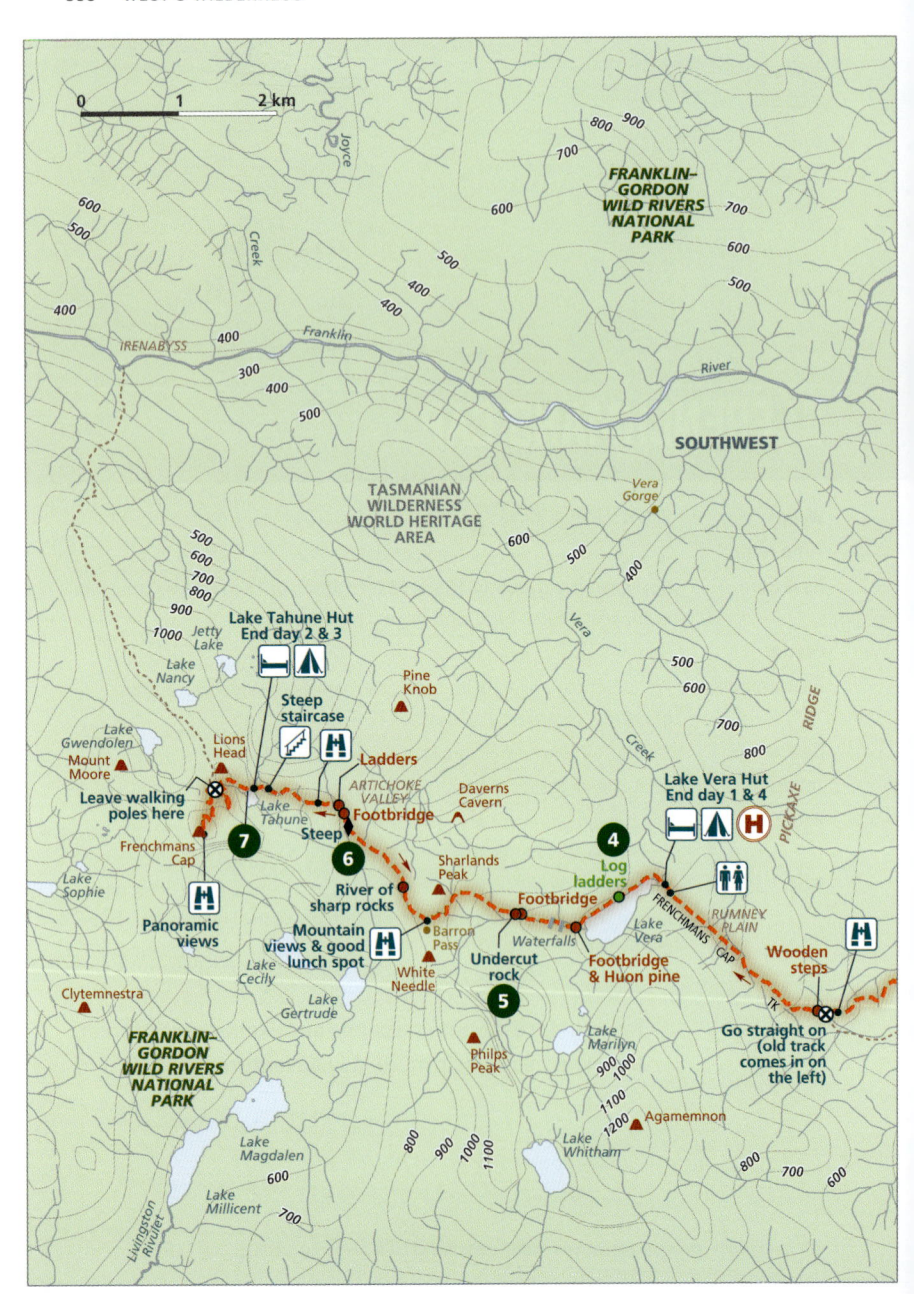

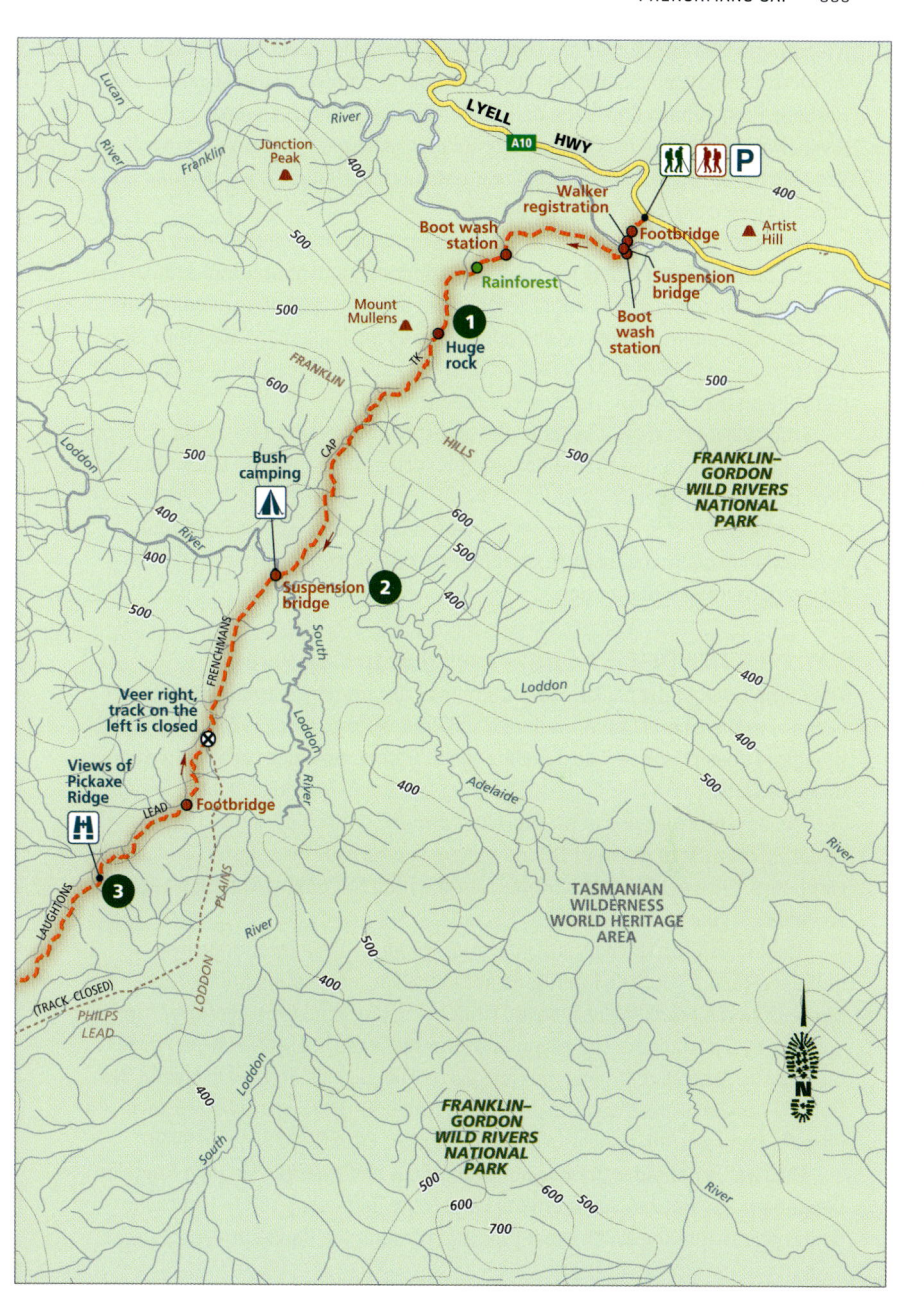

FRENCHMANS CAP 359

A landmark used by colonial-era ships sailing Tasmania's west coast, and by convicts attempting escapes from the hell-hole of Sarah Island in Macquarie Harbour, Frenchmans Cap is the dominant mountain in Franklin-Gordon Wild Rivers National Park, a part of the Tasmanian Wilderness World Heritage Area. The hike to the top of its distinct white quartz dome (1446m) is a multi-day adventure with sky-high WOW factor!

The Frenchmans Cap hike was for years notorious for the slog across the South Loddon (River) Plains (the 'Sodden Loddons') and photographs show hikers hauling companions out of thigh-deep bogs. As part of an ongoing 10-year upgrade jointly funded by entrepreneur and businessman Dick Smith and the Tasmanian Government, 4.6km of new track north of the Loddon Plains was officially opened in 2013. There is still mud though.

Embrace it and wear it proudly! Protect the environment by walking through bogs; don't step around them because this further degrades the track. Gaiters provide some protection.

The alternative to doing this walk independently is to join a guided tour. Tasmanian Expeditions (www.tasmanianexpeditions.com.au), part of World Expeditions, are a great option.

DAY 1: 15.7km (4–6.5 hours) – Lyell Hwy to Lake Vera

The name given to the peak this walk summits is commonly attributed to its likeness to the Liberty Cap worn during the French Revolution (1789–1799); this mountain doesn't doff its cap in deference to anyone so expect to have to work for its rewards.

The adventure begins at an overnight parking area on Lyell Hwy (A10), about 25km west of Derwent Bridge (where you turn off for Lake St Clair) and two hours' drive north-west of Hobart on the road to Queenstown. Don't leave valuables in your car.

Step down from the car park into thick forest, cross a footbridge over a gully, and record your trip intentions at the walker registration booth. Now descend to the Franklin River, saved from being dammed for a hydroelectricity scheme by a passionate campaign and river blockade in 1982-3, which gave birth to the Australian Greens political party. The genesis of the successful 'No Dams' Franklin protest was the unsuccessful 1966–1973 campaign to save Lake Pedder (see The Needles, page 371, and Mt Eliza Plateau, page 375).

The river is named in honour of naval officer and explorer Sir John Franklin, Lieutenant Governor of Van Diemens Land (now Tasmania) 1837–1843, who died trying to find the North-west Passage through the Canadian Arctic. Cross

FRENCHMANS CAP 361

Rocky track traverses the face of Sharlands Peak as you push on to Frenchmans Cap (visible in the top left of photo)

the one-person-at-a-time suspension bridge over the river and scrub and spray your boots at a cleaning station to limit the spread of pests and diseases.

The track climbs from here into drier eucalypt forest carpeted with pink common heath and coral fern. Fungi flourishes here too: clusters of toffee-coloured mushrooms, miniature red ones and more. A wide, compacted gravel track provides easy passage from button-grass plain to mossy forest waist-high with cutting grass.

Scrub your boots again (there's a brush), or walk through the water, at the next creek. Then start up onto Mt Mullens' shoulder. A huge rock, part-way up (*see* point 1 on map), on the left, colonised by moss and ferns and crowned with trees, is a gateway of sorts into a lusciously mossy forest pocket that could have been lifted from Middle Earth in *Lord of the Rings*.

The fern with broad fronds that look (and feel) artificial is the hard water fern. Crush a flat, diamond-shaped, green, celery-top pine 'leaf' (actually a branch) for a whiff of gin and tonic to tide you over for the hike.

Frenchmans Cap reveals itself for the first time about 3.5km into the walk as you crest the tea tree-topped saddle beside Mt Mullens, only to disappear again when you start downstream, between a creek and the tea tree, banksia and celery-top pines that climb the slope left of you. The track flattens out on boarded button-grass plain where misty mornings string water beads on spiders' webs spun between grass stalks. Over a low rise frothy with coral lichen, you've got flatter walking to a boots-wide suspension bridge over the Loddon River (*see* point 2 on map), 6.9km into the walk.

Bush camping (with no facilities) is permitted both sides of the Loddon, on foliage-quilted riverbank among beech and laurel trees, and white-flowering bauera bushes. This is an overnight option if starting out late. Fifty metres south along the west bank, the track turns right and a short pitch puts you back among button grass. Rooted track and duckboards traverse a boggy plain watered by multiple creeks. Watch for the wombats responsible for the cuboid droppings on the boards.

In closer wattle forest, you'll cross a creek browned by tannins from button grass, wattle and tea tree, which protect the plants from grazing by herbivores. In addition to making the plants bitter to taste, the natural chemical decreases the efficiency of herbivores' digestive systems. It is, though, a good source of drinking water for humans (some treat it, most do not).

The re-routed alternative to ploughing through the infamous Sodden Loddens (part of an ongoing ten-year upgrade of the track) is called Laughton's Lead. It begins about 2km from the Loddon River, where the closed old track goes left (see point 3 on map). Breaks in the trees to your right offer glimpses of Pickaxe Ridge as you tread new gravel track through tea tree and across a slope greened with mountain-berry bushes, grasses, she-oaks and long-leafed eucalypts. Shortly after another deliciously dark, mossy forest patch you pass the western end of the old track.

Rock and wood steps, some a stretch for shorter legs, climb steeply through rainforest whose every surface is thick with moss and lichen. It's quiet too, the only sounds being the puffing 'hiking birds' (the squelch of boots in mud!); in places the track is worn 40cm through peaty soil to base rock. Agamemnon (1238m), Philps Peak (1282m), White Needle (1117m) and Sharlands Peak (1140m) show themselves as you gain altitude, ducking back behind a nearer ridge as you tramp downhill from muddy spot to muddy spot. They remain out of sight as you extend your stride on fresh boarding and new, raised, crushed-quartzite track across a plain.

Frenchmans Cap and its companion peaks grab your full attention again on reaching a hill-side composting toilet, from where wooden steps drop to Lake Vera to end Day One.

Lake Vera Hut can accommodate 20 hikers but sleeping space cannot be booked. New, wooden tent platforms and a helipad, immediately north of the

Moonlight kisses the ridgelines

hut, make the best of the view. For a great warm-down after making camp, walk a few hundred metres further along the track among the she-oaks and fungi fringing Lake Vera.

As the Lake Vera Hut visitor book (an entertaining read) testifies, many hikers spend two nights at Lake Vera and do a big day walk from here to Lake Tahune, up Frenchmans and back. Although this reduces the weight you have to pack to Lake Tahune, it gives you a once-only chance to reach the top; so if the weather turns you are scuppered.

DAY 2: 7km (4–6 hours) – Lake Vera to Lake Tahune

Day 2 kicks off with an unforgettable walk-cum-clamber along Lake Vera's northwest bank: around mossy boulders; through beech trees, pandani, tea tree and climbing heath with flashy, pink bell blooms; along logs and half-logs (see point 4 on map); up and down rocks, roots and tree-trunk ladders with no handholds. It's not aerobically taxing but demands concentration so the going is slow. It is also exquisite; each time you think the rainforest can't get any more beautiful you'll turn a corner and think again.

About 1km from Lake Vera Hut you cross a creek. The bright green, almost fluffy fir-like tree to the left of the footbridge is a Huon pine, a physically unimpressive specimen of one of Tasmania's most prized and precious timber trees. The plant with elongated, serrated leaves is native laurel, a common understory rainforest plant.

A two-tiered waterfall awaits up rock and timber steps, boardwalk and exposed roots – and further up Vera Creek, another cascade emerges from behind a huge boulder that, like everything else here, is softened with moss. Continue uphill past a huge undercut lump of rock (see point 5 on map) deposited by a glacier way back and now crowned with trees and ferns. Walk-the-plank crossings of shallow gullies and fragile ground test your inner core.

An altitude gain of nearly 400m in just over 3km puts you (probably puffing) on Barron Pass, 950m above sea level. White Needle (1117m) pricks the sky to your left, Sharlands Peak (1140m) rears up on your right, and Frenchmans Cap sits directly ahead, lesser peaks stepping down from it into a valley floored with lakes. Lunch (or snack) breaks don't get more spectacular than this, especially in autumn, when the fagus (deciduous beech) covering the slopes turn gold and red.

Rested and rehydrated, step sharply down off the pass to the right and traverse the south-west face of Sharlands Peak, treading boards across the steepest places, and sometimes clambering backwards down rocks and trees.

The track crosses a river of sharp rocks as it works in and out of forest and across exposed cliff. Again, you'll need to watch every step.

Frenchmans Cap disappears and flatter track works over the rise hiding it, through pineapple grass and similarly hardy shrubs, and a flotilla of dead trees. Everywhere here are silver skeletons of King Billy pines killed in a catastrophic 1960s bushfire (see point 6 on map).

Having managed a steep, rocky gully and a few strategically placed bogs, you're on old boardwalk – this may have been replaced by the time of publication – crossing swampy Artichoke Valley, with the Overland Track's (see page 303) crenelated ridgeline on the northern horizon and Frenchmans Cap in view ahead. See the bite-like saddle to its right? You will climb part-way up a scree slope below that saddle on your way to the top.

Steep staircases descend to Lake Tahune Hut, camping platforms and composting loos-with-a-view. The hut, completed mid-2018, has micro-hydro underfloor heating powered by a waterfall below the lake. This keeps it at a luxurious 16–18°C year-round, eliminating the risk of fire from wood-burning stoves and the temptation for hikers to collect and cut wood to warm themselves. It will also slow the hut's deterioration from cold and damp.

A short walk west of the hut puts you on Lake Tahune's shore (see point 7 on map) among trees scruffy with old man's beard (Spanish moss). Tannin-stained water reflects the vertiginous rock enfolding the lake and Frenchmans Cap, directly overhead.

DAY 3: 4.8km return (3–5 hours) – Frenchmans Cap Summit

Weather permitting, today's walk will put you on the summit. It's only a few hours up and back but having the whole day to play with, and the next morning, gives you the best chance to successfully make the climb. Don't set out if rain is forecast or the cap is hidden in cloud.

The summit track heads west from the hut, descending a few metres to cross the creek running out of Lake Tahune before climbing non-stop to the top, initially through leg-scratching scoparia and pandani, and concertina-leafed deciduous beech. Lake Tahune appears below as you emerge from the trees and drops away quickly as you ascend a scree slope. Footpads through the rubble identify the old route up to the saddle but the track now turns left (south) about two-thirds of the way up, cairns marking a short traverse to firmer footing. Views unfold all around as you zigzag up the mountain.

About 1.2km into the climb you reach a junction where arrows point up a rock face to the summit and ahead to Irenabyss. Greek for 'chasm of peace',

TOP LEFT: *Beyond Barron Pass, rocky track navigates exposed cliff;* **TOP RIGHT:** *Crossing the South Lodden River;* **BOTTOM LEFT:** *Mushrooms colonise the forest floor;* **BOTTOM RIGHT:** *Camped at Lake Vera with Frenchmans Cap overhead*

Irenabyss is a magnificent Franklin River gorge 5km from here (and 1000m lower). Franklin River white-water rafters sometimes summit Frenchmans Cap as a 'break' from paddling. If you're fit and have enthusiasm and lots of daylight, you could add the gorge return hike to the summit walk.

This junction is a good place to leave walking poles behind a bush as hands are more useful from here. Walk up the rock face and along the track to the most challenging section: a clamber up a chute with narrow handholds and footholds. While this doesn't demand rock-climbing skills, some people find it near impossible solo. Work with your walking companions to get everyone up.

Snow can fall on Frenchmans at any time of year, which is beautiful on a sunny day and ups the adventure level under an atmospheric grey sky. Look for paper daisies poking through the white. Stop and look, too, at the assortment of cushion plants, lichens, moss and other ground-clinging plants. The creeper with strawberry-like leaves is a native raspberry and the bright-green bristling trees are King Billy pines. These beautiful, tough plants only emphasise that there is nothing soft about this country: it's steep, multi-layered, sharp-edged geology. Frenchmans Precambrian quartzite cap is some of the oldest exposed rock in Australia.

Prospector and early Tasmanian explorer Thomas Bather Moore made the first ascent of Frenchmans Cap from the west in 1887, later describing looking up at 'the most majestic cliffs of overhanging rocks that I have ever seen. Bold and rugged ... grandly sublime and indescribably beautiful.') The view from the summit, roughly the size of a footy oval and sloped towards a southern drop-off, is just that. On a perfect day, the Southern Ocean is visible to the south, beyond Mt Anne and layer upon layer of ridgelines, and lakes Cecily, Gertrude, Magdalen and Millicent reflect blue sky from the valley below. (Moore laid down that all western lakes should have feminine names to suit their capricious loveliness!) To the east is Barron Pass and the King William Range, and strung along the northern horizon are Overland Track peaks.

Having made the top, backtrack to Lake Tahune to celebrate!

DAY 4: 7km (4–6 hours) – Lake Tahune to Lake Vera

If a clear day looks likely, begin Day 4 in the dark, walking by torchlight, and catch sunrise from the plateau above Lake Tahune; the first rays backlight the dead trees before striking Frenchmans Cap, which glows red before fading to paler hues. With morning mist resting in the valleys, even rolling over the hills, that's impetus enough to get up early.

DAY 5: 15.7km (5–7 hours) – Lake Vera to Lyell Hwy

Retrace your steps from Day 1, remembering to fill in the walkers' registration book on your safe return.

WEST & WILDERNESS

62 DONAGHYS HILL

Walk:	2.4km out-and-back
Time required:	1 hour
Best time:	Clear day year-round – most spectacular when there's snow on the peaks
Grade:	Easy
Environment:	Eucalypt forest, cool temperate rainforest, button-grass heath, mountains
Best map:	This one
Toilets:	There are no facilities at the parking area. If you can't wait for a toilet elsewhere there are plenty of modesty bushes but TAKE YOUR TOILET PAPER AWAY WITH YOU!
Food:	Grab a scrumptious hamburger at the Hungry Wombat café at Derwent Bridge 35km east.
Tips:	Check out the wonderful day walks and boat cruise you can do at Lake St Clair, Australia's deepest lake, out of Derwent Bridge.

Reward-to-effort ratios don't get much better than this wonderful short walk in Tasmania's wild west.

Trees, clouds and ridgelines produce layered scenery

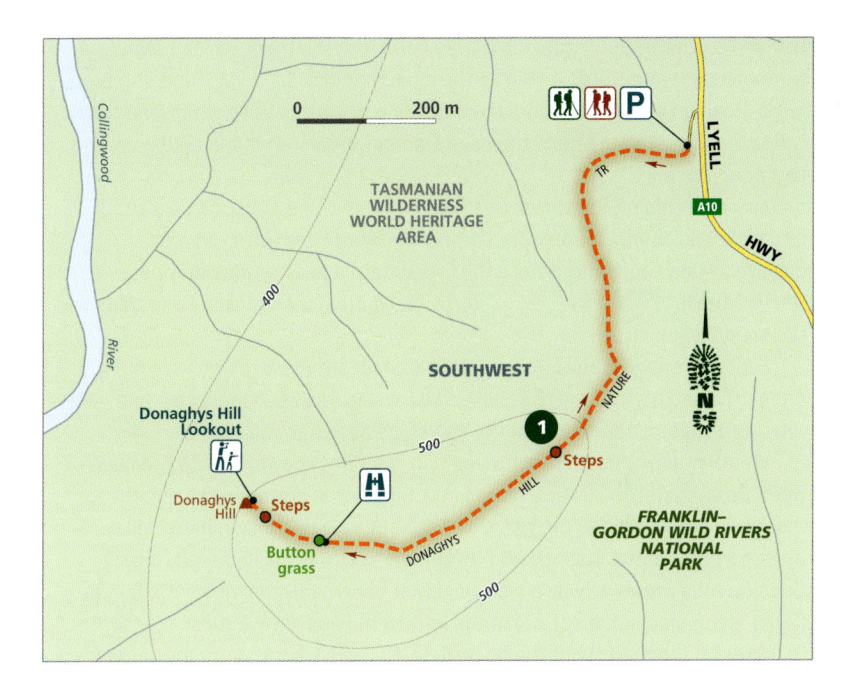

Donaghys Hill, in the heart of Franklin–Gordon Wild Rivers National Park, is a minnow compared with the surrounding mountains. But easy access makes it a standout place to get a taste of the Tasmanian Wilderness World Heritage Area without expending much energy on foot or with a paddle on an untamed river.

One of Tasmania's 60 Great Short Walks, the Donaghys Hill Lookout track starts on the southern side of the Lyell Hwy (A10) 51km south-east of Queenstown, 35km west of Derwent Bridge, and about 5.5km beyond the parking area for the challenging multi-day Frenchmans Cap hike (see page 357).

The 'hardest' part of this walk is the fairly easy, early climb on a broad compacted gravel track littered with leaves. This old alignment of the Lyell Hwy, which predates the road cutting, takes you through scruffy eucalypt and banksia forest carpeted with ferns; signs identify the dominant plants.

You get tantalising glimpses of mountain tops between the branches on your right until the track, now almost like a naturally cobbled footpath, narrows and swings right into dense cool temperate rainforest. Here grow myrtle beech (with variegated trunks), gum-topped stringybarks (the tallest trees), celery top pines (have a look, the leaves really do look like celery leaves) and tree ferns grow here. Tiny beech leaves polka-dot the track, which meanders through hard water ferns – they're the ones that look artificial – and fish bone ferns. Keep an eye out for fungi too, including beautiful yellow ones. The track traverses the south-eastern slopes of Donaghys Hill with steps taking you higher up the hill.

As well as hiding the views, this lush forest muffles all sounds except bird calls, the chorus loudest for early risers. About 1km into the walk, however, when you emerge from the forest onto a heathy ridge studded with button grass and the odd eucalypt, the hum of the Franklin River adds to the soundscape.

Fenced Donaghys Hill Lookout crowns the bluff ahead, steps (see point 1 on map) climbing through tea tree and banksias to a 360° mountain and valley view. Information boards name the geological features you can see.

Weather permitting, Frenchmans Cap (1443m) shows itself to the south-west, its unmistakable Precambrian quartzite dome crowning the encircling mountain profile. And 250m below to the south is the Franklin River Valley, meeting place of the Collingwood River and mighty Franklin, saved from flooding for a massive hydro-electric power scheme by the international 'No Dams' campaign and blockade in the late 1970s and early 1980s.

Soak up the majesty of the panorama, then walk back along the same track to your car.

Franklin River Valley from Donaghys Hill

WEST & WILDERNESS

63 THE NEEDLES

Walk:	3km out-and-back
Time required:	2–3 hours
Best time:	Clear, mild day
Grade:	Moderate (steep on unformed track but short)
Environment:	Mountains, exposed alpine plateau, heathland, views
Best map:	This one
Toilets:	None
Food:	None
Tips:	Wear boots (the track can be muddy) and take a jacket even on a sunny day; The Needles are exposed to the sometimes violent whims of south-west weather.
	An excellent and inexpensive base for walking in Tasmania's south-west is Giants Table and Cottages in Maydena (giantstable.com.au).

This cracker of a short walk in Tasmania's south-west rewards a bit of aerobic hill-climbing with views that are off the scale.

The jagged tooth-line that tempts hikers from their cars is not the top!

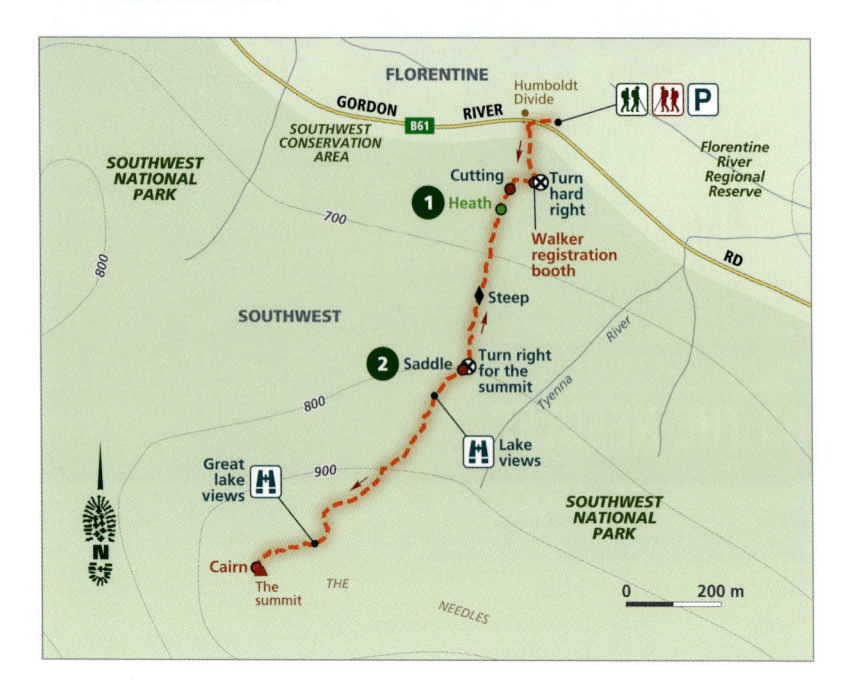

More suggestive of fangs than any recognisable sewing implement, The Needles sit 'grinning' above the high point of Gordon Bay Rd (C61) as it winds through Southwest National Park to Lake Pedder. Or perhaps it's a smirk, for hikers discover that the jagged tooth-line that tempted them from their car is barely half-way to the top!

This rewarding and fun short walk starts from the gravel parking area at the highest point on the scenic drive to lakes Pedder and Gordon, controversially flooded in 1972 to generate hydroelectricity; 19km from Maydena and 90 minutes' drive north-west of Hobart. A cairn and pink ribbon across the road at the western end of the parking area identify the start of the walk (there is no sign). Enjoy the view down the Florentine River valley to Lake Gordon before crossing – the road bends and is double-lined here so take care – and stepping into scrubby heath.

Beginning on a fire trail cut through flowering heath and strappy gums towards one of the most prominent Needles, you tunnel through tea tree to a cairn of white rocks about 20m in. Turn right here to a walk registration booth (it's worth recording your intentions even for such a short walk).

The view from the top of The Needles reaches to Lake Pedder

Your passage up the hill from here is also a track for water that runs down it from the surrounding slopes – and in places you've got mud among the compacted grass and rocks underfoot. Unformed rougher track made by feet and tied with pink ribbons pushes through banksia, mauve-flowering honey myrtle then climbs through striped alpine gums, cutting grass (not recommended as a handhold!) and banksias before landing you in a sea of wiry heath (see point 1 on map) with one of the biggest gauge Needles directly ahead and above. Spring and summer flowerings of yellow bush peas, cream mountain richea, mauve honey myrtle, white bauera, pink trigger plants and white alpine heath attract green-black-and-white Macleay's swallowtail butterflies. You'll pass occasional she-oaks too: the ones with the cones and tufty red flowers are female, those with pollen spikes are male.

As you climb, the view over your shoulder extends along the road west into the Florentine River valley and east along the Tyenna River valley. The track continues up onto a saddle (see point 2 on map) (the apparent top from the road, now 700m below) between two of the grey lumps of sloping layered rock thrust out of the heath that give The Needles their name, with another rising in front of you. An unsigned footpad goes left here to the base of one Needle but the summit is to the right.

There are no pink ribbons beyond the saddle but the well-worn, summit footpad, heading right and towards a ridge through tight, ground level heath, is obvious – at least in sunshine! This walk is dangerous in cloud cover or rain. As you walk on from the saddle you'll see lakes to the west; stop and look back, too, at those fantastic outcrops, Tim Shea (954m) rearing up from the other side of Gordon Bay Rd, and Mt Field West (see Tarn Shelf Loop page 38) on the horizon.

Having skirted a lumpy, protruding section of hill, on almost flat track above steep rocky slopes, you'll spot cairns marking your route up a ridge to the summit cairn, which looks tiny from here. Raw, rocky views accompany you towards the ridge through mounds of button grass. Five minutes of clambering brings you to the substantial summit cairn (1032m), to which you might want to add another rock.

You are encircled by the natural drama of valleys, lakes and mountains: flat tops to the north; Mt Mueller and the Mt Anne Range (see Mt Eliza Plateau page 375) to the south; the Wilmot and Frankland ranges on the far shores of lakes Pedder and Gordon. The car park is visible below and Maydena, in the Tyenna River valley, to the east. You will probably also see bald-patch logging scars on some slopes.

Absent from the climb, Tasmania's endemic scoparia thrives in the increased altitude up here, its bristling summer flower stalks adding foreground colour and texture to the summit view. The relatively easy pedestrian access makes this an ideal spot to watch the sun rise or set. Or you could just climb it in normal daylight and have lunch and a cuppa overlooking south-west Tasmania.

From the top, make your way back down the same way to your car.

TOP LEFT: *Alpine heath gives a suggestion of snow;* **RIGHT:** *Unformed rough track cut by feet pushes through heath scrub;* **BOTTOM LEFT:** *Yellow bush peas are among the many flowers that colour the slopes in spring and summer*

WEST & WILDERNESS
64 MOUNT ELIZA PLATEAU

Walk:	10km out-and-back
Time required:	5–6 hours (plus time up top)
Best time:	Clear, dry, mild weather (snow-bound in winter)
Grade:	Hard
Environment:	Button-grass plains, creeks, steep dolerite mountains, waterfall, lakes, cliffs, alpine plateau, steep rock clamber
Best map:	TASMAP's *Mount Anne Southwest National Park Walk Map and Notes* 1:40,000
Toilets:	In the car park and at High Camp Memorial Hut
Food:	None
Tips:	The Mt Anne Range is subject to foul weather with little warning. Whatever the forecast, pack wind- and waterproof clothing, food and water. Rain and misty cloud can make the last-leg clamber up onto Eliza Plateau slippery.

Soak up the cinematic view over Lake Pedder and Tasmania's south-west or unpick the tangle of wildflowers carpeting it in summer – that's the dilemma you face on reaching Eliza Plateau.

Lake Pedder spreads out below Mt Eliza

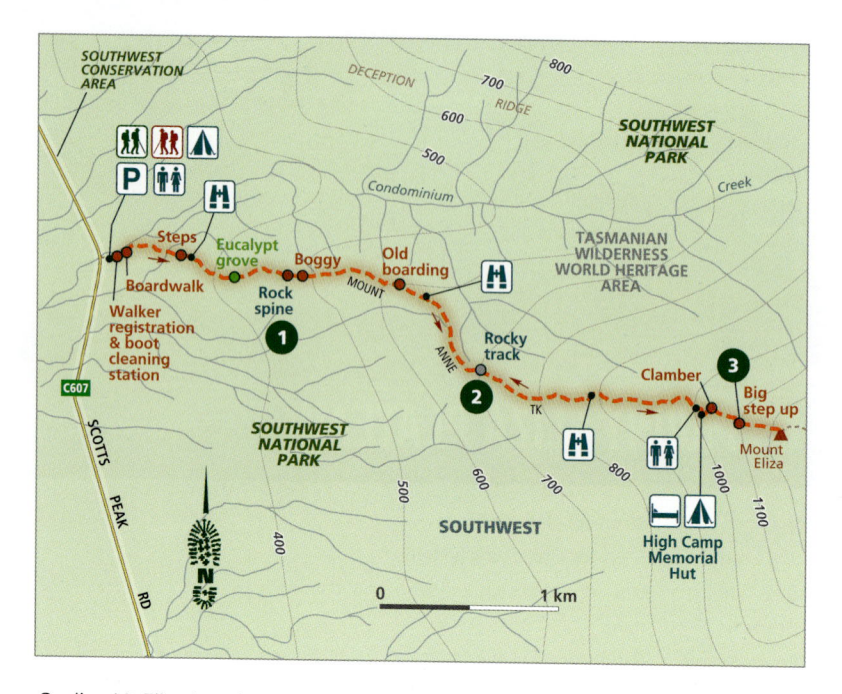

Scaling Mt Eliza is a shorter and less challenging alternative to bagging Mt Anne, the highest peak in Tasmania's South-west Wilderness. But everything is relative and reaching Eliza Plateau tests you mentally and physically. Some hikers channel mountain goats while others proceed more like sloths but if you are physically fit and prepared for the extremes of weather that put the wild in Tasmania's south-west, this is one hell of a day walk. It starts from a gravel parking area 21km south down Scotts Peak Rd and 127km (1.75h) west of Hobart. Travel via the Brooker (A1) and Lyell (A10) highways and the B62 and Gordon River Rd (B61) beyond New Norfolk. Scotts Peak Rd (C607) starts shortly before Lake Gordon.

The parking area sits beside beautiful Condominium Creek but there isn't a condo in sight, only peaks and ridgelines. With the rocky creek's tannin-tinted water on your left, head west through tea tree and eucalypts to a walker registration booth. Record your intentions and cross a gully to a boot-cleaning station. Feet scrubbed and sprayed, step eastwards on boardwalk. Ignore the footpad on the left immediately before a sign warning about the dangers of the climb, such as weather and rocks. This leads to a camping area beside the creek, to a sign.

Continue on the boardwalk which ends at a track you can trace towards a dramatic ridgeline dominated by Mt Anne (1423m) to the north. With peaks behind and on your left as well, cross button-grass flats fed by creeks, passing banksias, small eucalypts and honey myrtle shrubs (crowded with fluffy, mauve baubles in spring). Look out for small but show-off purple Tasmanian alpine lilies, a common endemic herb that also comes in rare yellow, as you start up a spur, about 500m into the walk.

The track becomes rockier, broken up with wood and stone steps, as you climb and Lake Pedder shows itself behind. The views compensate for the altitude gain and almost continuous climb to the top (remember to look back when you stop for a breather on the way up). About 600m up the spur the track veers round a rocky spine (see point 1 on map) projecting from the hill, at the top of which you are walking on exposed sedimentary rock layers some as thin as paper. To your left now is treed Deception Ridge, which runs east into Mt Anne (if you can see it for cloud) at the top of Condominium Creek valley.

Here the track is worn to bedrock and in places ground to sand underfoot. After rain you get boggy patches, some of which might muddy you to above your ankles.

The track continues along the creek side of the spur, an expanse of button grass and dwarf banksias dusted with white and yellow wildflowers in spring and summer. The track then narrows and walking poles come in handy with

Rock clambering and scrambling takes you to the top

roots and rocks on the only descent of note, around another rocky outcrop. Having trodden rotted boarding across a flat, resume climbing, on track worn 80cm deep to pinky grey-striped rock. (At the time of writing new, compound 'boards' had replaced some rotten sections.) And all the time Lake Pedder spreads behind you and Mt Eliza looms overhead.

The slope steepens and throws in a few step-ups as you ascend, again, to a mini saddle between multi-layered stone upended in Earth's upheavals and another rock spine (see point 2 on map), beyond which is ridgeline after ridgeline.

Continue climbing through heath with assorted shaped and textured leaves but all trimmed by wind and snow to only 70cm tall, up the spur to a saddle from which you'll see a scree slope to the right. As you round another outcrop on wider, flatter, less-steep track you'll see some more substantial trees sheltering below. Down there among scoparia bushes that festoon with flowers like Christmas candles during summer, about 4km into the walk, are unformed tent sites and a toilet with a Lake Pedder view. In spring, Tasmanian waratahs glow bright red among the green.

High Camp Memorial Hut, built in 1973 in memory of three members of the Hobart Walking Club, including photographer and conservationist Olegas Truchanas, sits among snow gums and myrtle beech 50m above the toilet. Hikers can sleep in the hut and previous residents have graffitied funny comments inside. The laziest of them have left toilet paper strewn around the hut too.

Look closely at the myrtles here. This cool temperate rainforest species grows at a range of altitudes from shrub to tree size and is seen on many walks in this book. These have perhaps the smallest leaves of any, the harshness of the conditions apparently affecting not just the size of the plant but also leaf area.

The real physical exertion starts now – with steep, rough track; rock clambering and scrambling to the top. About a hundred metres above the hut and tree line, you step up and over a huge boulder on which is a memorial plaque for Richard (Dick) Payling, killed in a fall near The Notch on the 26th February 2004. (The Notch, on nearby Mt Lot, is a notorious and particularly steep point on the multi-day Mt Anne circuit, up which most hikers haul their packs with ropes.) Stow or leave your walking poles and sticks below this boulder because they'll get in the way above it.

You gain 200m altitude over the next 700m or so and it's slow going following (and finding) a route marked by cairns up chunks, slabs and columns of dolerite embellished with lichen rosettes, but the heartening view over Lake Pedder and deep into the south-west rewards exertion.

When dry, the rock provides good grip so steeper, smoother slopes are often easier than they look. In rain it's a different experience and extreme care is needed. At one big step-up you can look right straight down on the huts and toilet and up Mt Eliza's rocky face. Scoparia and other flowering heath and even some snow gums find enough protection in cracks and hollows between the rocks to grow here despite the winter (and summer) snow.

On reaching a keep-like jumble of dolerite (*see* point 3 on map), where you can rest in the lee of jutting rocks, you'll see the odd cairn but essentially you'll need to find your own way over the battlement to navigate the last 200m or so.

Taking in Mt Anne, Lake Pedder and the wilds to the south-west, the view from atop Mt Eliza (1289m) recharges human batteries and soothes rock scrapes. Revel in it by exploring the plateau a little way towards Mt Anne and savouring your remoteness and vulnerability. Wildflowers unfurl across the plateau in summer and the vistas of mountain-backed flora can weary shutter fingers.

Lake Pedder and the Frankland Range, west of the water that is gilded by afternoon sun, fill your vision for much of the descent from Eliza Plateau, continuously distracting you from everything else around you including your next step. Mount Solitary, an island in Pedder sometimes transformed into a steaming volcano by well-placed cloud, was marooned by the controversial 1972 damming of the Serpentine and Huon Rivers, and flooding of the natural Lake Pedder, to generate hydro-electric power. Ever since, there's been occasional chat about the viability of draining it to restore its pink beach.

LEFT: *Rain stains an alpine gum cream and chocolate;* **TOP RIGHT:** *Rain beads on a snow pea flower;* **BOTTOM RIGHT:** *Lake Pedder from the Eliza Plateau track*

WEST & WILDERNESS
65 HARTZ PEAK

Walk:	8.7km out-and-back
Time required:	3-4 hours
Best time:	Mild, sunny day; can be cold and windy at any time of year and snowbound in winter
Grade:	Moderate (exposed alpine country and rock clambering near the top)
Environment:	Subalpine woodlands, ice-carved crags, lakes and moorlands
Best map:	This one or TASMAP's *Hartz Mountains National Park Map & Notes* 1:50,000
Toilets:	Flush toilets in car park
Food:	None
Tips:	Hartz Peak and the shorter Lake Esperance walk are popular on clear days so start early if you want the experience to yourself.
	Whatever the forecast, carry protective clothing and something to eat. The rock is slippery when wet and/or icy.

Get a taste – smell and feel too – for Tasmania's World Heritage South-west Wilderness from a natural lookout on a glaciated spine of dolerite.

Mountain rocket adorns the alpine plateau

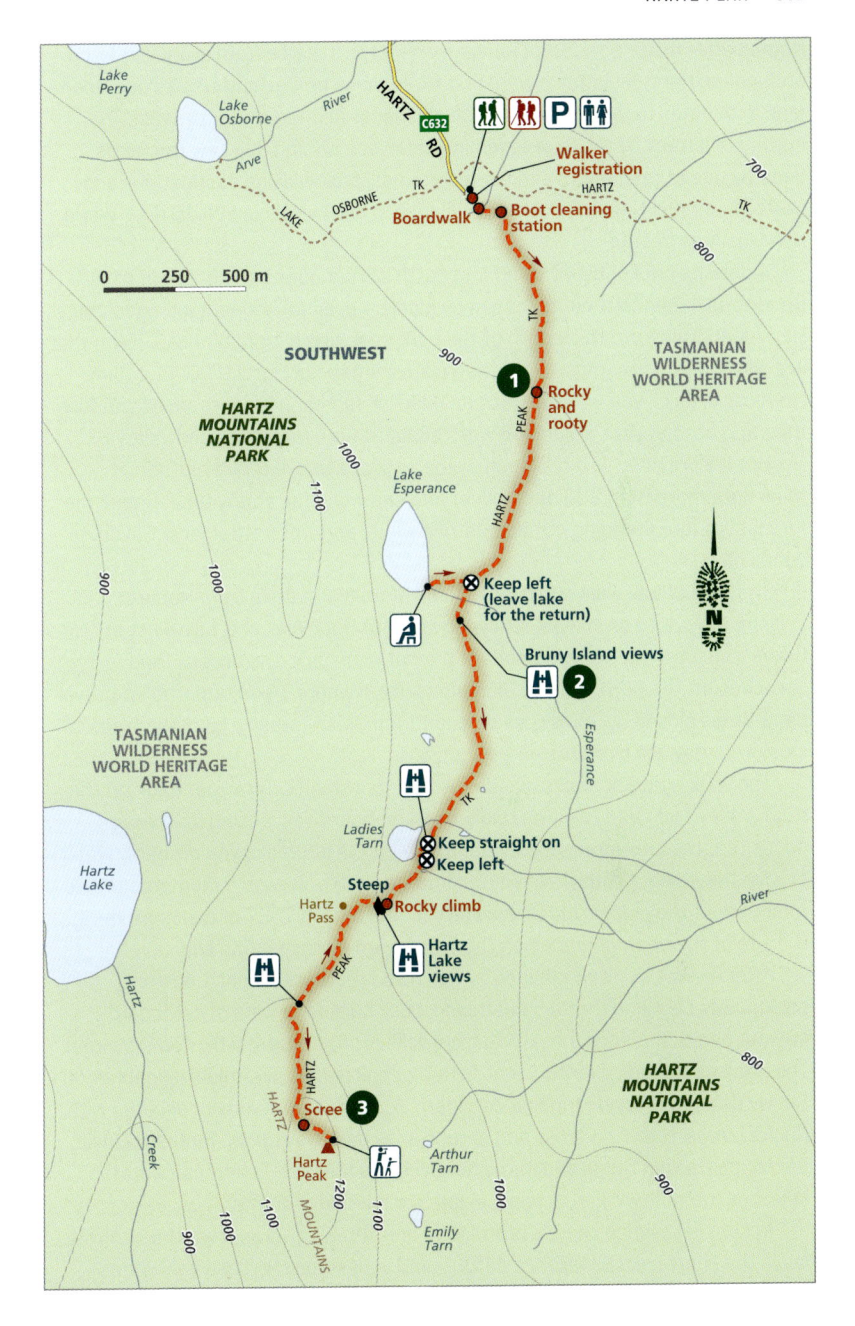

HARTZ PEAK 381

Named after the German Harz Range – where the 't' came from is unclear – the antipodean Hartz Mountains were first explored by timber-cutters seeking Huon pine and routes to Port Davey's forests deeper in Tasmania's south-west. The cutting of a track by the Geeves family (of Geeveston) in 1896 saw the range become one of Tasmania's earliest recreational bushwalking destinations and Hartz Mountains National Park was included in the Tasmanian Wilderness World Heritage Area in 1989.

A dolerite backbone intruded into Earth's crust during the breakup of the Gondwana super continent, shaped by glaciers over subsequent ice ages, the Hartz Mountains run the length of the park, reaching a highpoint of 1254m that is a window into the wilds. From the 'relative safety' of Hartz Peak, just 4km from car access, you can see into the heart of Tasmania's south-west and feel the sting of wind that whips and wails along remote ridgelines and valleys.

But it is 'relative safety'. Much of the park sits above 600m altitude. It rains here more than 200 days a year and snow can fall at any time. Check the forecast before stepping out and carry a wind- and waterproof jacket even on sunny days.

The Hartz Peak walk starts at the end of an 84km drive from Hobart. Exit the city south on the A6, following signs to Huonville, and turn west at Geeveston onto the C632, signed for the national park. The access road branches off the C632 about 13km along, from where 10km of potholed gravel sometimes closed by snow cuts through Tasmanian forestry land, the trees so close you may see lyrebirds on the run in.

The walking track starts beside the day-use shelter. Turn your back on the Huon Valley and head towards rocky rises, on boardwalk easing up through dense tea tree and young eucalypts, to the burble of creeks you probably won't see for the scrub. About five minutes into the walk you pass a memorial to two members of the pioneering Geeves family who died in 1897 of exposure here, the site of the original hut, when returning from a prospecting trip.

After a short climb roughened by rocks and roots (see point 1 on map), duckboards continue through heathland. Look back for a vista of cardboard-cut-out peaks and ridgelines rising from valleys often frothy with morning cloud. The track now heads directly towards Hartz Peak and its pyramidal neighbour Mt Snowy through ground-gripping coral fern, scoparia and stands of pandani with ringlet leaves. Note how trees and shrubs grow part-way up the fantastic Devils Backbone (to your right) and hardy heath covers the rest. Tasmanian waratah splashes the walk with red flowers in late spring–early summer.

In sunshine, when there's promise of breathtaking views from the summit, leave the short Lake Esperance detour until your return (in case conditions

The 360° view from Hartz Peak takes in Tasmania's spectacular South-west range

worsen). The track beyond the lake turnoff can have bogs even in dry weather and the damage caused by feet on fragile alpine plains is obvious. That's why it's important to walk through, rather than around, puddles and mud between old and new boarding – don't be a wally and deliberately walk off boarding just because you don't like the mud!

D'Entrecasteaux Channel, Bruny Island (see page 63) (see point 2 on map) and the Tasman Sea paint a stunning panorama to your left and are in full view from a plain dotted with tarns about 2km into the walk. Leave the side track to Ladies Tarn until your return, too, but look back along the boardwalk you're following before continuing.

A steep and stony step-up through assorted heath plants deposits you on rock-strewn Hartz Pass, a spectacular turn-back point. If not pushing for the top, tread a rough track, indicated by two rusty poles, right, for a view of Hartz Lake and south-west mountains that book-end Bruny Island, D'Entrecasteaux Channel and sea to the east. (The side track continues downhill to the lake.)

Ahead of you on Hartz Pass are the walk's first orange arrows, beyond which the summit track snakes up the peak. This final leg is exposed and often windy. You're at the mercy of unforgiving south-west weather so turn back immediately if you feel unsure.

Conical Mt Snowy summits to the east of Hartz Peak

The track works across the mountain's south-west face, presenting aerial views of Hartz Lake as you climb through fractured, upended and layered dolerite, where nothing grows taller than about 40cm except in protected pockets. Occasional cairns indicate the route up boulder scree (*see* point 3 on map) to a tiny saddle, from where you clamber the last 100m.

It can be screamingly windy up here with only a few sheltered spots behind rocks but persevere, because the view's a stunner: 360° taking in Bruny Island and the Huon River, Federation Peak and the Ironbound Range on the South Coast Track, and even Frenchmans Cap (*see* page 357) to the north. Experienced hikers can (and do) continue off-track from here to Mt Snowy but there are no markers.

From the top, retrace your steps to the car park, via Ladies Tarn and Lake Esperance. Five of Tasmania's 11 frog species are found in Hartz Mountains National Park including the moss froglet, discovered here in 1992, and frogs will probably serenade you on both detours.

A stone track leads to Ladies Tarn, whose clear, green water reflects fringing pandani and its rocky ridge backdrop. Further on, new boarding crosses a carpet of cushion plants to decking beside Lake Esperance. Cushion plants are actually slow-growing colonies packed so tightly they can maintain a constant internal temperature rather than freeze in winter conditions. Their aerodynamic mound shape also minimises wind damage. But these hardy plants are vulnerable to damage from humans. A boot print can take 30 years to repair.

Savour the mostly downhill run back to your car.

LEFT: *Boarding winds through heathland;* **RIGHT:** *A rocky clamber takes you to the top*

WEST & WILDERNESS
66 MYSTERY CREEK CAVE

Walk:	4.7km out-and-back
Time required:	2 hours
Best time:	Year-round
Grade:	Easy
Environment:	Leafy forest, old tramway, cliff-foot quarry site, limestone cave
Best map:	This one
Toilets:	None
Food:	None
Tips:	Flash floods can occur in Mystery Creek Cave (two high school students and a teacher died in the cave in 1990) and only experienced, well-equipped cavers should venture beyond the first cavern.
	Take a torch for viewing the cave structure.
	Allow time for a journey on Australia's southernmost railway, the historic Ida Bay Railway (www.idabayrailway.com.au).

Glow-worms hang out in the cave at the end of this lush forest walk along an early 20th century quarry tramway.

An axeman's support plank juts from the stump of a felled giant

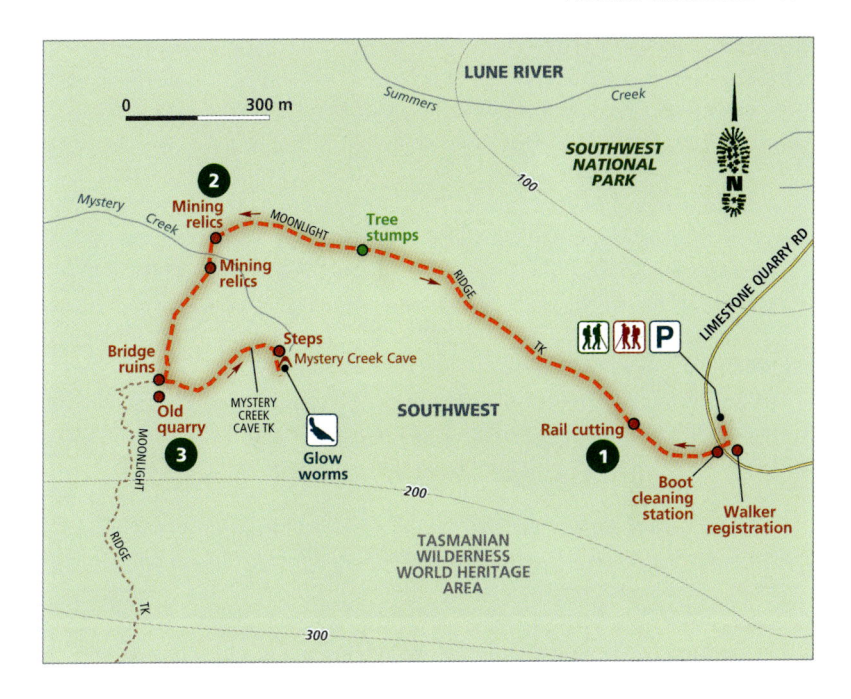

Mystery Creek Cave is a window (and, for some, a door) into one of Tasmania's most extensive limestone cave systems. The walk to it follows the route of a tramway built in 1919 to haul quarried limestone to the Deep Hole jetty at Ida Bay for the manufacture of calcium carbide, which was used in manufacturing and agriculture. (Convict-era settlers burned limestone to make cement and that remains its most common use.)

The cave and quarry are just inside the eastern boundary of Southwest National Park, 100km (75 minutes' drive) south-west of Hobart via Huonville and the Huon Hwy. Sixteen kilometres beyond Dover, turn right onto Lune River Rd and 500m beyond Ida Bay Railway Station turn right again, onto South Lune Road. About 4km along this poor grade, mostly unsealed road, turn left onto unsigned, unsealed Limestone Quarry Road. The walk starts where the road narrows to a vehicular bush track.

Walk up wooden steps left of the walker registration shelter (this is also the trailhead for the spectacular three-day hike over Moonlight Ridge to Mt La Perouse, in the Southern Ranges) and step out on a flat track beside a tree-fern filled gully. The huge stumps you pass walking from tall, slender trees into

TOP: *The mouth of Mystery Creek Cave opens into lush forest;* **LEFT:** *The track crosses rocky Mystery Creek;* **MIDDLE RIGHT:** *You'll find rusty relics in the old quarry;* **BOTTOM RIGHT:** *Tall trees tower over the fungi growing on them*

a railway cutting (see point 1 on map) roofed with fallen trunks testify to the age and stature of the trees that once inhabited this forest.

About 1.3km into the walk you'll come to a collection of mining relics, including broken bottles (see point 2 on map), an old pot, and a pair of battered boots. The track now narrows through the forest, and you'll see a rusty plate (one of many metal relics on the forest floor), as you approach and cross Mystery Creek.

Climbing slightly now, the track enters thicker forest and runs along a tramway embankment studded with timber cross-beams. Building foundations and bricks dating from quarrying times are visible down on the left. As the embankment rises further above the forest floor the walking track veers down its left side towards a grey cliff topped with eucalypts. You emerge from the trees in the old quarry at the foot of that cliff (see point 3 on map).

Track signage directs you left to Mystery Creek and right to the Southern Range but head right first, past the stacked, weathered timbers of an old tramway bridge, and tread rusty tramway tracks towards the quarried cliff. Then return to the junction and head east along the base of the cliff, past more abandoned quarrying equipment.

The track plunges back into shadow-filled forest of mossy trees and stumps, and on the right you'll pass the stump of a fallen giant, perhaps felled by lightning. Track and wooden steps skirt other huge trees as you work down into Mystery Creek gully. On warm days, there's a noticeable decrease in temperature as you descend.

You come to a sign warning of rock hazards, vertical drops and slippery uneven surface; it rightly explains that exploring the complex cave system requires difficult navigation and only experienced, properly equipped cavers should proceed beyond the first cavern. A steep, rocky and sometimes slippery clamber through the fern-filled and boulder-strewn cave mouth lands you in the first cavern, whose extent disappears into the darkness. Dry stalactites, other limestone formations, and a lurex-type glitter decorate the ceiling. Mystery Creek burbles across the floor, rounding chunks of rock that have fallen from above. Venture a few metres in, exploring the stonework with your torch.

What appears to be another cave level is visible to the left above the entrance while a glow-worm colony creates a miniature underground galaxy to the right just inside the cave mouth.

When you're done with star gazing, return to your car.

WEST & WILDERNESS

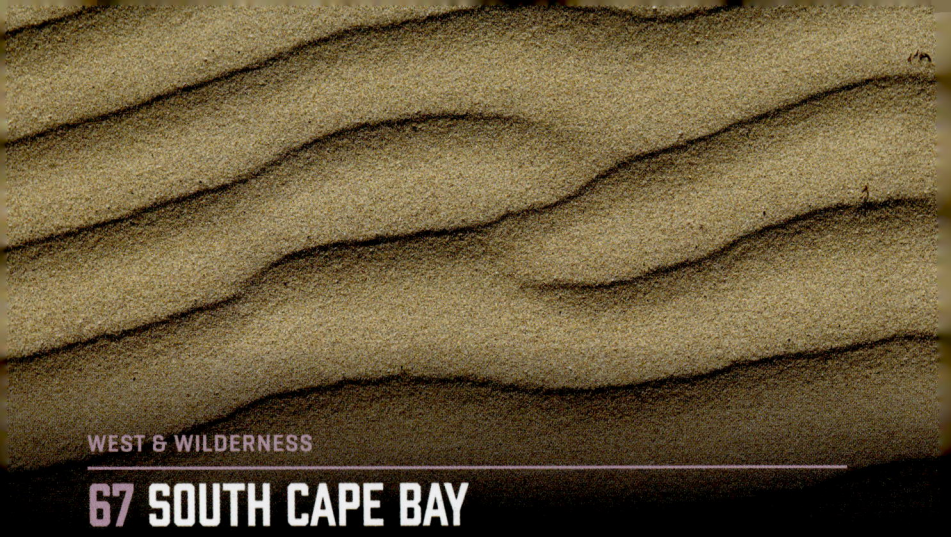

67 SOUTH CAPE BAY

Walk:	15km out-and-back
Time required:	5 hours
Best time:	Mild, clear day, year-round (can be very windy at the Bay)
Grade:	Easy–moderate
Environment:	Bay beach, creek, heath plains, eucalypt forest, riparian rainforest, coastal cliffs
Best map:	This one
Toilets:	Beside the park office on the southern side of Cockle Creek bridge
Food:	None
Tips:	For a bigger bite of Southwest National Park's wild grandeur without venturing far from civilisation and refuge from bad weather, extend this walk into an overnighter and camp at South Cape Bay or Shoemaker Bay, the next west along the South Coast Track.

Walk from Australia's southernmost road to its southernmost foot-accessible point and poke your nose over the edge of the continent.

The return walk to South Cape Bay from Cockle Creek is the eastern leg of the South Coast Track, a fly-in hike-out multi-day encounter with everything that Tasmania's wild south-west coast has to offer. A fairly easy, mostly flat walk

Perfect ripples form on the South Cape Bay beach

through forest and over expanses of coastal heath, this sampler leads from the southernmost road on continental Australia to a bay opening onto the Southern Ocean.

The journey starts from Cockle Creek, in Southwest National Park, Tasmania's largest and wildest park and one of the last remaining temperate wilderness areas on our planet. Cockle Bay is 1.5 hours' drive (119km) south-west of Hobart. Take the A6 from Hobart almost to Southport, continuing south on the C636 through Hastings and Ida Bay to (almost) the end of the road in Recherche Bay.

The South Cape Bay walk (and South Coast Track) starts immediately over Cockle Creek bridge just within the national park boundary. Follow a broad gravel track 50m along the creek to a junction, here turning right onto boardwalk that snakes 300m through strappling tea tree to a walk registration booth (sign in) and boot-cleaning station. (The root-rot fungus *Phytophthora cinnamomi* is a major threat to Southwest National Park, as is fire. Hard fuel fires are banned within the park.)

South-west Wilderness ridgelines and conical peaks appear on your right through the trees as you meander through eucalypts, banksias, tea tree and huge bunches of cutting grass over the gentle slopes of Moulders Hill. Rocky and lumpy with roots but fairly easy going, the track then descends into a fern

The track brings you out on a black bluff overlooking the Southern Ocean

392   WEST & WILDERNESS

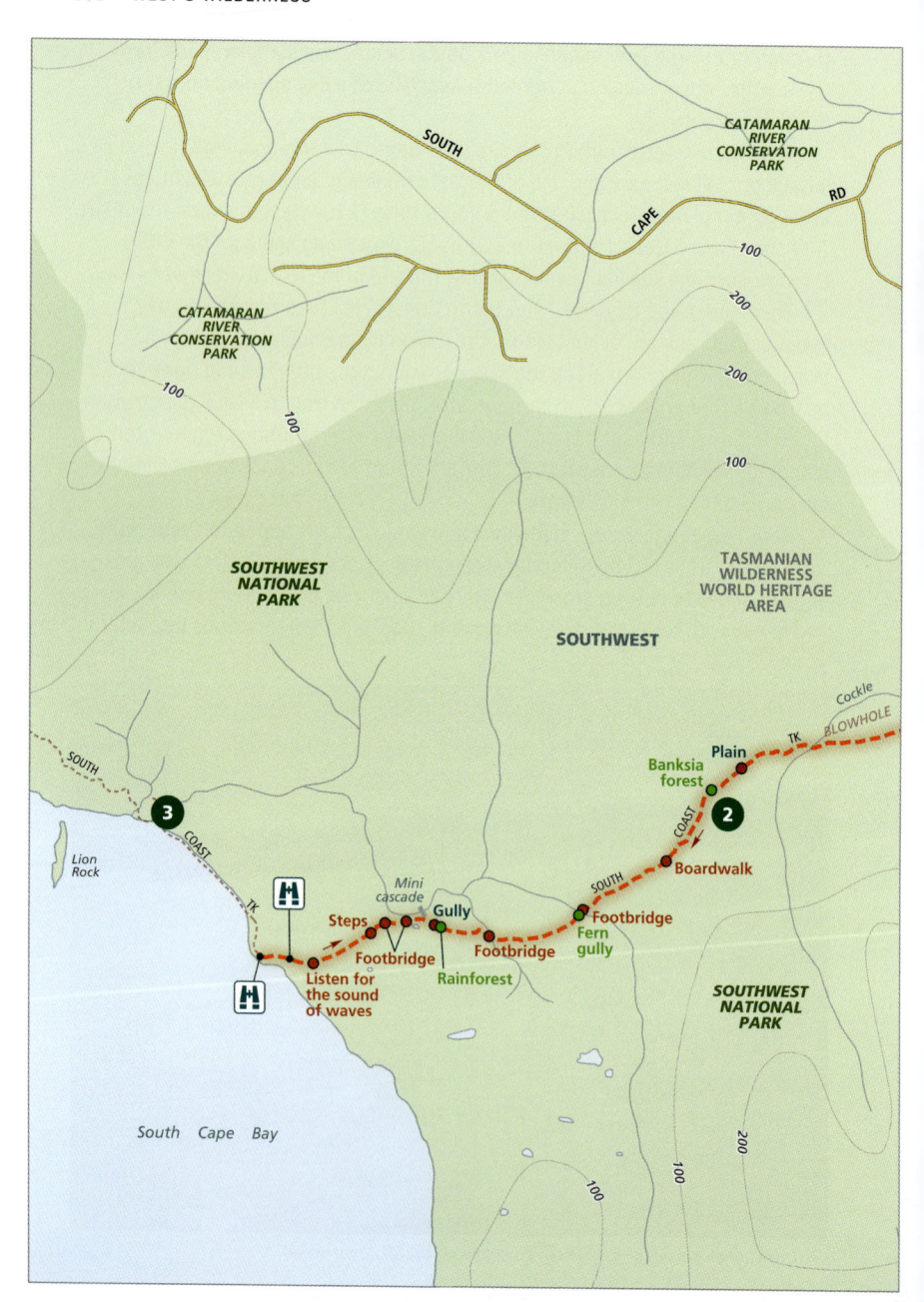

SOUTH CAPE BAY 393

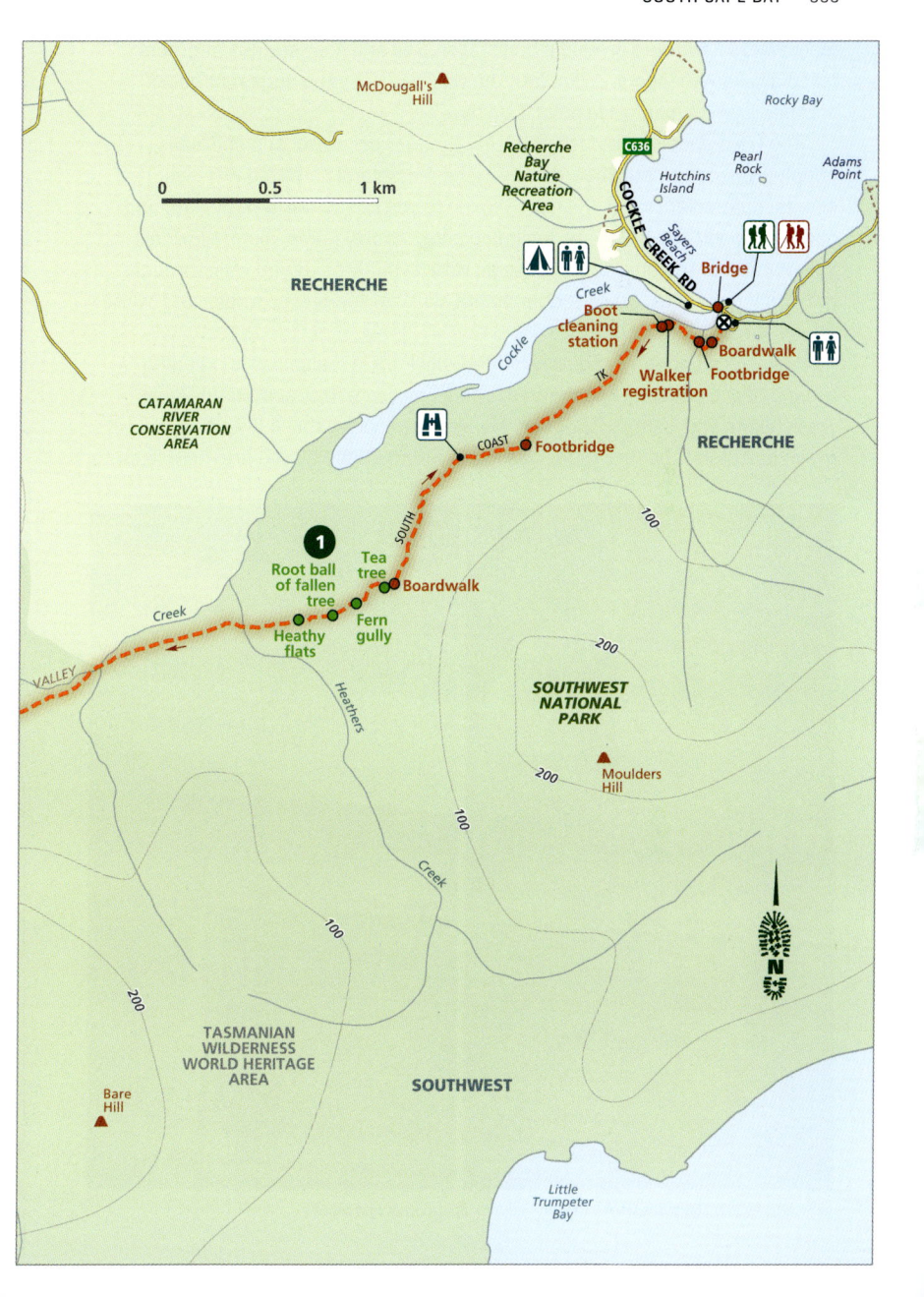

gully, where it detours around a huge fallen tree and past stumps of others felled by axemen. About 2.7km into the walk you pass the huge root ball of another toppled giant (*see* point 1 on map).

The track then leaves lush and leafy for drier eucalypts and she-oaks, popping you out on duckboards traversing marshland carpeted with assorted coastal heath plants. For the next 2km or so you cut across heathy flats and navigate islands of eucalypts, including cute scribbly gums, along Blowhole Valley. A few of the boards are loose so watch your step as you walk through red-topped grasses, grass trigger plants, daisies, and pretty purple-and-white fairies apron wildflowers.

Melaleuca Lagoon in Southwest National Park is the sole wild breeding ground of the critically endangered orange-bellied parrot and South Coast Track hikers and visitors flying into Melaleuca can view these blue-tipped vivid green parrots at the Bird Hide. Walking to South Cape Bay you are more likely to

LEFT AND RIGHT: *The track works through islands of eucalypt and moors*

see wedge-tailed eagles and gorgeous green rosellas, found only in Tasmania and on the Bass Strait islands. The eucalypt forest can be noisy with other birds reluctant to show themselves.

On route to South Cape Bay you often meet hikers finishing the South Coast Track; the weather they've experienced over the last week often determines whether they can raise a smile at you or not. And speaking of weather, if it's windy on this walk then a blow probably awaits you at South Cape Bay.

About 5km into the walk, marshland makes way for banksia forest (see point 2 on map). The track becomes sandy as you tread tea tree tunnels and push through bearded heath shrubs but you've got leaves underfoot along a deep fern gully. The track drops in and out of rainforest gullies before pulling away from the creek into a tunnel of tea tree. The waves are loud now as you continue through cutting grass, tea tree and bracken and the volume increases as you come over the top for your first view of the sea.

The track brings you out on a shaly black bluff overlooking the Southern Ocean and South Cape Bay to the right, and South East Cape, the southernmost landmass in continental Australia, to your left. This natural grandstand is composed of thin sedimentary layers that break off and move underfoot so take care, especially when it's wet, because it can be extremely slippery. From the front row you can see distinct eras of deposition in the cliff below; waves foaming over rock shelving at their base and bull kelp writhing in the swell too.

Cairns mark the path round the bluff to steps leading down onto the beach. You can walk about a kilometre along the sand for a closer view of Lion Rock (see point 3 on map) off the end of the beach and a taste of the wave spray – or remain up on the cliffs. Either way, allow enough time to walk back to Cockle Bay, and normal life, in daylight.

*Common heath (**LEFT**) and forest frilly heath (**RIGHT**) are two of the wildflowers you might see*

INDEX

A

Aboriginal culture 4, 14–15, 17, 59, 65, 68–9, 117, 141, 147, 153, 158, 173, 198, 250, 253, 291, 293, 334
Aboriginal middens 232, 250, 335
Acropolis, The 296, 301, 302
Adams Beach 195
Adventure Bay 66, 67, 69, 71, 72, 74, 77
Agamemnon 363
Ahrberg Hill 341
Alpha Pinnacle Conservation Area 24
Alum Cliffs & Brickworks 18–22
Anniversary Bay 252, 253
Anniversary Point 253
Ansons Bay 155
Apsley Gorge 156–9
Apsley River 157, 158, 159
Apsley Waterhole 156, 157
Archer's Knob 233, 235
Arm River Track 312
Arthur–Pieman Conservation Area 334
Arthur River 329, 331, 332
Arthurs Peak 112
Artichoke Valley 365
Asbestos Range 232, 233, 235
Asbestos Range NP *see* Narawntapu NP
Australian Convict Sites World Heritage property 97
Avon Creek 345

B

Backhouse Tarn 43
Baden Powell Scout Lodge 288
Bagdad 24
Bakers Beach 232, 233, 235
Ballroom Forest 266
Barn Bluff 242, 269, 287, 308, 310
Barron Pass 364, 367
Bass Strait 163, 169, 177, 179, 203, 205, 224, 242, 248
Bather Creek 345
Bay of Fires 152–5, 165
Bay of Fires Lodge Walk 153
Ben Lomond NP 227
Ben Lomond plateau 225, 228, 230, 242
Ben Lomond snow pole 225–30
Ben Lomond Village 225, 227
Ben Nevis 228, 230
Bert Nicholls Hut 317

Bert Nicholls Hut to Lake St Clair jetty 317
Bicheno 156, 157
Big Tree Reserve 54, 55
Binalong Bay 152, 153, 154, 155
Bird River 354
Bird River Bridge 354
bird-watching 2–7, 16, 22, 24, 60, 63, 65, 103, 110, 114, 117, 128, 141, 148, 155, 166, 179–80, 195, 203–5, 232–3, 235, 246, 256, 258, 291, 312, 320, 335, 394–5
Bishop and Clerk 128–9
Bivouac Bay 101, 103
Black Bluff range 243, 244
Black Rocks 333, 334, 336
Blackwood Camp 247
Blade, The 118
Blandfordia Hill 252, 253
Blowhole Valley 394
Blue Tiers Forest Reserve 163
Blue Tiers range 160, 163, 169
Bluff Hill Point 333, 336
Bluff Hill Point lighthouse 336
Bolts Spur 105
Bracknell 207
Brid River 192
Bridport 190
Bridport Walking Track 190–5
Broadview Hill 252
Browns Caves 26
Browns Caves Creek 26
Browns River 22
Bruny Island 6, 16, 20, 60, 62–77, 87, 106, 383, 385
Bryans Beach 146, 147, 148
Burgess Cove 248, 250
bushwalkers' code xi
Buttress Hill 349

C

Cameron Inlet 178–81
Camp Falls 106
Canoe Bay 103
canoeing 340
Cape Boullanger 128
Cape Hauy 80–4, 103, 106, 110, 111, 114, 117, 118, 120
Cape Pillar 82, 84, 88, 89, 93, 94, 106, 110, 114, 117–18, 120
Cape Queen Elizabeth, Bruny Island 62–6
Cape Raoul 17, 85–9, 92, 93, 110, 112
Cape Tourville lighthouse 136
Car Villa hut 227, 228, 230
Cartwright Creek 15, 17
Cataract Gorge 196–201
Cathedral Hill 251

Cathedral Mountain 314
Cathedral Rock (Tasman Peninsula) 117
Cathedral Rocks (Rocky Cape NP) 251, 252, 253
Caves Track 26, 27
C.C. Funk (shipwreck) 181
Central Highlands 210, 260–325
Central Plateau Conservation Area 324
Cephissus Creek 298, 300
Chalet, The 11, 13
Chasm Lookout 118
Chauncy Vale caves 23–7
Chauncy Vale Wildlife Sanctuary 23–7
Clemes Peak 106
Clumner Bluff 320
Coal Mines Historic Site 95–100
Coal River 30
Cockle Bay 391, 395
Cockle Creek 390, 391
Cockle Creek bridge 390, 391
Coles Bay 132, 134–5, 139, 142, 151
Collingwood River 370
Condominium Creek 376
Condominium Creek valley 377
Convict Trail 28
Cooks Beach 146, 147–8
Cooks Beach camp 142, 145
Cookville 70
Corinna 337, 338, 341
Corruption Gully 117
Counsel Beach 130
Cradle Mountain 114, 242, 262, 264–7, 269, 271–2, 281, 284, 286–7, 306, 308, 312
Cradle Mountain Huts Walk 306
Cradle Mountain–Lake St Clair NP 247, 262–6, 269, 274, 279, 282–8, 291, 294–302, 306, 307, 312, 320, 322, 324
Cradle Mountain Lodge 262, 267, 276, 277, 282, 303
Cradle Mountain Summit 282–8
Cradle Mountain Summit Track 271, 272, 288, 308
Cradle Mountain Visitor Centre 262, 267, 269, 273, 277, 279, 282, 303, 306, 307
Cradle Plateau 281, 284, 308
Crater Creek 281, 284, 307
Crater Falls 281, 284, 308
Crater Lake 272, 279, 281, 284, 287, 308
Crater Peak 287
Crescent Bay 110, 112
Crescent Bay & Mount Brown 90–4

Croquet Lawn Beach 195
Crotty 356
Cruikshanks Lookout 244, 246
Cuttys Creek 336
Cuvier River 293
Cyane Lake 302

D

Dale Brook 212
D'Alton Falls 316
Damascus Gate 322
Damascus Rise 323
Darlington 12, 124, 128, 130, 131
Deception Ridge 377
Deloraine 214, 216, 221, 279, 284, 320
Denmans Cove 110, 121
D'Entrecasteaux Channel 60, 63, 69, 74, 383
Derwent Bridge 289, 290, 294, 357, 360, 368, 369
Derwent River 2, 11, 12, 17
Desolation Gully 117
Devil's Backbone 382
Devil's Elbow 247
Devil's Kitchen 101–6
Devonport 232, 242, 250
difficulty rating (of walks) ii–iv, xii
distance (of walks) ii–iv, xii
Dixon's Kingdom Hut 318, 324
Dixons Track 219
Docks, The, to Killiecrankie 174, 182–87
Doctors Creek 336
Dolomieu Point 103
Donaghy's Hill 368–70
Donaghy's Hill Lookout 369, 370
Doona Falls track 252
Douglas–Apsley NP 157–9
Douglas Creek 312
Douglas River 157, 158
Dove Canyon 274
Dove Gorge 272–6
Dove Lake 262–6, 269, 271, 272, 275, 284, 286, 287, 308
Dove Lake car park 262, 264, 267, 269, 272
Dove Lake circuit 262–6, 269, 272, 308
Dove Lake High loop 267–72, 308
Dove River 275
Dover 387
Du Cane Gap 316
Du Cane Hut 314
Du Cane Range 290, 300, 302, 317
Duck Reach Power Station 201

INDEX

E
Eagle Tarn 41, 42, 43
Eaglehawk Neck 17, 97
East Coast 122–69
East Pillinger 354, 356
Edge Lookout 246
Ellarwey Valley 114
Evandale 227
Eve's Bath 27

F
Face Track (Cradle Mountain) 265, 269, 271, 286
Face Track (Mount Roland) 239, 242
Falling Mountain 317
Far Flung lookout 120
Federation Peak 385
Fergusson Falls 316
Fern Tree 5, 8
Fingerpost Track 5
First Basin 196, 198, 201
Fisherman's Wharf Lookout 259
Flat Rock 60
Flat Rock Reserve 24
Fleurieu Point 144
Flinders Island 117, 169–87, 195, 224, 230
Florentine River valley 372, 373
Fluted Cape, Bruny Island 63, 66, 67–71
Ford River gorge 230
Ford River Valley 230
Forest Stairs 246
Forestier Peninsula 97
Forgotten Lake 292
Fortescue Bay 80, 81–2, 84, 114, 117, 120–1
Fortescue Bay to Devil's Kitchen 101–6
Fossey Creek 240
fossicking 128, 184
Fotheringate Beach 175
Frankland Range 374, 379
Franklin–Gordon Wild Rivers NP 292, 357–67, 368–71
Franklin River 360, 366, 370
Franklin River gorge 366
Franklin River Valley 370
Frenchmans Cap 314, 357–67, 369, 370, 385
Frenchmans Cap summit 365–6
Freycinet Lodge 137
Freycinet Marine Farm 132, 137, 139, 142
Freycinet NP 134, 137, 139, 142–51, 284
Freycinet Peninsula 142–51
Freycinet Peninsula Circuit 144, 151

Frog Flats 311
Full Moon Creek 163, 164
Furneaux Islands 169

G
Gandalf's Staff 55, 56, 57
Gap, The 301
Gardens, The 155
Gates of Mordor 314
Geeveston 382
Glacier Rock 264, 269
Gladstone 166
Goblin Walk 164
Godfrey's Beach 259
Gottons Beach 195
Gould's Country 160
Gowrie Park 239
grade rating (of walks) ii–iv, xiii
Grants Lagoon 153
Grass Point 70
Great Oyster Bay 144
Great Western Tiers 207, 210, 213–14, 218–19, 221, 224, 238, 242
Green Point Beach 335
Griffiths Ridge 245–6, 247
Growling Swallet & Junee Cave 44–8
Gunns Plains 247
Guvy's Lagoon 27

H
Hanson's Peak 269
Hanson's Peak track 264
Hartnett Falls 316
Hartz Lake 383, 385
Hartz Mountains NP 380–5
Hartz Pass 383
Hartz Peak 380–5
Hastings 391
Hazards, The 134, 139–40, 144, 149, 150, 151
Hazards Bay 150
Hazards Beach 136, 139, 142, 144, 145, 149
Herod's Gate 322, 324
Hidden Falls 61
Higgs Track to Lady Lake 210–14
High Camp Memorial Hut 375, 378
Highfield 254
Highfield Lookout 259
Hill Point 154
Hippolyte Rock 117
Historic Richmond town 28–33
Hobart 2, 5, 6, 11, 12, 17
Hobart region 1–77
Horse Track 272, 284, 286, 287
Horseshoe Falls 36
Hugel River 293
Humbug Hill 154

Humbug Point State Reserve 153
Hunters Track 13
Huon Bush Retreats 58–60
Huon Pine Walk 341
Huon River 379, 385
Huon Valley 59, 60, 61, 382
Huonville 382, 387

I
Ida Bay 391
Ida Bay Railway 386, 387
Ida Clair ferry 290, 306
Innes Track 311
Irenabyss 365–6
Ironbound Range 385

J
Jacobs Ladder 225, 227, 230
Jaffe Vale 324
Johnston Tarn 43
Junee Cave 47–8
Junee River 47
Jurassic Crack 114

K
K Kol 42
kayaking 340
Kelly Basin 352, 354, 356
Kettering 63, 69, 74
Kia Ora Hut 314
Kia Ora Hut to Bert Nicholls Hut (Windy Ridge) 314–17
Killiecrankie 182, 185
Killiecrankie Creek 179
Killiecrankie Nature Recreation Area 184
King David's Peak 322
King William Range 367
Kingston Beach 18, 20
Kitchen Hut 271, 282, 284, 286, 287, 303, 308
Knyvet Falls 276
kunanyi/Mount Wellington 9–13, 70, 71, 106, 114
kunanyi/Mount Wellington summit 2–8

L
Labyrinth, The 290, 294–302
Ladies Tarn 383, 385
Lady Barron 174, 178
Lady Barron Creek 37
Lady Barron Falls 34–7
Lady Lake 210, 213–14
Lady Lake Hut 213
Lake Adelaide 320
Lake Adelaide Track 320
Lake Cecily 367
Lake Dobson 37, 40, 41, 43
Lake Dobson car park 40

Lake Elysia 302
Lake Esperance 380, 382, 385
Lake Fenton 43
Lake Gertrude 367
Lake Gordon 372, 374, 376
Lake Hanson 269, 284, 308
Lake Herbert 348, 349, 351
Lake Holmes 310
Lake Lilla 272, 279, 281
Lake Magdalen 367
Lake Millicent 367
Lake Murchison 349
Lake Nameless 213
Lake Newdegate 42, 43
Lake Ophion 302
Lake Pedder 360, 372, 374, 377, 378, 379
Lake Rodway 269
Lake Rosebery 346, 351
Lake St Clair 290, 293, 296, 300, 302, 306, 307, 317, 368
Lake St Clair Visitor Centre 289, 290, 293, 294, 296
Lake Salome 322
Lake Seal 41, 42, 43
Lake Tahune 357, 364, 365, 367
Lake Tahune Hut 365
Lake Tahune to Lake Vera 367
Lake Vera 357, 363, 364, 367
Lake Vera Hut 363, 364
Lake Vera to Lake Tahune 364–5
Lake Vera to Lyell Highway 367
Lake Webster 42
Lake Wilks 265, 271
Lake Will 310
Lake Windermere 310
Lakes Loop 277–81
Laughton's Lead 362
Launceston 196–201, 202, 203, 205, 242
Launceston region 188–235
Lee Archer Cave 253
Leven Canyon 243–7
Leven Canyon Regional Reserve 244
Leven Gorge 244
Leven River 243, 247
Lichen Hill 105
Liffey Falls 206–9
Liffey Falls car park 206
Liffey Falls State Reserve 206
Lighthouse Beach 334
Lightkeeper's Daughter, The 118
Lightning Tree 61
Lion Rock 395
Little Badger Hill 235
Loddon River 362
Loongana 247
Loongana Range 244

INDEX

Lost World 9–13
Lower Liffey camping area 208
Lower Sawmill Track 6
Lunchtime Creek 117
Lyell Highway to Lake Vera 360–4

M

Macquarie Harbour 354, 356
Maignon Blowhole 92
Maria Island 106, 124–31
Maria Island Walk 125
Marion's Lookout 264, 265, 269, 272, 281, 284, 287, 308
Marrawah 334
Marriotts Creek 53
Marriotts Falls 49–53
Mars Bluff 65
Mary Ann Cove 248, 250
Mawson Bay 334
Maydena 47, 371, 372, 374
Meander 216
Meander Conservation Area 216
Meander Falls 215–19
Meander River 207, 208, 216, 218
Meander Valley 210, 214
Melaleuca 394
Melaleuca Lagoon 394
Mersey River 316
Midway Creek 76
Miles Beach 65, 66
Miles Creek 65
Minotaur 300, 302
Mole Creek 242, 318, 322
Mole Creek Track 311
Montezuma Falls 342–5
Moon Valley Rim 160–4
Moonina Bay 65
Moonina Bay Hut 65
Moonlight Ridge 387
Mother Cummings Rivulet 216
Moulders Hill 391
Moulting Lagoon 148
Mount Amos 132–6, 139, 142, 149, 151
Mount Anne 367, 374, 375, 376, 377, 378, 379
Mount Barrow 228
Mount Brown 92, 94, 112
Mount Campbell 269
Mount Chappell Island 175
Mount Claude 238, 239, 240
Mount Donaldson 337, 339, 340
Mount Donaldson to Corinna via Savage River 337–41
Mount Doris 312, 314
Mount Eliza 376, 378, 379
Mount Eliza Plateau 360, 374, 375–9
Mount Farrell 348, 349

Mount Farrell & Lake Herbert 346–51
Mount Farrell Regional Reserve 349
Mount Field NP 34–7, 38–43, 44–8, 49–53
Mount Field West 374
Mount Fortescue 82, 118, 119, 120
Mount Freycinet 144, 145, 146, 148, 149, 150
Mount Geryon 301, 302
Mount Graham 144, 146, 148, 149, 150
Mount Hugel 292
Mount Jerusalem 323, 324
Mount Killiecrankie 184
Mount La Perouse 387
Mount Lot 378
Mount Maria 129, 130
Mount Mayson 139, 142, 151
Mount Misery 58–61
Mount Mueller 374
Mount Mullens 362
Mount Murchison 349, 351
Mount Nelson Signal Station 14, 15, 17
Mount Oakleigh 310, 311, 312
Mount Olympus 296, 298, 300, 317
Mount Ossa 114, 307, 310, 312
Mount Pelion West 310, 311
Mount Poimena 163
Mount Roland 234, 238–42
Mount Rufus 290, 292
Mount Snowy 382, 385
Mount Solitary 379
Mount Van Dyke 238, 239, 240, 242
Mount Wellington 4
Mount William NP 153, 165–9, 233
mountain-bike riding 164, 342
Munro Cabin 112, 114, 117, 118
Murchison Valley 301
Mystery Creek 389
Mystery Creek Cave 386–9

N

Narawntapu NP 168, 231–5
Narcissus Hut 284, 296, 298, 302, 317
Narcissus River 296, 298, 317
Narcissus Valley 317
Neck, The 63, 65, 66, 68
Neck Beach 66
Needles, The 360, 371–4
New Norfolk 376
New Pelion Hut 311, 312

New Pelion Hut to Kia Ora Hut via Mt Ossa 312–14
Nietta 244
Norfolk Bay 98, 100
North Bruny Island 62–6
North East Dundas Tramway 343
North Esk River 203
North Mount Lyell Railway Line 354, 355, 356
North–South Track 5
North–West 236–59
Notch, The 378
Nubeena 95
Nut, The 251, 254–9
Nut State Reserve, The 256

O

Oast House Track 130
Old Hobart Town 30
Old Hobartians Track 13
Old Man's Head 179
Old Pelion Hut 311, 312
Old Pier Beach 195
O'Neill Creek 240
Organ Pipes 5, 6, 11
Organ Pipes Track 6
Overland Track 114, 269, 271, 275, 279, 281, 284, 287, 288, 290, 293, 296, 298, 303–17, 365, 367
Overland Track Pass 206

P

Painted Cliffs 130
Pandani Grove Track 43
Panorama Track 6
park fees viii
Parthenon 300, 301, 302
Pelion Gap 312
Pelion Plains 311
Pencil Pine Creek 275, 276
Pencil Pine Falls 276
Penguin 247
Penguin Cradle Trail 247
Penguin Island 71
Perdition Plateau 117
Personal Locator Beacons (PLBs) 306
Philips Peak 363
Philosopher Falls 328–32
Pickaxe Ridge 364
Pieman River 329, 339, 341
Pillinger 352, 354, 356
Pillinger Point 352–6
Pine Forest Moor 310
Pine Valley 298
Pine Valley Hut 294, 296, 298, 300, 302
Pinnacle Track 6

Pipeline Track 8
Plains of Heaven 225, 228, 230
Platypus Bay 293
Platypus Tarn 42
Platypus Tarn Track 41
Plunkett Point 100
Poimena Day Use Area 160, 163
Policeman's Point 155
Pools of Bethesda 323, 327
Port Arthur 81, 87, 90, 92, 93, 94, 95, 98, 101, 103, 110–11, 112
Port Arthur Historic Site 92, 101, 107, 110
Port Dalrymple 203
Port Sorrell 234
Postman's Pass 251, 253
Premaydena 95, 97

Q

Quamby Bluff 211, 220–4
Quamby Bluff Conservation Area 221
Quamby Corner 220
Queenstown 348, 352, 354, 369

R

Radfords Track 5
Ranelagh 59
Raoul Bay Retreat 85, 87
Recherche Bay 391
Reedy Gully 199, 201
Reids Track 8
Remarkable Cave 90, 93
Remarkable Cave car park 90, 92
Retakunna Cabin 114, 119
Richmond 28–33
Richmond Bridge 31
Richmond Gaol 28, 32, 33
Ring River 343, 344
River Forth 311
River Forth Gorge 311
River Tamar 203, 205, 232
rock-climbing 6, 84, 89, 120–1, 184
Rocky Cape 248–53
Rocky Cape lighthouse 250, 251
Rocky Cape NP 119, 250
Rodway Range 41, 42
Ronny Creek 272, 279, 281, 284, 288, 307
Ronny Creek car park 277, 282, 284
Ronny Creek to Waterfall Valley Hut 307–9
Ronny Creek Valley 287, 288
Rosebery 342, 343
Russell Falls 35–6, 51
Russell Falls Creek 35

S

St Helens 152, 153
Sandy Bay 17
Sarah Island 354
Savage River 337, 339, 340
Savage River Walk 341
Sawmill Track 6
Schouten Island 147, 149
Schouten Passage 147
Seal Spa 118
Sentinel Lookout 201
Serpentine River 379
Shadow Lake 289–93
Sharland's Peak 363, 364
Sheffield 238, 242, 279, 284, 320
Shipstern Bluff 87
Shoemaker Bay 390
Shot Tower, Taroona 18, 20
Signal Point 98
Signal Station car park 14
Silver Falls 8
Sisters Beach 248, 252
Slide Track, Bruny Island 72–7
Snake Gully Track 199
Snowgum Track 40, 41
Solomon's Throne 323
South Arm Peninsula 71
South Bay Cape 390–5
South Bruny Island 63, 66, 67–77
South Bruny NP 70
South Cape Bay 390–5
South Coast Track 385, 390, 391, 395
South East Cape 395
South Esk River 198, 203
South Hobart 6
South Loddon Plains 360
Southern Ocean 148, 149, 150, 367, 391, 395
Southern Ranges 387, 389
Southport 391
Southwest NP 60, 371–4, 375–9, 386–9, 390–5
Sphinx Rock 5, 6
Split Rock 218
Split Rock loop 219
Springlawn 235
Springlawn Beach 232

Springlawn Lagoon 233, 235
Springs, The 2, 5, 7
Stacky's Bight beach 179
Standup Point 94
Stanley 254–9
Stanley Harbour 258
Strzelecki NP 174–7
Strzelecki Peak 172–7, 179 224
Strzelecki Range 175
Stumpys Bay beach 165
Styx Valley of the Giants 54–7
Surveyors Cabin 111
Swimcart Beach 153
Swimcart Lagoon 152, 154

T

takayna/Tarkine 328–32, 333–36, 337–41
Tall Tree Walk 36, 37
Tamar Island 202–5
Tamar Island Interpretation Centre 202
Taranna 97
Tarn Shelf 38–43
Tarn Shelf Loop 374
Tarn Shelf walk 40–3
Taroona 18, 20
Tasman Arch 82, 106, 120
Tasman Coastal Trail 103
Tasman Island 88, 89, 93, 112, 118
Tasman Island NP 103, 110
Tasman Peninsula 17, 66, 71, 78–121
Tasman Sea 393
Tasman Trail 106
Tasmanian Expeditions 360
Tasmanian Wilderness Experiences 306
Tasmanian Wilderness World Heritage Area 26, 54, 216, 284, 306, 320, 360, 369, 382
Tatnell's Hill 105, 106
Temple, The 323, 324
Three Capes Lodge Walk 110
Three Capes Track 81, 82, 107–21
Tim Shea 374

time required (for walks) ii–iv, xii
Tinkers Lookout 251
Tolkien Track – The Styx 54–7
Totem Pole 84, 120–1
Trappers Hut 320
Traveller Range 296, 317
Trevallyn Dam 199
Trevallyn Walk 199
Triabunna 124, 125
Trousers Point 175
Truganini 14–17
Truganini Track 15, 98
Tullah 346, 348, 351
Twilight Tarn 43
Twisted Lakes track 269
Tyenna River 51, 52, 53
Tyenna River valley 373, 374
Tyndall Beach 22

U

Ulverstone 244
Upper Blessington 227

V

Vera Creek 364

W

Wailing Wall 323, 324
Waldheim Chalet 279, 281, 288
Waldheim Hut 287
Walkers Creek 103
Walls of Jerusalem NP 296, 318–25
Waratah 331, 332
Watchtower Lookout 225, 230
Waterfall Bay 103, 106
Waterfall Bluff 106
Waterfall Creek 106
Waterfall Valley 308
Waterfall Valley Hut 309
Waterfall Valley to Windermere Hut via Lake Will 309–10
Weldborough 163
Wellington Park 5
Wells Creek 336
West & Wilderness 326–95
West Pillinger 356
West Point 334, 335

West Point State Reserve 334
West Point to Black Rocks 333–36
West Wall 322, 323, 324
Western Creek 214
Wet Cave 253
whale watching 88, 112, 117
what to take viii–x
White Hills 227
White Needle 363, 364
white-water rafting 247, 366
Whitemark 172, 174, 178, 179, 182, 184
Wild Dog Creek 322
Wild Dog Creek Camp 318, 322
Wilderness Expeditions Tasmania 306
Williamsford 343
Wilmot Range 374
Wilsons Promontory, Vic. 177
Windermere Hut 310
Windermere Hut to New Pelion Hut 310–12
Wineglass Bay 132, 134, 136, 144, 146, 149, 150, 151
Wineglass Bay & Hazards Beach 137–41, 145
Wineglass Bay beach 139, 151
Wineglass Bay camping area 151
Wineglass Bay car park 132, 134, 139, 142
Wineglass Bay Lookout 134, 139, 144
Wineglass Bay Track 139
Wombat Peak 281
Wombat Pool 272, 281
Wood–Maynard Loop 219
wukalina/Mount William 166, 168
wukalina/Mount William NP 153, 165–9, 233
Wughalee 114, 117
Wybalenna 173

Z

Zeehan 343
Zig Zag Track (Cataract Gorge) 198
ZigZag Track (kunanyi/Mount Wellington summit) 6

Published in 2018 by Hardie Grant Travel, a division of Hardie Grant Publishing

Hardie Grant Travel (Melbourne)
Building 1, 658 Church Street
Richmond, Victoria 3121

Hardie Grant Travel (Sydney)
Level 7, 45 Jones Street
Ultimo, NSW 2007

www.hardiegrant.com/au/travel

Explore Australia is an imprint of Hardie Grant Travel

All rights reserved. No part of this publication may be reproduced, stored in a retrieval system or transmitted in any form by any means, electronic, mechanical, photocopying, recording or otherwise, without the prior written permission of the publishers and copyright holders.

The moral rights of the author have been asserted.

Copyright text and photography © Melanie Ball 2018
Copyright concept, maps and design © Hardie Grant Publishing 2018

© Imprint and currency – VAR Product and PSMA Data
"Copyright. Based on data provided under licence from PSMA Australia Limited (www.psma.com.au)".

Hydrography Data (May 2006)
Parks & Reserves Data (August 2016)
Transport Data (November 2017)

The maps in this publication incorporate data © Commonwealth of Australia (Geoscience Australia), 2006. Geoscience Australia has not evaluated the data as altered and incorporated within this publication, and therefore gives no warranty regarding accuracy, completeness, currency or suitability for any particular purpose.

Assistance with research: The publisher would like to thank the following organisations for assistance with data and information: Australian Bureau of Statistics, Bureau of Meteorology, National Road Transport Commission, Tristate Fruit Fly Committee (after the Transport Commission), Tasmania Department of Infrastructure, Energy & Resources, Parks and Wildlife Service, Tourism Tasmania.

A catalogue record for this book is available from the National Library of Australia

Top Walks in Tasmania
ISBN 9781741175349

10 9 8 7 6 5 4 3 2 1

Publisher
Melissa Kayser
Project editor
Megan Cuthbert
Editor
Bron Willis
Proofreader
Brenda Thornley
Cartographer
Emily Maffei
Cover Design
Phil Campbell
Typesetting
Kerry Cooke, Eggplant Communications
Index
Max McMaster
Prepress
Kerry Cooke and Splitting Image Colour Studio

Printed in China by 1010 Printing International Limited

Disclaimer: While every care is taken to ensure the accuracy of the data within this product, the owners of the data (including the state, territory and Commonwealth governments of Australia) do not make any representations or warranties about its accuracy, reliability, completeness or suitability for any particular purpose and, to the extent permitted by law, the owners of the data disclaim all responsibility and all liability (including without limitation, liability in negligence) for all expenses, losses, damages (including indirect or consequential damages) and costs which might be incurred as a result of the data being inaccurate or incomplete in any way and for any reason.

Publisher's Disclaimers: The publisher cannot accept responsibility for any errors or omissions. The representation on the maps of any road or track is not necessarily evidence of public right of way. The publisher cannot be held responsible for any injury, loss or damage incurred during travel. It is vital to research any proposed trip thoroughly and seek the advice of relevant state and travel organisations before you leave.

Publisher's Note: Every effort has been made to ensure that the information in this book is accurate at the time of going to press. The publisher welcomes information and suggestions for correction or improvement.